ARISTOTLE'S N

In this engaging and accessible introduction to the *Nicomachean Ethics*, Aristotle's great masterpiece of moral philosophy, Michael Pakaluk offers a thorough and lucid examination of the entire work, uncovering Aristotle's motivations and basic views while paying careful attention to his arguments. Pakaluk gives original and compelling interpretations of the Function Argument, the Doctrine of the Mean, courage and other character virtues, *akrasia*, and the two treatments of pleasure. The chapter on friendship captures Aristotle's doctrine with clarity and insight. There is also a useful section on how to read an Aristotelian text. This book will be invaluable for all student readers encountering one of the most important and influential works of Western philosophy.

MICHAEL PAKALUK is Associate Professor of Philosophy at Clark University, Massachusetts. He has published extensively in the history of philosophy, including Plato, Aquinas, Hume, and Reid, as well as in political philosophy, philosophical logic, and early analytic philosophy.

CAMBRIDGE INTRODUCTIONS TO KEY
PHILOSOPHICAL TEXTS

This new series offers introductory textbooks on what are considered to be
the most important texts of Western philosophy. Each book guides the
reader through the main themes and arguments of the work in question,
while also paying attention to its historical context and its philosophical
legacy. No philosophical background knowledge is assumed, and the books
will be well suited to introductory university-level courses.

Titles published in the series:

DESCARTES'S *MEDITATIONS* by Catherine Wilson

WITTGENSTEIN'S *PHILOSOPHICAL INVESTIGATIONS* by
David G. Stern

WITTGENSTEIN'S *TRACTATUS* by Alfred Nordmann

ARISTOTLE'S *NICOMACHEAN ETHICS* by Michael Pakaluk

ARISTOTLE'S
NICOMACHEAN ETHICS

An Introduction

MICHAEL PAKALUK

Clark University, Massachusetts

CAMBRIDGE
UNIVERSITY PRESS

CAMBRIDGE UNIVERSITY PRESS
Cambridge, New York, Melbourne, Madrid, Cape Town, Singapore, São Paulo

CAMBRIDGE UNIVERSITY PRESS
The Edinburgh Building, Cambridge CB2 2RU, UK

Published in the United States of America by Cambridge University Press, New York

www.cambridge.org
Information on this title: www.cambridge.org/9780521520683

First published 2005

Printed in the United Kingdom at the University Press, Cambridge

A catalogue record for this book is available from the British Library

ISBN-13 978-0-521-81742-4 hardback
ISBN-10 0-521-81742-0 hardback
ISBN-13 978-0-521-52068-3 paperback
ISBN-10 0-521-52068-1 paperback

For
niko-*Max*

Contents

Preface

I vividly remember my first encounter with Aristotle's *Nicomachean Ethics* in my first semester of college. I was assigned the text as part of an introductory course in the history of philosophy. My professor, Ed McCann, had said in lecture that it was widely accepted that Aristotle and Kant towered above all other philosophers, on account of their depth and comprehensiveness. So I had the highest expectations as I went off to the library, the text of the *Nicomachean Ethics* in hand, to grapple with Aristotle's thought.

But lulled perhaps by the soft hum of the heating system in the library, or by the plush comfort of the leather chair into which I had sunk, I simply could not stay awake while reading. I would read a chapter or two of the *Ethics*, then nod off to sleep; then wake up and read another chapter; and then fall asleep again; and so on. During my brief periods of wakefulness, it was my impression that I was following the argument, and that what Aristotle was saying was, after all, commonsensical – a very common first impression of the *Ethics*, as it turns out. And yet really I was hardly understanding the text. What was happening was that the seeming obviousness of Aristotle's claims allowed me to run my eyes over the text fairly quickly, and yet the density and concentration of the underlying argument, to the extent that I did grasp it, caused a kind of intellectual overload, from which I would then escape by falling asleep.

This experience, although not entirely pleasant, gave me a wary admiration for the *Ethics*. It seemed a serious work – difficult and appropriately challenging – while also being congenial and in many respects evidently right. My troubles in understanding the text seemed completely compatible with my professor's high estimation of Aristotle. But I was impatient with myself: I wanted truly to understand the *Ethics* and *learn* what it had to offer.

Sooner than I could have imagined, I had another chance. In my second semester, not knowing quite what I was getting into, I sought to enroll in and was accepted into a seminar on political philosophy for upperclassmen. One of the first readings for the seminar was Aristotle's *Ethics*. Each member of the seminar was required to give a presentation during the semester, and I rather foolishly volunteered to give the presentation on the *Ethics*. It was unwise, of course, for me to offer to give one of the first presentations of the semester in an advanced seminar designed for upperclassmen, but I imagined that by agreeing to do the presentation I could *force* myself to acquire an understanding of the *Ethics*.

I soon came to realize, however, the bind that I was in. In a kind of panic, and without a plan or system, I started reading quickly through secondary literature on the *Ethics*, hoping to find some interpretative key. I came across an article – I cannot remember exactly what or by whom – which claimed that the *Ethics* is from first to last "teleological" in outlook. That is correct, but I had no idea then what "teleological" meant. No matter: in my presentation to the seminar, I parroted the claim, and I used this theme, which I did not understand, to introduce and summarize the rather vague points I made about the text. Needless to say, I was completely dumbfounded when the professor, Nathan Tarcov, led off the discussion following my presentation by asking me to define what I meant by "teleological"!

I would be assigned the text a third time before my undergraduate years were over, this time, oddly enough, in a course entitled "Nonscientific Knowledge." The professor for this course, Hilary Putnam, a philosopher of science, assigned the *Ethics* as a kind of culmination of the argument of the course, which was directed at breaking down any sharp distinction between "facts" and "values." Earlier we had examined arguments from Iris Murdoch's book *The Sovereignty of the Good* for the claim that words that indicate a person's character (for instance, "kindly," "persevering") are not purely evaluative but are also essentially descriptive. Assertions that use words that purport to say how the world is also carry with them an evaluation. Aristotle's *Ethics*, the professor claimed, was a kind of star example of this, and the system and intelligence of the *Ethics* showed that ethical discourse of that sort, although not "scientific," could nonetheless constitute a kind of knowledge.

Naturally in such a course we did not read the *Ethics* with great attention to detail. What left a lasting impression upon me, rather, was my professor's high regard for the *Ethics*. He remarked in lecture that the *Nicomachean Ethics* would probably be the book he would take with him to a desert island if he were allowed just one book. He even claimed that one could find in the *Ethics* not merely "non scientific knowledge" but also *wisdom* about human life – the only time in my college career, in fact, that I had heard a professor acknowledge the existence of something like wisdom.

So during college I was taught the *Ethics* from three very different approaches: by a historian, as a basic text in ancient philosophy; by a political philosopher, as a seminal text in political thought; and by a philosopher of science, as a paradigm of organized but "non-scientific" understanding, and perhaps even as an instance of wisdom. My experience, which is not unusual, was a witness to the power and general importance of the *Ethics*. There were any number of other courses in economics, sociology, government, and religion in which I might have enrolled and encountered the *Ethics* yet again.

The *Ethics* seemed a text I personally could not escape. It fascinated me; I continued to admire it, while being intrigued by what I did *not* understand about it. I went on to study it carefully in various courses as a graduate student and eventually, almost against my intention, wrote a dissertation on it. I say "against my intention," because my plan was to write my thesis in systematic political philosophy – an argument, I conceived, for the importance of "civic friendship" in political society. But to do this, I had to study the notion of friendship, as a preliminary. And to study friendship, I needed to master the very best discussion of the subject, which happens to be found – wouldn't you know? – in books 8 and 9 of the *Ethics*. And that turned out to be the topic of my dissertation.

I suppose it is the definition of a fundamental text that it is preliminary: it is what one should ideally read and master before going on to study and think about other things. By this definition, Aristotle's *Ethics* counts as one of the most fundamental texts in Western thought. It lies at the root of moral philosophy, political theory, behavioral science, and economics, besides being of pervasive and continued influence in literature and culture generally.

Not surprisingly, many books have been written about so fundamental a work. Why, then, am I offering yet another? The explanation is provided by my own experience. I have tried to write a book that would save a student today some of the labor I needed for reading and understanding the *Ethics*. My aim has been to formulate and then pass on something of what I have learned in grappling with the *Ethics* during these years. For instance, there is a particular art or skill of reading Aristotle, which involves being able to see that he is proposing an argument, in a sentence or passage, and then to reconstruct that argument for reflection and evaluation. The density and concentration of Aristotle's thought is difficult for a beginning student to appreciate, not least because hardly anyone else writes in this way; nearly every sentence plays a role in some argument or other, and every word plays a specific role in the sentence, as in a carefully crafted poem. I try to explain how Aristotle writes and give hints for recognizing arguments.

And then there are distinctive methods of analysis which Aristotle employs but which will be alien for us, because although these methods have analogues in ordinary language and commonsense, they are not explicitly formulated or directly relied upon in most systematic thought of the last several centuries, and they seem intractable by the usual methods of logical analysis. The most important of these are Aristotle's notions of "focal meaning," "analogy," "categories" of predication, and reduplicative predication. These are absolutely fundamental for understanding Aristotle, and yet readers whose education has led them to regard either classical mathematics or first-order logic as an adequate framework for reasoning – that is, nearly all of us – will find these notions obscure. We are tempted to pass over, dismiss, or change through reformulation precisely those claims of Aristotle that one must treat as central, if one is to understand his thought. My aim in this book, rather, has been to give special attention to these methods of analysis and the claims which make particular use of them.

It seems to me, too, that a student of Aristotle needs help in discerning what might be called the "high themes" of the *Ethics*. In this work the forest is sometimes just as difficult to see as the trees.

What are Aristotle's intentions? How does a particular difficulty appear to *him* (not to *us*)? Why exactly is he taking the approach that he does? What is the upshot of a particular series of arguments or claims? Aristotle does not mark his text with chapter headings. He rarely announces what he is attempting to show. Frequently, to understand a section of argument requires that we see that a particular presupposition is in place, motivating Aristotle's investigation. A beginning student could easily knock his or her head against the *Ethics* for hours on end and not make much progress in discovering such things. A chief aim of this book, then, has been to clarify as much as possible the proper context and relevant presuppositions of Aristotle's discussions.

On a related point, I should say that I reject, both for the purpose of this book, and as correct doctrine on Aristotle, the common view that the *Ethics* is a collection or cobbling together of separate treatises or discussions, lacking genuine unity. It seems clear to me that the most useful working hypothesis for a student is to presume that the *Ethics* possesses great integrity and is skillfully and intelligently arranged, because surely we will not discover what order the work actually has unless we persevere in looking for it. The error of attributing order when there is not any is not particularly harmful, although it can be philosophically fruitful; but the error of too quickly supposing discontinuities in the text can be harmful and is usually unfruitful. Throughout this book I aim to draw attention to some of the many connections and cross-references which, I believe, bind the *Ethics* together.

As regards passages in which there is no suspicion of disunity or editorial manipulation, it seems similarly the most useful working hypothesis to hold that Aristotle is saying something plausible, interesting, and possibly profound, even when all kinds of objections and difficulties present themselves. It has been said that the sign of a great philosopher is that "the smarter you get, the smarter he gets." Aristotle is certainly a great philosopher. Generally, then, interpretations which would present Aristotle as saying something uninteresting or ill-considered risk revealing more about the interpreter than about the text being interpreted. It is a relatively easy matter to raise problems about what Aristotle says; it is difficult, in contrast, to see how these might be resolved or settled. My approach, then, is generally to take for granted that students will see difficulties and to presume that what they need particular assistance in, rather, is seeing how, in the face of these, Aristotle may nonetheless be saying something valuable.

Everyone who writes an introductory book in philosophy is aware that some delicate decisions need to be made about how much to bring in secondary literature, and about whether the standard views are to be considered, even when the writer regards such views as mistaken. These determinations, it seems to me, are relative to one's purposes. If one's goal is to prepare students, who already have a grounding in philosophy and some familiarity with the *Ethics*, for graduate study or future scholarly work, then it is quite necessary that they be introduced systematically to the best secondary literature, and that they know which views are the "standard" views, and which prominent alternative positions have been proposed. That a major scholar has put forward a view is reason enough to consider it, then, even if that view appears false.

But my goal in this book is in contrast relatively modest. It is simply to provide a clear, accessible, and comprehensive introduction to Aristotle's *Ethics* for a student with a minimal background in philosophy and ethics, and who will probably go on to do something other than academic work in philosophy. It has therefore seemed wise to keep to a minimum any explicit consideration of secondary literature (apart from the bibliographical notes that follow each chapter) and even in some cases, when this has served the purpose of the book, to give relatively slight attention to interpretations which have nonetheless been widely accepted among scholars.

My reluctance explicitly to discuss the scholarly literature should not be taken as a sign that I consider myself as somehow above or beyond reliance upon it. By no means is this true. At every step of my education I have relied upon the writings of scholars and commentators; I would be a fool and ungrateful not to regard myself as thoroughly indebted to the contributions of others. Moreover, and obviously, it would be self-defeating for someone who has himself contributed publications to the secondary literature – and is now putting forward a new work of scholarship – to depreciate work of that sort. Rather, I conceive of my approach as once again one of economy: I hope to save students some labor in the fields of scholarship, although without doubt someone must do that work, if not students themselves, then others. And sometimes due respect for scholarship takes the form of, for the moment, passing over it.

Not that I always adequately recognize my indebtedness; in fact, I must confess an intellectual debt that has for a long time needed acknowledgment. When I wrote my Clarendon Aristotle volume on *Nicomachean Ethics*, books 8 and 9, now seven years ago, I thought of that as *not* a "dissertation book" – which was correct. And on those grounds, in something of an adolescent conceit of philosophical independence – which was not correct – I omitted acknowledgment in print of my dissertation supervisors, Sarah Broadie and John Rawls, who had contributed to the book indirectly through their help with the earlier dissertation. Broadie was my mentor; the very rare combination of analytic clarity and philosophical depth in her own work remains an ideal that I would be pleased to imitate. Rawls was an extraordinarily generous teacher and, as is now well known, a remarkable historian of philosophy, who taught me and other students by his own example how to read great philosophical texts with seriousness and integrity. To be able to acknowledge my gratitude to them is itself a cause of gratitude.

I am conscious that particular parts of this book have been shaped by discussions with Victor Caston, Patrick Corrigan, Anthony Price, and Stephen White. I owe a general intellectual debt to Jennifer Whiting, my teacher, and through her to Terence Irwin, in matters of interpreting the *Ethics*. My thought on the *Ethics* has otherwise been particularly shaped by the writings of David Bostock, John Cooper, Robert Heinaman, Richard Kraut, Gavin Lawrence, and Nicholas White. I am grateful as well to students at Clark University and Brown University, where much of the material of this book was first tested.

For financial assistance in completing this work I wish to thank the Higgins School of the Humanities at Clark University and the Earhart Foundation. The book was drafted during a sabbatical leave, generously provided by Clark University. When I needed a sabbatical from that sabbatical, I retreated to The Currier's House in Jaffrey, New Hampshire, where Nancy Lloyd, the Innkeeper and herself an author, provided much appreciated and refreshing hospitality, for which I am very grateful. I additionally thank Gisela Striker for sponsoring my position as a Visiting Scholar at Harvard during that sabbatical year, and David Sedley for arranging a brief visit too in the Classics Faculty of Cambridge University.

I am much indebted to Hilary Gaskin at Cambridge University Press for her unflagging helpfulness and keen editorial insight. An anonymous press reader gave useful suggestions as regards the penultimate draft. Anthony Price generously read a large portion of the typescript and offered many perceptive comments. My son, Maximilian Pakaluk, to whom this book is dedicated, read carefully and discussed with me the entire typescript, to its great improvement.

Jay Delahanty's friendship proved an indispensable support in the final months of revision.

Above all I thank my dear wife, Catherine Ruth, for her devotion and life-bringing love, and for her willingness to see with me whether it isn't true after all that *amor con amor se paga.*

CHAPTER I

Reading Aristotle's Nicomachean Ethics

THE BASIC STRUCTURE OF THE *NICOMACHEAN ETHICS*

The *Nicomachean Ethics*, Aristotle tells us, is a search or an investigation (1.6.1096a12; b35; 1102a13). It poses a question at the start, looks at various possible answers along the way, and concludes with a definite judgment. The treatise therefore has something of the shape of a detective story.

What Aristotle tells us he is looking for, and what he wants us to join with him in looking for, is what he calls the "ultimate goal" of human life. Informally, we might think of this as what counts as "doing well" in life, or what it is for someone to be in the true sense "a success." To attain our ultimate goal is to achieve "happiness." Practically speaking, the ultimate goal in life is something toward which we would do well to direct everything else that we do. We reasonably *prefer* this to anything else. Our ultimate goal, we might think, is something we can *rest satisfied in*: when we attain it, we require nothing more.

Is there such a goal which is the same for all, and, if so, what is it? This is the basic question of the *Ethics*.

It is useful to think of any search as involving four basic elements. Suppose, for instance, that a detective wished to establish the identity of a person who committed a murder. First, she would formulate a description of the murderer, or *criteria* that the murderer satisfied: she might have deduced, for instance, from examining the crime scene, that the murderer wore cowboy boots and walked with a limp. Secondly, she would draw up a list of suspects, or a *field of search* – those people who just possibly committed the murder. Thirdly, she would question and *examine* those suspects one by one. While doing so – and this is the fourth step – she would *apply her criteria*, seeing whether they picked out just one suspect as the murderer, the suspect who, as it turns out, wears cowboy boots and walks with a limp.[1]

Aristotle's search for the ultimate goal of human life follows similar lines. First, at the beginning of the *Ethics*, he formulates criteria which, he thinks, an ultimate goal must satisfy: he maintains that it must be *most ultimate*; *self-sufficient*; and *most preferable* (1.7.1097a25–b21).[2] Secondly, he identifies a field of search: in the famous Function Argument of 1.7 (1097b22–1098a20) he argues that our ultimate goal is to be found among those activities that we can perform only through our having good traits of character, or the virtues. This is what he means when he says, in the oft-cited tag, that the highest human good is "activity in accordance with virtue" (1098a16–17). Thirdly, he proceeds to examine one by one the virtues and their characteristic activities, such as courage, generosity, and justice. This project occupies the bulk of the treatise, books 3–6. Fourthly and finally, after looking at some supplemental topics, Aristotle applies his original criteria and argues in 10.6–8 that the intellectual activity which is an expression of the virtue of "philosophical wisdom" (*sophia*) is the ultimate goal of human life:

> The activity that we carry out with our minds, a kind of perceptual activity,[3] seems to excel over all others in goodness. It aims at no goal beyond itself. It has its distinctive pleasure (which augments the activity). And, clearly, the self-sufficiency, freedom from necessity, effortlessness of the sort that human nature can attain, and anything else that is attributed to a blessedly happy person, are achieved through this activity. This, then, would be a human being's ultimate happiness ... (10.7.1177b19–26)

Thus, the *Ethics* consists of three main sections, as well as a fourth, which discusses side topics. An outline of the treatise would look something like this:

THE ULTIMATE GOAL OF HUMAN LIFE
   Criteria and Field of Search (1.1–12)

---

[1] Of course it might happen that more than one suspect met the criteria.
[2] We shall look at these criteria more closely in the next chapter.
[3] Aristotle strictly says that this sort of activity is "theoretical" or "contemplative," that is, it is a kind of seeing or insight. At this point, it is least misleading to call this a kind of perception, not meaning by this any sort of *sense* perception.

THE VIRTUES AND THEIR CHARACTERISTIC ACTIONS
  The Origin, Definition, and Classification of Virtue (1.13, book 2)
  The Relationship between Virtue and Action (3.1–5)
  The Virtues (3.6–6.13)

    A. Character-Related Virtues
      1. Courage (3.6–9)
      2. Moderation (3.10–12)
      3. Generosity (4.1)
      4. Magnificence (4.2)
      5. Magnanimity (4.3)
      6. Minor character-related virtues (4.4–9)
      7. Justice (5.1–11)

    B. Thinking-Related Virtues (6.1–13)
      1. Demonstrative knowledge (6.3)
      2. Craftsmanship (6.4)
      3. Administrative skill (6.5)
      4. Good intuition (6.6)
      5. Philosophical wisdom (6.7)
      6. Minor thinking-related virtues (6.9–11)

SIDE TOPICS
  Self-Control and Lack of Self-Control (7.1–10)
  Bodily Pleasure (7.11–14)
  Friendship (8.1–9.12)
  Pleasure Generally (10.1–5)

HAPPINESS RECONSIDERED (10.6–8)[4]

THE FUNDAMENTAL IDEA OF THE ETHICS

But if the treatise is a search for our ultimate goal, then why – we might wonder – is it called a treatise on "ethics"? Does "ethics" not have to do with obligations, rules, principles, and duties? Why not

---

[4] The last chapter of the treatise, 10.9, seems to be a transitional chapter, the purpose of which is to argue that the study of the ultimate good for a human being leads naturally into the study of laws and political institutions. It links the *Ethics* to the *Politics*.

call it instead a treatise on "the purpose of human life," or "what we should all be striving for"?

The treatise gets its name because of the *manner* in which Aristotle searches for the ultimate goal. As was mentioned, Aristotle holds that our ultimate end is to be found among those of our actions that we can carry out only as a result of having good traits of character, or the virtues. And the Greek word which means "pertaining to traits of character" is *ēthikē*, the source of our word "ethics." Aristotle's treatise is about "ethics," then, in the historic and original sense of that term.[5] (It is called "*Nicomachean*" after Aristotle's son, Nicomachus, but whether because it was dedicated to Nicomachus or because Nicomachus was the editor, we do not know.)

But this only leads to the more important question: why does Aristotle hold that our ultimate goal is "activity in accordance with virtue"? Since this is perhaps the most distinctive and fundamental claim of the *Ethics*, it is good to have an initial understanding of what Aristotle meant by it, and what his reasons were for his holding it. I shall examine these matters more carefully in the next chapter, but a brief introduction is useful here.

Aristotle's claim is based on a principle which he takes over from Plato and which might be called the "Interdefinability of Goodness, Virtue, and Function." By the "function" (*ergon*, literally "work" or "task") of a thing, understand its characteristic activity or achievement. According to Plato, we can identify the function of a thing by considering what that sort of thing alone can achieve, or can achieve better than anything else (*Republic* 352e). For instance, the "function" of a knife is to cut: cutting is something that a knife alone achieves, or achieves better than any other available instrument.[6] If you were to pick your way through a drawer in a kitchen, from the shape of a knife you might be able to see that its distinctive task is to cut; some other implement is designed to crush garlic; something else works to flip pancakes or hamburgers; and so on. You could hardly cut an apple with a flipper, or crush garlic with a paring

---

[5] This in turn should serve as a warning in our approach to the treatise: we should not presume at the start that Aristotle is concerned with what *we* mean by "morality" and "ethics."

[6] The point is even clearer with specialized knives: you will not be able to prune a tree, or prune it well, except with a pruning knife.

knife, or flip pancakes with a garlic press. Each sort of implement has its own job to do, and this is its "function." Plato and Aristotle look at the kinds of things that exist in nature in much the same way. A kind of thing would not exist, unless it had some distinctive role to play.

Clearly a thing carries out its "function," in this sense, either well or badly: one knife cuts well; another cuts poorly. What explains the difference? A knife that cuts well will have features or "traits" that make it cut well; a knife that cuts poorly will lack those same features – such things, obviously, as the blade's *taking a sharp edge*; its *holding a sharp edge*; its *having the right shape and size* for the sort of cutting it is supposed to do (small and thin for paring; large and wedge-shaped for dicing; etc.); and so on. It was natural for a Greek speaker of Aristotle's time to call these traits, which make a thing do its work well, the "virtues" of a thing of that sort.

The relevant Greek word is *aretē*, which means broadly any sort of excellence or distinctive power. In Aristotle's time, the term would be applied freely to instruments, natural substances, and domestic animals – not simply to human beings. If you were going into battle, for instance, you would seek a horse with "virtue," in order to draw a chariot that had "virtue," made of materials that had the relevant "virtues." The term connoted strength and success, as also did the Latin term *virtus*. Our English word, too, in its origin had similar connotations. Something of this original significance is still preserved in such idioms as "in virtue of": "The knife cuts *in virtue of* its sharpness."[7]

Any knife that has all of these good traits, and any other "virtues" that it should have, will as a result be a *good* knife, whereas a knife

---

[7] Because the Greek, *aretē*, could be applied in this wide-ranging way but it is no longer natural to use our word "virtue" in this way, some commentators recommend that *aretē* be translated instead as "excellence." The term "excellence" makes it clear at once that *aretē* is not a specifically moral term, and that it has something to do with distinction and special achievement. Yet it could be said, as against this, that it is likewise unnatural for us to use "excellence" to refer to such traits as generosity and justice. And, as I said, the English term "virtue" is not lacking in suggestions of strength and power. My own view is that it is better to try to reclaim the word "virtue," restoring it in part to its earlier meaning, by deliberately retaining the word in discussions of Greek ethics – keeping in mind all along what the term actually means.

that noticeably lacks one of them will be a *bad* knife. If this is so, then the notions of *function, kind, virtue,* and *goodness* are interdefinable, a relationship which can be expressed in the following claim:

The Interdefinability of Goodness, Function, and Virtue. A *good* thing of a certain kind is that which has the *virtues* that enable it to carry out its *function* well.

A second important principle that Aristotle presupposes is that there is some close relationship between *goals* and *goods*: he believes that for something *to be a good* simply is for it, somehow, *to be a goal.* (This claim, in contrast, seems *not* to have come from Plato. It looks to be original with Aristotle, even though in the opening of the *Ethics* he denies special credit for the insight.)

Suppose now that we take a goal to be *something at which other things are directed.* It would follow that the good of a thing would be that at which other things involving it would be directed. Consider the parts of a knife, for instance. We see that they are designed so that each contributes to the task of cutting: the knife has a blade of a certain length, which is made out of a particular material, and is mounted on a handle in a certain way, all so that it can cut. The goal of a knife, then, would seem to involve cutting. If a goal is a good, then the good of a knife would seem to involve cutting. It is odd, perhaps, to say that something like a knife has a good. But then we might say that if a knife were a living thing, then its good would be to cut. What it would aim to do, the achievement it would most basically seek, would be somehow to engage in cutting.

Of course, a rusty or broken knife will not cut very well or safely. A knife with a dull blade might not even be able to cut at all. We could hardly tell the function of a broken knife, and it would seem misguided in any case to say that it attains the goal of a knife. We would not look to a broken or rusty knife to see what the point of a knife was. So it seems more appropriate to say that the goal or good of a knife is not simply *cutting,* but rather *cutting well.*

However, to cut is the function of a knife, and, as I have said, something carries out its function *well* only through its having the "virtues" of that kind of thing. Thus, it would be most appropriate to say that the ultimate goal of a knife is to engage in cutting *in the way that a knife cuts when it has the "virtues" of a knife.* Consider the difference between a knife in a good condition – sharpened, safely constructed, and well maintained – and a knife in a bad condition – rusty, poorly made, or damaged. Consider the difference that being in good condition makes for cutting: what the good knife can achieve that the bad knife cannot. The ultimate goal or good of a knife will be located, then, precisely in that difference of achievement. The ultimate goal or good of a knife will consist in what a knife can achieve precisely through its being sharp, safely constructed, and well maintained.

The *Ethics* is essentially Aristotle's application of a similar line of thought to human beings rather than knives. Aristotle thinks that, however much we might disagree about the justice or rightness of particular actions, we find ourselves in general agreement as to what counts as a good human being. This is reflected in how we use the word "good": we are generally agreed in applying the word "good" only to those persons who have such traits as generosity, courage, fairness, and so on, and who do not noticeably have any traits that are contrary to these. We do not disagree that the fact that someone is generous or fair-minded provides us, to that extent, with a reason for calling that person "good."

So we are generally agreed, Aristotle thinks, on what counts as a good trait or "virtue." But the line of thought developed above would indicate that the ultimate goal of a human being, just like that of anything else, would consist in our carrying out our function well; and our carrying out that function well, as in other cases, is found in what we can achieve precisely through our having those traits that make us good: the "virtues" of human beings. Thus, Aristotle thinks, the way to become clearer about the ultimate goal of human life is to examine more carefully what it is we can achieve or carry out precisely through our having the virtues. The human good will be found among activities such as these, just as the point of being a knife can be discerned in what it is that a good knife in particular can accomplish.

This is the fundamental idea of the *Ethics*, and this is why Aristotle devotes the bulk of the treatise to a careful – and, he thinks, *exhaustive* – examination of the various human virtues and their characteristic actions.

A FIRST DIFFICULTY — AND THEN FOUR OTHERS

Selection or Collection?

Yet as soon as this fundamental idea is sketched, an ambiguity appears in what I have said. I said that Aristotle thinks that our ultimate goal will be found among those of our actions that we can do only as a result of our having good traits of character. But "among" could mean either of two things – either that *one* such action is our ultimate goal, or that *all* such actions are our ultimate goal. Either there is just one virtue, such that the actions that we can achieve through having that particular virtue constitute our ultimate goal; or any virtue is such that the actions that we can accomplish only through having that virtue constitute our ultimate goal. On the former, we are looking for one sort of virtuous activity as being the ultimate goal; on the latter, we are looking for every sort of virtuous activity as belonging to the ultimate goal. On the former, we should identify the ultimate goal by "selecting out" one activity in accordance with virtue; on the latter, we do so by "collecting together" all such activities. Is Aristotle advocating that we settle the matter by Selection or by Collection?

Here is an analogy. Suppose someone were to say, "The ultimate goal of a physician is to heal patients by employing medical skill of the best sort." That is a vague claim so far, because we do not know what "medical skill of the best sort" is. Suppose that the person who makes this claim then goes on to discuss all the various types of medical skill: skill in setting bones; skill in treating intestinal problems; skill in brain surgery; and so on. When he has finished enumerating and examining all of the specialties and sub-specialties in medicine, he could do either of two things. He could select out one such skill and say something like the following: "The best sort of medical skill is seen in the work of a brain surgeon, since brain surgery aims at health in the best and most important part of the body." Or he could collect together all of these skills and maintain: "The best sort of medical skill is found in someone who combines into one all of these various abilities – a family practitioner – since that sort of physician aims at all-round healthiness."

In the same way, it is not entirely clear whether Aristotle examines the various virtues and their activities with a view to selecting out one of them or collecting all of them together. This is a fairly well-worn controversy among scholars, and standard names have been given to the different views. An interpretation of the *Ethics* which takes Aristotle to be selecting out one sort of virtuous activity is typically called a "Dominant End" or "Intellectualist" interpretation ("Intellectualist" on the grounds that that activity is distinctive of the human intellect). An interpretation which takes Aristotle to be collecting together all virtuous activities (and perhaps even including other things besides) is typically called an "Inclusivist" or "Comprehensivist" interpretation.

At first glance, it looks as though the *Ethics* has no uniform view. In book 10, as we saw, it looks as though Aristotle intends to *select*: the ultimate goal of human life, he maintains there, is the sort of activity we can engage in through having the virtue of philosophical wisdom (*sophia*). But book 1, with its famous Function Argument, and also the fundamental idea which motivates the treatise would seem to commit Aristotle to *collection*: if the ultimate goal of human life is what a good human being can achieve through his having the virtues, and if there are many virtues, then the ultimate goal of human life, it seems, should include *any* sort of action that we accomplish through our having a virtue. And it is difficult to understand how virtuous actions could otherwise have the weight that they do for Aristotle: as we shall see, he thinks we should do them for their own sake, and that frequently we should be prepared even to die rather than do something contrary to a virtue. But why should this be appropriate, unless *all* such actions were somehow included in our ultimate goal?

A complicating problem is that Aristotle himself seems aware of the ambiguity of Selection versus Collection, and he seems even deliberately to cultivate or prolong the ambiguity. Consider the following passages:

The human good turns out to be activity in accordance with virtue, and if the virtues are several, then in accordance with the best and most ultimate virtue. (1.7.1098a16–18)

All these things [sc. goodness, usefulness, pleasure] belong to the best sorts of activities, and these, or the best one of them, we claim, is happiness. (1.8.1099a29–31)

And presumably it's even necessary, if there are unimpeded activities corresponding to each condition, that, regardless of whether happiness is the activity of all of them or of some particular one of them, that, if it's unimpeded, it's the most preferable thing. (7.13.1153b9–14)

Regardless, then, of whether the activities of a mature and blessedly happy human being are of one sort or are several in kind, the pleasures that bring these to completion would properly be said to be "human pleasures." (10.5.1176a26–28)

It has frequently been pointed out that Selection and Collection need not be regarded as exclusive. Aristotle's view of the human good might be that it consists of a variety of activities, but as having a certain ordering, with only one such activity being first or at the top. Happiness for us, then, would be to engage in that first-ranked activity, while having all the other virtues and putting them into practice as appropriate. So perhaps Aristotle does not regard Selection and Collection as exclusive; perhaps he prolongs the ambiguity because he thinks he never needs to dispel it.

The Problem of Order

And yet, if we accept this solution, we seem to be led directly into another difficulty, which similarly seems to make its appearance at various points in the treatise. We may call it the "Problem of Order."

The problem arises in the following way. There are many things that we apparently do for their own sake, for instance, watching a good movie; solving a puzzle for the fun of it; or giving someone a gift as a "random act of kindness." Aristotle, in fact, goes so far as to say that every truly virtuous act is carried out for its own sake (2.4.1105a32). Apparently his view is that there cannot be "ulterior motives" behind a truly generous action: we perform such an action simply to "show generosity" (as we might say), because it is an inherently good thing to be generous.

This attitude seems fairly important in friendship as well. In a true friendship, Aristotle says, we show affection for another person "for his own sake": we recognize his good traits; appreciate and admire them; and then we want to benefit him somehow, simply because of what we like about him (cf. 8.2.1155b31, 8.3.1156b10). Clearly, "ulterior motives" have no place in a true friendship: it is not a true friendship, it seems, if we befriend someone in order to get something out of him.

But now juxtapose this with the idea, which Aristotle also endorses, that we do everything that we do for the sake of happiness (1.2.1094a19), and two difficulties arise.

First, it begins to look as though "ulterior motives" are inescapable. Someone who gives a gift as a "random act of kindness" would then also be promoting his own ultimate good, according to Aristotle. Even a true friend would not do good things for his friend simply for the sake of that friend; he would do them also for the sake of his own good. But then Aristotle's view begins to look disturbing. Some scholars have even claimed that it is incoherent: does it make any sense to say that you love someone "for his own sake, for your sake"? Or that you do something "for its own sake, for your own sake"?

Secondly, if we do whatever we do for the sake of some ultimate goal, what will prevent our concern with that goal from swamping every other consideration and every other value? Suppose we do X for the sake of Y. Then it might seem that X is a mere means to the achieving of Y. Thus, if we could obtain Y without recourse to X, then we would do so; and X becomes unimportant. Now apply this to the case at hand. Suppose that we act virtuously and love our friends for the sake of our own ultimate good. Then it seems that these actions are mere means to our own happiness, and, in those cases in which we *could* achieve our happiness by dispensing with these things, there is no reason why we *would* not do so. In particular, it looks as though nothing would prevent us from acting non-virtuously or treacherously when doing so would advance our own ultimate interests.

Both of these issues involve the Problem of Order in the *Ethics*, because both are concerned with the general problem of how it is possible that we pursue a variety of goods for their own sake, when these goods have a certain ordering – some of them being sought for the sake of others. It is clear, as I said above, that any attempt to combine Selection and Collection would run straight into this problem.

Egoism versus Altruism

The Problem of Order seems related to another difficulty involving "Egoism" (or self-love, self-interest) and "Altruism" (or love of others, benevolence, other-regarding attitudes). Aristotle says that each of us aims above all at the ultimate goal of human life, or happiness, and that we aim at everything else for the sake of this (1.7.1097a34–b6). But does he mean that each of us aims at *his own* happiness, or at happiness in some general sense? It seems that he holds the former: he thinks, for instance, that each person should prefer his own happiness to that of others (8.7.1159a12) and love himself most of all (cf. 9.8). But if so, then Aristotle apparently holds that human action is in some fundamental sense egoistic.

But then he needs to explain why we at least *seem* to act altruistically, and there would seem to be roughly three alternatives:

1. Appearances are deceiving: although we appear to act altruistically, in fact all of our actions are expressions of self-interest. This is the view that Aristotle seems to adopt when he maintains that seemingly self-sacrificial actions, such as giving a gift to a friend, are really actions in which a person gains a benefit for himself, because in giving away a mere material possession, the giver gains for himself a distinctive and better ethical good (9.8.1169a18–b1). Apparent self-sacrifice, then, is in reality a form of acquisitiveness.

2. A virtuous life requires a kind of *replacement* of motives: each of us begins life aiming at his own happiness above all, but through the right sort of ethical education and training, this motive can become supplanted by new and distinct motives, involving altruistic regard for the welfare of others. Some of Aristotle's remarks on moral education suggest that he holds this view – that we can acquire the virtues only if those responsible for our upbringing impose the appropriate altruistic attitude upon us, before we are in a position to accept or reject it rationally (see, for instance, 1.4.1095b4–6).

3. A virtuous life involves the merging or contrived coincidence of egoism and altruism: although each of us begins life aiming at his own happiness, we can after all acquire *friendships*, and a friendship may be understood as simply a social structure in which it becomes impossible to draw any sharp distinction between the good of the one friend and that of the other. Some scholars have thought that Aristotle's extended treatment of friendship in books 8 and 9 is intended, in part, to respond to the Problem of Egoism and Altruism in this way.

A problem related to that of Egoism and Altruism is whether Aristotle thinks that the ultimate goal of human life is something that people can reasonably seek individually, or only in a group, and, if in a group, then whether someone achieves that goal if the group does. For instance, "walking on the moon" is not a goal that someone can reasonably seek on his own. A person can succeed in walking on the moon only if he is a member of a large cooperative enterprise which takes this as its goal, namely the "Space Program." Yet at the same time, it seems that any member of the Space Program can "claim credit" for walking on the moon when it succeeds in placing an astronaut on the moon. It seems that the entire Space Program and all of its members achieve this goal of walking on the moon, even though only a handful of astronauts actually do the walking.

Does Aristotle think of the ultimate goal of human life in this way? As we shall see, he apparently writes the *Ethics* for legislators and political leaders. Does he think that the ultimate goal of human life is something that people can reasonably seek only as citizens in a political society which takes that as its goal? And, if so, does he think that *all* of the members of such a society can claim to achieve that goal, if *some* of its members do?

Moral objectivity

Call "conventionalism" in ethics the view that ethical requirements are ultimately based only on human decision or agreement. Aristotle rejects this view (see 1.3.1094b14–16; 5.7.1134b18–20), and is, to that extent, an "objectivist" in ethics, and yet his reasons *why* are not entirely clear.

That he rejects conventionalism is not surprising given the Function Argument: as we saw, Aristotle believes that human beings have a definite, common, and objective nature, and that, as a result, we have in common some ultimate goal. He also likes to use sense perception as a model for sound judgment in ethical matters. For instance: "a good person is especially distinctive because he sees the truth in each case" (3.4.1113a32–33); "in any particular case, things *are* the way they *seem to be* to a good person" (10.5.1176a15–16). Language like this seems to suggest that ethical attributes are somehow based on the nature of things.

Yet Aristotle says little to explain or justify such a view. What is it about reality that is perceived when a good person perceives correctly some ethical attribute? Aristotle variously describes virtuous actions as "noble" or "admirable" (*kalon*); "fitting" (*prepon*); or "fair" and "equal" (*ison*); but he does not give criteria or standards for these things. Does he have a view, which he presupposes and is implicit in what he says, or has he simply not given sufficient thought to this matter at all? The latter would be strange, since Aristotle's predecessors in ethics, Socrates and Plato, precisely insisted that thoughtful people should be able to give definitions of ethical attributes.

It has been a common view in moral philosophy since at least David Hume in the eighteenth century that moral judgments cannot be about objective features in the world. Ethical attributes seem not to be observable, as are physical attributes. And there seems to be a yawning gap between physical "facts" and ethical "values": notably, ethical principles are prescriptive, in contrast with the descriptive laws that are formulated by natural science. But if ethics is discontinuous with science, yet science comprises our knowledge about the world, then ethics would not involve knowledge about the world. Ethical opinions, it might seem, would merely be the expression of our subjective interests and likings. Aristotle is not unaware of this sort of view, since several of his predecessors held something similar, but he shows little sympathy for it. In the *Ethics* he apparently presupposes that moral phenomena are entirely of a piece with natural science. If ethical judgments are distinctive, it is because they are practical, not subjective (see 6.1–2).

The Problem of Objectivity seems related to the Problems of Order and of Egoism and Altruism. We can say, roughly, that if there were "objective" grounds for counting something as inherently worthy of our pursuit, then this being so would presumably remain true even if we pursued it also for the sake of our happiness. These "objective" grounds might conceivably place *constraints*, even, on our pursuit of that other thing. Suppose, for instance, that it were somehow objectively "fitting" (say) to repay a gift from a friend before initiating a gift exchange with a stranger, all things being equal. Then, if we were to choose the former over the latter, we might be doing so *both* because it (simply) is "fitting" *and* because doing that contributed to our own good. It would make sense to say something like, "Yes, I'm pursuing my own happiness, but not in such a way as to do anything unfitting, say, favoring a stranger over a friend with gifts." That *seems* to be the way Aristotle views the matter, but, as was said, the nature and grounds of his view seem to be largely unexplained.

The Problem of Guidance

A related problem involves how we are to decide which action or course of action is right. Aristotle emphasizes that ethics is a practical discipline. He insists that its purpose is not simply to help us understand goodness and badness, and right and wrong, but also and more importantly to help us actually *to become good* and *to do what is right.* "The point of these lectures," he says, 'is not knowledge but action' (1.5.1095a5–6); "We're not engaging in this task simply to theorize, as in other disciplines: we're not inquiring in order to *know* what goodness is, but rather *to become good* ourselves, since otherwise there wouldn't be any point" (2.2.1103b26–29). "In practical matters the point is not simply to examine various things and to know them, but rather to *do* them. It's hardly enough to 'know things' about virtue: we have to try to acquire it and put it to use – unless you suppose there's some other way of becoming good" (10.9.1179a35–b4).

But apparently we could not put his teaching into practice, as Aristotle intends, unless we had some definite, practical advice, which we could actually follow. Yet there seems to be precious little of that in the *Ethics.* And what Aristotle *does* tell us seems empty or too vague to follow. In many of his discussions of particular virtues, he describes the behavior of a virtuous person simply by giving what seems an uninstructive list: for instance, a courageous person fears the things that he should fear, at the right times, to the right degree, and in the appropriate manner (e.g. 3.7.1115b15–16). In other places, Aristotle says that a person who has a particular virtue will act "in the way that a person with practical wisdom would advise" (e.g. 2.6.1107a1–2).

Perhaps it is unavoidable in matters of morality that we rely on authorities at some point: to put Aristotle's teaching into practice, then, we would have to find a person with good judgment, and simply follow what he tells us. Yet on this view as well a difficulty threatens: how do we identify such a person? Aristotle says that a person cannot have good judgment in such matters unless he has all of the other virtues (see 6.13). So, to identify a person with good judgment, we would need to identify first a person who had courage. But how could we identify a courageous person, unless we knew what counted as courageous? – which is exactly what we supposed we lacked.

Another way to state the Problem of Guidance is as follows. We might think that people typically learn to do what they regard as right through being given precepts or commands (the Ten Commandments); lists of duties (such as, in past centuries, books on the "Whole Duty of Man"); solutions of problematic cases (what is known as "casuistry"); a balancing of authoritative opinion (as in the Talmud); or bits of common wisdom (such as the Book of Proverbs). Or, again, we acquire convictions about right action by being shown examples of correct action in stories or in the biographies of exemplary women and men. But the *Ethics* neither contains anything like that nor refers us, apparently, to these sorts of guides. (Consider Plato, in contrast, who gives, for instance, detailed advice about the sorts of stories a young person should be exposed to, in *Republic*, books 2–3.) It seems that Aristotle neither gives such practical advice himself nor tells us where we can find it. Someone might read his treatise with great care, it seems, and agree with all of its conclusions and yet not have the slightest idea of what to do next.

BACKGROUND FOR THE *ETHICS*: ARISTOTLE'S LIFE AND WORKS

Could we perhaps get some help in resolving these difficulties by knowing the context of the *Ethics*? It is good in any case to know something about Aristotle's life and works, especially for someone who is approaching Aristotle for the first time precisely through a study of the *Ethics*.

Aristotle's life

When Martin Heidegger, the German existentialist philosopher, lectured on Aristotle, he would begin by saying, "The man was born, he worked, and then he died," and then turn directly to a discussion of philosophical matters, on the grounds that Aristotle's biography was irrelevant to his philosophy. But an acquaintance with the basic facts of Aristotle's life can at least help us to understand better some of Aristotle's interests and preoccupations, even if they were of little help in analyzing or evaluating his arguments.

Aristotle was born in 384 BC in Stagira, a small town on the coast of the Aegean Sea, about two hundred miles north of Athens. Aristotle's father, Nicomachus (after whom Aristotle would eventually name his own son), was a physician. Although medical science was a very crude affair in those days, nonetheless, with this background, we can presume that Aristotle from an early age would have been given the best available education, with special attention to biology and natural science. Moreover, we might expect that he would have been trained to have something of the outlook of a physician: an eye for detail; a hard-headed practicality; a concern with effective action; and an interest in both general principles and the idiosyncracies of their application in particular cases. This kind of temperament is in fact immediately evident in the *Ethics*, and medical examples abound. In general Aristotle tends to think of ethics as analogous to medicine. Plato taught that virtue was a kind of health of the soul; Aristotle, with a background in medicine, takes this analogy very seriously.

Stagira was close to Macedon, the most powerful dominion in the rugged mountain country to the north of Athens, and Aristotle's father served as court physician to Amyntas II, then King of Macedon, the father of Philip of Macedon and the grandfather of Alexander the Great. From an early age, then, we may imagine that Aristotle was at ease with the influential types of people who frequent royal courts: advisors, stewards, military men, generals, and law-makers. The *Ethics* seems in fact to be a course of lectures designed for people like that: as was said, it seems intended for an audience of would-be rulers, legislators, and advisors.

Aristotle was still a child when his father died. He was placed under the protection of one Proxenus, who apparently gets the credit for sending the seventeen-year-old Aristotle to study with Plato in Athens, a decision with world-changing implications. Plato, a follower of Socrates, had won renown by writing a brilliant series of dramatic intellectual discussions, or "dialogues," in the newly devised, cutting-edge discipline of "philosophy," and we may speculate that Aristotle was drawn to study in Athens after reading some of these dialogues.[8]

Plato had formed a research group, named the "Academy," after the public garden by that name, where its members would typically meet. Members of the Academy devoted themselves to systematic mathematical research but also, in a creative and critical spirit, to more broadly philosophical studies. This is the group that Aristotle would have joined: elite, priding themselves on rigorous argument (an inscription over the door of the Academy read, "No one unskilled in geometry may enter"), and committed to the primacy of the intellect and the supreme reality of the objects of thought. Aristotle's *Ethics*, no less than the rest of his writings, bristles with a kind of confidence in reasoning and a love of argument. Clearly Aristotle treasured and collected arguments, keeping them on hand like so many tools or weapons. And we might suppose that his early experience in the Academy served as a kind of model for him, of how human life should ideally be lived: good friends, freed from cares of business or troubles of war, engaged in a common and even competitive search for the truth.

Plato was apparently away when Aristotle arrived: off in Sicily on one of his desperate attempts to win the favor of the tyrant there, Dionysius, and convert him into a "philosopher-king," Plato's ideal ruler. Eudoxus, it seems, was left in charge of the Academy, and perhaps he would have been Aristotle's first instructor. The views of Eudoxus are frequently discussed in the *Ethics*, in each case with apparent admiration and respect.

Since Aristotle would be associated with the Academy for twenty years, he surely had many opportunities to study with Plato himself. It is sometimes claimed that throughout this period Aristotle was a fervent and even doctrinaire follower of Plato, and yet the idea seems implausible. The history of thought would suggest that someone with Aristotle's talents would almost certainly have arrived at his own distinctive ideas while a young man, near the beginning of his intellectual life. And since the Academy tolerated and even encouraged

---

[8] Aristotle would go on to write dialogues of his own, presumably in imitation of Plato's. But these have since been lost.

dissent and pluralism in philosophy, there is no reason to think that a young recruit like Aristotle would fall directly in line behind Plato. Yet this is not to deny that Plato was a great influence on Aristotle: in nearly all of his treatises, perhaps especially in the *Ethics*, Aristotle is wrestling with, attempting to refute, or developing ideas that originate with Plato.

Plato died in 347, when Aristotle was thirty-seven and, we may presume, just reaching his intellectual prime. That same year, Aristotle left the Academy, along with Xenocrates, another leading thinker of that school, and went to live in Assos on the northwest coast of Asia Minor (modern day Turkey). Some have speculated that Aristotle was disappointed that Speusippus had been selected instead of him as the next head of the Academy and left in a huff. (Not that we should suppose that Speusippus would have been preferred for philosophical reasons alone: he was the more natural choice, being twenty-five years Aristotle's senior and an Athenian citizen, whereas Aristotle's status in Athens was that of a "metic" or resident alien, lacking many legal rights relevant to serving as head of the school, such as the right to own property.) In any case there would have been overriding political reasons for a move: at about that time, Philip of Macedon had begun waging a brutal military campaign which appeared to threaten Athens; anti-Macedonian sentiment had become fierce; and Aristotle, with his connections to the Macedonian court, and as a resident alien, would have been in an uncomfortable situation if he had remained in Athens.

In Assos Aristotle enjoyed the friendship of King Hermias, marrying his niece and adopted daughter, Pythias, with whom he had a daughter (also named "Pythias"). Under the patronage of Hermias, Aristotle joined forces with Xenocrates and two other alumni of Plato's Academy who lived in the area, Erastus and Coriscus, to form a philosophical research group. (It is thought that Aristotle began his comprehensive biological treatises at this time, since a disproportionate number of examples from his biological treatises apparently involve species that are peculiar to the area.) This arrangement was to be short-lived, however, since in 345 the Persians invaded Assos, captured Hermias, and executed him; Aristotle and his colleagues escaped to the nearby island of Lesbos.

Deeply moved by Hermias' death, Aristotle composed a hymn to
Virtue personified in honor of his slain friend, which he was said to
have sung every evening after dinner, for the rest of his life. The point
of the hymn seems to be that heroic persons such as Hermias achieve
the immortality they implicitly long for, because through their
virtuous deeds they are eternally remembered by immortal gods.
That Aristotle would compose and regularly recite such a hymn is
revealing: it shows the strength of his devotion to his friend; his
esteem for virtue; and his generally pious outlook. Aristotle evidently
shared with many of his fellow Greeks a strong sense of the "divinity"
of admirable achievement.[9]

The next several years of Aristotle's life seem to have been fairly
unsettled, in part because of his changing relationship with the
Macedonian court: after Lesbos he moved to Macedon, as tutor to
thirteen-year-old Alexander the Great; and after that once again to
his hometown of Stagira for a short period. His wife, Pythias, died
during this time. Aristotle then developed a close relationship with
one Herpyllis, who came from Stagira, and they had a son
Nicomachus, whom I have mentioned.

In 334, when he was fifty years old, Aristotle returned to Athens,
perhaps at the insistence of Alexander the Great, where he established
in apparent competition with the Academy his own philosophical
community, which met in the Lyceum, a public gymnasium. Like the
other teachers who met there, Aristotle originally lectured in one of
the shaded walkways of the gymnasium, called a *peripatos*, which
is the origin of the term "Peripatetic," later applied to followers of
Aristotle's philosophy. The school soon acquired the use of nearby
rooms and these came to be known, by transference, as the "Lyceum."

It is not implausible to count Aristotle's school as the first university: it apparently had an exceptional library; rooms for collecting
specimens and doing scientific research; and, for classes, there were
morning and afternoon lectures by Aristotle, who was engaged in the

---

[9] Compare these provisions from Aristotle's will: "They should dedicate my mother's statue of
Demeter at Nemea, or wherever they think best. Wherever they put my tomb, they should
collect and place the bones of Pythias, as she herself requested. Because Nicanor returned
safely, he should put up stone statues 4 cubits high in Stagira to Zeus the Preserver and
Athena the Preserver, in fulfillment of my vow."

ambitious project of giving an account of everything that was then known. It was presumably at this time that Aristotle either wrote or put into near-finished form his various foundational treatises in almost every important area of knowledge: linguistics, logic, physics, chemistry, biology, psychology, earth science, astronomy, ethics, politics, constitutional theory, philosophy of law, rhetoric, literary criticism, and philosophy proper (which Aristotle labelled "metaphysics" – literally "what one investigates after one has mastered physics").

The vigor of Aristotle's thought, and the tone generally of the research in the Lyceum – wide ranging, inquisitive, relentlessly curious – are captured in a compilation of research questions and tentative hypotheses called the *Problemata*. Here are a few selections, taken at random:

Why do men generally themselves yawn when they see others yawn? Is it because, if they are reminded of it when they feel a desire to perform any function, they then put it into execution, particularly when the desire is easily stirred, for example, that of passing urine? (Problem 7.1)

Why is it that the bases of bubbles in water are white, and if they are placed in the sun they do not make any shadow, but, while the rest of the bubble casts a shadow, the base does not do so but is surrounded on all sides by sunlight? (Problem 16.1)

Why does a large choir keep better time than a small one? Is it because they look more to one man, their leader, and begin more slowly and so more easily achieve unity? For mistakes occur more frequently in quick singing. (Problem 19.22)

Why is it that in law courts, if equal votes are given for the two adversaries, the defendant wins the case? Is it because the defendant has remained unaffected by the action of the plaintiff, and in a position of equality with him he would probably have won? (Problem 29.15)

Why is it that one sneezes more after one has looked at the sun? Is it because the sun engenders heat and so causes movement, just as does tickling the nose with a feather? For both have the same effect; by setting up movement they cause heat and create breath more quickly from the moisture; and it is the escape of this breath which causes sneezing. (Problem 33.4)

The final year of Aristotle's life was spent in exile. After Alexander's death in 323, Athens rebelled against Macedonian rule and began a purge of pro-Macedonian elements in the city. Aristotle understandably regarded his own life as at risk. Commenting that he did not want Athens "to sin twice against philosophy" by executing him as it did Socrates, he retreated to Chalcis in Euboea, to an estate belonging to his mother's family, and died within a year, at sixty-three years of age.

Aristotle's works

As mentioned, Aristotle had encyclopedic aspirations as a philosopher: his complete works in two volumes amount to about two thousand pages of detailed observation, thorough classification, astute analysis, and careful argumentation. Yet these treatises represent only a portion of his works. Aristotle apparently wrote not only analytical treatises for use within his school (the so-called "akroamatic" works), but also more popular discussions, many of them in dialogue form, which were published and intended for a wide readership, but which have since been lost except for a few fragments. The internal writings are unpolished for the most part and have something of the character of lecture notes. The *Nicomachean Ethics* falls within this class.

How much of Aristotle's vast work does someone need to know in order to appreciate the *Ethics*? Fortunately, very little at the start. Aristotle regards ethics as a relatively autonomous discipline, with its own principles and procedures, and therefore as only occasionally needing to rely on results from other disciplines. And when any such additional material *is* needed, Aristotle himself tends to introduce it for the reader, in a commonsense manner, and without going into more detail than is strictly required. But there are three special connections between the *Ethics* and other works in the Aristotelian corpus, which should be mentioned here.

The *Ethics* is first of all closely related to Aristotle's *Politics*. The opening chapters of the *Ethics* declare that the project of that treatise is really a matter of "the art of government" or (as we might say) "political science" rather than "morality" in any narrow sense; and the final chapter looks very much like a bridge passage, leading to a discussion of politics. For these and other reasons some scholars have even held that these two treatises were intended to form two parts of a single inquiry.

Secondly, Aristotle's *Rhetoric* is at times useful for understanding the *Ethics*. The *Rhetoric* is a handbook in techniques of persuasion, and many of the argument forms that Aristotle examines and recommends there are employed by Aristotle himself in the *Ethics*. Moreover, the analyses of various emotions that Aristotle gives in the *Rhetoric* – because a rhetorician, he thinks, should be able to exploit various emotional reactions in his listeners – can often shed light on discussions of the emotions in the *Ethics*. And the *Rhetoric* reveals much about how Aristotle understood the typical person of his time – what beliefs he took to be generally plausible, what motives he took to be widespread.

Finally, the *Nicomachean Ethics* is closely related to the *Eudemian Ethics* – they even overlap. Four separate treatises have come down to us ascribed to Aristotle: not only the *Nicomachean Ethics*, but also the *Eudemian Ethics*, the *Magna Moralia* (or "Great Ethics"), and *On Virtues and Vices*. Scholars agree that *On Virtues and Vices* is not authentic: it reads like a somewhat crude attempt to synthesize Platonic and Aristotelian ethical ideas. The authenticity of *Magna Moralia* has been defended by some, but the general consensus of scholars is that it was written by one of Aristotle's followers and is a kind of digest of the *Nicomachean* and the *Eudemian Ethics*. However, the latter is apparently authentic: some scholars maintain that it dates from very early in Aristotle's career; others hold that it comes from late in his life and should be regarded as Aristotle's most mature thought on the subject.[10]

A perplexing puzzle arises from the fact that the two works share three books: *Nicomachean Ethics* 5, 6, and 7 are the very same as *Eudemian Ethics* 4, 5, and 6. To which treatise, then, did these so-called "common books" originally belong? And which treatise was written first? The topic has many difficulties and is far from settled: what a beginning student of the *Nicomachean Ethics* needs to know is simply that the *Eudemian Ethics* exists and that interpretations of the former can sometimes be helped by consulting parallel passages

---

[10] A once popular view, but perhaps still worthy of serious consideration, is that the *Eudemian Ethics* is not authentic and is rather something like an early commentary on portions of the *Nicomachean Ethics* from within Aristotle's school. Of course, even on this last view it would have significant authority.

in the latter. Yet at the same time, it should be said, that sort of consultation is typically of limited use, because the obscurities or difficulties one finds in the *Nicomachean Ethics* are often mirrored in the *Eudemian.* For instance the *Eudemian Ethics* similarly seems undecided between Selection and Collection. At the opening, it seems to support Collection, since it maintains that the goal of human life is to acquire all-round virtue and put it into practice. However, in its concluding sentences, the treatise tilts decisively toward Selection, since it argues that, once someone has acquired all-round virtue, he should place this virtue in the service of a suitable end, which, it maintains rather bluntly, is contemplation of God:

Whatever preference for, or acquisition of, things that are by nature good will best lead to the intellectual contemplation of God (whether goods of the body, or wealth, or friends, or any other good), this is the best; and this is the best target to aim at. Likewise, whatever deficiency or excess in us hinders our service to, and intellectual contemplation of, God – this is bad. (1249b16–21)

I should mention a fifth writing on ethical subjects attributed to Aristotle: the *Protrepticus.* Unlike the others, this work has not been passed down by ancient editors as included in the body of Aristotle's teaching. As mentioned, Aristotle wrote philosophical dialogues and other works of a more popular nature, which have largely been lost. Yet in the case of one such work, the *Protrepticus,* or "Exhortation to Philosophy," scholars believe that lengthy extracts have been preserved in the writings of a later author, a neo-Platonist philosopher named Iamblichus, who lived nearly six hundred years after Aristotle. When these passages are judiciously selected out and put into a cogent order, as modern editors have done, they have a reasonable claim to be regarded as a good representation of some of Aristotle's more popular ethical thought.

What one finds in the *Protrepticus,* so reconstructed, is an impassioned defense of the primacy of intellectual activity and the importance of devoting oneself to a life of study and culture. The *Protrepticus* unabashedly defends a Dominant End view of the human good. A few extracts capture its spirit well enough:

Human beings, then, possess nothing which is divine or blessed, except for this one thing that is of any worth, namely, that in us which involves mind and intelligence. This is our only immortal possession; this alone is divine. Because we share in this ability, then, even though a human life is feckless and burdensome, we are so wonderfully outfitted, that a human being looks to be a god in relation to the other animals ... So then we should devote ourselves to philosophy, or we ought to bid life farewell and leave this scene, since everything else seems, at any rate, a kind of nonsense on a grand scale and puffery.

Elsewhere in the reconstructed *Protrepticus* Aristotle praises Anaxagoras because, when asked why it made sense to be born and to be alive, he replied, "Simply to see the heavens and stars within it, and the moon and sun." Aristotle (if the reconstruction is correct) then comments on this approvingly: "He answered this way because he held that everything else was of no worth whatsoever."

ARISTOTLE'S METHOD

What is the best way to do philosophy? Should we attempt to identify a foundation of indubitable truths and build up from there, as Descartes did? Or should we perhaps aim to clarify and criticize our beliefs by tracing them back to sense experience, in the manner of Locke and Hume? Or does philosophy involve largely the analysis of concepts that we already possess and cannot do without? Clearly, each philosopher has his own conception of what counts as a good philosophical method. In fact, it seems difficult to distinguish sharply *method* from *content* in philosophy: depending upon what one takes philosophy to be *about*, a different sort of *manner* of doing philosophy will seem appropriate. Aristotle, too, has his own distinctive methods, and, since these are especially prominent in the *Ethics*, it is helpful for a beginning reader to be acquainted with them.

We may note five distinctive strategies which constitute Aristotle's method.

"Saving the phenomena"

One of Aristotle's most basic presuppositions in philosophical investigation is that human beings are built by nature to discover the truth. We are, he thinks, truth-seeking and, indeed, truth-finding animals. Because of this, each person's considered opinion counts, for Aristotle, at least as a kind of pointer toward the truth, and opinions which are particularly widespread, or which he regards as held by intelligent and careful thinkers, are especially good pointers toward the truth.[11] Aristotle calls these more reliable opinions "endoxa" (pronounced EN-doksa; singular *endoxon*). The *endoxa* in any subject are the opinions of "the wise" and of "the many," which need to be taken into account in theorizing about that subject. *Endoxa* are to be contrasted with "random" or "chance" opinions about a subject, which are not especially interesting or important.

Aristotle, in effect, takes human beings to be "measuring instruments," which give "reports" relevant to determining the truth in any subject. A satisfactory theory in that subject will have to account for the reports given by these different "measuring instruments."

We tend to think that data relevant to constructing a scientific theory about the world are, as it were, read accurately off scientific instruments: for instance, we say that *a scale* measures a substance as weighing 3.2 grams; or that the velocity of a baseball is reported *by the radar gun* at 92 miles per hour. But Aristotle would conceive of these reports, rather, as the considered opinions of the persons who use these instruments: the (very reliable) opinion of the person trained to use the scale is that the substance weighs 3.2 grams; the (extremely trustworthy) opinion of the person skilled in radar gun use is that the ball was traveling at 92 miles per hour. For Aristotle, data are inseparable from opinions, and opinions are themselves data. This is the reason why he sometimes refers to the relevant, reliable opinions in some subject matter as the "appearances" (*phainomena*): that is how things appear to be, to those observers whose opinion needs to be taken into account.

Aristotle insists that a good theory "saves" or "preserves" the appearances: that is, it either *vindicates* these opinions, by counting them as correct, or it *accounts for* them, by explaining why they are mistaken. His procedure is not unlike how we deal with scientific data. Suppose that scientists are doing an experiment which generates a set of data points, most of which fall along a curve, but a few of which are radically off the curve. In writing a scientific paper about

---

[11] Aristotle seems to think that what *most people* hold is *very likely* to be in substance true; and what *everyone* always thinks is *certainly* true.

this experiment, the scientists would have to discuss both sorts of data points. They would have to discuss how the points that fall along the curve tend to confirm their hypothesis, and they would have to give an account of why the points that fall off the curve do not disconfirm this hypothesis, by suggesting some source of the error – some mistake in measurement, or a predictable perturbation, or something of that sort. Similarly, Aristotle insists that a good philosophical theory must explain also why people have the false opinions that they do, why those opinions have exactly that form.

This approach has two important implications for Aristotle's philosophy. First, he tends to view his own thought as the end-point of a process of philosophical development. When he discusses a subject, he typically begins by surveying the views of his philosophical predecessors, which supply many of his "data." (These surveys are, by the way, the first recorded "literature searches.") He supposes that he needs to account for these various views in the manner explained. Thus, he aims to construct a theory that somehow incorporates and supersedes everything that came before. But note that if this is done well, it will *look* as though everything that came before was simply a preparation for his own view.[12] Secondly, Aristotle tends not to be a "revolutionary" philosopher but rather an irenic, coalition-building sort of philosopher. Given his method, which relies so much on the considered opinions of others, it would simply not be open to Aristotle to conclude, in the manner of a Descartes or a Wittgenstein, that all earlier philosophers dealing with some subject were completely misguided and speaking nonsense.

It is sometimes claimed that Aristotle's approach in this regard limits him to conventionality and conservativism in theorizing, that his philosophy can amount to no more than describing what we already think and clarifying our concepts. But this would be an unwarranted view, just as much as it would be unwarranted to claim that a scientific theory can be no more than a simple summary of results obtained in experiments. Scientific theories will often postulate principles or entities which go beyond the available obser-vations, precisely in order to account for those observations; likewise,

---

[12] But note that Aristotle does *not* subscribe to some kind of Hegelian view of the inevitable *progress* in thought toward his own formulations.

nothing hinders Aristotle from formulating a theory which goes beyond the *endoxa*, precisely in order to account for them. Indeed, as we shall see in the chapters that follow, Aristotle will frequently arrive at a theory that requires us to reinterpret radically the *endoxa* that originally gave rise to that theory.

Aporia and lusis

If the reliable opinions or *endoxa* about a subject provide the *data* for theorizing, according to Aristotle, then what provides the *motive* for an investigation is *wonder*. Aristotle thinks that our efforts to understand the world begin with wonder and are prompted along the way by wonder, essentially by the same kind of puzzlement that a child feels who keeps on asking "Why?"

Aristotle has a technical term for what usually occasions this sort of wonder: he calls it *aporia*, literally "a blockage." *Aporia* is a kind of difficulty or perplexity. Aristotle goes so far as to say that philosophers should actively seek out this "blockage": that, when we find it, we should revel in it and feel the full resistance of the difficulty, and only once we have done so, will we be in a position to find our way through to a solution. Naturally enough, Aristotle calls the solution to such a difficulty a *lusis*, a "breaking through" or "dissolution" of the blockage.

In a fascinating passage from his *Metaphysics*, Aristotle uses some striking comparisons to explain this method of "*aporia* and *lusis*": it is like discovering how to break free from bondage; or getting a clearer glimpse of where you are aiming to go; or reaching a judgment in a legal case after having listened carefully to advocates on opposing sides press their case:

Those who wish to be free and clear should first work their way through the relevant perplexities. For to be free and clear is to loosen a bond that had previously constrained us, and it's impossible to loosen a bond that's unfamiliar. But a difficulty in thought makes evident this bond involving the subject matter. Why? Because insofar as we are perplexed, we're very much like those who are in bondage, because it's impossible to move forward in both directions at once.

That's why it's necessary to have examined carefully in advance all the difficulties – for these reasons, and also because those who investigate without having first worked their way through the difficulties are like people who have no idea in which direction they should walk. Additionally, they don't know whether they've found what they're looking for. Why? Because that sort of person has no clear goal. But the goal is clear to someone who has already worked through the relevant perplexities.

Furthermore, you'll be better at reaching a verdict if you're like someone who has heard the contending lawyers in a case and all the relevant arguments. (995a24–b2)

There is a close connection between Aristotle's concern with "saving the appearances" and his method of *aporia* and *lusis*. Frequently the reliable opinions on a subject will appear to contradict one another.[13] Since both views will have some merit, this appearance of a contradiction will cause perplexity: Which of the two views, we wonder, is correct? Thus the one method complements the other, and in a famous passage from the *Ethics* Aristotle presents them as two components of his general approach:

As in other cases, what we should do is set down how things appear to people (the *phainomena*), then, after going through all the difficulties (*aporiai*), to vindicate – that's the best case – all of the reliable opinions (*endoxa*) about the subject, but, failing that, we should vindicate the bulk of them, or those that are most authoritative. The reason is that, if the difficulties are dissolved and the reliable opinions are preserved, then our view will be sufficiently established. (7.1.1145b3–7)

It is likely that these features of Aristotle's method developed naturally out of the dialogue form of Plato. A good philosophical dialogue will employ characters who hold representative yet disparate views: since the views are representative, they serve in effect as *endoxa*; and since these views are disparate, their juxtaposition generates perplexity and constitutes an *aporia*. Indeed, a well-constructed dialogue would be a good way of "surveying all the difficulties beforehand," in the way that Aristotle recommends, before arriving at a satisfactory resolution.

Central-case analysis, or "focal meaning"

As mentioned earlier, one of Aristotle's basic assumptions in the *Ethics* is that *to be a good* and *to be a goal* amount to the same thing.

---

[13] A clear example would be from 8.1: "people who are alike become friends."; but also "people who are unlike each other become friends."

Thus the *Ethics*, which is concerned with human goods, deals throughout with goals. Aristotle thinks that things that are trying to reach a goal need to be classified in a distinctive way, and this is what underlies his frequent use of "central-case" or "focal-case" analysis (as it is called) in the *Ethics*.

Central-case analysis is to be contrasted with the standard method of classification in Aristotle, which involves genus/species trees. For example, here is an elementary example of such a tree:

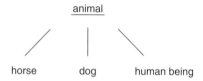

In this case, *animal* is the genus, and *horse*, *dog*, and *human being* are the species. The species fall under the genus, and are classified under it, because they all display the characteristics of the genus. It is a characteristic of any animal that it moves and perceives; similarly, a horse moves and perceives; a dog moves and perceives; and a human being moves and perceives. What makes a horse a species of animal, is that it has additional characteristics, besides those it has in common with all animals, and which set it apart as a distinct sort of animal.

Genus/species classifications correspond to "definitions" of the sort that are looked for in Platonic dialogues. When Socrates asks his interlocutors to define a term such as "piety" or "courage," he is looking for necessary and sufficient conditions for the application of a term to a thing. To define piety is to say what an action cannot lack if it is to be an act of piety (a necessary condition), and what, if an action has it, qualifies that act as an act of piety (sufficient condition). For every pious act, Socrates maintains, there will be something that it has in common with every other pious act and with nothing that is not pious.

Contrast this sort of classification and definition with "central-case" analysis, involving things all trying to attain some goal. Suppose you are walking through a park the day after there was a political rally for an unpopular candidate. You notice the bare spots in the grass where the crowd trampled it down; you notice, too, bare and brown spots where tables and platforms were set up. But then you see an area where there is a concentration of rotten tomatoes, eggs, and broken water balloons scattered around the ground. From the way these things are scattered, you can see exactly where the unpopular speaker was standing. The reason is that people were aiming at him, but they threw these things at him with varying degrees of success. That he was the target, then, serves to unify these data, and your observations generate the following classification:

In this case there is clearly nothing in common among the tomatoes, eggs, and balloons, which makes us group them under the heading of "garbage," other than that they were all orientated toward a single goal. If we wish, we can call all three sorts of things by the same name, "garbage," but this would not be because all three shared some characteristic which they and only they possessed. One could not construct necessary and sufficient conditions for the use of "garbage" in this sense. Not even location relative to the spot where the podium is would suffice, since some things close to that spot would not be "garbage thrown at the speaker," and, no matter how far away from the spot we looked (within limits), we might still find there something that was intended to hit the speaker.

Another example like this – a closer analogy to what one finds in ethics – is the sort of classification that might be found in a medical textbook: the healthy condition of the body or an organ would be the central case, and then various diseased conditions, or disease agents, are grouped around this and understood in relation to this. The syphillus bacterium, the polio virus, and prions have little in common considered in themselves, but they can nonetheless be meaningfully grouped together as disease agents affecting the brain.

Note that, in this case, as in other instances of central-case analysis, there is an important asymmetry: the derivative cases must be understood in terms of the central case (a sickness is a failure of *this* healthy function), but the central case can be understood on its own, without reference to the derivative cases (a textbook on healthy function need not go on to discuss diseases), and the derivative cases are typically not illuminated by any other derivative case taken just on its own (a textbook on one sort of pathology needs to make reference to health but not to other sorts of pathology).

Aristotle's favorite example of central-case analysis is in fact an example chosen from medicine. We apply the term "healthy," Aristotle observes, to all of the following: urine, food, a living body. But these – certainly healthy urine and healthy food – have little in common which serves to explain why we call them "healthy"! Rather, our use of the word "healthy" requires a central-case analysis: the central application of the term is to a living body in good condition, and other things are called "healthy" because of their relationship to this central case: healthy food is food that *produces* a healthy body, and healthy urine is urine that is *produced by* (and therefore is a sign of) a healthy body.

Appropriate variation in accuracy

Aristotle seems at various times to mean at least four things by what he calls "accuracy" (*akribeia*). These may be illuminated by a simple example, say, of a master carpenter trying to explain to an apprentice how to measure and cut a piece of wood. Suppose the carpenter tells the apprentice: "Take some wood, measure it, and cut it like so." This command could involve more or less "accuracy," in Aristotle's sense, in at least four dimensions:

- Accuracy of *measurement.* How precisely should the apprentice measure and cut the wood – for example, down to an eighth of an inch, or sixteenth, or thirty-second?
- Accuracy of *specification.* Suppose different sorts of wood should be cut in different ways (hard vs. soft wood; maple vs. oak vs. pine vs. ash; etc.), then the carpenter could make his instruction more accurate by adapting what he says to the sort of wood he intends.

- Accuracy of *qualification.* Typically, an instruction contains an implicit condition or qualification: "Do this (that is, unless so-and-so holds)." So the carpenter's instruction is more "accurate" to the extent that he makes such conditions explicit: "Here's how to cut the wood when it's damp," or " . . . when it's slightly warped," or " . . . when the saw is dull"; and so on.
- Accuracy of *explanation.* Typically, we give reasons for what we say, reasons which we state explicitly or regard as implicit. A command will be more or less "accurate," the more or less extensive one's supporting reasons. For instance, a carpenter with little formal education might say simply, "Handle damp wood in this way because of its dampness," but a carpenter with a background in biology and chemistry might go on to explain how the moisture in damp wood penetrates the cells and changes how the saw mechanically affects the cells, and so on.

Aristotle thinks that general claims in ethics admit of similar variations in accuracy. Consider a rule such as: "One should repay a debt first, before giving a gift to a friend" (which Aristotle seems to accept). But, we may wonder, does this principle hold no matter what the value of the debt or gift? Perhaps it holds only for relatively large sums but not for sums below a certain amount? ("Accuracy of measurement.") And perhaps it makes a difference to what sort of person one owes the debt (e.g. friend or stranger), or to what sort of person one is contemplating giving the gift? It might, for instance, be correct to give a gift to a *very close* friend before repaying a debt to a *complete* stranger. ("Accuracy of specification.") Or suppose there were some unusual conditions: the person to whom you owe the debt is dishonest and likely to misuse the money when he gets it, but the person to whom you want to give the gift had given *you* a large gift the year before? ("Accuracy of qualification.") And how exactly should the principle be stated, anyway? Should it be stated, perhaps: "Because justice is more necessary than friendship, we should (in general) repay debts before giving gifts" – thus giving the reason why? And should more be said about what this supposed "necessity of justice" amounts to? ("Accuracy of explanation.")

Aristotle maintains that generally the degree of accuracy that one seeks should be appropriate to: (i) the nature of the thing that one is talking about; and (ii) one's purpose in stating a generalization (see 1.7.1098a26–33). It is not always the case that the greater the accuracy the better; rather, one must seek what is appropriate (see 1.3.1094b22–27). For instance, a carpenter who is cutting pine to frame out a wall will not be as accurate in taking measurements, nor should he be, as a carpenter cutting oak to build a fine cabinet. (Note that typically accuracy will be affected in the same way by the nature of the material and the craftman's purpose, because one chooses the material *given* the purpose one has in mind: we do not use oak to frame a wall, or rough pine to build a fine cabinet.)

The subject matter of ethics, Aristotle thinks, "admits of great variation and unpredictability" (1.3.1094b14–16). Furthermore, he thinks that the purpose of ethics (as we have seen) is practical – it aims at making persons good, rather than simply at knowing what goodness is – and therefore it needs only as much accuracy as is effective for achieving that practical goal. These two constraints, he thinks, work together to make accuracy in ethics fairly limited. What this means is that our statements of ethical generalizations will typically succeed in holding only "for the most part." They will not articulate what holds "always and everywhere, without exception" thus: "*For the most part*, we should repay debts before giving gifts." (But note that our putting a generalization in this way would not necessarily rule out our being able to state the rule with greater accuracy, if circumstances or purposes warranted it.)

Another way of understanding this is that a generalization in ethics typically states a tendency or propensity, which manifests its effect only if "other things are equal" (*ceteris paribus*): for example, "In battle, courage is beneficial to the soldier who has it" means, strictly, "In battle, to the extent that a soldier has courage, to that extent he fares better," or "Other things being equal, a soldier in battle is better off if he is courageous." This would not rule out cases in which a courageous soldier does something that leads to his death, when a coward would have run away and remained safe.

It is sometimes claimed that Aristotle's views on the inaccuracy of ethics imply that he thinks that there cannot be any universally binding or exceptionless ethical principles. That (as we have seen) he gives no list of ethical rules seems to support this view: what better explanation of his not formulating any such rules, than that he thinks they do not exist? Yet Aristotle *does* seem to think that there are some principles of that sort: he apparently maintains in a famous passage that adultery, theft, and murder are always wrong (2.6.1107a14–17). Moreover, it would be strange if a practical discipline had *no* exceptionless rules. Even in a discipline which is fairly inaccurate, it seems always possible to find *some* class of actions which are so outlandish that they can just be ruled out, *tout court*. Consider again the carpentry example: that we cannot cut soft pine with precision does not rule out our formulating such exceptionless principles as "You should never try to cut a pine board with the *side* of the saw" or "You should never try to produce a *straight* cut in pine by turning the saw at a *45 degree angle*." It seems plausible enough that Aristotle viewed adultery, theft, murder, and other such actions as equally outlandish for human beings: actions of that sort are so different from what we are supposed to be attempting, that they can simply be ruled out, *tout court*.[14]

Starting points

From Aristotle's point of view, none of the methodological points we have so far discussed would involve anything peculiar to ethics: saving the phenomena, exploring difficulties, central-case analysis, and variation in accuracy will be relevant, he thinks, to most disciplines (mathematics being an exception). Aristotle, as I have said, does not think of ethics as a special domain (the realm of "values") that is especially strange or intractable, in comparison with other fields of investigation.

The same would apparently hold for his remarks about "starting points" or "first principles" (*archai*, pronounced ARK-eye, or *archē*, ARK-ay, in the singular). He presents these remarks as if what one finds in ethics is of a piece with what one finds anywhere else. Here is the famous passage from 1.4:

Let's not lose sight of the fact that arguments *from* first principles differ from those *to* first principles. Plato was right when he used to worry about this

---

[14] It is noteworthy that such rules are practically irrelevant, also, for moral education. A parent usually does not find himself having to remind his child not to murder. If he did, educating the child for virtue would already be a lost cause.

and would try to figure out "Is this path going away from the starting points, or back toward them?" (It's just as on a racetrack: are we racing from the judge's bench to the turning point, or back in the other direction?) Why the concern? Because one needs to start from things that are known, yet these are of two sorts: those that are known *by us*, and those that are so, simply. It's safe to say, then, that *we*, at any rate, should start from things known *by us*. That's why no one can profitably listen in on lectures concerning admirable and just actions (or generally, what pertains to the art of governance) unless he's been brought up correctly. The reason is: "that this is so" is a first principle, and if that is sufficiently evident to him, he won't at the same time require *"why* this is so." He's the sort of fellow, then, who either (i) already has or (ii) can easily acquire first principles. But someone for whom neither of these things is the case should listen in, rather, on Hesiod's remark: "The best person of all is someone who understands everything for himself; a good person, too, is the fellow who accepts on trust the well-spoken word of another; but the person who neither grasps something for himself, nor arrives at heartfelt conviction through listening to others – he's a waste of a human life." (1095a30–b9)

The passage is difficult, but what Aristotle seems to mean is something like the following. To engage in reasoning in ethics, as in anything else, one needs to start somewhere. But these starting points have to be kept "fixed" for our reasoning to move forward: it cannot be the case that, at one and the same time, one *works from* the starting points and also tries to justify them, by *reasoning to them* – that is like being unclear about in what direction to move on the race track.

Here is an example, taken from the very next chapter in the *Ethics*. Aristotle maintains there that a person who devotes his life to accumulating the pleasures that come from eating, drinking, and sex is living the life of a slave or a brute animal and that, for this reason, such a life can be dismissed immediately as not a candidate for human happiness (1.5.1095b19–20). But is this view a starting point of an argument or a conclusion? Presumably, Aristotle regards it as a starting point: he takes it as obvious that that sort of life should be rejected as "bestial." But one might well wonder why. *Why* is it bestial? What do we mean by calling it so? What in fact differentiates a distinctively human life from the life of a non-human animal? If, in asking these questions, we keep that starting point fixed, not wavering in our conviction that that sort of life is bestial, then well and good. In that case what we are doing is engaging in ethical reasoning *from* the starting point, to try to determine *why* that is so. (And Aristotle's answer would presumably rely on the argument, which we shall consider later, that only "activity in accordance with reason" is distinctively human, cf. 1.7.) But if, in asking these questions, we are calling into question that starting point – "Is it *really* the case that such a life is bestial? How can I know that? What *reasons* can you give for making me think that?" – then we are no longer treating it as a starting point. Rather, we are acting as though now we are reasoning in the other direction, *toward* that claim, as if it were a conclusion. Aristotle is concerned, rightly and perceptively so, that those who listen to his lectures do not reject offhand what he has to say because, without their realizing it, they slip from the one sort of questioning to the other.

That they do not slip in this way, Aristotle thinks, will generally be possible only if they have received a good upbringing. Here too, Aristotle apparently does not take himself to be saying anything peculiar to ethics: it happens all the time that someone unskilled in logic or mathematics, when he is asked to prove a theorem, ends up assuming (going away from) what he was meant to prove (go towards). And it is easy to imagine similar sorts of confusion in natural science: the clinician says "This patient is clearly displaying a familiar symptom of X" and the poorly trained resident says, "Why?," not meaning "What's the cause of the symptom?" (reasoning away from) but rather "I don't see that. Why do you say so?" (reasoning to).

Note that Aristotle holds that a starting point can be either something that we "see directly" ourselves, or something that we recognize as true because of someone's say-so. Appeals to authority, he thinks, do have weight in ethics, and in other disciplines, at least when it comes to introducing starting points. Thus, a student in ethics might say "Oh, yes, that sort of life is bestial – my mother told me that" or even (today) "That's obviously bestial – Aristotle dismissed it as such." Similarly, when the clinician says "This patient clearly is displaying a familiar symptom of X," the resident might think to herself, *I'm unsure about it myself, but I remember the famous doctor X saying something like that in a similar case – I'll defer to that judgment.*

PRACTICAL ADVICE FOR READING THE *ETHICS*

Lecture notes?

The text of the *Ethics*, for the most part, is written with extraordinary care, in the sense that every word has a function; every word seems to be chosen over alternatives for just that particular function it can perform; and the meaning of the text (when one finally succeeds in construing it, which may be difficult) is extremely clear and precise. It seems written with as much care as any fine poem and, consequently, it has great power and force. This is one reason why the *Ethics* is considered a great masterpiece and amply repays intensive study.

Given that this is so, it might seem strange that scholars commonly refer to the treatise as "lecture notes." In fact, we do not know how the treatise came to be written. Does it consist of Aristotle's own notes for lecturing? Was it dictated by Aristotle to someone else (perhaps to his son, Nicomachus)? Or was it written down and edited by someone who attended Aristotle's lectures? We simply do not know. However, there are features of both the content and the style that suggest some relationship to lectures. As to content: Aristotle refers to the audience of his investigation as "listeners," suggesting oral delivery (e.g. 1.3.1095a5); and he frequently summarizes and recapitulates in the manner of a lecturer. As to style: the text has various features that are more appropriate to something like notes than to polished writing, which can be enumerated as follows.

1. *Compression.* Aristotle's writing is extremely concise and sometimes drastically abbreviated. Translators will fill out his language to a greater or lesser extent, depending upon how literal they aim to be. Here is an example from book 1. Aristotle writes, literally, "For the vegetative shares not at all in reason, but the appetitive and generally desiderative shares in a way, insofar as it listens to reason and can yield. Thus, then, also to father and to friends we say 'to have reason'" (1.13.1102b29–32). But what Aristotle means, and the way the passage will be translated, is:

In sum, the "plant-like" part of the soul doesn't have any share in reason at all, but the part which has desires and which generally strives after things does share in reason, in some manner, namely in the way in which it can listen to reason and yield to what reason says. This part "has reason," then, in just the same way as we say that someone who listens to his father or friends, and who yields to what they say, "has reason."

Sometimes, that Aristotle writes with such compression has great philosophical significance: in many places in the *Ethics*, as we shall see in various chapters below, a single, compressed sentence is intended to present an entire line of argument.

2. *Density of argument.* The text of the *Ethics* consists of closely packed, interesting arguments, one after another. It is difficult enough to *read* it and follow all of the arguments; it would be impossible to hear it being read and do so, hence the supposition that it was meant to be elaborated upon in lectures. Here is an example. In the midst of a fairly elaborate argument, Aristotle includes the following consideration:

It seems also that Eudoxus was correct in his defense of pleasure's claim to highest honors. That pleasure is not praised, even though it is a good, indicates, he thought, that it's *better* than those goods that are praised. But only God and The Good are that sort of thing, he thought, because it's to these that all other goods are referred. (1.12.1101b27–31)

If we examine the passage carefully, we see that it contains a very interesting but dense argument ascribed to Eudoxus, which might be set out more fully as follows:

   (i) Goods are divided into two kinds: higher goods and lower.
  (ii) Higher goods are those to which lower goods are referred.
 (iii) All goods that are referred to any other good at all are referred to God and The Good, and only to these.
  (iv) Thus, the only higher goods are God and The Good.
   (v) Lower goods are praised; higher goods are not praised.
  (vi) Pleasure is a good.
 (vii) Pleasure is not praised.
(viii) Thus, pleasure is a higher good.
  (ix) But pleasure is not God.
   (x) Thus, pleasure is The Good.

Clearly, this argument within an argument is itself complex and extremely interesting, requiring careful attention. An unwary reader could easily breeze right over it. A reader therefore needs to pause frequently when studying the text, pulling apart and analyzing such arguments in detail. (And, as if this is not bad enough, Aristotle will frequently pile up a long series of dense arguments like this, one after the other, connecting them tersely with "Furthermore," "Moreover," "Again," or "Additionally.")

3. *Reasons come after.* When people lecture they characteristically assert things first, and then give the reasons in support of what they say afterwards (not that people do this only in speaking, but that this is especially prominent in speaking). The *Ethics* has this character throughout: conclusions come first; premises come second. This requires that we pause as we read and be prepared to read through passages repeatedly, and *backwards,* trying to discern the logical order of the argument.

4. *Variations in texture.* The *Ethics* consists of segments of text which play a variety of functions: arguments; digressions; dialectical objections; lists of the opinions of others; exercises in classification; and so on. Typically these will not be clearly marked, so an intelligent reader must be sensitive to them and try to sort passages correctly while reading.

5. *Purposes implicit.* Aristotle gives very few signposts to mark his discussions. He will normally not tell us, for instance, why he discusses subjects in the order in which he discusses them, or how an apparently off-topic discussion in fact fits well into the overarching argument. A reader has to supply these signposts. Again, this is characteristic of lecture notes: the teacher knows what his purposes are and will make them explicit when actually delivering the lecture.

An example worked out

After I have flagged these characteristics of Aristotle's text, it seems useful to give a brief example of how to read the *Ethics* taking these things into account. The very first thing that a student must do is to presume that there is an intelligent structure to the text, because it is difficult to discern Aristotle's arguments, and if a reader lacks the conviction that intelligent structure is there to be discovered, then it is unlikely that he will persevere in finding it. That the *Ethics* has an intelligent structure, both in general and in its parts, is no wishful thinking or charitable make-believe; rather, it is a sound working hypothesis, which will be repeatedly confirmed when it is adopted.

Since, as we are supposing, the *Ethics* has an intelligent structure, then we must take care to understand passages in their appropriate context: we should try to understand the function that a word is meant to play in a sentence, that a sentence is meant to play in an argument, that an argument is meant to play in a broader discussion, and that a broader discussion is meant to play in some overarching line of thought.

As an example, we shall consider chapter 1.12, which I select because it is one of the shortest chapters in book 1, and because I will not be examining it later in this book. The steps one should take in reading this or any other passage in the *Ethics* are:

(i) Place the passage in context and identify the function of the passage as a whole.

(ii) Construct a *divisio* (as medieval commentators called it) of the text, by identifying its principal parts and what the function is of each part.

(iii) Construe the arguments within each part.

We apply these to 1.12 as follows.

(i) 1.12 discusses a question that at first seems trivial and even silly: is happiness the sort of thing that should be praised? Aristotle's answer is that, no, happiness is not the sort of thing that should be praised. We praise only those goods that we can regard as contributing to some *other* good; happiness is that for the sake of which we do everything else, and to which all other goods are referred; thus, happiness cannot properly be praised. Rather, Aristotle thinks, happiness is something to be honored or accounted "blessed."

So much for what Aristotle maintains. But can we put the chapter in context? Its context is book 1, and book 1, as we shall see, is concerned principally with formulating a definition of happiness. In fact, the book may be divided into two almost equal portions: the first part leads up to that definition (1.1–7), and the second part leads away from it and is meant to confirm the definition (1.8–12). 1.12 falls in this second part. Now, after Aristotle formulates his definition, he tries to confirm it by checking it against other things that we believe or would say – *phainomena*, in the broad sense discussed above. And he considers three sorts of *phainomena*: (a) other things we believe or say that happiness is; (b) the subjects of happiness: *to whom* do we apply or not apply the term "happy"?; and (c) what we predicate or say *of* happiness. 1.12 falls in this last category. Thus, we can place the chapter in context in the following way, by locating it within a general outline of book 1:

BOOK 1: HAPPINESS

  I. Preliminaries to the definition of happiness (chs. 1–6)
  II. The definition of happiness itself (ch. 7)
  III. Confirmation of the definition (chs. 8–12)
     i. Consistency of the definition with other things said about happiness (ch. 8)
     ii. Consistency of the definition with what we take to be the scope of the term "happy" (chs. 9–11)
     iii. Consistency of the definition with what things we say of happiness (whether we praise or bless it) (ch. 12)

Notice that once we place 1.12 in its proper context, then Aristotle's thesis no longer seems quite so trivial or silly. The chapter, we can see, is part of a methodical examination of how we use the term "happiness," but whereas chapters 8–11 consider how the term is used in the predicate position ("_____ is happiness," or "_____ is happy"), chapter 12 quite interestingly changes focus and considers it in the subject position ("happiness is _____").

(ii) We may next develop a *divisio* of the text, which is an account of the inner structure of the text we are examining. It is an intelligent parsing of the text. This is a difficult process, which will usually have lots of false starts. Here is a suggestion as to how it might be done in this particular case. A *divisio* as we understand it consists of outline-style headings together with the text that falls under each heading.

Book 1, Chapter 12
Should Happiness Be Praised?

Introduction
Now that these matters are settled, let's consider whether happiness is the sort of thing that should receive praise or honor instead. (<It has to be one or the other>, because obviously happiness is not a potentiality.)

What is implicit in praising something
It seems that everything deserving of praise is praised because it is (a) a certain sort of thing, and (b) related to something in a certain way.

Two arguments in support
(first argument) Evidence for this: we praise a just man, a courageous man, and generally a good man together with his good character, because of his actions and accomplishments; we praise a man with physical power, running ability, or other <athletic talents>, because he has a certain sort of constitution and is related in some way to something good and worthwhile.
(second argument) This is also clear from the praises we direct at the gods: our praise looks ridiculous when it's referred back to ourselves; but the reason this happens is that (exactly as we've claimed) one can't praise something without referring it to something else.

We reserve blessing for goods that are higher than those that are praised
If praise is for things of that sort, then it's obviously not for the best things. Rather, something greater and better is for these.

Two arguments in support
(first argument) And that's precisely what one observes: we *bless* the gods and *count them happy*; we do the same with the most godlike of men; and we do so also with those good things that are most godlike. The explanation is that no one praises happiness in the way that we praise (say) justice, but we *bless* it, since we take it to be something more godlike and better.
(second argument) It seems also that Eudoxus was correct in his defense of pleasure's claim to highest honors. That pleasure is not praised, even though it is a good, indicates, he thought, that it is *better* than those goods that are praised. But only God and The Good are that sort of thing, he thought, because it's to these that all other goods are referred.

Clarifying remarks about our practices of praise
So then: *Praise* is directed at good *traits*. Why? Because it's as a result of our good traits that we characteristically do admirable actions. But *encomia* are directed at admirable *achievements*, whether of the body or of the soul.

Editorial remark
(But to discuss these matters in detail, it's safe to say, is more the job of someone who's been trained to give encomia.)

Thesis, which confirms Aristotle's definition of happiness
As for us, given what's been said, it's clear that happiness falls in the class of things that are honorable and that have the nature of a goal.

A parenthetical remark giving an argument in addition to that of the chapter

(Another reason why it's plausible to place it there: happiness is a first principle or starting point. Why? Because it's for the sake of a first principle or starting point that everyone does everything else. But we hold that the first principle and cause of <all other> goods is something honorable and godlike.)

Note that 1.12 provides a good example of what I above called "variation in texture": the chapter contains arguments, digressions, statements of a thesis, classifications, editorial comments, and so on. Some of this work of producing a *divisio* will already have been done by the translator, if the text has been divided into paragraphs which correspond correctly to the argumentative structure of the text. But a student should be aware that our original Greek manuscripts consist simply of a continuous string of letters, with no word spacing or punctuation. Even to mark a paragraph is to propose an interpretation of the text, and there is no guarantee that translators will do this correctly.

(iii) After we have discerned the structure internal to the chapter by constructing a *divisio*, such as the one given above, we are in a position to analyze and critically examine passages within the chapter, such as Eudoxus' argument, which was analyzed above. Of course, our analysis will be guided by our sense of what the function of the passage is supposed to be: what the passage is supposed to achieve; what Aristotle is trying to establish and why. Indeed, many mistakes are made in interpreting Aristotle's arguments because their broader context and precise function are not first grasped correctly. In that case it is common for interpreters to suppose a mismatch between Aristotle's argument and his conclusion: they puff up the conclusion and consequently find the argument lacking, or they underestimate the force of the argument and miss the significance of the conclusion. But Aristotle is remarkably skilled in argument and has an extremely clear sense, akin to that of a mathematician, of what is needed to establish a point. His writing displays usually a great efficiency: he says what he needs to establish his conclusion, and he says no more than that.[15]

---

[15] In trying to appreciate Aristotle's *Ethics* today, additionally a project of extension and transposition is required. Most of what Aristotle discusses in the *Ethics* is meant to apply to all human beings: he is above all interested, as he says, in the *anthrōpinon agathon*, that is,

FURTHER READING

There are several treatments of the *Nicomachean Ethics* in general which are to be recommended for different reasons. Bostock (2000) is valuable as a sourcebook of difficulties and problems. Broadie (1991) gives a demanding and philosophically deep reading of the work. These books are perhaps best suited to advanced undergraduate and graduate study. Some of Broadie's best particular insights can be easily gleaned by beginning students from the notes she provides to a recent translation of the *Ethics* by Broadie and Rowe (2002). Urmson (1988) is a selective overview. Much scholarship of the recent past has started from or responded to Hardie (1980). Kraut (1989) discusses much of the *Ethics* while considering what I have called the Problem of Selection versus Collection, and the Problem of Order.

The Problem of Selection versus Collection is raised well by Hardie (1965); Ackrill (1974) makes a famous case for Collection; Heinaman (1988) makes perhaps the best case for Selection. Lawrence (1993)

"the goodness that is distinctive of human beings generally" (in contrast to what is good for the gods or for non-rational animals). We can possess and enjoy this because we are rational and have minds, and he thinks that both male and female human beings are like this.

Nonetheless, Aristotle writes his *Ethics* for leaders and aspiring politicians who, he presumes, will be male. He furthermore regards male human beings as providing the best specimens of humanity, and he thinks that only they can exhibit virtue in its fullest form. Thus, throughout the *Ethics*, when discussing paradigmatic cases of the various virtues – courage, magnanimity, justice – he invariably has in mind males. (A noteworthy exception, however, would be his discussion of love and friendship, where he often cites females as providing the best examples.) In the *Politics* Aristotle maintains that females have virtues that are analogous and complementary to male virtues, but in the *Ethics*, although he refers to this view in 8.9–12, he is not much interested in exploring these differences.

We do not share Aristotle's views of the primacy of males; and in some respects we are very much interested in the different approaches that males and females might take to the ethical life and the moral reasoning. Thus, to appreciate his views, and to give them the most charitable form today, we need in some cases to extend what he says, so that it applies to both male and female indifferently; and in other cases we need to transpose what he says, to find something analogous but interestingly different, which we might think tends to be true of how females in particular approach ethics.

Accordingly, translations of the *Ethics*, and commentaries, should strike a sensible compromise. When Aristotle is speaking of human beings generally (*anthrōpoi*), then one should avoid language which gives the impression that he means males solely, thus "extending" his remarks implicitly. Yet when it is clear that Aristotle intends what he says to apply to males alone, and the point could not without anachronism or twisting be extended to females also (for instance, many of his comments about courage have this character), then one needs to make the intended referent of his remarks clear, and allow readers to "transpose" his remarks as they see fit.

introduces a valuable distinction that perhaps allows a compromise. The Problem of Egoism and Altruism might be looked at through the work of Annas (1977 and 1993), and also Irwin (1988a). The Problem of Moral Objectivity and the Problem of Guidance tend to be raised by scholars in connection with concerns about Aristotle's method. On this see Barnes (1980), Bolton (1991), and Irwin (1981). A vigorous argument that Aristotle may consistently be committed to some universal norms, even though ethics lacks "accuracy," is made by Kaczor (1997).

A speculative and provocative attempt to relate Aristotle's life to his philosophy, especially his politics, is found in Chroust (1973). That Aristotle began his philosophical career as a Platonist and then broke away through doing biological research is the famous developmental thesis proposed by Jaeger (1948). Any consideration of the relationship of the *Nicomachean* to the *Eudemian Ethics* must start with Kenny (1978). The *Protrepticus* currently is best studied simply by looking at the passages culled together among the fragments of Aristotle at the end of volume II of Barnes (1984).

Two articles of Owen (1960 and 1961) are seminal for considerations of Aristotle on "appearances" and "focal meaning"; on the former topic, see also Nussbaum (1982). Burnyeat (1980) gives a provocative and influential account of the "that" and how it must be instilled in education. Perhaps the best way to study how to attempt a *divisio* of an Aristotelian text is simply to look at examples in Aquinas (1993).

CHAPTER 2

The goal of human life
(Nicomachean Ethics, *book 1*)

I have said that the *Ethics* has the form of a search, and that a search has four distinguishable steps: formulating criteria for what is sought; identifying the field of search; examining that field; applying the criteria. Aristotle takes the first two steps in book 1. He sets down criteria which, he thinks, the ultimate goal of human life must satisfy, and he identifies in a general way his field of search, by arguing, as we have seen, that the ultimate goal of human life involves some "activity in accordance with virtue." More precisely, he does both of these things in chapter 7, which is the pivotal chapter of the book. After book 1, he then conducts his search, by looking at the various virtues and their characteristic activities.

A word about terminology is in order. Aristotle refers to the ultimate goal of human life variously as: "the good"; "the human good"; "the practically attainable good"; "the best thing"; "the highest thing"; and "the ultimate (or 'last') good." Clearly, he regards it as a kind of end point, and whether we imagine this as the end point of a vertical ("highest"), horizontal ("last"), or evaluative ("best") sequence is irrelevant.[1]

He also calls it *eudaimonia* (you-dye-mone-EE-ah) and says that people would agree in calling it this. "*eudaimonia*" was a popular term, not a technical term in philosophy, which meant literally to be blessed by a spirit or god (see 9.9.1169b7–8), or to be blessed as regards one's own spirit. Since the term involves the notion of blessing, it carried along with it suggestions of prosperity and good fortune (*eutuchia*) – "making out well." It is typically translated into

---

[1] We should keep in mind, however, that Aristotle perhaps wished to maintain a distinction between a mere "human good" and the *ultimate* human good.

English as "happiness," although some commentators prefer "flourishing," "doing well," or even "fulfillment." "Happiness" will do well enough, so long as we keep in mind some basic differences between how Aristotle (and his fellow Greeks generally) understood *eudaimonia*, and how we tend to think of happiness:

1. *eudaimonia* is something stable. It is not therefore a fluctuating feeling, but some kind of lasting condition.
2. *eudaimonia* is objective, that is, someone might suppose he has *eudaimonia* but be wrong about it.
3. *eudaimonia* is universal. It is similar for all human beings, not something different for each person.
4. *eudaimonia* has some relationship to divinity, either because it comes from the gods, or it is a condition like that of the gods.

IS THERE AN ULTIMATE GOOD?

I omitted to say that a condition of searching for something is verifying that it actually exists and so can be found. Aristotle does not neglect this preliminary step. In fact, the first several chapters of book 1 argue that there is such a good to be found and argue also against some false conceptions of this good.

But how might one establish that there is a best good? "Best" is a superlative and typically we understand a superlative term through the comparative: the *tallest* mountain is that mountain which is *taller* than any other.[2] In the same way, we might understand the *best* good as that good which is *better* than any other. So a best good exists, if there is some good that is better than any other good.

But comparisons presuppose a ranking, and how can we rank one good as *better* than another? We might have a chance of answering this, if we had a grasp of what we wanted to compare. But what is a *good*, anyway? Aristotle's preliminary answer is contained in the very first lines of the *Ethics*: "Every method of production and every type of inquiry, similarly also every action and purpose, seems to aim at

---

[2] If we define it as "that mountain than which none is taller" (compare Socrates' understanding of the Delphic oracle, Socrates is the human being "than whom none is wiser"), we leave open the possibility that more than one mountain is "tallest."

some good. That is why people have declared, correctly so, that goodness is what anything aims at."

Before considering why Aristotle says this, we should look briefly at the common charge that Aristotle commits a crude fallacy in this passage at the very start of his treatise. This charge is fostered by translations (also allowable) which render the second line above as something like: "That is why people have declared, correctly so, that the Good is what everything aims at." If we translated the line in this way, Aristotle would be using "the Good" as a name for a particular thing, and he would be claiming that everything aims at it. However, this conclusion would not follow from his opening claim. From "Each thing aims at some good or other" it would not follow that "There is some single good at which all things aim." Compare: from "Every road leads somewhere" it does not follow that "There is a single place to which all roads lead." (This fallacious inference is called a "Quantifier Shift" fallacy by logicians, since it involves an illicit shift from an expression of the form "Every ... some ... " to one of the form "Some ... every ... ")

But we *need* not take Aristotle to be reasoning in this way, and therefore we *should* not. We may take him, instead, to be proposing a definition, rather than arguing that there is some particular good at which all things aim. What Aristotle wishes to claim, in effect, is that "good" should be defined as "aimed at." To be a good is to be a goal (or an "end"). To confirm that this is his purpose, note that the rest of the chapter presupposes this identification. In the immediately following sentence, Aristotle continues: "But a certain difference is evident among *goals*." He has dropped talk of "goods," and now will in fact speak only of "goals" for the remainder of the chapter. His introductory lines are designed not to give a grand argument, but to replace talk of goods with talk of goals.

Let us return, then, to our concern about comparisons of goods. If goods are goals, we can determine whether one *good* is better than another, if we can determine whether one *goal* is better than another. But then how might we rank goals in this way? To clarify this, Aristotle makes a simple point, which he thinks draws attention to the relevant principle of comparison. In some cases, Aristotle observes, what we aim at is simply an action itself (say, a difficult dance move); but in other cases, in contrast, what we aim at is some accomplishment or "work" separate from our actions (say, a house to be constructed). Consider now cases of the latter sort: "In cases in which there are particular goals apart from the actions," Aristotle observes, "it is the nature of the accomplishment to be better than the activity" (1094b5–6). The house that a carpenter builds, for instance, is *better than* his movements in building the house; obviously so. But why do we hold that? Because those movements are *for the sake of* the house. The carpenter makes motions that he understands will produce certain effects, and he makes those motions precisely because they will do so. He therefore chooses the motions "for the sake of" the effects. It is because his actions are for the sake of the effects that the effects are better. Thus Aristotle proposes the following principle of comparison: when X and Y are goals, and X is for the sake of Y, then Y is better than X.

Note that the "for the sake of" relation establishes a ranking, too, among the actions and products of a practitioner of any discipline. A housebuilder acts for the sake of the building of the house, and this implies an order, and a basis of comparison, for everything that he does, as a builder. Similarly, a physician acts for the sake of the health of the patient, which serves as a standard of comparison. However, what about these goals themselves: a house, health, a vessel, military victory, and so on? These are very different in kind, and each is the aim of a separate discipline. Is there some way in which *they* can be ranked? Aristotle maintains that indeed they can, insofar as one such discipline is subordinate to the other. (What he means by "subordinate" is not fully explained. He means, at least, that the higher discipline in some way directs and decides how to make use of the achievements of the lower discipline.) In such cases, the goal of the higher discipline, he says, is better than that of the subordinate discipline, because here too the latter goal is "for the sake of" the former.

Once Aristotle in chapter 1 has thus explained in a tentative way the comparative, "better," he can construct a description of the superlative, "best," and argue that something satisfies that description: the best goal would be that which is the goal of the highest discipline, if such a discipline exists.

So his argument in chapters 1 and 2 has the following general form:

1. Each discipline has a goal (or good) at which it aims.
2. The higher the discipline, the better its goal (or good).
3. If there is a highest discipline, then there is a best goal (or good).
4. There is a highest discipline.
5. Thus, there is a best goal (or good).

Premise 1 is asserted in the opening lines of the treatise and was in any case a commonplace in Aristotle's time. Nothing could even count as a discipline ("craft," "skill," "art," "method of production") unless there were some sort of good that it reliably and intelligently sought. Medicine, for instance, simply is the reliable and intelligent promotion of health; shipbuilding is the reliable and intelligent production of ships; and so on. (In contrast, rhetoric, as Socrates argues in the *Gorgias*, at 463a–466a, is not a discipline, because there is no definable good at which it aims.) Premise 2, as we have seen, is the main principle of comparison of goals (or goods) that Aristotle develops in chapter 1. Premise 3 relies upon Aristotle's definition of the superlative, "best," in terms of the comparative, "better." It would seem that premise 3 is what Aristotle is presenting in the difficult passage at the opening of chapter 2:

If, then, there's some end of practical matters, which we wish for on account of itself, and other things on account of this (and it's not the case that we choose everything on account of something else, since thus they proceed indefinitely, so that striving is empty and vain), it's clear that this would be the good and the best thing. (1094a18–22)

We should understand this not as an argument that there is a best thing, but as a definition of the best thing – of the condition that would suffice to establish that there is a best thing.[3]

The defense of premise 4, then, occupies the remainder of chapter 2. Aristotle argues that there is a highest discipline, and if there is a highest discipline, then the existence of a highest good is established. He refers to this highest discipline as *politikē technē*, literally, "the art of governance." Understand *politikē technē* to be whatever expertise

---

[3] If we took just this sentence as an argument that there is a best thing, then Aristotle once again would be committing a Quantifier Shift fallacy. Thus we should not take the sentence in that way, if we need not do so.

we look for in a legislator or political leader; it is the knowledge or understanding that should be put to use in framing laws and governing political society well. The phrase might also be translated "leadership ability," "political skill," or even "statecraft." That there is some such expertise that political leaders should have is a constant theme in Plato (for instance, in *Republic*, book 1, and the *Alcibiades*). Aristotle takes this for granted, but the idea is also deeply related to important ideas in his own philosophical outlook. Aristotle famously regards human beings as meant by nature to live in political society (which is the force of the phrase "political animal"); but then there is something that nature is aiming at, in so contriving it that we live in political society; and, if so, then this can and should be made the object of human intelligence and skill.

Another way of understanding Aristotle's view, that political authority should be based on expertise, is to take him to be proposing an alternative. Certainly we take laws to have the greatest "power" in society: the laws of political society trump all other rules and procedures. But this power is either based on expertise or not. If not, then laws are the mere expression of force, the "rule of the stronger" – in which case their authority is undermined, since we have no reason to obey the law simply because it is set by the more powerful person or group. Thus obedience to law is intelligible only on the supposition that law is the expression of some sort of expertise.

Since Aristotle takes it for granted that obedience is intelligible only if it is obedience to expertise, he concentrates in chapter 2 on establishing that political expertise is the highest authority: it directs, he claims, even the most respected skills and methods of production; it directs what should be investigated and to what extent by the various sciences (even if it does not constrain those sciences in the results that they reach); and furthermore it directs our particular actions and omissions (1094a27–b6).[4] Since it is the highest authority, and this authority is the expression of some expertise, and every sort of expertise aims at something, then whatever it aims at, Aristotle

[4] Notice the implicit induction in Aristotle's three considerations. Political authority governs methods of action (both practical and speculative), as well as particular actions that may not fall directly under any method, and therefore its goal "envelops those of all the others" (1094b6).

concludes, is the highest good. So a highest good does indeed exist – and soon afterward he will add that it is appropriate to refer to this good as *eudaimonia*, "happiness" (1095a18).

The argument, although ingenious because indirect, will probably not strike us as entirely convincing, because we do not take it for granted, as Aristotle did, that expertise (or "knowledge," "true insight") provides the only suitable basis for reasonable obedience in political society, and it is not obvious to us that any other basis must similarly have a definite aim or goal.[5]

ENDOXA REGARDING THE BEST GOOD

In book 1 of the *Ethics*, and indeed for much of the treatise itself, Aristotle makes progress in his investigation by shifting back and forth between what might be called "formal" and "material" considerations. A "formal" consideration is one that is concerned with what sort of thing, generally, one is seeking; a "material" consideration is concerned with what, in fact, satisfies a general description. After he has established, to his satisfaction, that there is some good that plays the role of highest or last in a sequence – a formal result – Aristotle then turns to consider *what* in fact such a good might be – a material question. He does so by, as we might expect, considering opinions or *endoxa* about the ultimate good, to which he has already given the label *eudaimonia*, "happiness."

He straightaway wishes to put aside shifting or particular views about happiness, because these do not even have a chance of being the right sort of thing. This is why (after some methodological digressions in 1.3–4) Aristotle makes use in chapter 5 of the device of "ways of life." We may understand a "way of life" as a manner of structuring one's life consistently around the pursuit of some single goal, and, furthermore, it is the sort of thing that many people could in principle pursue together. Entire societies in general might be

---

[5] We might put the point in the following way. Aristotle is presupposing that "good" is prior to "right," but other philosophers, such as Kant and more recently Rawls, have argued that "right" is prior to "good," that is, there is no goal that reasonable authority aims to bring into existence; rather, the exercise of reasonable authority is its own goal. We shall not consider in this introductory text the interesting question of whether Aristotle's notion of practical reason is ultimately not very different from a Kantian view.

devoted to some "way of life," in this sense. Thus, a "way of life" carries along with it a conception of happiness as something that is stable and universal, which is what was wanted.

Aristotle identifies three principal "ways of life," although he mentions one other incidentally as well. Each implies a conception of the highest good, as in the following table:

Way of life	Highest good
Life of ease	Pleasure
Life of civic involvement	Honor
Life of attaining insight	?
Life of money making	Wealth

Note that, consistent with his view in chapters 1–2, he is taking a "highest good" to be a *kind* of thing or activity, which is acquired or achieved at intervals, with respect to which everything else that one seeks may reasonably be taken as directed, and which one may in turn reasonably regard as not directed to anything beyond it. To regard *ease* as one's highest good, for instance, is to take the periodic achievement of relaxation to account for everything else that one does, and for this in turn not to be accounted for by reference to anything else.

He then subjects pleasure, honor, and wealth to criticism, concluding that none of these could reasonably be regarded as a highest good in this sense. He regards this conclusion as obvious the moment one gives the matter some thought and hardly wishes to devote much time to arguing for it. No doubt he regards the ground as well covered already by the standard protreptic arguments that Socrates used to give, followed by Plato, that we should not devote ourselves to such things as money, pleasure, or reputation (cf. *Euthydemus* 278e–282d). (The best and fullest development of arguments like this may be found in a much later work by Boethius, *The Consolation of Philosophy*, which belongs to the same tradition.) Aristotle himself seems to have repeated these sorts of arguments in his popular writings, to which he seems to refer (1096a9–10), including presumably his *Protrepticus*.

By "pleasure" he means specifically pleasures associated with the comforts of the body and the satisfaction of bodily desires. (Later, in 10.1–5, he will argue that there are other kinds of pleasures, which are pleasures, he thinks, in the proper sense of the term, and that these are intimately connected with happiness.) As I said in chapter 1, Aristotle dismisses this alternative more through a disdainful description of it than through any explicit argument: it should be evident, he thinks, that such a life is slave-like and fit for a herd animal (1095b20). It is true that the Function Argument, which he gives later, implies that we should reject a life of ease: the argument maintains, in effect, that a human being is principally his faculty of reasoning and that, therefore, someone who devotes his life to care of the body places his true or real self in a position of servitude to the body. But this argument has no more force than its premise, that the faculty of reason is distinctive and especially valuable, and to agree to that is *already* to reject a life centered around bodily pleasures. To take the *argument* to count against that way of life, as pointed out earlier, would be to confuse *arguing to* with *arguing from* a starting point.[6]

Aristotle's criticism of the life of civic involvement (literally the "political life") shows how he allows that a widespread belief may nonetheless not be entirely coherent and may become unstable when examined rationally. Societies centered around this way of life take honor and good repute as the reason for everything else that people do. But honor looks somehow dubious as a good: it is not clear that we can actually possess it, since honor exists only insofar as it is being conferred by others.[7] Moreover, it is not reasonable to value honor unless it is awarded by someone who has good judgment and knows the relevant facts – but this indicates, Aristotle claims, that we value honor *for the sake of* what a competent judge recognizes.[8] This is some good trait of character, or virtue. Thus when the life of civic involvement is subjected to rational criticism, Aristotle thinks, we see that it

[margin note: Value / Honor]

---

[6] It is not clear that someone who lives a life devoted to bodily ease and pleasure would even wish to defend it rationally – that is just how he lives. And if he *did* take up a rational defense of it, then it would seem that he would be led, rather, to fix on something else as his aim (say) *power* or *distinguishing himself* over others.

[7] Honor is a relation, *from* the person who gives it, *to* the person who receives it, and, on Aristotle's view of relations (see *Categories* 8), it would exist, then, in the person who gives it.

[8] Note Aristotle's move from "X is a condition for reasonably valuing Y" to "we value Y for the sake of X." But is this inference valid?

should in fact regard virtue, not honor, as the highest good. No one can reasonably value honor, without valuing even more the virtue which receives the honor.

Yet virtue cannot be the highest good, that is to say, it makes no sense to take *having become a good human being* as that accomplishment toward which everything else can reasonably be directed, and which is not reasonably directed in turn to anything besides it. Why? Because suppose someone has become a good human being. Then by hypothesis he would have achieved the ultimate good, and therefore the life that he lives would be a happy life. But now suppose that such a person falls into a coma for the rest of his years, or that he is captured by the enemy and subjected to torture for years on end. If simply *having become a good human being* were the point of it all, he would have achieved that, and his life would be happy. But it would be absurd, Aristotle rightly says, to regard someone in a coma or suffering ceaseless tortures as living a happy life.

Note that, at this point in the argument, it looks as though Aristotle is maintaining that if one further correction is made, then the conception of happiness implicit in a life of civic involvement will be sufficient. Take the ultimate human good to be not honor, or virtue, but rather the *exercise* of virtue under suitable conditions – "activity in accordance with virtue," which is Aristotle's own conception. But, if so, then is it Aristotle's view that people *do* attain happiness through a life of civic involvement, even if they are not always clear about what that happiness actually is? Or does Aristotle think, rather, that once someone becomes clear that it is some *activity* (or, better, "rational activity") that he should be aiming at, then he is inevitably faced with the question of *which* activity is the best, and, in answering that question, he will be led away from a life of civic involvement? The latter in fact seems to be Aristotle's view, and the dialectic of 1.5–7 has this general direction and force.

As for a life devoted to business ("the life of moneymaking"), wealth is obviously not the greatest good, since it is *for the sake of* something else and, therefore, something else is better than it. Moreover, that sort of life can be dismissed because it essentially involves necessity and compulsion (1096a6) – it is a "rat race," as we say. (Here we see manifested for the first time Aristotle's conviction that there is a deep connection between happiness and free time, "leisure," a thought that will acquire a very great importance in his final remarks on happiness in book 10.) The other prominent way of life mentioned by Aristotle is the *bios theōrētikos*, literally "a life devoted to seeing" or, more naturally, "a life devoted to achieving insight." It is not clear what Aristotle means by this, or even what he means in saying that he will be investigating it in "what follows." There are two alternatives, depending upon whether we understand this "seeing" which such a life aims at in either a narrow or a broad sense. (i) Understood narrowly, this "seeing" would be the insight and understanding that one gains through philosophical and scientific study, especially (Aristotle thinks) in those disciplines that deal with unchanging things: mathematics, astronomy, and theology. Aristotle's discussion of that sort of life seems contained largely in the final chapters of the treatise, 10.7–8, and the phrase "what follows" would then mean "what follows eventually." (ii) Understood broadly, this "seeing" would be *any kind* of appreciation of beauty or fittingness, in which case one might suppose that *any activity* where beauty or fittingness were a condition, or overriding constraint, would be one that belonged to this way of life. As we shall see, Aristotle takes it to be a mark of any virtuous action that it somehow aims at a kind of beauty or nobility in action, and he thinks that someone who acts virtuously thereby "gains" this nobility for himself. Now if this is the broader sort of "seeing" and corresponding way of life that Aristotle has in mind, then *all* of the books of *Ethics* that follow are a discussion of the *bios theōrētikos*, and the phrase "what follows" would mean "what follows immediately."

A DIGRESSION ON THE LOGIC OF GOODNESS

But if, when we think about it, we see that bodily pleasure, comfort, honor, reputation and wealth cannot reasonably be taken as the point for which we do everything that we do, what else is there to strive for? What other good could count as the highest good? A large part of the persuasiveness of Aristotle's own account comes simply from the elimination of these familiar alternatives. It might look as though Aristotle's view is the only one left standing.

However, before he puts forward his own view, Aristotle argues at length against one last alternative, a view derived from Plato, that the highest good is a separately existing Form of the Good, which is the source and cause of the goodness of all other good things. Aristotle perceptively remarks that views like this have a certain appeal, precisely because they portray the highest good as something beyond ordinary life and ordinary apprehension, and people are in some sense aware that they have not in fact gotten it right – that the goods generally pursued as the highest good are not really the highest (1095a25–28).

Plato's view is based on logical considerations about the use and meaning of words, which is why Aristotle regards his discussion of that view as something of a digression, better suited to a logical or metaphysical treatise. But the digression is important, since it criticizes a view of goodness that can easily seem appealing. For our part, by understanding why Aristotle rejects Plato's theory, we understand better Aristotle's crucial claim that to be a good is to be a goal.

(*Warning. The following section is philosophically heavy going! If, like Aristotle, you think that logical investigations have no proper place in ethics, but if, unlike Aristotle, you do not count fervent Platonists among your closest friends, then feel free to skip to the next section, on p. 67 below.*)

Plato's view consists basically of three claims:

1. Goodness is uniform: all good things are good in the same way.
2. There is a separately existing Form of Goodness or "Goodness Itself."
3. Expertise in goodness involves intellectually perceiving this Form of Goodness.

Let us first consider Plato's reasons for these claims and then look at Aristotle's criticisms of them.

   1. *Goodness is uniform.* Some words ("singular terms") we apply to one thing only, for instance, we apply the term "Socrates" only to the individual Socrates. But other words ("universal terms") we apply to more than one thing, for instance, we apply the term "pale" to Socrates before he gets some sun, but also to Agathon similarly, or to anyone else who has a pale complexion. Now Plato presumes, understandably enough, that there has to be some reason why we

apply a word to some things but not to others. Speech is intelligent; we do not fashion words arbitrarily. Therefore, when we apply a universal term to some objects but not others, there has to be a reason why this is so. As Plato understands it, the definition of a word is meant to supply this reason. The definition of a word picks out some characteristic that is possessed by everything to which that word is properly applied, and which is lacking in everything to which the word is not properly applied (see *Euthyphro* 5d). All things properly called by a universal term therefore have this characteristic in common. They are the same *sort* of thing and similar in form. Paleness in Socrates is the same sort of thing as paleness in Plato, and all pale things are uniform insofar as they are pale.

The word "good" is clearly a universal term, since we can apply it to more than one thing. Moreover, we pick out some things as good, but not others. Thus, there has to be a reason why we apply the word as we do. Thus, on this line of thought, goodness would be like paleness: each good thing has some definite characteristic which it has in common with all and only other good things. Good things are uniform in goodness.

It follows from this that comparative statements involving goodness are remarks about differences in degree. To say that "Socrates is more pale than Plato" is to say that the very same characteristic that is found in both of them, which is responsible for their being pale, is found in Socrates to a greater degree than in Plato. Similarly, to say that one good is better than another is to say that the former has goodness to a greater degree.

2. *There is a separately existing Form of Goodness.* Plato is of course famous for his Theory of Forms, the view that there are intelligible, non-material, unchanging paradigms of the attributes that we recognize in the changeable objects that we perceive through our senses. His chief argument for the existence of Forms, called the "One Over Many," takes its start from the uniformity which, on his view, underlies our use of universal terms. When the same name is applied to several objects and thus they all share in a single characteristic, then, it seems correct to say, *there is some one thing which all of those objects are.* However, this one thing cannot be identified with any of the particular objects, or with any feature of any of these objects: each of these things is an individual, yet the "one thing which all of those objects

are" is obviously universal. So this one thing must be distinct from each of the individuals, yet somehow present in them. Call this the Form: it exists separately from the individuals; individuals *participate* or *share* in that Form; and when we apply the universal term to an individual, we are doing so in virtue of the individual's participation in the Form.

The One Over Many Argument similarly would establish that there is a Form of Goodness. We apply the term "good" to various objects. Therefore, there is some one thing, Goodness Itself, which all of them are. This cannot be identified with any of the particular good things, or with the particular goodness that each of them has. Rather, it is separately existing and intelligible. To say that any particular thing is good, then, is to say that it participates or shares in the Form of Goodness, which serves as a kind of paradigm of any good thing.

3. *Expertise in goodness involves intellectually perceiving the Form of Goodness.* One of the reasons why Plato posited the Forms is that he thought that we could have knowledge only if the Forms existed. His reasoning was as follows. We have knowledge of something only if we cannot be wrong about it. But anything that is changeable is something we can be wrong about. Why? Because it might change when we are not perceiving it. Thus, our knowledge must be of things that cannot change. But everything we perceive in this world is subject to change. Thus, knowledge must be of unchanging objects that are not in the perceptible world, and these are the Forms. Knowledge is always a perception of a Form, and corresponding to each Form there is a certain kind of knowledge which consists simply in the perception of that Form.

Since Forms account for our knowledge, it follows that there will be a single sort of expertise corresponding to each Form, which deals with all and only those individuals that participate in that Form. Thus, there will be a single expertise that deals with all good things, insofar as they are good; moreover, if Xs are one sort of good thing and Ys are another sort of good thing, then the expertise that deals with Xs, insofar as they are good, will be the same as the expertise that deals with Ys, insofar as they are good.

Aristotle argues against all three of these Platonic claims in 1.6. His criticisms rely on his doctrine of the "categories"; therefore, this doctrine needs first to be explained. The doctrine of the categories

Ladybird Beetle

is that there are several highest kinds or genera of things; it is perhaps best explained in relation to the notion of genus–species classification, familiar from biology. Consider a particular living thing, say, the ladybird beetle which, as I type, is crawling on the table top next to my computer. I know that this insect is not the only one of its kind; in fact, it belongs to a particular species of insects, all alike in important ways. Since I am not an entomologist, I cannot say which of the 350 North American species of ladybird beetles it belongs to. But whatever species it is, that species as well is not something utterly unique: it belongs to a higher kind (coccinellidae, in fact, the family of ladybird beetles). Yet all beetles, similarly, are alike in certain ways and belong to the kind "coleoptera." Now coleoptera are themselves a kind of insect, which is a kind of animal, which is a kind of living thing, which is a kind of ... thing. And that would appear to be the highest kind of all: things.

But this is precisely what Aristotle denies by his fascinating doctrine of "categories." He maintains that there are *several* highest kinds: besides "things," or *substances*, as Aristotle calls them, there are also *qualities* (being "such like"), *quantities* (being "so much"), *relations* (being "of" or "toward" something), aspects of *time* and *place*, and (Aristotle thought) a few other highest classes or "categories." (His longest list is of ten such categories.) These categories are exclusive, in the sense that no item in one category belongs also in another: a substance is not a relation; no quantity is a quality. But, more importantly, precisely because the categories are (as Aristotle holds) highest kinds, there is no class of which items from two distinct categories are both members. In cases in which it might look as though there was a class spanning various categories – because we can apply one and the same word to items in different categories – then we can be assured, Aristotle thinks, that that word is being used in different senses. For instance, we might think that the word "existent" can be applied across the various categories, since we can say such things as "A substance is an existent"; "A quality is an existent"; "A relation is an existent"; and so on. But Aristotle would insist that the word "existent" varies in sense along with these various assertions. To say that a substance is an existent is to say that it is a separate and independent thing; to say that a quality is an existent is to say – very differently – that it is a "such like" of a substance; to say that a relation is an existent is to say that it is some aspect of a substance that is "of" or "toward" something else.

Thus, if categories are highest kinds, any word applied to items in different categories is not used uniformly, and it does not pick out one and the same characteristic in its various uses. This is the basis for Aristotle's objection to the first claim of the Platonic theory. Goodness is not uniform, Aristotle insists, because there are items that we call "good" in each of the categories:

> The term "good" is used in as many different ways as the term "is." It's used in the category of "what" (e.g. God, mind); and of "what sort" (e.g. the virtues); and of "how much" (e.g. the right amount); and of "relative to something" (e.g. what is useful); and of "time" (e.g. the right moment); and of "location" (e.g. the right place, and other things of that sort). Hence it's clear that "good" used generally does not signify a single thing shared in common – because if it did, then "good" would not be used in all the categories but rather in one alone. (1096a23–29)

Of course, if the word "good" is not used in the same way in its various applications, then it is implausible to claim that "there is one single thing that all particular good things are," and thus the One Over Many is blocked, and, as against the second claim of the Platonic theory, there is no basis for postulating a Form.

But Aristotle adds another criticism of this second claim in the Platonic theory, and, in order to understand this criticism, we need to understand first what is traditionally known as the Third Man objection to the Forms. The Third Man objection is that the One Over Many argument implies a vicious regress. The objection proceeds as follows. According to the One Over Many, whenever a term can be applied to various members of a class, then we may postulate a Form, distinct from the members of that class, which all of the members of that class resemble, and in which they participate. Consider then the class of individual human beings. We can apply the word "human" to each of them; thus, according to the One Over Many, we may postulate a Form, call it "Human Itself," distinct from any particular human being, which all human beings resemble, and in which they participate. Suppose, then, that this Form exists. If it does, then it looks as though we can formulate now a new class, consisting of all individual human beings, together with Human Itself. But the word "human," it seems, can now be applied, not

merely to all the individual men, but also to the Form, Human Itself.
After all, individual human beings participate in and resemble this
Form, and resemblance seems to be symmetric. Moreover, the Form
is supposed to be a paradigm of the things that participate in it, but
surely a paradigm exhibits in a preeminent way the feature of which it
is a paradigm. Thus, it seems that we can say that Human Itself is
"human." However, if we say this, then the One Over Many directs
that we should now postulate a third thing, a "Third Human"
("Third Man"), distinct from both the individual men and the
Form of Human Itself, in which these other things share. Why?
Because, recall, the One Over Many directs us to postulate a Form
whenever we can form a class of items all called by the same name.
But now observe that, for comparable reasons, the word "human" can
apparently be applied to this Third Human as well. But then it is
clear that there is an infinite regress of Forms: on Plato's theory, we
are compelled to hold that there exist individual human beings;
and that there exists the Form of Human; and that there exists
the Form of {human beings and the Form of Human}; and that
there exists the Form of {human beings, the Form of Human, and
the Form of {human beings and the Form of Human}}; and so on,
without end.

To block this absurdity, it would be enough to say that the One
Over Many allows us to postulate a Form only when the items to
which a single word is applied are all "on the same level." Individual
human beings are "on a level" – they are all perceptible particulars –
but the Form of Human is clearly on a different "level": it is somehow
prior and has a different status. Thus one could not apply the One
Over Many to the class consisting of both the particulars and the
Form, and the regress would be blocked. One might even insist that
the word "man" varies in meaning, depending upon whether it is
applied to something prior in status or not. And these things are
apparently what some Platonists said. They tried to escape the Third
Man regress by maintaining that a single Form should not be
postulated when a term was used of items that could be ranked as
prior and posterior with respect to what was picked out by that term.

Suppose that a Platonist were committed to responding to the Third
Man problem in this way. But then, as Aristotle points out, this would
now imply that we should not postulate a Form of Goodness at all! His

argument once again relies on the doctrine of the categories. The categories themselves display priority and posteriority, Aristotle notes, because substance is prior to the other categories (and, most evidently, it is prior to the category of relation). By this he means that any term applied both to a substance and to an item in some other category is used in a prior sense as applied to the substance, and in a posterior sense as applied to that other item. For instance, if one says "This ladybird beetle exists" and one also says "The redness of the beetle's shell exists," the word "exists" as used in the former sentence indicates something that has a kind of priority over what the word "exists" indicates in the latter sentence. (Elsewhere Aristotle explains this priority as dependence in definition: the redness exists *in* the beetle; thus, one cannot define the redness without mentioning that *in which* it exists; but one can define the beetle without mentioning the redness.) But if the categories in this way display priority and posteriority, and the word "good" is used of substances as well as items in the other categories, then goodness exhibits priority and posteriority, and the One Over Many would not apply. Thus:

It was the practice of those who introduced this opinion not to postulate "Ideas" [or Forms] for things in which the application of a term displayed priority and posteriority. (That's why they didn't posit an Idea for the numbers.) But the term "good" is applied to what is in the category of "what is," and "what sort," and "relative to something." But what exists in its own right, sc. substance, is prior by nature to what is relative to something. Why? Because the latter is something like an offshoot or concomitant of what exists. It follows that there would not be any Idea that is common to these. (1096a17–23)

Aristotle's objection to the third claim in the Platonic theory, namely that expertise in goodness is to be explained by knowledge of a Form, then proceeds as follows. Consider goodness simply as it is found in a single category, say, the category of time. Goodness as regards time is just *appropriateness* of time; it is good timing.[9] If the Platonic theory were correct, then there should be a single expertise pertaining to good timing generally. But this suggestion is absurd.

[9] This limitation of the argument to a single category is necessary simply to get the argument off the ground. Aristotle is putting forward what is called an "*a fortiori* argument," an argument from the stronger to the weaker case: if his point holds of goodness in a single category, then *a fortiori* it holds of goodness generally.

[margin note: Revise this Paragraph]

Good timing as regards health – *when* to perform surgery, *how long* to administer a drug, and so on – falls under the expertise of medicine. Good timing as regards warfare – *when* to attack, *how long* to hold a position, and so on – falls under the expertise of military strategy. Other decisions about other sorts of good timing similarly belong to other sorts of expertise. Moreover, it is clearly not the case that, in mastering one sort of good timing, one has mastered them all. Thus, if even as regards the particular sort of goodness that is found in a single category there is no single expertise, it cannot be the case that expertise in goodness amounts to grasping the Form of Goodness.

These are Aristotle's objections to the Platonic view that are directed at the principal claims of that view. But Aristotle also raises additional objections to the Platonic view, to the effect that the Form of Goodness cannot play the role that the highest good plays. In particular, those features of a Form which, on the Platonic view, are supposed to make it a suitable object of knowledge, would render unaccountable how the Form of Goodness would be the highest good. Here is how that argument proceeds. The highest good is better than any other good; hence, if the Form of Goodness were the highest good, as Plato maintains, it would have to be better than particular good things. Now a Form, as I said above, is meant to be a suitable object of knowledge: things in this world are changeable and pass away, but a Form is unchanging and eternal. However, a Form must be the same sort of thing – the same "in definition" – as the things that participate in it, otherwise it would not be the case that knowledge of those things was the same as knowledge of that Form. (The same result is implied also by the One Over Many argument. If the Form is simply that "single thing which all of the several individuals are," then it has to be the same in definition as those individuals.) So, for example, if the Form of White is to account for our knowledge of white things, then, on Plato's theory, two conditions must hold: the Form must be the same "in definition" as any particular white thing; the Form must be eternal. But, Aristotle points out, neither of these conditions could explain why the Form of Goodness was better than individual good things. Insofar as it is the same "in definition" it is equally good, no better and no worse. And that its goodness lasts forever does not imply that it is more of a good than some good which exists only briefly. An eternal thing in principal could even conceivably have an attribute to a lesser degree than a similar thing that existed only briefly. Thus, there is a conflict between the two roles that the Form of Goodness is supposed to play. Its role as an object of knowledge does nothing to account for how it can play the role of the highest good: "A good-itself and a particular good will not differ at all, precisely as good. And it's not going to be by lasting forever that a good-itself is a greater good than a particular good thing, if white things that last a long time aren't whiter than those that last only briefly" (1096b2–5).

Aristotle concludes his criticism of the Platonic theory with further arguments that the Form of Goodness could not play the role of a highest good. His most fundamental point is that, since the Form of Goodness, like any form, is supposed to be a non-material, unchangeable, and separately existing thing, it seems not to be the sort of thing that we could attain or possess; yet the highest good, if it is indeed that for the sake of which we do everything else that we do, has to be something of that sort (1096b32–35).

A Platonist might respond that even if the Form of Goodness is not something we can attain or possess in this life, nonetheless knowledge of it is extremely important, because the Form of Goodness is a kind of paradigm of goodness: since it is such a paradigm, if we become familiar with the Form, then we are in a better position to recognize and thus possess the individual goods that we *are* capable of attaining in this life. And Aristotle concedes that there is some plausibility in this reply. But he thinks that the practice of those various disciplines that aim at particular goods shows that the reply is misguided. If knowledge of the Form were indeed important for recognizing and acquiring goods, Aristotle maintains, then each discipline would *already* have included a training in this knowledge in the standard course of training for that discipline. For instance, geometry is important for architecture, as architects have discovered, and thus training in geometry is required of all prospective architects. But clearly no discipline requires training in knowledge of the Form of Goodness.

Moreover, it is implausible to say that knowledge of the Form of Goodness would lead to a greater or *more refined* proficiency in any discipline. The reason is that such knowledge would presumably be extremely general in character, since presumably it would involve what *all* goods have in common. Yet, that sort of knowledge would be useless for advanced practitioners of any special discipline. Typically, expert proficiency in a discipline involves skill in applying the principles of that discipline to unusual or special cases; for example, the best physicians are those who practice medicine in teaching hospitals, which handle rare and atypical illnesses, whereas the treatment of very common diseases requires no special skill. To claim, then, that knowledge of the Form of the Good might constitute the difference, or part of the difference, between an ordinary and an expert practitioner in a field, would be like saying that someone could attain advanced proficiency in medicine by studying something as generally applicable as arithmetic.

It is unfortunate, but telling, that Aristotle shows little interest in proposing his own positive account of our use of the word "good." His remarks on this topic are brief and cryptic:

> But then how *is* the term used? At any rate, it doesn't look as though "good" is one of those terms which, by mere chance, has a variety of different uses. Is it perhaps that all the various uses originate in some single thing, or have their point in connection with a single thing? Or, even more so, are they based on analogy? For instance, sight : body :: mind : soul. (1096b26–29)

It is difficult to know what he means by this. Is he suggesting that, after all, there is a single standard of goodness for the universe, yet that things are called "good" not by participating in it, but only insofar as they tend to it – the doctrine that he seems to put forward in the discussions of the Prime Mover in the *Metaphysics*, book 12, where he does discuss the goodness of the universe (albeit only briefly)? His mention of analogy would then cover how we relate and group together those things, other than the Prime Mover, which we regard as good: we count sight and the mind as goods, for instance, because each plays a similar *role* – the role, perhaps, of somehow bringing that in which it is found into a *closer relation with* the Prime Mover. But given the brevity of the passage, it is difficult to have confidence in any interpretation of it.

CRITERIA OF GOODNESS

By the beginning of chapter 7, then, Aristotle takes himself to have shown that an ultimate human good exists, and that the common views about this good, and also the Platonic view, are mistaken. So chapter 7, in a sense, marks the beginning of his own search for this good. His first task is to propose criteria which, he thinks, the ultimate good must satisfy, and which therefore will serve to identify the ultimate good (1097a15–b21). (He will not actually apply these criteria until much later, in 10.6–8.)

It is not clear whether Aristotle intends to give three criteria or only two: he seems to give three, but in the summary of his own remarks, he mentions only two (1097b20–21).[10] The three criteria which he seems to give may be summarized as follows:

1. Ultimacy (1097a25–34): the highest good is that for the sake of which we seek everything else and is not itself sought for anything further.
2. Self-sufficiency (1097b6–16): the highest good itself implies no further need.
3. Preferability (1097b16–20): when compared one by one with any other good, the highest good is in every case preferable.

Let us consider each in turn.

1. *Ultimacy.* This criterion seems to be a refinement of what Aristotle had already said in chapters 1 and 2. As we saw, it is a basic principle of the *Ethics* that to be a good is to be a goal. So a criterion of the highest good would be that it was most of all a goal. But what would it be for something to be like this? Aristotle first introduces a word to signify that something reasonably plays the role of a goal: he calls such a thing goal-like, *teleion,* from the Greek word, *telos,* which means "goal" or "end." He then claims, in effect, that something becomes more or less goal-like, depending on what side of the "for the sake of" relation it is found: to the extent that a thing is that for the sake of which we do other things (call this the "goal augmenting" side of the relation), to that extent it is more goal-like; to the extent that a thing is sought for the sake of another thing (call this the "goal diminishing" side of the relation), to that extent it is less goal-like.

Now consider the following classification of goals, which Aristotle seems to adopt from Plato's *Republic* (357b–358a):

---

[10] And furthermore he does not seem to make use of the third criterion in book 10.

(i) those sought only for the sake of something else;
(ii) those sought on account of themselves as well as for the sake of something else; and
(iii) those sought only on account of themselves and not for the sake of something else.

Aristotle maintains that any member of (ii) will be more goal-like than any member of (i), on the grounds that members of (i) are always on the goal-diminishing side of the "for the sake of" relation, but members of (ii) are sometimes on the goal-augmenting side of the relation. But similarly any member of (iii) (and Aristotle's language at 1097a32 shows he is suggesting that there will be only one member in [iii]) will be more goal-like than any member of (ii). Aristotle thinks that this licenses our saying that a member of (iii) is "goal-like without qualification," that is, it never enters into the "for the sake of" relation in such a way as to diminish its claim to be a goal.

Note that this is something of a counterintuitive result. We might have thought that something in class (ii) would be the most valuable of all. Is not something that both leads to good things, as well as being itself good, better than something which is merely itself good? But Aristotle is claiming that a careful consideration of the principle on which we count anything as good at all suggests otherwise.

The Criterion of Ultimacy is perhaps most naturally understood as directing us to use Selection to identify the ultimate goal. As I said, Aristotle's general picture of a goal is of something that regulates our activity in a cyclical way, through its being repeatedly attained: for instance, a general conquers one city, and then he moves on to his next military objective; a physician cures one patient, and then she cures another. But note that these goods exercise control over only certain sorts of behavior, and not others: it is only when he is waging war that the general's activity is governed by the goal of victory; it is only when the physician is seeing patients (or is "on call," ready to see a patient) that her actions are directed by the goal of health (that is, of some particular patient or other). On this pattern, then, it would be natural to take the "most goal-like goal" to be simply some good, the periodic attainment of which would similarly give structure to *all* other activities without exception.

Nonetheless, some scholars have argued that the Ultimacy Criterion favors, rather, Collection. In Greek, the word *teleion* can mean also "complete" or "perfect," that is, not lacking anything of note, or not lacking anything which might reasonably be regarded as due to a thing. Suppose that Aristotle understands *teleion* in this sense. Then he is maintaining that goods are better or worse, the more or less complete they are. If a more complete good, as one might think, collects together less complete goods, then the best good would be the most complete good and the most inclusive, containing within it, presumably, every good worth attaining.

But there are two difficulties with the latter interpretation of Ultimacy: (i) Given the importance so far, for Aristotle's argument, of the principle that to be a good is to be a goal, it would be strange for him at this point, and in a passage which so much resembles the opening passage, to use the word *teleion* – which has the same root as the word for "goal" (*telos*) – in the very different sense of "complete," and to do so without any warning. (ii) As we saw, Aristotle explains Ultimacy with reference to the "for the sake of relation." But it is not typically the case that when one thing is sought for the sake of another, then the latter includes the former and is in that sense more complete. For instance, we seek money for the sake of food and clothing, but food and clothing do not *include* money; again, we exercise for the sake of health, but health does not *include* exercise. So it simply seems inapt to understand a more *teleion* good, in Aristotle's sense, as generally a more inclusive good.

2. *Self-sufficiency.* Aristotle begins his consideration of this criterion with an intuitive remark, "good which is goal-like seems to be self-sufficient" (1097b8), and it is helpful for us also to get an initial, intuitive grasp of this criterion.

To the extent that something is a goal, it seems, we can *rest* in it once it is attained. Our reaching a goal should *satisfy* us. Our reaching that goal should not itself bring with it further needs or yearnings. What self-sufficiency in this intuitive sense amounts to can be better appreciated, perhaps, by contrast with something that is not like that. In this regard it is helpful to consider the famous image of the leaky jars, from Plato's *Gorgias*, which is intended to draw just this contrast. In the *Gorgias*, the character Callicles claims that a happy life would be a life in which someone constantly increases his needs but manages also to increase correspondingly his ability to satisfy them. Socrates in effect objects that such a life would not be happy, because it would not involve self-sufficiency.[11] To establish his point, Socrates introduces the image of the jars:

> Suppose there are two persons, each of whom has many jars. The jars belonging to one of them are sound and full, one with wine, another with honey, a third with milk, and many others with lots of other things. And suppose that the sources of each of these things are scarce and difficult to come by, procurable only with much toil and trouble. Now the one person, having filled up his jars, doesn't pour anything more into them and gives them no further thought. He can relax over them. As for the other one, he too has resources that can be procured, though with difficulty. But his containers are leaky and rotten. He's forced to keep on filling them day and night. The alternative is that he suffers extreme pain. Now, given that the life of a moderate person is like the former, and the life of a self-indulgent person is like the latter, are you saying that the life of the self-indulgent person is *happier* than that of the moderate person? (493d–494a, Zeyl translation with modifications)

A life similar to that of the leaky jars would not be self-sufficient, and therefore could not be a happy life, because it would involve no goal which implied rest, and what it did aim at, in its attainment, would immediately imply further need. The intuitive idea of self-sufficiency, then, includes the notions of *rest* and *absence of further dependence*.

Aristotle's definition of a self-sufficient good, "that which makes a life worth choosing on its own and in need of nothing" is obscure and difficult to understand. (Does he mean that *the good on its own* makes a life worth choosing, or that the good makes a life *worth choosing on its own*?) But if we take the two parts of the definition to correspond to the two elements of the intuitive idea of self-sufficiency, then he would be claiming that a self-sufficient good is something such that its attainment implies a rest from effort and does not imply further need. As I said, Aristotle conceives of a goal as an activity that is repeated periodically, and which serves to give direction to other things that a person does. If so, then such an activity would be self-sufficient, to the extent that it could be understood as a kind of rest

---

[11] Socrates begins his response by asking, "Then is it not correct to say, as people do, that those who want nothing are happy?" (492e) – to which Aristotle's formulation at 1097b15 is perhaps an allusion.

from exertion, and to the extent that that activity itself implied no need of something outside itself.

The Self-Sufficiency Criterion, so understood, seems most naturally to direct us to use Selection to identify the ultimate good: the more self-sufficient an activity, the less it would become combined with or require other activities or goods, and the more it alone would satisfy us. We typically want to dispense with other things when we come upon something that has the marks of self-sufficiency. (For instance: a music lover discovers some especially great piece of music and begins to listen to that alone, regarding other pieces in her collection as inferior and dispensable.) And any highest good arrived at through Collection, in contrast, would seem less Self-Sufficient. Would it not require more effort to safeguard and preserve a vast variety of goods? And is it not the case that the more goods to which we are beholden, the more likely that our regard for these goods will imply reliance on other things outside that set?

Yet some scholars have argued that the Self-Sufficiency Criterion implies a highest good gained through Collection. Their argument is as follows. According to Aristotle, a good is self-sufficient, only if it makes a life in need of nothing. But what could make a life in need of nothing, strictly? Surely, only some kind of composite good could do this, a good which included anything that one might reasonably ever need or could want. For if a life lacked any such good, then someone who lived that life would remain in need of that good. Thus, only the sum total of *all* goods, as possessed over a lifetime, could constitute a good that was strictly self-sufficient.

But there are three difficulties in this argument. (i) In the philosophical context in which Aristotle wrote, a self-sufficient life connoted simplicity and austerity, yet a good arrived at through Collection threatens to be extravagantly large. (ii) Again, in that context, the self-sufficiency of a good was taken to have an effect on our desires, causing desires we had for other goods to fade away or seem insignificant. Yet Collection apparently takes our desires as fixed and looks for the most expansive satisfaction of those desires. (iii) It seems that the sort of composite good required by this interpretation simply could not exist: even a very large composite would not be strictly self-sufficient in this sense, since it would always lack some good that might reasonably be desired. However, the highest good, Aristotle insists, has to be a possible good, which we can in fact attain (1096b34).

Note that, since the Self-Sufficiency Criterion is meant to apply to *goods*, not to the *persons* who attain, possess, or enjoy goods, there is nothing about the possession of a self-sufficient good that implies a solitary life, as Aristotle points out at 1097b14–15.[12] A non-self-sufficient human being might attain, along with others, a good that was itself self-sufficient.

3. *Preferability.* It looks as though Aristotle gives a third criterion as well, namely, that the highest good is the sort of thing which, when compared individually with any other particular good, is always preferable to the other: "Furthermore, *eudaimonia* is the most prefer-able of all goods, assuming it is not counted along with anything else. (If it is so counted, then clearly it is more preferable with the addition of the littlest good thing. An incremental addition produces an excess of good things, and the greater good is always preferable.)" (1097b16–20).

This criterion is apparently taken from Plato, who makes use of it at the beginning of the *Philebus* (20d–22e), although Plato does not restrict comparisons to goods taken individually: Plato allows comparisons of composite goods. Aristotle apparently criticizes Plato for this later in the *Ethics*, pointing out that if we use this test for composite goods, then nothing whatsoever could count as the most preferable good, because, no matter how great the composite, it would always be possible to fashion a good that was preferable to it, by adding yet another good (10.2.1172b28–35).[13] Note that, if Aristotle thinks of the highest good as something that should be compared individually with other particular goods, then he appar-ently favors Selection.

But this third criterion has also been taken to support Collection. We took the passage to be ruling out comparisons involving composite

---

[12] Consider: there is nothing about the imagery of casks that restricts the use of non-leaky casks to hermits living on their own: there might be families or communities that were collecting their honey and milk in non-leaky jars, as much as individuals.

[13] This of course looks very much like the difficulty we found in the Comprehensivist interpretation of the Self-Sufficiency Criterion. We should note, however, that Aristotle's remarks in 10.2 are difficult to interpret, and some scholars deny that they have the sense given here.

goods. Yet it is possible to understand the passage to be advocating them: "Furthermore, *eudaimonia* is the most preferable of all goods, assuming that it is not counted along with anything else. Yet if it *were* so counted, then clearly it would be more preferable with the addition of the littlest good thing." In that case, the passage would in effect be saying that anything that we regard as happiness, but which could be improved upon by the addition of some good, would not yet be happiness – because happiness is the most preferable good. So we would need to keep adding goods to some candidate for happiness, until we arrived at a composite good that could not be improved upon, and then that would be the highest good. (Note that, on this latter interpretation, Aristotle would not be putting forward a third, distinct criterion. His point about Preferability would simply be a rephrasing of what he had said in connection with Self-Sufficiency.)

THE FUNCTION ARGUMENT

After Aristotle gives criteria by which to pick out the highest good, he delimits his field of search in the famous Function Argument (1097b22–1098a20). Before the Function Argument Aristotle has done little more than provide criteria for identifying the highest human good; after the Function Argument he gets to work examining the particular virtues and their characteristic activities. Therefore, the purpose of the Function Argument, as I said, is to argue that the highest human good is to be found among those things that we can do only because we have the virtues. The Function Argument identifies virtuous actions as the field of search to which we should apply the criteria he has given.

Here is how the argument begins:

But to say that the best thing is happiness (one would think) is to say something that, plainly, everyone accepts. What one wants is that something be said more clearly about *what happiness is*. This might just be possible, if we could identify the work to be done [*ergon*] by a human being. Why? Because in the case of a flautist, a sculptor, or any maker – and, generally, in the case of any occupation for which there is some definite work to be done – the "good" and the "well done" seem to reside in the work; and so it would seem also in the case of a human being, if indeed there is some definite work to be done by him. (1097b22–28)

We have already looked at the basic reasoning of the Function Argument: the function or "work" of a thing (*ergon*) is that for the sake of which it exists; therefore, the achieving of this work, or, more precisely, its doing so *well*, is its good; but only a good thing of a kind achieves its function well; and it is through its having the relevant virtues that something is a good thing of its kind; thus, we can see what the good of a thing is, if we look at what that kind of thing can achieve only insofar as it has those virtues that make it a good thing of its kind. In particular, we can see what the human good is, if we look at what a human being can do only through having those traits that make someone a good human being. A virtue is a trait that makes a thing of a certain kind good and in view of which we call a thing of that kind "good." Thus, the Function Argument directs us to examine the various virtues and the sorts of actions that are distinctive of them. But let us now look at the argument in more detail and consider especially how Aristotle might respond to some standard objections to it.

Aristotle does not take seriously the possibility that human beings do not have a function. After all, he takes nature generally to act for the sake of goals; indeed, he thinks that changeable things would have no reason to change in one way rather than another, except to achieve some goal; and he considers that human beings, as being placed in some sense at the summit of the changeable world, would especially act in order to achieve some goal. Nonetheless, he does give two very compressed arguments for the premise:

[i] Or do you suppose that the *carpenter*, or the *shoemaker*, has some definite work or action to perform, but that the *human* doesn't, and, rather, he's by nature unemployed? [ii] Don't you think that, just as there plainly is some definite work to be done by the eye, the hand, the foot, and, generally, by each of the *parts* of a human being, likewise, beyond all these, there is some definite work to be done by a human being? (1097b28–33)

It is not clear what Aristotle's argument is in (i). He could simply be drawing attention to the *names*, "carpenter," "shoemaker," "human," and arguing that we would not have a name for this distinct kind, *human*, if either it did nothing distinctively or what it did was indistinguishable from what other things did. One might object that we can fashion a name for a kind of thing simply through using a *description* of what that sort of thing is, and thus in naming things we do not therefore need to rely on some conception of the ends at which it aims, its "work" or function. But Aristotle might very well deny this; he might insist that every conception of a *kind* of thing involves the formulation of an ideal, at which things of that sort, it is supposed, are meant to aim, and which they achieve only "for the most part."

Or perhaps what Aristotle is emphasizing in (i), rather, is the distinction between acquired and natural functions, and the priority of the latter over the former: we could not *acquire* any role, such as being a carpenter or shoemaker, if we did not originally have a role that was *not* acquired: art imitates and completes nature (see *Physics* 2.8.199a15–18); therefore, any learned occupation is simply the giving of some specific form to our natural "occupation" as human beings.

The argument in (ii) seems to be that we would not have been equipped with parts which have special work to do if there were not some work or function to which these were to be directed, because, as Aristotle thinks, "nature does nothing in vain" (see, for instance, *De caelo* 1.4.271a33). If a human being as a whole had no distinctive function, then nature would be operating much as we would if we built a machine by taking a valuable component from a car, another from a computer, another from a camera, and placed them together for no purpose or point. It also seems to be suggested by the argument that it would be incoherent to attribute a function to a part at all, if the whole lacked a function, since a part of a thing needs to be defined with reference to the whole. (The function of the human eye is properly specified as "seeing in order that __," not merely as "seeing," where we would place in the blank space what the function of the organism is in which this capacity to see is located.)

How plausible is the view that human beings have a function? To believe some such thing, must we also be committed to a teleological framework, such as Aristotle's philosophy of nature? Perhaps not: there are commonsense analogues to Aristotle's viewpoint, such as how we tend to think about "talents" that people have. We tend to think that if someone has some extraordinary ability, which sets her apart from others, in music or sports for instance, then it would be unfortunate or somehow wrong if she were to leave this talent completely undeveloped. We suppose that whether she could be accounted a "success" in her life may very well hinge on how she makes use of this special talent – that she might after all fail and "waste her gifts." The Function Argument can similarly be understood in this sort of intuitive way, but now with respect to the "talents" of the human race as a whole. What special talents set us apart from other animals? Would we not be "wasting those gifts" if we lived no differently from animals that lack the ability to think and to direct their behavior through thinking?

The next part of the Function Argument aims to say just what the work or function of a human being is, by looking for something that is distinctive of us:

> Well enough, but then what could this be? *Living* is clearly something shared even with the plants, but one seeks something that belongs only to human beings. Yet in that case a life involving mere nourishment and growth has to be put aside. Some sort of life involving perception comes next, but plainly that too is something shared with other things – with horses, oxen, and with every animal. The only alternative, then, is that the work to be done by a human being is some sort of life displayed in action of the part of us which possesses reason. (1097b33–1098a4)

As we saw (pp. 4–5 above), in supposing that the function of a thing is distinctive of it, Aristotle is following Plato, who maintained in his own Function Argument at the end of *Republic,* book 1 that the function of a thing is what it alone can do, or what it does better than anything else. And the first thing Aristotle does is to turn Plato against himself. In his own Function Argument Plato held that the function of a human being (or, more precisely, the human soul) is to live (see *Republic* 353d). He said this because he was presupposing that souls generally constitute a uniform kind, a view which was consistent with his belief in reincarnation across species.[14] Yet this view hardly yields a distinctive function of human beings, as Aristotle points out: mere living is not something we alone do, or which we do best of all.

It is commonly objected that Aristotle's own candidate for the human function, "a life involving reason" is likewise not distinctive,

---

[14] Aristotle in contrast in the *De anima* holds that souls differ in kind and form a series – souls with higher powers contain within them the capacities of souls that have lower powers only.

at least on Aristotle's terms, because he believed that there are gods, and that the gods are rational and alive. So they too live "a life involving reason"; thus this is not distinctive of us and cannot be our function. But his saying, more precisely, that our function is a "kind of life *displayed in action* (*zōē praktikē tis*) of the part that possesses reason" seems intended to block that objection. Aristotle, as we shall see later (see chapter 4 below), thinks that only human beings *act*. He does indeed believe that there are gods which are living, rational beings, and who initiate change in the world, but they do so not through discrete movements but through other things' continually being attracted to them (see *Metaphysics*, book 12). *Action* is distinctive of human beings; it is the mode of agency that is distinctive of the kind of being we are, as Aristotle insists elsewhere in the *Nicomachean Ethics* (3.3.1112a31–33; 3.5.1113b16–19; and see also *Eudemian Ethics* 1223a4). So to live a life *consisting of actions* that involve reason, even on the supposition that gods exist, would indeed be distinctive of human beings.

Sometimes it is also objected that mere distinctiveness cannot be a guide to the function of a thing, because there are many things that are distinctive of us, which it would be absurd to count as part of the human function, for instance, playing checkers or theft. But this seems a frivolous objection, because the function of a *kind* has to pertain to what is common to members of that kind, and such things as playing checkers and theft are not like that. Moreover, the objection is at this point out of place, since Aristotle is here relying on an intuitive view of human reasonability; later he will tidy things up and make them more precise, giving arguments that amusements cannot be regarded as the goal of a human life (see 10.6), and that injustices such as theft are not instances of the good operations of human reasonability (see 2.6 and 5.2).

After stating what he takes to be the human function, Aristotle makes two qualifications:

> But "the part of us which possesses reason" can mean either: [i] that which is responsive to reason; or [ii] that which has reason and thinks things out. And since "life" is also meant in two senses, one should take it as referring to the actualization, since that's the principal sense of the term. So assume the work to be done by a human being is: *rational or not irrational actualization of the soul.* (1098a4–8)

The first qualification introduces some elementary psychology, which Aristotle will make use of later, in 1.13 and 2.1 (cf. especially 1103a1). There are two ways, he thinks, in which a human being may be said to be reasonable: either through simply exercising his faculty of reason ("the part which has reason"), or through exercising some other faculty in a manner consistent with or responsive to reason. Both of these are ways in which we *act*, and thus both are distinctive of us. This point too seems intended as a response to Plato. Aristotle presumably introduces this qualification to make it clear that by "life of the part which possesses reason" he is not identifying a human being simply with his mind, as Plato did.[15]

Aristotle's second qualification makes the obvious point that, for instance, to remain always asleep would not be to achieve the human function. The point applies generally to any function and not simply to the human function: merely having a potentiality or power could not count as the "work" of a kind of thing; the "work" or function of a thing would have to be, rather, the actualization of a power or capacity.[16]

Next comes the passage where Aristotle makes his crucial point about the interrelatedness of function, virtue, goodness, and good achievement of a function. His remarks are extremely compressed in the Greek; the following translation tries to state explicitly his thought:

But we don't mark a distinction between the kind of work to be done by X, and the kind of work to be done by a *good* X: for instance, we don't mark a distinction between the kind of work to be done by a *harpist*, and the kind of work to be done by a *good harpist*. And we speak in this way, then, not making any qualifications, in all cases. Yet we *do* mark what gets added to the work through the *good* traits of a practitioner. To wit: we say that "the work to be done by a harpist is to play the harp" but "the work to be done by a *good* harpist is to play the harp *well*." (1098a8–12)

If this is the correct way of rendering this very compressed passage, then Aristotle is basically making a plea for consistency in usage: we

---

[15] Thus the "or" in the phrase "rational or not irrational actualization of the soul" should be understood inclusively.

[16] Note that, as mentioned, Aristotle uses the same word, *energeia*, for both "actualization" and "activity" or "action"; the reason is that the human soul is actualized, he thinks, precisely through its actions.

should qualify neither side of an assertion ("The work of a harpist is to play the harp") or both sides equally ("The work of a good harpist is to play the harp well"). The reason why Aristotle wishes to emphasize this is that it has the following important consequence: if anyone with a function should reasonably take as his good the doing of that function *well*, then he should take as his good the achieving of that function in the way that a *good* practitioner of the function does.

It is important to appreciate how Aristotle intends this claim to be put to use. We can see this by comparison with a usual but incorrect way of construing the Function Argument. Often the argument is understood as having the following basic form:

1. The function of a human being is activity in accordance with reason.
2. A good human being, that is, someone who has the virtues, carries out this function well.
3. Thus, the ultimate good for a human being is acting in accordance with the virtues.

The argument, so understood, is clearly a *non sequitur*. The premises tell us what a *good human being* does; the conclusion is about what the *good for a human being* is. Aristotle begins the *Ethics* by wondering what the ultimate goal of a human being is, that is, what is or should be the purpose or goal of all of our striving. But the Function Argument, when construed as above, only specifies what it is to live as a good human being, namely to live in accordance with the various virtues. But then Aristotle would not have answered his original question so much as changed the subject. He would have confused what it is to live as a good human being, with what is good for a human being.

Yet this difficulty, it seems, can be avoided if we take the basic form of the Function Argument, rather, to be the following:

1. A good human being, that is, someone who has the virtues, carries out the human function well.
2. For something to carry out its function well is for it to attain what is good for it.
3. Thus, a good human being attains what is good for him.

On this interpretation, we take premise 2 to be precisely what Aristotle is insisting upon at 1098a8–12.[17] Aristotle would not be arguing in the Function Argument that having the virtues makes a human being good. This he takes for granted. Rather, he is arguing that only someone with the virtues achieves the human function in the way in which it can reasonably be accounted as a goal – that is, achieving that function *well*. Moreover, since he takes being a goal to be equivalent to being a good, he is presupposing that the good for a thing simply is its achieving its function well.

The text of the Function Argument then continues:

But if this is so, that is, if we set it down that:

[1] the work to be done by a human being is a certain kind of life; and that

[2] this is an actualization and action of the soul, involving reason; and that

[3] to do these things well and correctly is the work of a good human being; and that

[4] each sort of worker succeeds at doing his work *well*, by making use of the virtue appropriate to a worker of that sort;

then, if this is so, the good appropriate for a human being turns out to be: actualization of the soul as brought about by virtue. And if there are several virtues, then it is: actualization of the soul as brought about by the virtue which is best and is the most end-like.[18] But add: in a life which has the nature of a goal. Why? Because "one swallow does not make a spring," and neither does a single fine day, and thus a single day does not make someone blessed and happy, and neither does a brief span of time. (1098a16–20)

---

[17] Note that, on this way of understanding it, the premise saying what the human function is drops out. What that premise does is simply to direct us to look at those good traits of a human being which lead us to say that he is a "good human," rather than "healthy" (because his body works well), or "keen sighted" (because his eyes work well). In all of these respects he is good, but not good *qua* human.

[18] The phrase "as brought about by virtue" renders *kata tēn aretēn*. This is more usually rendered "in accordance with virtue." But such a translation is too imprecise, since something can be in accordance with some principle or cause, even if not in fact the result of that principle or cause. Aristotle looks at virtues as real causes and principles of action. They are powers of acting. Admittedly, these *powers* have distinctive and characteristic manifestations, which may be said to be conformable to or "in accordance with" the typical manifestation of a power of a certain sort. But what Aristotle has in mind in the Function Argument are actions of the sort that we accomplish *precisely through* the operation of some virtue.

Thus, the Function Argument contains four steps: (i) an argument that human beings have a function; (ii) the identification of the human function, as rational activity; (iii) the qualification that the function is accomplished by a good human being; and (iv) the conclusion that the ultimate good of a human being is to be located in virtuous activity.

It is worth noting that Aristotle first states the Function Argument as though there were just one human virtue. He does this in deference to Plato, and in recognition of the Platonic origins of the argument, because Plato thought that there was only one human virtue. (Indeed, Plato generally held that each sort of thing had just one virtue that enabled it to achieve its function well.) But Aristotle thinks that there are various human virtues, so that various things would be contained within "the human good." That would be why he adds the clause, "And if there are several virtues ... " He is apparently assuming that we could not act coherently if we had irreducibly multiple highest goals. Thus he is supposing that, in order to identify the *ultimate* human good, we would need somehow to operate upon this diverse "human good" – again, either by Selection or by Collection – in order to arrive at a single good that is highest. This is why he adds, "as brought about by the virtue which is best and which is most end-like." This phrasing is perhaps most naturally understood as instructing us to apply, to the various activities characteristic of the virtues, the criteria of the highest good that he had supplied immediately before the Function Argument.[19]

A LIFE THAT IS GOAL-LIKE

The remaining chapters of book 1, although they contain some bewildering passages and raise interesting questions about the relationship between happiness and material prosperity, are generally straightforward. But we should briefly give some attention to Aristotle's qualification that the human good is "activity in accordance with virtue in a life that is *teleion*" (1098a18). The phrase is

[19] Here again I have kept with the reading of *teleion* as "goal-like," for reasons given above. But, as I said, the term *may* mean "complete," and Ackrill (1974) argues strongly that it does so here.

usually translated as "in a complete life," but given the context of book 1 perhaps strictly means "in a goal-like life." The qualification can be understood in at least three senses:

1. *Chronologically.* Aristotle means a "sufficiently long" life, as the proverb cited by Aristotle suggests. This is perhaps the most natural interpretation, but it seems unsatisfactory, because mere length of time would seem to be the sort of thing that Aristotle would regard as an accident. (Aristotle even says earlier that maturity, not length of time alive, is the crucial thing for ethics, 1095a7.)

2. *Developmentally.* Aristotle means a life in which one reaches "maturity," and he has in mind some standard of maturity against which a life can be measured. For instance, elsewhere Aristotle maintains that a living thing has grown to maturity only when it becomes capable of reproducing its kind (*De anima* 415a23–28). He might therefore think that moral "maturity," and thus the right sort of life, requires that we develop in virtue to such an extent that we succeed in inculcating virtue in others, say, through prudent leadership and wise legislation.[20]

3. *Teleologically.* Aristotle means that a life cannot be a happy one if it is not "goal-like," that is, if it cannot be intelligibly taken as a goal. Whether a life could be intelligibly taken as a goal would depend on how it was constructed. Very different sorts of lives, and even relatively brief lives, could be goal-like, if they contained what they needed on their own terms. The famous choice of Achilles would illustrate just this point: he had to choose between two goal-like lives, one involving glorious death in battle at an early age, the other involving long years of undistinguished accomplishments. Either sort of life has its point and "makes sense"; either is intelligible as a goal.

It is debated, once again, whether the fact that Aristotle adds this qualification tends to favor Collection. One might think that it does not, since, on that interpretation, completeness would be already built into the human good, so that it would seem to be *impossible* to attain the human good in any context that was not complete. On the

---

[20] This would be similar to a standard of happiness advocated by Plato in the *Symposium*, cf. 206bff.

other hand, one might argue that it does, on the grounds that by adding the clause Aristotle is simply reinforcing, as regards temporal extension, a notion of completeness that he has been assuming all along.

In much of the second half of book 1, Aristotle is intent on arguing that a happy life needs a minimum of material goods. Much of this seems motivated by the popular association, which has already been noted, between *eudaimonia* and *eutuchia*, "prosperity," "making out well." His view is that goods are equipment for the activity that constitutes happiness; thus, obviously, a complete lack of such goods would impede our activity and consequently our happiness, because happiness is an activity. Some minimum of such goods is therefore a necessary condition of happiness (and later, in 10.8, he will argue that the minimum is very modest). But no amount of material goods, he thinks, could itself make someone happy, because happiness requires virtuous action; moreover, no lack of them could make someone unhappy, because, similarly, unhappiness requires bad action.[21]

A strange problem Aristotle discusses in the final chapters of book 1 is whether someone can become unhappy because of (for instance) sufferings that befall his relatives after he dies. That he takes the problem seriously is a sign of his commitment to the objective character of happiness. If happiness is something objective, then someone could fail to be happy, or cease being happy, without his knowing it. For instance, suppose that while a happy woman is asleep, terrorists kidnap her children, torture them horribly, and then put them to death. When the woman awakes, Aristotle would apparently maintain, she would no longer be happy, although she would not yet *know* that she was not happy. But if we adopt this sort of view, why should we not also hold that someone who lived a happy life could cease being happy because of sufferings that befell her relatives after her death? True enough, she would not then *know* that she was no longer to be accounted happy, yet happiness, we are supposing, is not subjective.

---

[21] Thus, although whether we are happy, according to Aristotle, depends to some extent on luck, whether we are *unhappy* does not – an important distinction not always observed by commentators who speak of "moral luck" in Aristotle.

Aristotle surprisingly does not say, as we might expect (see 3.6.1115a25–27), that someone who is dead simply does not exist, so that she is no longer either happy or unhappy, and cannot therefore change with respect to either condition. Rather, he speaks of the sufferings of the living as somehow being able to "reach through" to the dead. They do reach through, he believes, but not so much as to be able to make someone cease to be happy. This is an odd claim – what could "reaching through" mean except that the dead somehow learn of or perceive the sufferings of the living?

The difficulty, like much of book 1, seems to presuppose a Platonic background. Plato held that the souls of the dead, if they were not reincarnated, continued to exist in a divine realm, where they would associate with the souls of other good persons and with the gods in unalloyed blessedness. This blessedness would be threatened, if the sufferings of still-living relatives had the same weight for the dead as for the living. However, if this is indeed the context for Aristotle's discussion and solution, then it is strange that nowhere else in the *Ethics* does he raise the related question – even to dismiss it – of possible consequences of good and bad action after death. That the souls of the deceased are judged for their deeds by the gods after death was a widespread popular belief and repeatedly asserted by Plato (see, for instance, *Republic* 612b–614b); and Plato thought, furthermore, that a belief in that sort of judgment served to reinforce our motives for virtuous action. But Aristotle strikingly shows no signs of interest in the question, even as something supplemental to ethics in the strict sense.

FURTHER READING

Kraut (1979) contains an excellent discussion of what counts as an objective conception of *eudaimonia*. Aristotle on goodness may be looked at through Ackrill (1972), on goodness in the various categories, and N. P. White (1988), on goodness as goal-like.

As regards the criteria of the ultimate goal, and their implications, I have already mentioned Ackrill (1974) as giving the basic argument for Collection, and Heinaman's critique (1988). One might mention also Price (1980) as attempting to sketch an approach to Collection that would render it immune to the more usual criticisms. Bostock

(2000) at 21–25 gives a useful summary of how the criteria might rather seem to favor Collection rather than Selection.

Two challenging and subtle studies, suitable for more advanced work, are Lawrence (1997), on Preferability, and Wedin (1981), who takes a very different view of the opening sentence of 1.2 than advocated here, regarding it as linked to 1.7.

There are many valuable discussions of the Function Argument, but perhaps the best of these are Gomez-Lobo (1991) and Lawrence (2001). Whiting (1988) is helpful in defusing some common objections. The presentation of the Function Argument sketched above was intended to bypass a famous charge of fallacy put forward in a brief article by Glassen (1957). Glassen's point raises the deeper issue of whether expedience and moral principle coincide, and for a discussion of this in an Aristotelian spirit, see P. Foot (2001).

For the relationship of happiness to material goods, Cooper (1985), Irwin (1985), and especially S. M. White (1992) are worth consulting.

CHAPTER 3

Character-related virtue (Nicomachean Ethics *1.13 and book 2*)

The state of Aristotle's argument near the end of book 1 of the *Ethics* is as follows. There is an ultimate goal of human life, namely whatever is the aim of that expertise which is required in order reasonably to govern political society. We can be assured that there is such an aim, and such an expertise, Aristotle supposes, because political society is a natural form of association for human beings and therefore has a definite purpose or goal. We can identify three (or perhaps only two) criteria which such a goal must satisfy: it must have the marks of Ultimacy, Self-Sufficiency, and (perhaps also) greatest Preferability. We can also identify, roughly, the general sort of thing that this ultimate goal is going to be: as Aristotle maintains in the Function Argument, the ultimate goal of human life involves some activity which a human being can accomplish only through his having a trait that contributes toward someone's being a good human being. Such a trait is a "virtue," so the ultimate goal of human life is some "activity in accordance with virtue." We can determine the ultimate goal of human life, then, by looking at activities of that sort and seeing which of them satisfy the criteria of Ultimacy, Self-Sufficiency, and greatest Preferability.

So Aristotle's next step must be to examine the various activities of that sort. But before he can do this, he must first distinguish the various virtues, which would require also that he say what sort of thing a virtue is. And this is what he aims to accomplish in book 2. Book 2 of the *Ethics* is concerned with defining virtue, and with distinguishing the various virtues.

PARTS OF THE SOUL AND PARTS OF VIRTUE

This task so described, however, is actually begun in 1.13, where Aristotle offers a preliminary analysis of human virtue. As I have said, Aristotle follows Plato in supposing at first that the virtue of a thing is something unitary and singular. A virtue is "what it is about a thing which makes it such that it perform its function well." Things have unified functions, and therefore we might suppose that "what it is about a thing which makes it such that it perform its function well" would also be something unified. Nonetheless, Aristotle allows that virtues typically admit of some kind of analysis. How they do so may be made clear by a simple example.

An electric coffee maker is an appliance which, we may say, has the function of *brewing coffee*. If such a coffee maker brews coffee *well*, then there is something about it which makes it such that it brews coffee well. We can gesture in a general way at what this is, by referring to it as the "virtue" of the coffee maker: "This excellent coffee maker brews a great cup of coffee because it has the 'virtue' one looks for in a coffee maker."

But this "virtue" is not simple; it admits of analysis. That it admits of analysis is clear if we consider that the function of a coffee maker also admits of analysis. The function of a coffee maker, we might say, is *to send very hot water through ground coffee*. But this consists of a variety of steps, each of which may be accomplished either well or poorly. If the coffee maker does that particular step well, then there is something about the coffee maker which makes it so that it does that step well, and thus there is a virtue of a coffee maker, of sorts, for just that step. For instance, a very good coffee maker will filter the water, grind the coffee in the right sort of way (with a burr grinder) immediately before brewing, and heat the water to exactly the right temperature. Thus, corresponding to these three aspects of its function, there would be three "virtues" of that sort of a coffee maker: what it is about it that makes such that it filters the water well; what it is about it that makes it such that it grinds the coffee correctly; what it is about it that makes it such that it heats the water to the right temperature.

Of course, another way of analyzing the function of a coffee maker, and discovering different aspects of the "virtue" of a coffee maker, would be simply to look at its physical parts. It is a truism that form and function in an instrument are related: each part of an instrument will have its distinctive purpose or function. So we could take the appliance apart and simply observe that it had a reservoir for water with a filter, a heating element for heating the water, and a grinder for grinding the coffee on the spot. Each part would have its own function, contributing to the function of the whole, and thus each part would have its own virtue, contributing to the virtue of the whole.

Note that these parts would be *separable* parts: you could remove the filter, or heating element, and replace it with another, if you wished. Yet it is not always the case that the parts of an instrument are separable: an ice-cream scoop, for instance, cuts a portion of ice cream out of the carton with its smooth convex face, and it shapes that scooped ice cream into a neat ball with its smooth concave face, and yet its convex face is not separable from its concave face. So we must not take our use of the word "part" in these contexts as implying separability in "location" (as Aristotle would say).

Note too that not every part of the electric coffee maker contributes to the function, or virtue, of a *coffee maker*. For instance, the electric cord supplies the power for the appliance, but it plays no role in the brewing of coffee. Admittedly, it is something *good* about an appliance if its electric cord works well, and it is something *bad* about an appliance if its electric cord is faulty. But a coffee maker is not a *bad coffee maker* if its electric cord is faulty, and neither is a coffee maker a *good coffee maker* insofar as its electric cord works well. It is not the case, then, for every part of a certain kind of thing, that if that part works well, then, to that extent, we will say that a thing of that sort is "good," without qualification. We will say that it is "good," perhaps, but only adding a qualification: "The thing can't brew coffee worth a fig, but its *cord* is first rate, at least."

Thus, some parts of an instrument or appliance (e.g. the water filter, the heating element) are such that, if they are good, their being good contributes to that instrument's being good, without qualification; and other parts of a thing (e.g. the electric cord) are such that, if they are good, their being good contributes to that instrument's being good only in a qualified way. As regards the former sort, what it is about a part like that which makes it such that it is good, or the "virtue" of that part, will be a part of the virtue of the instrument as a whole. As regards the latter sort, what it is about a part like that which makes it such that it is good, or the "virtue" of that part, will not be a part of the virtue of the instrument as a whole.

(We might want to say that the goodness of this latter sort of part is no more than a "condition" for the operation of the instrument.)

The virtue of a good coffee maker, when thus analyzed, includes such things as its being such that it filters water well; and its being such that it heats the water well; and its being such that it grinds the coffee well. But the virtue of a good coffee maker does not include, for instance, its being such that it receives electric power well.

Aristotle reasons about human virtue in a similar way. His presupposition is that it is unitary, but he thinks that it admits of analysis, which we can carry out by reference to the parts of the human soul, where the goodness of only some of these parts, however, contributes to the goodness *of a human being*.

Why does Aristotle turn to parts of the "soul" at this point? Why not the parts of a human being? Well, clearly, the relevant parts are *not* the parts of the human body. It is good that a person's heart works well; and that someone's heart works well is something good about him. But that someone's heart works well provides no reason at all for our regarding *him* as good. Our calling someone "good" or "bad" (when these terms are used without qualification) has nothing to do with whether any part of his body is diseased or malformed: "That crook may be the worst criminal in history, but his *heart* is as healthy as can be." The goodness or badness of a part of the human body makes no contribution to the goodness or badness *of a human being*.

But what does Aristotle mean by a "part" of the soul? Is not the soul (if there is such a thing) something simple and uniform? The "soul" (*psuchē*), for Aristotle, and indeed for any Greek speaker of his time, as I have said, was simply the principle or cause of life in an animal, whatever that might turn out to be.[1] Plato admittedly regarded the soul as an incorporeal substance, which was capable of independent existence apart from the body: this was the basis of his belief in reincarnation and the immortality of the soul. But whereas Aristotle agreed with Plato that the soul is not a body – because the soul *activates* the body, it must be something different from it – he

---

[1] Thus the notion of a "soul" is not a specifically religious notion; indeed, it is primarily a biological notion. Many of Aristotle's contemporaries thought that the soul was something corporeal – a kind of fine, gaseous substance; and it was a common, popular belief that the soul was something like a vapor, which, when it was separated out from the body at death, was liable to be scattered and destroyed.

generally resisted the conclusion that the soul is therefore a substance that can exist on its own apart from the body. The soul of an animal may be conceptually and even causally different from its body, Aristotle insisted, without its being the sort of thing that, generally and in its entirety, can exist on its own.

The soul in this sense will have different "parts" if there are different sorts of activity of life for which it may be taken to be responsible. But how do we mark out some sorts of activity as different in the relevant sense? For Aristotle, nature largely does this for us already. Plants display one kind of activity only, "nutritive activity," which consists in such things as taking in nourishment, growing, and exhibiting controlled decay. We may therefore postulate, Aristotle thought, a "nutritive" part of the human soul (*to threptikon*, cf. 1102b11), since indeed the life of a human being also involves activity of nourishment, growth, and measured decay. This part of the soul works well, and therefore has its own "virtue," when we have good digestion, sleep well at night, develop strong bones and muscles, and so on. But it is clear that the goodness of this part of the soul is irrelevant to whether a human being is good. It is good that someone sleeps well at night, but we are not disposed to say that he is *good* (a good man, a good human being) because he sleeps well at night. So this part of the soul is of no use in analyzing the virtue *of a human being*.

Aristotle thought, similarly, that we can easily enough take the activity of *thinking* to be attributable to a distinct part of the human soul, because this activity, too, exists on its own in the world: divinities exist, he thinks (gods, and the First Cause), which display this sort of activity alone. Thus, if this activity or something like it is found in a human being, we should postulate some distinct part or aspect of the human soul as being responsible for it. (We need not accept his theology to see the force of his conclusion, since thinking in various ways looks to be quite different from other activities of living things. Indeed, for most of us it takes an effort to look upon *thinking* in human beings as something akin to a biological function, to be classed with digestion or sensation.)

But even if we were to grant that there is some distinct part or aspect of the soul that is responsible for thinking, should we hold that this part has much to do with human goodness? Is not goodness in thinking like goodness in digestion – a desirable thing to have, but not relevant to whether someone is simply *good* or *bad*? Is it not clear that someone could be a brilliant thinker, but a terrible human being, or a real saint but mentally dull? We do not, after all, seem to treat intellectual ability as if it were a human virtue: when we meet an exceptionally *smart* person, we are not, to that extent, disposed to say that she or he is a *good* person.

But Aristotle takes a different view. He believes that the goodness of the thinking part of the human soul – "thinking-related virtue" (*dianoētikē aretē*, 1103a5, 15) he calls it, or "intellectual virtue" – does indeed make its own contribution to human goodness. He thinks that human virtue must be analyzed in such a way that it includes "thinking-related virtue," and he devotes book 6 of the *Ethics* to discussing virtue of that sort. This view is understandable and perhaps not so far from what we also hold, once we suppose that goodness in thinking is more than cleverness or quickness, and that it involves such things as "good judgment," "insight," "understanding," "intellectual depth," and even some sort of "wisdom" (see the list at 1103a5–6).

A thorough analysis of human virtues, Aristotle thinks, should include one further part of the human soul. He calls this the part which does not "have reason" but which somehow "attends" to reason and "submits itself" or "responds" to reason (1102b31, 1103a3).[2] His procedure in distinguishing and appealing to this part of the soul is curious. We might have thought that Aristotle would at this point simply rely on his investigations in the *De anima*, where, besides the thinking and nutritive (or "plant-like") parts, he also distinguishes parts responsible for sense-perception, for bodily movement, and for desires for food, drink, and reproduction – in short, the powers or faculties that, in an elementary psychology, we might think were to be found in animals generally. Call this the "animal side" of human nature. Aristotle cannot simply rely on what he says elsewhere about this "animal part," for the following reason. One cannot plausibly

---

[2] It is not particularly clear from the text, and there is much dispute among commentators about precisely what Aristotle means in saying that there is a part which properly "has reason." Does this mean that it can grasp explanations or definitions? Or that it can formulate them? Or that it is capable of *reasoning*? And so on. But these refinements seem largely irrelevant to Aristotle's point here, which is very basic.

claim that this animal side, like the nutritive part, is completely irrelevant to human goodness, since clearly it *is* relevant somehow: how someone experiences emotions, or perceives things, or the manner in which his body comes into play in an action, can be relevant to whether he is a good or bad human being. But neither can one claim that this animal side is *in all respects* relevant, since such things as whether our eyesight is good or bad or whether we can move quickly or not are irrelevant to whether we are good or bad.

Aristotle therefore has to make some kind of selection of this "animal side" and claim that it is relevant in some respects and not others. This he does precisely through this notion of a part of the soul that is able to "listen to" and "respond" to reason. Insofar as our activity of perceiving, feeling emotions, and moving is such that it listens and responds to reason – or *could have* listened and responded, if we had acted differently in the past – then this activity is something different in kind, Aristotle thinks, from other animal activity. This part of the soul too exists on its own in the world, in a certain sense. Aristotle says that this part listens and responds to reason as if to a father (1102b32, 1103a3); he apparently has in mind how an immature child obeys his parents naturally and with a very imperfect grasp of their reasons for requiring something. An immature child, then, not yet having reached the "age of reason" (as we call it), would be an instance of this part of our nature existing in a way in isolation from the part of our nature that "has reason."

How is this part which does not "have reason" but which can "listen" and "respond" to reasons relevant to whether someone is a good or bad human being? Why is the goodness of this part not akin to good digestion – valuable but morally irrelevant? To establish that it is relevant, Aristotle brings in the case of someone who has to battle to achieve self-control. Consider someone who *thinks* that he should act in a certain way, and who therefore *wishes* to do this,[3] but who consistently

<hr/>

[3] When Aristotle remarks, "It seems, then, that there's a twofold division in the non-rational part of the soul as well: the vegetative part shares in reason not at all; but the part which is appetitive and generally desiderative somehow does share in it" (1102b28–30), we should not take him to mean that appetites and desires are found only in the non-rational part, that the rational part of the soul does not in any respect have desires, or that it in no way aims at or tends to anything. (This is a view that was championed by David Hume.) Rather, Aristotle thinks that there is such a thing as rational desire, which we exemplify in acts of wishing and choosing.

Table 3.1

Part of the human soul	Part of human virtue
The part that has reason	Thinking-related or "intellectual" virtue
The part that does not have reason but which can listen and respond to reason	Character-related virtue
The part that does not have reason and which cannot listen or respond to reason	– none –

has strong impulses to do something else, and so either fails to do what he wishes or succeeds but only with difficulty. Each time he suffers from such conflict, we ascribe the thinking and wishing to the same aspect of him as before, and we take the contrary impulses to be yet another expression of the same thing in himself. So we treat the conflict as though it originates from two different and persistent parts. The impulses that oppose thinking and wishing, we concede, might not have been so strong, or might not even have existed; we therefore suppose that the part to which we attribute them is somehow persuadable by reason. Moreover, we take someone to be worse, to the extent that he finds acting as he thinks and wishes something difficult. A good human being would have no impulses *that might not have been present had he acted differently* and that conflicted with what he thought he should do. So, the fact that this part is duly persuaded and submissive, Aristotle thinks, is indeed a good that contributes to human goodness, and thus the goodness of this part is a part of human virtue.[4]

So Aristotle gives us a minimalist psychology in 1.13, which he uses to provide an analysis of human virtue (see table 3.1).

---

[4] Aristotle's ideal of moral excellence diverges from a common view today, namely that virtue and moral commitment are most evident, and most admirable, when someone struggles successfully to do what is right against his inclinations to the contrary – because (it is thought) when someone's inclination diverges from what is his duty then he cannot have any ulterior motives for what he does, of the sort that would diminish the moral purity of his motives. Aristotle holds, in contrast – and this was the common Greek view – that a person is in a better condition, if *everything* about him that can be committed to duty is so committed, and that, if a person *could* have made it so that his inclinations were aligned with his duty, but did not do so, then he is to blame for his being in this worse condition.

THE SHAPE OF BOOK 2

Aristotle begins book 2 by remarking, "The virtue specific to human beings therefore has two parts: the thinking-related part and the character-related part. The former begins to exist and increases largely through our receiving instruction. That's why it needs experience and time. The latter is a side-effect of our becoming accustomed to behave in characteristic ways" (2.1.1103a14–18). He discusses thinking-related virtue, as I said, in book 6, and particular character-related virtues are discussed in books 3–5.

As a prelude to this latter discussion, he gives in book 2 a general introduction to character-related virtue, which has the following structure:

The *origin* of character-related virtue (chapters 1–4)
The *definition* of character-related virtue (chapters 5–6)
The *classification* of character-related virtue (chapters 7–9)

One might wonder why Aristotle discusses the origin of character-related virtue before giving a definition of it. Is it possible to determine *how* something comes into existence, without first getting clear about *what* it is? But Aristotle evidently thinks he has already picked out this sort of virtue well enough, with his notion of the virtue of "the part of the soul that listens and responds to reason," and he can plausibly suggest that some commonly used names of virtues, such as "generosity" and "moderation," are meant to pick out precisely that sort of virtue (1103a6). So we have some kind of an initial grasp of what this sort of virtue is. And then Aristotle believes too, reasonably enough, that we often get a better intuitive understanding of something by seeing how it comes into existence (cf. *Politics*, book 1), after which we are in a better position to define it.

But to some extent, also, his procedure is meant to mark out his own approach to virtue from what might be called a broadly "Socratic" approach. Socrates apparently held that virtue is equivalent to knowledge: to be courageous, for instance, is the same as knowing what it is to be courageous. Socrates' reason for holding this can be captured in the following line of thought. No one willingly chooses to do something bad, Socrates thought. Thus, if we recognized an action as, say, courageous and therefore good, or cowardly and therefore bad, then of course we would do the one and avoid the other. But to be able to recognize an action as courageous requires being able to say whether a particular action is courageous or not, and why. But this is to be able to say what all courageous actions have in common, and what all actions that are not courageous lack. But this is simply to give a definition of "courageous." Yet to be able to give a definition of a thing just is to have knowledge of it. Thus, to know what it is to be courageous implies actually being courageous.

On this view, once someone has the relevant knowledge, then the virtue follows immediately. There is no particular task or concern of acquiring a virtue, other than simply acquiring the relevant knowledge. Being good, then, would not be unlike being skilled in a mathematical discipline such as geometry: when someone knows geometry, he is simply no longer capable of making stupid, ungeometrical inferences; in the same way, when someone knows what courage is, he is simply no longer capable of acting in a non-courageous way.

However, once Aristotle has distinguished a part of the soul that has reason from the part that merely "listens" and "responds" to reason, virtuous action does not follow immediately from knowledge of virtue, and it becomes an issue of how this latter part becomes suitably responsive. It clearly becomes so other than through instruction, as in geometry. And it makes sense to think that we can best understand what exactly this sort of responsiveness amounts to, by seeing first how it comes into existence. Aristotle's repeated emphasis on the practical outlook of his investigation is of a piece with this departure from the Socratic view: "The point of what we're doing here is not simply to see what's true, as in other discussions. Our goal is not to know the definition of virtue, but to become good" (1103b26–31).

Book 2 begins with a couple of brief arguments against the view that we acquire character-related virtue by nature, because Aristotle is presupposing that if he eliminates this view, then he has effectively established his own. The reason is that Aristotle standardly recognizes four ways in which things can originate: nature, human deliberate purpose, necessity, and chance. That good traits of character arise randomly is absurd, since then happiness as well would arise randomly (see 1.9). If their origin were necessary, then no one could be praised or blamed for them (or so Aristotle thinks: cf. 3.5). Thus, if they do not arise by nature, they must arise through human deliberate purpose, which in this case would presumably take the form of some kind of training.

The notion that virtues arise by nature additionally needs to be argued against, because Aristotle has some sympathy with the view, and he thinks that it is in some sense true. He will later say, in 6.13, that human beings generally are equipped by nature ("straight from birth," 1144b6) with tendencies supportive of right action. As a consequence it is appropriate to speak of "natural justice," "natural moderation," and "natural courage." Such virtues are not, however, true or full virtues (and we should always refer to them with the qualification "natural"), because they need to be kept checked and directed, as Aristotle goes on to argue, by sound practical reasoning, in which case they are transformed into virtues in the strict sense. But if someone with merely natural virtue does not develop into a truly virtuous person in this way, then these natural tendencies will eventually lead him astray – and perhaps do so to a greater degree, the more striking his natural gifts originally were.

There was a common Greek idea that some people were especially distinctive in "natural virtue," perhaps because of their ancestry. We find scattered throughout the Platonic dialogues characters who, clearly, are meant to exhibit merely natural virtue in a striking way: Charmides, for instance, in the dialogue by that name, is depicted as having a noteworthy, natural moderation; Alcibiades, a natural magnanimity; Lysis, a natural amiability. Plato held that natural virtue was insufficient on its own and that, unless it was supplemented by ethical knowledge, it would expose someone to great moral corruption, Alcibiades being the star example of this. Aristotle presumably agrees but in 2.1 merely remarks, tersely: "Although we are naturally equipped to acquire the virtues, they attain full development in us through training" (1103a25–26).[5]

---

[5] Good traits of character naturally acquired are in this respect similar to good traits of physique that someone comes upon naturally: a young man might be a natural athlete in a sport and distinguish himself among untrained peers, but he will need to undergo training to compete against the best, and he will certainly need to continue in training if he wishes to remain a good athlete after he reaches maturity.

Something should be said about Aristotle's notion of "training" generally. We might tend to associate with this word how a man trains a dog or how a drill sergeant trains fresh recruits, a process involving constant oversight and the immediate dispensations of rewards or punishments for behavior adjudged acceptable or not. Aristotle's notion is subtler; it resembles, rather, the view of Montaigne or Hume about the pervasive force of "custom." The Greek word often rendered as "training" means something like "becoming accustomed," "becoming habituated," "getting used to." This can indeed happen in a strongly directive way – Aristotle would prefer an athletic coach as a model for this rather than a drill sergeant. But typically it happens indirectly, and it is most effective when indirect; for instance, parents send their child to a music camp where they know that standards are high and that other campers there have strong career ambitions in music, thinking that their own child, through spending some weeks at the camp, will "become used" to approaching his or her own musical studies in that way.

Of course Aristotle would insist that even when it happens in this indirect way, "training" is still something that has to be *imposed* by people who have authority upon those who are under their care. This is why he writes the *Ethics* for aspiring leaders: the *Ethics* is not a self-help manual, nor does Aristotle think that we could, practically speaking, become good human beings through our own efforts, any more than someone could on his own train himself to become a concert pianist. Even when indirect, training involves the imposition and acceptance of some kind of discipline or law, although admittedly the force of that discipline or law may indeed be felt only lightly; for instance, students at the music camp may practice their instruments for four hours each afternoon because, they think, "that's just what we do here," when originally campers' doing so was a requirement for remaining in good standing, imposed by camp administration.

THE ACQUISITION OF CHARACTER-RELATED VIRTUE

Aristotle makes five fairly practical observations in 2.1–4 about the acquisition of character-related virtue. He does not argue for them, but he seems to expect his listener to agree with them as he points them out.[6] Presumably he takes these remarks to have force, in part, because of an implied contrast with how we acquire knowledge and skill in speculative subjects such as geometry. If character-related virtue were simply a matter of thinking in the right sort of way, it would not be acquired in the way that it is.

1. *We acquire a character-related virtue by performing actions similar to those of people who have that virtue* (1103a31–b6). Aristotle puts the point pithily: "What we can only do by practicing, we practice only by doing" (1103a32–33). He gives as analogues the way people become good at building houses or playing the lyre. In learning such a skill, one at first attempts to carry out a "performance" typical of the skill all at once, even if one does so ineptly – say, one tries with fumbling success, and under the guidance of an expert, to build a section of a wall, or play a simple melody – and then over time one becomes more exact and steady in that very same sort of "performance." With acquiring knowledge it is different: no one becomes expert in geometry by doing whole proofs at a go but in a fumbling way, hoping to get better at proving things simply by repeating such performances.

2. *We acquire a character-related virtue not by performing certain kinds of actions, but by performing them in a certain way* (1103b6–21). Given observation 1, we might think that there were certain kinds of actions which were such that, if we simply carried them out, then we would acquire a character-related virtue. Compare the old joke about the man carrying a violin who asked a New Yorker how to get to Carnegie Hall and was told, "Practice! Practice!" – as if to suggest that if one were simply to *play the violin*, then one would eventually become good at it. But Aristotle points out that some people keep on playing a musical instrument and as a result become, instead, *bad* at playing that instrument (1103b9). So the *manner* in which one performs an action of a certain sort is crucial for acquiring a good trait: those who repeatedly perform that sort of action well become in that respect *good*; those who do so poorly become in that respect *bad*.

This has two important implications as regards character-related virtues. First, we should expect that each such virtue will have a

---

[6] In offering these remarks, however, he *does* rely throughout on analogies between, on the one hand, character-related virtue, and, on the other, practical skill and bodily fitness – which amount to arguments of sorts.

"domain" of action, that is, a class of actions such that one acquires that virtue, or acquires a contrary vice, depending upon whether one carries out actions in that. class well or poorly. These "domains" would then serve to differentiate virtues. And Aristotle lists some such domains in a preliminary way: "it's by our carrying out exchanges of goods with others that some of us become just, others unjust; it's by what we do when threatened by dangers, and by our developing habits of being afraid or feeling confident, that some of us become courageous and others cowards" (1103b14–16). Second, we should anticipate that in such things there would be two ways in which one could go wrong, because success consists in the correct *manner*, but manner suggests *degree*, and degree suggests striking a *balance* and adjusting things correctly. If what is at stake, in becoming a good lyre-player, is *how* one practices the lyre, then one might go astray by either rushing to strike a note or hesitating; by playing a note sharp or playing it flat; by adding too much emphasis or too little; and so on. Observe that here too there is an implied contrast with how we acquire a skill or knowledge in a subject such as geometry: becoming skilled at geometry is not a matter of doing some *other* thing well; and success in geometry is not a matter of degree – either one gets it right, or one has simply failed to reason geometrically.

3. *Acting well in a domain involves, initially at least, the avoidance of contrary extremes* (1104a11–27). This observation follows naturally from the preceding. Aristotle's remarks here might at first appear fatuous:

If someone runs away from and fears everything, and stands firm against nothing, he turns into a coward; if generally someone fears nothing, but rather rushes at everything, he becomes a rash person. Similarly, if someone satisfies his every liking and resists nothing, he turns into a self-indulgent person; but if he avoids all pleasant things, as toughened country folk do, he turns into someone who lacks sensitivity. (1104a20–25)

We might wish to protest that there is a large gulf between running away from everything and rushing toward everything: how is it helpful to be told, as practical advice, to encourage behavior that falls in between? But Aristotle's remarks are pointed and have considerable force if we understand them as directed against the Platonic view of virtue. On that view, there would be only one condition opposed to each virtue, because virtue is knowledge, and knowledge is opposed by one thing only, ignorance. Furthermore, this ignorance would be shifting and random, just as someone unskilled in geometry typically has some confused smattering of geometry. Aristotle's remark in contrast is intended to establish that for any character-related virtue there are <u>two conditions that</u> were contrary to it, and that these are settled and determinate.

Nonetheless, Aristotle's remarks are helpful even if understood as a piece of practical advice. A rock climber walking the length of a thin mountain ridge might usefully be reminded: "Hey, this is not like a cliff – you can fall off here either to the right or to the left." Balancing correctly is something different from clinging correctly. Moreover, one goes a long way toward discovering the *right* rule for action, simply by being directed to look at *some* rule which flexibly modulates behavior: it is not bad advice, for someone who wants to keep at a healthy weight, to be told simply, "Watch what you eat and get regular exercise." That is to say: follow *some* rule. The reason is that a rule is a kind of limit, and action which is not adapted to some kind of rule tends to be unlimited. If someone eats "when he feels like it," never not eating because some discipline or rule restricts this, then there is nothing in principle which keeps him from eating continually: it is as if he *is* eating always. Or if someone fails to get out of bed to do his morning exercise because "he doesn't feel like it," then why should he ever exercise? It is as if for the moment he has adopted the principle: never exercise.

4. *There is a kind of momentum in action: to the extent that someone acts well or poorly in a domain, to that extent he becomes more disposed to act in that way* (1104a27–b3). Aristotle supports this claim with a comparison involving fitness: people become strong by lifting heavy weights, and the stronger they become, the better they are at lifting weights. Likewise, "it's by refraining from enjoying pleasures that we become moderate, and once we have become so we are especially able to refrain from them" (1104a33–35). He does not attempt to give an explanation for why this is so. The closest he comes is the slightly metaphysical language he uses in a summary passage: "the things from which a virtue took its start are the very same things concerning which it finds its actualization" (1105a14–16). This language suggests that a virtue (and a vice) involves some kind of propensity to fulfillment – presumably taking the form of our being prepared to regard

something as good and to favor it – and that therefore to the extent
that someone has a virtue, to that extent he favors performing actions
which would strengthen that virtue. Aristotle presumably regards this
as holding generally for the sort of thing a virtue (or vice) is – a
"habit" or "disposition," something about us which makes us accustomed to something (cf. 1103b20–22). Note that there are two
important implications of this principle. First, in any domain corresponding to which there is a character-related virtue, a person who is
active in that domain will tend to develop either that virtue or one of
the contrary vices. Mediocrity is not, as such, easily sustainable;
someone who is not improving will be getting worse. Second, virtues
and vices, once developed, are stable: someone who has a virtue and is
disturbed in such a way that he acts for the moment out of character
will tend to return to acting virtuously; and similarly someone who
has a vice (cf. 1.10.1100b12–16; 8.3.1156b12).

5. *When someone regularly performs actions similar to those of people
who have a virtue, and if he actually* likes *acting in that way, we can be
assured that he indeed has that virtue* (1104b3–9). "The pleasure or pain
that is a side-effect of action," Aristotle says,

should be used as a sign of a person's character. Consider a man who is
denying himself bodily pleasures: if he's pleased to do this, he has self-
mastery; but if he's bothered by it, he's a self-indulgent man. And consider a
man who is standing firm when confronted by frightening things: if he's
pleased to do this, or, at least, not distressed by it, he has courage, but if he's
distressed by it, he's a coward. (1104b3–8)

This remark follows from the preceding point and from Aristotle's
notion of "becoming accustomed" generally. His idea is this. The first
step in acquiring a virtue is typically that someone perform actions like
those of people who have the virtue because he is directed to do so by
some discipline or rule. This rule will attach rewards to observance and
punishments to infractions. When we perform an action thus required
by a rule *because* of the reward,[7] we are taking pleasure in something
other than the action, but which is accidentally attached to the action.
After repeatedly performing actions of that sort, however, we can

---

[7] Or even, one suspects, *simply because it is required by the rule*, that is (Aristotle would say), *by
some authority who makes the rule*, since finding pleasure in the good pleasure of that authority
is still not taking pleasure in the action itself.

change so that we *want* to perform actions like that.[8] If we have indeed acquired the relevant character-related virtue, which (recall) pertains to that part of our animal nature which is responsive to reason, then as regards the performing of this action we would have no divided affections – there would be nothing within us which would rather not perform *that action*. Thus the attitude of someone who has the relevant virtue, toward the action, is unalloyed liking.[9] That someone is simply pleased in performing the action itself, then, is a sign of the full development of the relevant character-related virtue.

Note that, when describing this growth in character, it is natural that we speak not simply of the pleasure or pain that an agent takes in his action, but also of his feelings of "satisfaction" or "dissatisfaction" in performing it, or his "liking" or "disliking" what he does. In fact the Greek terms for "pleasure" and "pain" can cover all of these subjective states. It is clear that Aristotle understands these terms in this broad way when he argues at length, in 2.3, that every character-related virtue deals in some way with pleasures and pains (1104b9). We might express Aristotle's general outlook in that chapter as follows. Since there is a subject who acts and feels appropriately or not, then there will be subjective responses, of pursuit or avoidance, associated with these actions and feelings, and thus virtues must take these subjective responses into account as well. To receive a "good upbringing," then, is to be disciplined in such a way that one's subjective responses come into a good alignment with what one objectively ought to do: a person has been correctly brought up when he has come to like doing what he should do and to dislike doing what he should not do. Elsewhere, Aristotle compares this process to how we develop an objective understanding of the world, starting from a subjective perspective: "That's how the process of learning occurs in everyone, through things that are less knowable by nature, to things that are more knowable by nature. This is our task;

---

[8] Aristotle does not at this point attempt to explain how we so change, except insofar as this is implicit in his language of "actualization" of a virtue.

[9] This is not to deny, on Aristotle's reckoning, that the circumstances surrounding some virtuous action may be extremely repugnant: thus a courageous person likes the *courageous action* that he performs, without any division in his affection, yet he might recoil at the *wounds* he thereby receives (see 3.9). Clearly, Aristotle's maintaining such a view requires that he have a theory of action which allows him to count the agent's *courageous action* as one thing and his *getting wounded* as something else.

just as, when it comes to action, our task is to start from things that are good for the individual, to make it so that things that are generally good are good for him" (*Metaphysics* 1029b3–7).

We are now in a position to understand Aristotle's reply, in 2.4, to a difficulty that might have seemed to arise in connection with observation 1 above. Is it not circular to say that people become virtuous by performing virtuous actions – since they would have to be virtuous *already*, to perform a virtuous action in the first place? Aristotle replies, in effect, that the phrase "acting virtuously" has two senses: it can mean either (i) performing the sort of action that someone who is virtuous would perform, or (ii) performing that sort of action, but *as a virtuous person would do it*. And Aristotle's claim is that, by performing actions of the former sort, we become such that we perform actions of the latter sort.

That we can perform actions of the former sort, without yet being such that we are capable of the latter sort, is clear: as we have seen, people who are not yet virtuous can perform actions of the former sort because they are *required* to do so. There is a similar gap even in the case of a skill; for instance, someone who is learning the trumpet will, on occasion, play his audition piece, or parts of it at least, with complete accuracy. But he does not therefore play it *skillfully*: he plays the piece skillfully, only when he both plays the piece with accuracy and *typically* plays the piece with accuracy. (Then he has "mastery," as we say.) This requires a change *in him*, a development of his skill. Similarly, a young person placed in good company will do the right sorts of things because everyone else is acting that way, and because he wants to get along with and win the approval of others. However, he is not yet acting virtuously: he has to become the sort of person who performs such actions consistently and as an expression of a stable character. This requires that he understand the action correctly and aim to perform the action for what it is; also that this understanding and purpose not be transient but rather the expression of something stable and well-established in him (1105a31–33).[10]

---

[10] The exact interpretation of these conditions is controversial. I offer here a commonsense interpretation of them, since I take the context in which they are proposed not to be especially technical and simply to be giving a clarification which Aristotle thinks should be obvious by that point.

THE DEFINITION OF VIRTUE OF CHARACTER: ITS GENUS

"After these matters we ought to consider what a virtue is" (1105b19), Aristotle remarks at the opening of 2.5, thereby moving from a discussion of the *acquisition* of character-related virtue to a formulation of a *definition* of it.

In his logical work, the *Topics*, Aristotle holds that in order to formulate a good definition we must, first, give the more general class to which something belongs (its *genus*), and, second, identify its sub-class within that general class (its *species*), by saying what distinguishes that thing from other things within that general class (its distinguishing *property*). He follows exactly that procedure here, arguing first (in 2.5) that a character-related virtue is in general a "state" of the soul, and second (in 2.6) that what distinguishes a character-related virtue from other such "states" is that it is somehow "intermediate." His full definition may be found at 1106b36–1107a2: "The upshot is that virtue is a state involving deliberate purpose, which occupies an intermediate position, as that is determined by reason and as someone with practical wisdom would determine it."

We should keep in mind that this is meant to be a definition of character-related virtue only, not thinking-related virtue. Thus when Aristotle begins his argument by claiming that "There are three things that arise in the soul – emotional responses; capacities; and states" (1105b20), we should presume that he intends to be referring to that part of the soul to which virtue of character pertains, namely that part of the non-rational part which is responsive to reason. Obviously Aristotle holds that one might also find in the soul thoughts, beliefs, and particular rational acts, such as acts of wishing or consenting.

As regards the responsiveness of the part of the soul that does not have reason but listens and responds to it: we are such as potentially to have a response, and that is a "capacity" in the soul; or we are such as actually to have it, and then that is an actual "emotional response"; or we are such as to have it in a certain way, and that is a "state" (*hexis*) and the sort of thing Aristotle thinks a virtue is. His arguments that a virtue is neither a capacity nor an actual response are straightforward and based on ordinary language considerations: we would not justify a claim that someone is a good (or bad) person by pointing to his *having* an emotional response of some kind ("he's a bad man – look, he's angry, isn't he?"), or to his being *able* to have it ("he's a bad man – look, he's capable of becoming angry"). If so, then it follows that a virtue is a "state," – as was effectively shown already by Aristotle's remarks about how we acquire a virtue, when he claimed that acting virtuously involved the *manner* in which one acted.

Aristotle's claim that virtues are "states" raises a question about the relationship between virtues and the emotions. "A state," Aristotle says, "is that by which we are disposed to respond with an emotion well or badly. For instance, as regards becoming angry, if we are disposed to become intensely or weakly angry, then we are badly disposed, but if we are disposed to do so in an intermediate way, then we are well disposed" (1105b25–28). Does this remark imply that (i) Aristotle thinks that all virtues of character have to do with the modulation of emotions, and that (ii) Aristotle holds that virtues are correlated one-to-one with emotions, with each virtue making us such that we have that emotion correctly? Alternative (i) is clearly false: Aristotle says in many places that virtues deal with *actions* as well as emotions (1106b16–17; 1108a30–31, b18–19; 1109a23, b30; 1111a2–3; 1115b20); he introduces the notion of character-related virtue in 2.1, as we saw, precisely by describing virtues as directive of *actions*; and in 2.3 he argues at length that virtues are concerned, also, with likes and dislikes, not insisting in that context that these are always related to emotions. He does not restrict the domain of a virtue to the modulation of emotion, then, as the above remark might be taken to suggest. And (ii) seems false as well, because there are several virtues that Aristotle later mentions and discusses, such as generosity and magnanimity, which do not evidently deal with any particular emotion; and there are some emotions in the list at 1105b21 (such as "yearning," *pothos*) to which no virtue is correlated. (But then why does Aristotle explain a "state" as "that by which we are disposed to respond with an emotion well or badly"? Presumably because he is looking among things "in the soul," and therefore he aims to say what a state is only by reference to things "in the soul.")

What precisely does Aristotle mean by a "state"? The corresponding Greek term, *hexis*, means literally "a having." (That is why, traditionally, it was translated as "habit," from Latin *habere*, "to have," and why in older books the virtues are sometimes explained as being "good habits.") Aristotle in his doctrine of the virtues evidently wishes to rely upon three important connotations of the term *hexis*, which our word "state" largely lacks:

1. "*Hexis*" connotes having a *firm grip* on something, and therefore signifies something that has stability. In other contexts Aristotle uses the term simply to signify an enduring and deeply rooted quality of a thing rather than one that is transient and superficial. For instance, to sculpt a shape out of the block, but not to paint it a color, would be to impose a *hexis* upon the block. So the term connotes stability and permanence.

2. The term also connotes *possession* and in this sense is to be contrasted with *use*. Aristotle relies on this contrast when he makes a distinction between someone's merely having a virtue and his actualizing that virtue through performing an action characteristic of it. When someone with a virtue performs a corresponding virtuous action, he "puts to use" the virtue: a sleeping hero merely possesses courage; that same hero in the heat of battle is additionally using it. Thus, the term *hexis* connotes something potential and hidden, which can make itself manifest but need not do so.

3. The term also connotes having a kind of persistent orientation, whether this orientation is passive or active. A *hexis* can be simply a passive disposition (a "passive power," in the language of the eighteenth century) to respond in certain ways, given certain circumstances or stimuli, such as the readiness of an electric door to open if someone interrupts the photoelectric beam. Or a *hexis* can be active and directive (an "active power"), aiming to realize a certain kind of result regardless of circumstances: a sandpiper combing the beach for mollusks throughout the day shows an active *hexis* of looking for food.[11]

Aristotle takes a virtue of character to be a *hexis* in all three of these senses: it is a stable trait, built up and established, as we have seen,

---

[11] Aristotle looks upon a craft or skill (*technē*) as a *hexis* which is in this way active. In fact, Aristotle tends to speak as if it is the craft or skill, not the craftsman, which is the cause of the order and structure shown in its product: when a skilled sculptor makes a statue, it is that man as having the skill which is properly the cause (cf. *Physics* 2.3). Similarly, when Aristotle speaks of a virtue or vice as a *hexis*, he is regarding it as what is properly denominated the cause of the consequent control of actions and emotions.

through some kind of "training"; it is a condition that need not be actualized; and it is analogous to a skill (such as house building or military strategy) insofar as it works toward a definite goal in a disciplined way.

THE DEFINITION OF VIRTUE OF CHARACTER: ITS SPECIES (THE DOCTRINE OF THE MEAN)

Of course a vice as well as a virtue is a *hexis*; thus, to define a virtue, one needs to add its distinguishing property, which, according to Aristotle, is that it is goal-directed (*stochastikē*, 1106b28) toward a mark that is intermediate between extremes. This is his famous Doctrine of the Mean.

The Doctrine of the Mean seems to have two components: (i) each virtue itself, as a state, is intermediate between two other states, a vice of excess and a vice of deficiency; and (ii) any correctly felt emotion or action correctly carried out falls between those that would go astray because of some sort of excess and those that would go astray because of some sort of deficiency. We may take these two components to correspond to Aristotle's explanation of a virtue in 2.6, where he introduces the Doctrine. "Every virtue, as regards that of which it is a virtue," Aristotle says there, "brings that thing into a good condition and renders its work good" (1106a15–16). We may take (i) as relevant to the clause "brings that thing into a good condition," and (ii) as relevant to the clause "renders its work good." As regards (i), Aristotle apparently thinks of a virtue as akin to physical health: it is a kind of balance and beauty of the soul, involving suitable proportion. A vice, in contrast, involves some kind of distortion or exaggeration (when it involves excess) or stuntedness and deformity (when it involves deficiency). And there is a certain congruity between the actions or emotions to which a state gives rise and that state itself. A disproportion in the soul leads to disproportionate actions and emotion.

It is disputed whether the Doctrine of the Mean is meant to be a practical rule of thumb, or simply a principle of classification, which helps us discover and classify virtues and vices – two vices correlated to each virtue. Aristotle apparently intends it to be both. As we saw, the Doctrine is first introduced in 2.2, precisely after he has announced that his interests are practical; and then it is explained more fully in 2.6, where Aristotle's concern is, rather, to define virtue, with a view to developing a good classification of virtues and vices.

The Doctrine of the Mean, construed as a practical principle, should not be taken as a counsel of moderation: "Always feel moderate amounts of emotions and do moderate actions." Such a principle would be unworkable – what counts as a moderate amount? – and it would frequently give results contrary to what would be characteristic of virtue, because there are many occasions in which it would be correct not to feel anything of an emotion at all (or not to engage in some action at all), and many other occasions in which it would be correct to feel an extreme degree of an emotion (or do something in some extreme way); for instance, it would be right to respond to an egregious injustice with passionate concern and extreme indignation.

One might object that, nonetheless, it is useless to be told that correct actions and emotions fall between extremes. Is this not too vague to give any guidance in practice? But presumably the Doctrine of the Mean is not itself meant to give advice; rather, the Doctrine is a schema which shows the general form that advice involving character-related virtue needs to take. You want advice about how to be courageous? Then avoid reckless boldness on the one hand and cowardice on the other. You want advice about how to use your money? Then avoid extravagant self-indulgence on the one hand and miserliness on the other. And so on.

Of course, one might object that advice like that still looks too vague: what, after all, counts as reckless boldness or cowardice? But Aristotle might insist, in reply, that such advice can always be made more specific, by supplying examples and paradigms relative to some context that one has in mind; yet what the Doctrine of the Mean implies is that, however specific one makes the advice, it still takes the form of pointing the way between two extremes. For instance, suppose someone wants to know, more specifically, what counts as courageous in *this* sort of circumstance in battle? Then he has to be told something like: "Avoid *this* sort of recklessness (the sort that *so-and-so* showed) and *this* sort of cowardice (such as doing *that*)."

Aristotle introduces the Doctrine of the Mean by saying: "In everything that comes in distinguishable increments, continuously ordered [literally, 'in everything that is continuous and divisible'], it is possible to take more, less, or an equal amount, where these are considered either with respect to the thing itself or relative to us" (1106a26–28). Thus, to get a better grasp on the Doctrine we need to consider (i) what for Aristotle are the "distinguishable increments," with which a virtue deals, and (ii) what Aristotle has in mind when he speaks of what is an equal amount "relative to us."

A simple answer to (i) is that the "distinguishable increments" are merely the various degrees of an emotion. For instance, gentleness aims at and achieves a degree of intensity of anger that is intermediate; courage aims at a degree of intensity of fear that is intermediate; and so on. This view is at home with the view, mentioned above, that the virtues modulate emotions and are therefore correlated one-to-one with emotions. We saw above that there were strong reasons for thinking that this view is not Aristotle's. And then there are additional difficulties with this view involving the Doctrine of the Mean in particular; for instance, Aristotle seems to articulate no notion of "degree of intensity" of an emotion, nor is it easy to see what this could be; also, Aristotle later claims that courage deals with *two* emotions, boldness and fear, so that (on this view) there would be two "means" aimed at by courage, and therefore courage would actually consist of two virtues.

A more satisfactory answer is to hold that the "distinguishable increments" to which Aristotle refers are concerned with what might be called the "particulars" of an action or emotional response. We can understand the "particulars" of an action or emotional response in the following way. Any action (or emotional response) is necessarily something complex, and, to be described completely, one needs to use a complex description. One must specify at least the agent, object, instrument (if any), manner, time, place, duration, reason (the special circumstances which trigger or qualify the action), and purpose. Here is an example of such a description. "For over an hour, at Agamemnon's command, Odysseus without hesitation held his ground vigorously using only a sword against ten attacking soldiers, for the sheer glory of it." This description gives duration ("for over an hour"), occasion ("at Agamemnon's command"), agent ("Odysseus"); timeliness ("without hesitation"); object ("held his ground"); manner ("vigorously"); instrument ("only a sword");

indirect object ("ten attacking soldiers"); and purpose ("for the sheer glory of it"). Aristotle apparently thinks that an individual action is not completely described until it is described in all such dimensions.

Call these things, which need to be specified to pick out any individual action, the "particulars" of that action or emotional response. Aristotle gives various lists of such particulars (cf. 1106b21–22; 1109a28; 1111a3–5; 1135a25, b33).[12] Each of these particulars may be regarded as falling within a range of options that constitute "distinguishable increments continuously ordered": it is possible, for instance, that more or fewer persons be the object of one's action (or more or fewer sorts of persons; or sorts which comprehend more or fewer persons); or that the action be initiated sooner or later; or that it last for a shorter or longer time; or that it be done more or less in a certain manner; or that it employ more or fewer instruments (or instruments that are more or less appropriately chosen); or that the circumstances that trigger the action be reckoned by the agent generously or strictly; or that the agent's motive be better or worse (or more or less accompanied by ulterior or less admirable motives). And this would hold true of an emotional response as much as an action.

The Doctrine of the Mean in this more complex version then becomes: (a) people who characteristically go astray as regards particulars of an action (or emotional response) fall into two distinct groups, namely, those that go too far, and those that do not go far enough; moreover, (b) a person tends to go astray in one such direction as regards all of the particulars if he tends to go astray in that direction as regards any one of them. Consider, for instance, becoming angry at a perceived injustice. Some people go astray by characteristically remaining angry longer than is appropriate. The Doctrine of the Mean tells us that: (a) these are a distinct class from those who tend to be angry for a less than appropriate time, and (b) those who tend to remain angry too long also tend to be angry at

---

[12] He seems to regard them as roughly related to his ten categories, mentioned in chapter 2 above. Note, by the way, that it is more natural in the first instance to regard these as pertaining to actions than to emotional responses, as against the notion that virtues modulate emotions only.

more persons than is justified, and on more occasions, and with greater intensity, and so on.[13]

The Doctrine of the Mean so understood requires that there is a fact of the matter as to what counts as too much, as opposed to too little, in some dimension, and that the non-rational but responsive elements in us, relevant to that virtue, are somehow able to recognize this and pursue it across the various particulars of an action or emotional response. There has to be a fact of the matter that, for instance, remaining angry at a certain slight for ten days as opposed to five is to show *more* anger: one's showing that much anger cannot simply be the same as showing *less* of something else (say, irascibility). Also, anger must be the sort of motive that is somehow capable of taking these various real instances of being greater as related to one another, because there is no *reason* why someone who stays angry for *longer periods* of time should also become angry at *more* persons than he should. Irrational generalizations of this sort, then, have to be attributed to the non-rational part of the soul, and, when we do so, we say that someone is acting "out of anger." (One might say: the Doctrine of the Mean so understood is more a theory of *irrationality* than of rationality.)

So far I have discussed what Aristotle means in saying that a virtue is a "state" that is intermediate between extremes. As we saw, he qualifies this by saying that what counts as intermediate depends upon the agent: it is "relative to us." But what does he mean by this? The remark seems intended simply to rule out the absurd thought that the appropriate intermediate is a fixed quantity determined solely by consulting the dimension under consideration. For instance, on this absurd thought, the intermediate number of persons who should be the object of any action of ours would always be *half* the number of human beings who exist – about 3 billion – because half is intermediate between the entire world population and no one. Since Aristotle's remark merely rules out that kind of absurdity, its function, then, would be to allow room for all kinds of reasonable

---

[13] Actually, Aristotle thinks that anger is an exception in important respects to the general rule for virtues and vices (see 4.5.1126a11–12), but insofar as it does conform to that rule, it does so in a clear way.

relativity, as his analogy with physical training should make clear, and we may distinguish various sorts:

1. Relativity as regards the agent's degree of virtue. Aristotle points out that stronger athletes require more food and a more demanding program of exercise; one might suppose, then, that persons with better established virtue would need to meet higher expectations in order to act correctly. There are actions that show more or less daring, generosity, magnanimity, amiability, and so on, and we can imagine our expectations for someone changing, and our willingness to excuse or grant a pass, depending upon the degree of his virtue.

2. Relativity as regards human nature. The most terrifying objects, such as earthquakes, are beyond human capacity to endure, according to Aristotle (3.7.1115b27); "a courageous person is undaunted," he says, "*as far as being human goes*" (1115b10–11). But one might suppose that gods or divinized heroes could stand fast and avoid panic even in the midst of an earthquake. What can be expected of an agent, and what would be blameworthy, is therefore relative to his nature.

3. Relativity as regards age, gender, and capacity for freedom. Aristotle holds in the *Politics* (1.13) that what should be expected of human beings will vary with their gender, immaturity, and whether they are fit to be free (or are "natural slaves," as he thinks some human beings are). He puts forward a similar view in *Ethics* 8.12. He holds, for instance, that what in most cases counts as an extreme display of fear and other emotions in an adult male would fall within acceptable extremes for a female (cf. 9.11.1171b6–12). We might reject these views but accept the analogous view that reasonable expectations for conduct should be relative to a person's connate temperament.

CLASSIFICATION AND OPPOSITES

Once he has articulated his definition of a virtue of character as itself being an intermediate condition, Aristotle is in a position in 2.7 to classify the virtues, by postulating a virtue for important human motives and goods and by identifying two vices corresponding to

Table 3.2

Field	Mean (Virtue)	Excess	Deficiency
Fear	courage	cowardice	\<unnamed\>
Boldness	courage	rashness	cowardice
Felt desire	self-mastery	self-indulgence	insensibility
Wealth as a good	generosity	dissoluteness	stinginess
Wealth as a good – large-scale use	magnificence	pomposity	shabbiness
Honor as a good – large-scale honor	magnanimity	self-inflatedness	small mindedness
Honor as a good	\<unnamed\>	over-ambitiousness	unambitiousness
Anger	mildness	irascibility	spiritlessness
Sociability – truth	"truthfulness"	posturing	self-depreciation
Sociability – humor	wittiness	buffoonery	boorishness
Sociability – enjoyment	"friendliness"	obsequiousness	contentiousness/ morose bearing
Shame	having a sense of shame	nervousness	shamelessness
[feelings of vengeance]	righteous indignation	envy	exulting in wickedness

each, one involving excess and the other deficiency. Table 3.2 expresses his results. (It differs, however, in always giving the name of the character trait, whereas Aristotle sometimes gives instead the name of the person who has the trait; and of course different translations will use different terminology.)

Aristotle clearly intends this list to be exhaustive: see 3.5.1115a5. But then on what principle is it constructed? Presumably he is picking out "domains," and thus virtues, but if we do not know the principle on which he picks them out, we can have no guarantee that the list is exhaustive.

One suggestion is that Aristotle is operating here with a notion of a "basic good," and he thinks each such good defines a domain of a virtue. Thus, one might suppose that there are basic goods that involve mere life, such as security from harm (courage) and bodily sustenance and pleasure (self-mastery). Then there are basic goods that are sought through life in society generally, such as wealth (generosity, magnificence) and honor (magnanimity, measured ambition). Then there are basic goods that are sought among the society of friends in particular, such as a good reputation (sense of shame), good conversation (truthfulness, friendliness, wit), and sympathy (righteous indignation). If we are equipped with natural motives and impulses for seeking these goods, then the character-related virtues would be states by which these motives and impulses are harmonized with reasonable prescriptions for the seeking of these goods in common, in political society.

This seems well and good. And yet Aristotle seems to leave out important virtues. He makes no mention of such traits as loyalty, tactfulness, discretion, optimism, team-spirit, willingness to forgive, quickness at showing mercy, or (as are important particularly for us) tolerance and humility. Moreover, we might wonder whether there are good traits that are "broader" and more pervasive than virtues: call these fundamental moral "attitudes" or "outlooks" rather than virtues, as, for instance, moral seriousness, reverence, a proper regard for the past, gratefulness, love of nature, a sense of wonder, docility, and sensitivity to beauty. These apparently have no place in his scheme.

Aristotle's table of virtues and vices is innovative, compared to the philosophical tradition before him, insofar as it postulates *two* opposing conditions for each virtue. Thus after giving the table, Aristotle (in 2.8) aims to account for the common view that each virtue has just one opposite. He says that in those cases in which it looks as though there is only one vice, we simply do not notice easily the other vice, for one of two reasons: either (i) the manifestations of the one vice are so similar to the virtue that we do not count it as a vice (rashness, for instance, is very much like courage, because it leads the person who has it to confront the enemy rather than run away); or (ii) we are so much more inclined naturally to the one vice rather than the other, that we hardly count the other vice as a real possibility (it is so unlikely that we would end up insensible as regards pleasures of food, drink, and sex, that we do not even think of that condition as being opposed to self-mastery, as it in fact is).

An astute observation is Aristotle's claim that a person at any extreme tends to think of himself as occupying the intermediate position, and therefore he assimilates the true intermediate to the opposite extreme. (This would be another way in which we might reduce the three possible conditions to only two.) Thus, for instance, a timid person regards the actions and decisions of a truly courageous person as rash; a rash person looks upon a courageous person as excessively timid and cowardly.

Aristotle returns to practical considerations in the final chapter of book 2 and gives three bits of shrewd practical advice: (i) We should aim to hit the intermediate mark, not by going directly for it, but by trying to avoid the extreme to which we are most inclined. (ii) In matters in which we have tended to go astray and therefore are already on the path to developing one of the extreme conditions, we should try to perform actions that depart from the intermediate in the other direction. Aristotle likens this to how we straighten out a bent stick by bending it back in the opposite direction. (But then is Aristotle saying that we should do wrong in order to make ourselves right? How could these corrective actions not be wrong, if they depart from the intermediate mark, just as much as do the wrong actions which we have already committed?) (iii) We can get a good sense of the extreme to which we are most inclined by attending to what pleases and displeases us: "In all matters the greatest diligence has to be exercised in relation to what is pleasant for us and the pleasure we feel" (1109b7–8). And since we are not "impartial judges" when our own pleasure is involved, we should try to make ourselves impartial, by thinking about what is fitting and required in the circumstances, as if no pleasure came from our action or emotion at all: "By simply dismissing the pleasure we'll be less likely to go wrong" (b11–12).

Given the essentially practical nature of ethical inquiry, Aristotle surely regarded these applications of his definition of virtue as important confirmations of its correctness.

FURTHER READING

Price (1995) has a good discussion of divisions of the soul in Aristotle and in other ancient writers. As regards the acquisition of character virtue, Burnyeat's (1980) influential discussion of character education, very different from what is offered here, has already been mentioned. Kosman (1980) is also relevant and illuminating.

Aristotle's definition of virtue and particularly the Doctrine of the Mean may be well studied by looking first at Hursthouse's critique

(1980–1) and then the worthy defense of Curzer (1996). Urmson (1973) is important as influencing later discussions.

For consideration of the philosophical viability of the notion of virtue, MacIntyre (1994) is something of a modern classic; Foot (1978) is centrally important; and Geach (1977) gives an accessible overview.

CHAPTER 4

Actions as signs of character
(Nicomachean Ethics *3.1–5*)

Let us review the argument to this point. In book 1 Aristotle argues
that the ultimate goal of human life is some "activity in accordance
with virtue," and he sets down criteria that he thinks the ultimate goal
must satisfy. In 1.13 and 2.1 he analyzes human virtue into thinking-
related and character-related virtue, and in the remainder of book 2
he constructs a list, which he regards as exhaustive, of particular
character-related virtues. One would think that his next step would
be to examine these virtues individually. In fact he puts this off until
3.6. Instead, in 3.1–5 he undertakes a discussion of human action and
the psychology underlying human action.

This is not a digression, as it might seem, because Aristotle's
discussion of human action follows naturally from, and is even
required by, various claims that he had put forward in book 2.
Recall that, as Aristotle sees it, the discipline of ethics is practical:
its aim is that we become good and live well. But, as he has just argued
in book 2, we cannot become good unless we acquire the virtues of
character. As we saw, Aristotle thinks that we generally acquire the
virtues through being directed, by those in authority over us (by our
parents when we are immature, and by legislators, even when we are
mature citizens), to do actions characteristic of those virtues and to
refrain from actions characteristic of the contrary vices.

But now consider this task from the point of view of those in
authority. They direct the actions of those under their care, Aristotle
had said, by attaching rewards and punishments to actions.
Presumably these rewards and punishments should be assigned
appropriately, given the goal which is aimed at. Then presumably
the reward should be greater, the more someone's action evinces
good character, and the punishment should be greater, the more

someone's action evinces bad character. That is, reward and punishment of action should be sensitive to the character of the person who did the action. Thus it is of great importance that those in authority judge appropriately when, and to what extent, actions are signs of underlying character. Aristotle's discussion of human action in 3.1–5 seems intended precisely to assist us in making judgments of that sort.

Again, Aristotle had pointed out in 2.4 that there is a gap between performing actions that are characteristic of virtue, and actually acting virtuously. For someone to act virtuously, Aristotle had said, a person furthermore needs to perform such an action (i) with understanding, (ii) aiming to do it for just the sort of action that it is, and (iii) as something characteristic of him. But how can we be assured that these further conditions obtain? When should a virtuous-looking action be counted as a virtuous action? Aristotle's discussion of human action is meant to provide guidance here.

Again, Aristotle had defined a character-related virtue as "a state involving deliberate purpose, which occupies an intermediate position, as that is determined by reason and as someone with practical wisdom [a *phronimos*] would determine it" (2.6.1106b36–1107a2). The definition mentions "deliberate purpose" (*prohairesis*, or "choice," as it is commonly rendered), presumably because a virtue is some stable condition of purposive action. But then what is "deliberate purposiveness"? More generally, how precisely does some non-rational element of the soul become persistently persuadable by, and docile to, rational indications? How are rationality and non-rationality harmonized, in a human being, through character-related virtue? Aristotle's account of human action, and of the role of *prohairesis* or "choice" in human action, is meant to provide some insight into this.

Thus, far from being a digression, Aristotle's account of human action is a necessary follow-up to his definition of virtue and a preliminary to his discussion of particular virtues.

OVERVIEW OF 3.1–5

Aristotle's first step (in 3.1) is to identify those conditions in which an action is not a sign of a good character, or a sign of a bad character, because it is not a sign of the agent's character at all – because the action, in an important sense, is not even his action. It is something that he *happened to do*, but it is not his *action*.

He supposes that there will be two such conditions: when someone is forced to act as he does, and when he does not know what he is doing. Why just these two conditions? Aristotle's underlying idea is that an action involves (i) our introducing changes in the world (ii) in order to achieve some goal. (See his remarks at 1110a12–18; 1111a22–24; 1112a31–33, b31–32; and 1113b18–19.) If we are forced to do something, then we ourselves do not introduce the changes, and condition (i) fails. And if we are ignorant, then what we take to be achieving through an action is not in fact what we succeed in achieving, and condition (ii) fails. We might say: force misdirects the initiation of change; ignorance misdirects its aim. Compare: that an archer's arrow misses the target is not something ascribable to the archer if either (i) someone had moved his arm at the last moment or (ii) someone had shifted the target when he was not looking.

Yet there are spurious cases of force and spurious cases of ignorance. Distinguishing the spurious from the genuine is important, because the spurious cases are often brought forward in attempts to excuse bad action. The claim that "I didn't know what I was doing" in some cases should excuse and in others should not; likewise "I had to do it" or "I had no choice." Thus Aristotle takes pains to become clear about precisely what kind of force and what kind of ignorance severs the relationship between action and character.

If an action, then, is neither genuinely forced, nor genuinely performed because of ignorance, it is the agent's action indeed. Aristotle's term for the class of things done in that way is *hekousion*, and he calls an agent as acting in that way *hekōn*. He uses these terms very broadly, to apply to any sort of living agent whatsoever: children and animals, as well as adult human beings, may move in a way that is *hekōn* and do what is *hekousion*. Basically, for a living thing to do something in this way is for it to do it "of its own accord." It is to that extent a "self-mover," as Aristotle refers to this elsewhere.[1]

What it is for a living thing to do something "of its own accord" will vary, of course, depending upon what is so acting. What it is for a snail to do something "of its own accord" will naturally be

---

[1] See Furley (1980) for a full discussion.

different from a horse's doing something in that way, which will be different from a human child, who will act "of his own accord," once more, differently from an adult. Since to act "of one's own accord" is, as I have said, to have an aim and then to initiate action with a view to achieving this aim, then living things will in different ways act "of their own accord" insofar as they differ in these respects. A non-rational animal will grasp the end of its action only through perception and imagination, but a rational animal will do so through reason as well; a non-rational animal will take steps to achieve that end instinctively and automatically, but a rational animal will do so additionally through deliberation and seeking counsel.

This is Aristotle's notion. For lack of a good, one-word English equivalent, translations will typically have it that an action in that class is "voluntary" or "willingly" performed. These terms are the best available, and yet they are not quite suitable, since we would not say that a dog when it fetches a ball, or a snail as it slides across the ground, is acting "voluntarily" or "willingly." These terms bring in the notions of purpose and will, and we apply them generally on analogy with human action, which typically is *hekousion* through being purposeful and willed.

As was said, in marking out this very broad class of actions performed when an agent is acting "of its own accord," Aristotle has so far identified only a necessary condition for making an inference from action to character: an action cannot be a sign of someone's character at all, unless it was something that the agent did when he was acting of his own accord. Yet this gives no help in discerning whether an action is a sign of good character or bad. To see this, consider an example which Aristotle gives in his discussion of courage (in 3.6–9). There Aristotle distinguishes true courage, where someone remains at his post in battle simply because to do so is good and admirable, from various false forms of courage, including "civic courage," where someone remains at his post because he does not want to be ridiculed later for being a coward. Someone who kept to his post out of this false form of courage would be acting "of his own accord" just as much as a truly courageous person. But it would be misguided for a legislator or general to reward both of them equally.

So, then, how exactly can we discern whether an action that looks to be courageous is a sign of genuine courage, or rather is indicative of a false form of courage? To do so, one needs an account of distinctively human action, which Aristotle provides in 3.2–4. His view, roughly, is that a distinctively human action is one in which (a) the agent begins with a conception of some good to be sought as a goal; then (b) working back from there in thought, through a process of deliberation, he arrives at a conclusion about a particular action that he can do to advance that goal; after which (c) he then chooses that action precisely with a view to advancing the end in that way. We might say, in very rough outline, that a distinctively human action will display a certain *sensitivity to goods,* and a *preference* or ranking of some sorts of goods over others. An action indicates good or bad character, or a tendency to develop one of these, depending upon what sort of sensitivity and preference it displays. For instance, the soldier who remains at his post out of merely civic courage is either insensitive to the goodness of remaining at one's post simply because it is admirable to do so, or he is sensitive to this but gives a higher ranking to avoiding the bad opinion of his peers. Either of these conditions would suggest that his action was not a result of the virtue of courage.

In 3.5, the final chapter of the passage we are considering, Aristotle takes up the question of whether we can also be said not simply to perform particular actions, but also to acquire the character that we have "of our own accord." Grant that a coward whenever he acts in a cowardly way does so of his own accord: one might still wonder whether he has acquired his *cowardice* of his own accord. If not, then it might seem that he cannot, after all, be held responsible for his cowardly action. The problem becomes pressing because Aristotle has admitted that something more is required, for an action to be distinctively human, than that someone perform it "of his own accord." If this "something more" is not after all something that we have or acquire of our own accord, then it may look as though we cannot hold a coward responsible for his cowardly action, and the entire arrangement by which persons in authority reward and punish those under them will look pointless. This is why Aristotle concludes his discussion of action by arguing that we are indeed responsible for our character, bad character as well as good.

FORCED ACTIONS

Sometimes it is easier to arrive at a difficult notion by first marking outer boundaries and saying what definitely does *not* count as the thing we mean. What is meant is then indicated by contrast. This is Aristotle's general procedure in 3.1: he gets at the difficult notion of acting "of one's own accord" by looking at what is commonly thought to make an action *not* of one's own accord: force and ignorance. Let us look first at force.

Force seems straightforward: A's action is forced if some power or agency outside A initiates the action, rather than A himself: for example, someone else takes his hand and makes it press a button, or a puff of wind pushes him aside. Such an action, Aristotle says, is one in which "the person who does something, or has something done to him, contributes nothing" (3.1.1110a1–3).[2]

One might wonder whether we need a second category of forced actions, overlooked by Aristotle, for things that we are compelled to do, but would not mind doing. To see why, we need to jump ahead slightly in Aristotle's exposition. When Aristotle later discusses actions performed through ignorance, he distinguishes two sorts of such action: those that we perform *unwillingly*, and those that we perform only *non-willingly*. An action *unwillingly* performed out of ignorance, he says, is one which I am later distressed by, when I find out the truth about what I did (e.g. I am aghast at having inadvertently injured my best friend); an action only *non-willingly* performed out of ignorance, is one that I do not later find distressing (e.g. I do not mind so much that I inadvertently harmed an enemy). Should we make, then, a similar distinction as regards force and say that a forced action is "unwilling" if contrary to what the agent wants,

---

[2] The text admits of being understood as: "the person who does something, or feels something, contributes nothing," thus allowing that emotions as well as actions can be forced. But this translation is probably to be rejected: (i) Aristotle's examples concern only actions; (ii) he firmly puts aside suggestions that internal motives can be forced (1110b9, 1111a25); (iii) in any case, it seems difficult to see how we could make no contribution at all to an emotion. Someone might say that the pain someone feels when injured, or fear evoked by a sudden fright, are "beyond his control"; but Aristotle would count them as nonetheless experienced "of our own accord," because that is how our animal nature is supposed to act in such circumstances. We are animals, in part, and so feeling pain or fear would be something that *we* are doing.

and only "non-willing" if the agent wants to do what he is forced to do? Imagine, for instance, a survivor of a boat wreck, drifting about at sea on a raft with a makeshift sail. He has no control over where the wind takes him; therefore, in whichever direction he goes, he is "forced." But should we say that when it blows him away from land, where he wants to go, he does it "unwillingly," but when it blows him toward land, where he would not mind going, the action is still forced but something he does "non-willingly"?

Here the distinction seems pointless, and Aristotle was apparently right to have omitted it, because in practice it would be irrelevant: anyone being forced to do what he wanted would typically contribute something, in which case it would not be forced, by Aristotle's definition. A manhandled fellow who was being dragged where he wanted to go anyway would surely stop struggling and walk there himself. Similarly, the man in the boat would take action to catch the wind and steer the boat in the right direction, when the wind was blowing him toward land.[3]

After considering genuine cases of force, where something from the outside makes someone do something, Aristotle looks at a spurious case. These are actions where we are faced with a "choice between two evils" and therefore have to do something we would otherwise not have wanted to do. Aristotle gives the example of a captain of a trading ship who, in the midst of a storm, orders that the cargo be thrown overboard in order to save the ship and its crew. In no way would a captain lightly jettison the ship's cargo: chances are that the ship had been at sea for several months, and the crew had endured all kinds of dangers, precisely in order to bring that cargo back safely; in throwing the cargo overboard, then, they render that effort senseless. Given this context, the captain would justify his action by saying such things as, "I had no choice," or "The storm forced me to do it," or "That's the last thing I wanted to do. I resisted doing it at every point, and did so only when I was compelled." Moreover, looking on, someone might excuse the captain and say something like, "To the extent that it was up to him at all, he wouldn't have thrown the cargo

---

[3] And then, curiously, we redescribe what exactly counts as the agent's action. When the wind pushes the boat in a favorable direction, and the man in the boat merely steers it, we count the entire motion of the boat as his action. Indeed, most sailing is like that.

overboard." Thus it might look as though something outside him, the storm, were responsible for the action. The captain contributes nothing but rather is, as we say, a "victim of circumstances."[4]

But Aristotle insists that actions like that are performed of the agent's own accord and not forced. He does so by appealing to his positive conception of action "of one's own accord." Recall that someone acts "of his own accord" if he (i) introduces changes in the world (ii) in order to achieve some end. But both of these conditions hold in the case of the jettisoned cargo. Condition (i) holds because the captain "initiates the movements of parts of his body" (1110a16) which cause the cargo to be thrown overboard: he speaks words and gives the command, which initiate that action. Condition (ii) holds as well because, Aristotle says, the agent's goal in performing an action is to be determined "with respect to the moment it is done" (a13–14). Although at any point previously in the voyage the captain would not have wished to toss the cargo overboard, nonetheless, when the storm arises, because jettisoning the cargo is the only way to save the ship and its crew, that *does* become what he wants to do. Aristotle points out that it is precisely because such actions are of the agent's own accord that we can evaluate them – praising the captain for coolly making a difficult decision in unusual circumstances; or blaming him for valuing his cargo so highly that he waited too long to jettison it, jeopardizing the passengers; and so on.

Aristotle does, however, concede that there is an important respect in which the agent does not perform such actions of his own accord, so that they may be regarded as "mixed." That Aristotle picks out such actions and gives them this special label might seem unmotivated or arbitrary: are not mixed actions simply ordinary cases of acting out of mixed motives? The captain desires the safety of both the cargo and the ship, but he cannot have both – nothing strange about that. But Aristotle's emphasis on this class of actions makes sense when placed in the correct context. Recall that Aristotle

---

[4] The other example Aristotle gives of a forced action is of a tyrant who has your family in his power and will treat them well only if you do some shameful action that he orders you to do. Aristotle merely poses the case and does not say what the correct thing to do would be in such circumstances. It is sufficient for his purposes that this is a case in which whatever course of action you take would be one that you would justify by saying, "I had no choice."

conceives of character as an active disposition to perform, or to refrain from, acts of various sorts, in various domains. These dispositions will typically involve the pursuit of multiple goods, but with an implicit ordering. An action which involves a "choice of two evils" forces the agent's ranking to become explicit, requiring that he act uncharacteristically against a lower ranked good. It is this latter characteristic which makes such actions in an important respect not performed of the agent's own accord. That is to say, a mixed action is one that, if taken in isolation, would be "out of character." For instance, a peaceable man kills in self-defense. That he would kill anyone is entirely out of character for him: typically, he is kindly and friendly toward others, simultaneously promoting the good of others and his own good. But these goods have an implicit ordering, and, when he is attacked and faced with a choice between his own life and that of his attacker, that ordering becomes explicit. Circumstances require him to act against a good that he otherwise promotes. But he regrets having to do so – it is not at all what he "wants" – and perhaps he even weeps over it after the fact.

Thus a mixed action is not something like: in the abstract you would like steak for dinner but, given your health, you will take chicken. Properly speaking, it is an action in which someone does something which, in usual circumstances, would be characteristic of vice: killing someone; destroying valuable goods; and so on. And Aristotle's view is that whether or not an action of that sort in fact indicates bad character depends upon the ranking that is revealed. To jettison goods in order to save persons is a ranking of the sort which is implicit in many virtues. But a ruthless pirate captain might instead have thrown some prisoners overboard to save his precious cargo, showing a reverse ranking. That *both* captains might explain, "I had no choice", for these opposite courses of action, confirms that what is operative here is something different from force in the strict sense.

ACTIONS RESULTING FROM IGNORANCE

Aristotle thinks that ignorance as well as force can render an action not done of one's own accord – but only ignorance of a certain sort, and not ignorance for which we are responsible.

His view may be well illustrated by a simplified example. You are selling your old car to someone for $2000 cash, which the buyer gives you in hundred-dollar bills. You take this to be a fair price, and it is fairly agreed upon. When you arrive home, however, and count the money again, you see that some bills had stuck together and in fact you had mistakenly been given $2200. We can imagine two reactions: you are upset that you were overpaid and effectively got something for nothing; or you are pleasantly surprised to find that you have a couple of hundred extra dollars that you had not counted on (it is "found money"). If you react in the first way, then you are not the sort of person who would deliberately try to get something for nothing; in fact, you will probably take steps to return the extra money. If you react in the second way, an onlooker might judge that you are indeed the sort of person who might very well in other circumstances, aim to do something dishonest.[5] As it is, you would hesitate to return the money, and perhaps you plan to return it only if the buyer realizes his mistake and asks you about it.

Aristotle distinguishes, as I have said, between actions resulting from ignorance which are *unwillingly* effected from those that are *non-willingly* effected, because his concern is with drawing inferences about character from someone's actions. If because of ignorance an agent does the sort of thing that a person with bad character would do, but when he learns the truth he shows distress, then we may judge that the action was out of character for him. If he later shows no regret, then, even if we cannot say he *would* have performed that action in those circumstances had he known the truth, we can nonetheless infer that it is the sort of action that he *would* perform.

There are spurious as well as genuine cases of acting because of ignorance. Spurious cases are where the ignorance is "culpable": the agent himself, if he had acted as a person with good character would, or if he were taking care to act virtuously, would not have ended up ignorant. We may be ignorant of (i)particulars or (ii)moral generalities. Aristotle holds that ignorance of particulars is sometimes not culpable, but ignorance of moral generalities is always culpable.[6]

---

[5] An onlooker might judge this even if it is true that if you had found out the mistake when the buyer was still around, you would have returned the extra $200 without hesitation.

[6] Aristotle first introduces the distinction between culpable and non-culpable ignorance as that between acting "because of ignorance" and acting "in ignorance" or "while ignorant" (1110b24–25).

As regards (i): consider the following somewhat fanciful but illus-trative scenario. Suppose it is well known that recently issued hundred-dollar bills have a tendency to stick together; and you sell your car on a humid summer evening, when it is clear from other purchases made that such bills are tending to stick together. Someone who was intent on being fair, and who definitely did not want to receive more money in a large transaction than was agreed upon, would take care to count the bills repeatedly and carefully. If you did not take these steps, then your ignorance later on (of the extra money that you were in fact paid), rather than blocking an inference from your action to your character, might actually allow such an inference to be drawn: your ending up with more money in your pocket than you thought might suggest that you lacked the relevant virtue of fairness (or "justice"), since that trait would have led you to take sufficient care not to be overpaid.[7]

Your not knowing that you were paid $2200 is ignorance of particulars. But someone might plead ignorance of some relevant moral generality. Suppose someone finds that he was overpaid by $200 and, when challenged about not returning the extra sum, he responds, "Why did I keep that extra money? Because I simply was not aware that a seller should receive only the amount fairly agreed upon." Or suppose someone pleaded ignorance of the relevant prin-ciple of comparative worth, "I didn't realize that, in a business deal, one should prefer fairness to monetary gain." Would ignorance like that always be culpable?

Aristotle apparently thinks so. In an obscure passage, he seems to distinguish two types of ignorance of generalities: (i) ignorance of the relevant "universal," and (ii) ignorance of what is "advantageous" (as he calls it), as this is revealed in a person's choice (1110b30–33). It is not clear exactly what Aristotle has in mind in this passage, or whether the passage expresses some definite distinction. But it seems plausible to understand these two types of ignorance in con-nection with what Aristotle has already said about judgments that concern character. As mentioned earlier, Aristotle thinks that any virtue involves both a sensitivity as regards what things are properly

---

[7] The example here is admittedly fanciful, but the phenomenon is common. This disposition to seek out information reasonably taken to be relevant to a relatively serious action is what is commonly known as "due diligence."

good in a domain, and a disposition to rank goods in a certain way (that is, a settled purpose of seeking some goods with a view toward other goods). Take "ignorance of the universal," then, to be someone's lacking the appropriate sensitivity: for instance, a merchant who simply fails to "see" or "acknowledge" that fairness in an exchange has any worth at all. Take "ignorance of what is advantageous" to be someone's failing to rank goods correctly, regardless of whether he has the relevant sensitivity: for instance, a merchant who indeed recognizes that fairness has value, but who nonetheless regards making money as preferable to fairness. Clearly, neither of these types of ignorance would render an action something that is not performed of an agent's own accord. When an action is not of the agent's own accord, as we have seen, the inference from action to character is blocked. But we can indeed draw conclusions about someone's character if he acts out of these sorts of ignorance, because, as Aristotle points out, such ignorance is itself constitutive of bad character (1110b32).

Aristotle goes into some detail about the sorts of non-culpable ignorance of particulars that would block the inference from action to character. Naturally enough, he appeals to the same list of "particulars" of an action (or an emotional response) that he had developed in stating the Doctrine of the Mean. If virtuous behavior requires that we avoid extremes in each of these respects, then we are capable of acting non-virtuously in any of these respects, and, therefore, also capable of being excused, on account of ignorance, for going astray in any of these respects. To take just one example: to act justly, we have to pay our bills on time, but we can be non-culpably ignorant of the payment date for a bill – say, there is a printing error on the statement, giving the wrong day of the month – and it is not the case that a virtuous person could reasonably have been expected to act in such a way as to discover the error. It is easy to imagine corresponding cases as regards the other dimensions of an act, and Aristotle supplies his own examples.

DELIBERATE PURPOSE OR "CHOICE" (*PROHAIRESIS*)

As was said, Aristotle wants to examine when and how we can draw inferences from a person's action to his character. That the action is performed of the agent's own accord is a necessary condition of our drawing such an inference. But so far this is only a negative result. We

want to know more than this; we want to know what we should be
attending to, when we attempt to draw a conclusion about character
based on actions. What gives us the most *information* about the
agent's character? Aristotle tells us to look at the *prohairesis* of the
agent. Actions performed with *prohairesis* are a subset of those actions
that are performed of an agent's own accord: children, animals, and
adults in reflex responses move of their own accord but do not act
from *prohairesis*. According to Aristotle, *prohairesis* seems to be "the
most distinctive mark of virtue, and better than actions for discerning
character" (1111b5–6).

The term *prohairesis*, as I said, is often translated "choice," sometimes "decision," "intention," or even "deliberate purpose." But the
meaning of a word is given by its use. As much as possible, I shall keep
the word untranslated at the start, to see how Aristotle uses it, and
then from this we may find English equivalents as appropriate.

Aristotle explains what *prohairesis* is by distinguishing it from: (a)
felt desire (or "appetite," *epithumia*); (b) vigor (or "lively spirit,"
thumos); (c) wish (*boulēsis*); and (d) opinion (*doxa*). This list comes
from Plato; thus, in arguing that there is some additional and distinct
thing, *prohairesis*, which is important in moral action and evaluation,
Aristotle is self-consciously arguing for a significant change in the
Platonic account of the soul. For Plato each of these items can
indicate either a particular *event* or a *power* in the soul: *thumos*, for
instance, can mean either some particular person's spiritedness on a
definite occasion, or the general capacity of showing spiritedness,
which is part of human nature. Aristotle similarly seems to use the
term "*prohairesis*" in both ways, to mean either a particular exercise of
prohairesis, or a general power or faculty of exercising *prohairesis*, with
the context indicating which of these is meant.

Aristotle's procedure is to establish that *prohairesis* is something
distinct from each of the other four by finding, in each case, assertions of the form: "*prohairesis* is F but ___ is not F," or "*prohairesis* is
not F but ___ is F" (where "F" stands for some attribute). That is, he
is presuming that if two things are the same, they will have the same
attributes; hence, if an attribute applies to one but not the other, then
they are distinct.[8] What is most important for present purposes is

---

[8] This is the principle known as "Indiscernibility of Identicals."

that, from each statement of the above form, we learn something about what Aristotle takes *prohairesis* to be, and this then allows us to piece together Aristotle's doctrine of *prohairesis*.

For instance, Aristotle begins by comparing *prohairesis* to felt desire (or "appetite"). He makes five claims (1111b12–18):

1. *prohairesis* is not found in non-rational animals, but felt desire (appetite) is.
2. *prohairesis* does not govern the action of someone who shows weakness of will, but felt desire (appetite) does govern such action.
3. *prohairesis* governs the action of someone who shows willpower, but felt desire (appetite) does not govern it.
4. *prohairesis* is found in opposition to felt desire, but felt desire (appetite) is not found in opposition to felt desire.
5. *prohairesis* is properly for things not insofar as they are either pleasant or painful, but felt desire (appetite) is properly for things only insofar as they are pleasant or painful.

A word about Aristotle's method is helpful here. Frequently when Aristotle makes an observation about something that is not itself directly observable, what he has in mind, as supporting that claim, are the sorts of things we are disposed to say, and the sorts of things that it would be ridiculous for us to say, about that thing.[9] Aristotle's presupposition is that, by paying attention to our habits of speaking, we may be led to appreciate simple and obvious truths (but not easy for all that) which are embodied in our ordinary ways of speaking and are therefore already implicitly accepted by us. Thus it is frequently a useful exercise for a reader of Aristotle, in order to get a better grasp of what Aristotle is saying, to try to think of observations about our own habits of speech that would underwrite his assertions.

So, for instance, consider claim 1, that animals besides human beings have felt desire (or appetite) but lack *prohairesis*. Neither felt appetite nor *prohairesis* is perceived; and animals are incapable of introspection or reporting on the results of their introspection. So on what grounds can we claim such a thing? We can understand the claim as underwritten by

---

[9] In this regard, there are great affinities between Aristotle's approach to philosophy and the approach of what is called "ordinary language philosophy," especially the work of J. L. Austin, who indeed modeled himself on Aristotle.

the naturalness of our saying such things as, "The dog had a strong desire to eat from that bowl of dog food," but the oddness of saying, "The dog *chose* to eat from that bowl of dog food." Again, it makes sense to say, "Anticipating the pleasure of it, he yearned for just a taste of that ice cream," but it makes little sense to say "Anticipating the pleasure of it, he *chose* just a taste of that ice cream" – which tends to support claim 5. Likewise it makes sense to say, "In the end, he *chose* something other than what he wanted," but it would be odd to say, "In the end, he *wanted* something other than what he wanted" – which tends to support claim 4.

Note that, if we so wished, from claims 1–5 we might begin to generate something like a positive account of *prohairesis*: (1) it essentially involves reason; (2) it is a kind of power; (3) it is a kind of power which can vary in effectiveness; (4) it involves acting with a view to "all things considered"; and (5) it takes as its object something which is viewed as good on reasoned grounds.

Aristotle only very briefly argues that *prohairesis* is distinct from spiritedness: "Much less is it spiritedness, since those actions that we perform on account of spiritedness seem least of all to be ones that are under the control of *prohairesis*" (1111b18–19). His point seems to be that, to the extent that we attribute an action to spiritedness, to that extent we do not attribute it to *prohairesis*. If, for instance, we were to remark about someone's action, "His quick temper got the best of him when he punched the wall," we would to that extent not be disposed to say, "Punching that wall is something he chose to do." Yet if choice and spiritedness were the same, then we would be just as disposed to attribute the one as the other.

Aristotle gives four arguments that *prohairesis* is not the same as a wish for something (1111b19–30):

1'. *prohairesis* does not aim at impossible things, but wish does;
2'. *prohairesis* does not aim at something the agent himself cannot bring about, but wish does;
3'. *prohairesis* aims at things contributing to an end, but wish does not (except by aiming at the end), whereas
4'. *prohairesis* does not aim at the end (except by aiming at things contributing to an end), but wish does.

Again, we should interpret Aristotle's view by finding habits of speech that tend to underwrite these claims. For instance, as regards 1': it would make sense for someone looking out at the beauty of the Grand Canyon, and reflecting on the sheer goodness of being alive, to say something like, "I'm wishing right now I could gaze on this forever." But if someone were to say, rather, "I'm choosing now to gaze on this forever," we would take him to have an insane view of his own capacities. In support of 2′, consider that "I'm hoping that the Red Sox win this game," (said by a fan watching the game) would make sense, but if someone were to say "I'm *choosing* that the Red Sox win this game," we would have to take this to mean something other than it seems to say – for instance, "I'm placing a bet on the Red Sox."

Aristotle supplies his own examples relevant to 3′: "I wish to become healthy" is appropriate but "I wish to take the medicine" is not, in the same sense. (We would have to interpret the latter assertion in the sense, "I'd like to be able to take the medicine.") Similarly, "I am wishing to be happy" makes sense, but "I am *choosing* to be happy" makes little sense. (We would have to take the latter to mean: "I am adopting some specific means which I take to produce happiness.") Generally a claim about wishing, which superficially has the same form as some intelligible claim about choosing, would have to be given an entirely different meaning, for it to make sense as well.

Note that from observations 1′–4′ we can conclude that *prohairesis* is a power or faculty that has within its scope only things which I regard as capable of being brought about through my actions, with a view to achieving some good. As regards this last point: I could not say that I was displaying *prohairesis* (say) in lifting my hand, unless there were something that I aimed to achieve by doing so, even if my aim were merely the trivial one of showing that I might lift my hand for no other aim than that.

Aristotle reserves his largest battery of arguments for distinguishing *prohairesis* from opinion (*doxa*): to display *prohairesis*, he insists, is not to think or to believe that something is the case (1111b30–1112a13). He has some fairly decisive arguments that *prohairesis* is not the same as opinion in general: we can have an opinion about anything whatsoever, including things that cannot be altered by human action, and certainly about things that cannot be altered by one's own action (e.g. necessities in nature), and even about things we ourselves take to be impossible (you can *believe* such things as

"A round square is a square"). But it would obviously make no sense to say that I *choose* anything like that.

In response to these objections, someone might urge that *prohairesis* should be identified, not with belief in general, but with beliefs about a certain class of things. Suppose, for instance, that we took it to be correct belief about the goodness or badness of actions that are within our power. What could be said against this? Aristotle once more gives five arguments:

1''. By exercising *prohairesis* as regards a good or bad action available to us, we become either good or bad; but by our merely thinking that a good or bad action available to us is good or bad, we do not ourselves become good or bad.

2''. The content of *prohairesis* is limited to "X is to be sought" or "X is to be pursued," but the content of our opinions as regards the goodness or badness of actions available to us takes a variety of other forms, such as "X is good," or "X is expedient for Y," or "X is good if done in the manner Y."

3''. We evaluate a *prohairesis* by judging whether it is *proper* or *correct*; but we evaluate a belief, even one concerning the goodness or badness of an action available to the agent, by judging whether it is *true.*

4''. People are most properly said to display *prohairesis* for what they *know* to be good, but we are not said most properly to *believe* that which we *know* to be the case (in fact, once we can be said to know something, it is typically inappropriate to say that we believe it).

5''. Some people with bad character nonetheless still recognize what they ought to do: what through their *prohairesis* they acknowledge as the best thing for them to do is not the same as what they *think* best for them to do.[10]

From these observations we can continue to build up our positive theory: *prohairesis* initiates an action, making the person who has it responsible for the action (from 1''); the content of *prohairesis*

---

[10] Aristotle's official doctrine seems to be that, to the extent that someone has a vice, to that extent he loses his grasp on what he ought in fact to do (see chapter 8 below). But often Aristotle speaks, in an informal way, as he does here, as if even bad persons still in some way recognize the correct principle governing their actions.

involves this initiation of action, and its content is somehow implicit in this initiation (from 2″); thus it is essential to *prohairesis* that it be practical, that it aim to effect a change in the world (from 3″); it resembles a resolution or a judgment, or, at least, it is at odds with the suspension of judgment and assent that can accompany belief (from 4″); and *prohairesis* is something that can be more or less *settled*, and thus it need not be dislodged even by the recognition that it is misguided (from 5″).

Now putting together all of the positive theory so far gleaned about *prohairesis*, we arrive at something like the following characterization: *prohairesis* is a rational ability; it operates from an "all things considered" perspective; it varies in effectiveness (resolve, strength); and it is essentially practical, in that it is directed at actions immediately within my power. It expresses a kind of practical judgment as regards the goodness or badness of things, in the very seeking of them. Particular acts of *prohairesis* will be particular acts of this sort. (It is evident, then, that various English equivalents will be suitable in different contexts. For instance, the power or faculty of *prohairesis* may sometimes be best rendered as "will"; a particular act might be rendered as " act of will," "choice," "decision," "purpose," or even "intention".[11])

Aristotle appears to hold that everything distinctive about *prohairesis* is captured by pointing out its relationship to deliberation, since he concludes 3.2 as though offering a summary: "Is the upshot of all this, at very least, that an action performed with *prohairesis* is one that is previously deliberated about? The reason: *prohairesis* implies both our being able to give an account and our thinking things through. Even the name looks like it signifies this – as suggesting that *this* is *worth choosing prior to those other things*" (1112a15–18). The sense of this remark seems to be that it is precisely through our deliberating in

---

[11] Many scholars avoid using the term "will" in describing or rendering Aristotle's theory of *prohairesis*, on the grounds that the notion of a distinct faculty of the "will" is an innovation in Western thought that much postdates Aristotle. However, in ordinary language we use the term "will" broadly and not always as implying some theory or special philosophical view. One might think that the persistence of the term in ordinary language attests to some reality to which it corresponds. There is a rough overlap between this usage and some uses of *prohairesis* in Aristotle; in these cases, to avoid the term "will" tends to obscure, and we can use that term while keeping in mind the necessary caveats.

advance of an action that the action may be said to embody or display a preference for one good rather than others.[12]

DELIBERATION

It follows that we need to understand Aristotle's notion of deliberation (*bouleusis*, literally "taking counsel") as having exactly the richness and content that can account for the distinctive features of *prohairesis*. Yet what Aristotle says about it seems disappointingly sketchy and furthermore difficult to apply to practical reasoning.

Aristotle begins by asking what sorts of things we may be said to deliberate about. Here again we have to take his remarks to be underwritten about how it would be natural to speak. For instance, suppose some cosmologists spend an afternoon debating theories about the origin of the universe: we would not naturally describe their session as "*deliberating* about the formation of the universe," although they might be said to be deliberating about how to write a scientific paper on the subject together, or how to test a theory experimentally. Again, mathematicians cannot properly be said to *deliberate* about theorems, though they might be said to deliberate about how best to prove a theorem. Likewise, it would be nonsense for a group of Americans to gather together and *deliberate* about what policies should be enacted in Britain (we would have to take them, say, to be imagining themselves in the British parliament). As Aristotle observes, we reserve the word "deliberation" for cases in which people are considering matters that are up to them to achieve.

But so far this picks out only the general class, since not even everything up to us is an appropriate object of deliberation. For instance, I am not *deliberating* about which letters to type as I type the manuscript for this book, nor are you deliberating about what words those letters spell. On the other hand, I am deliberating about how best to explain Aristotle's ideas, and you perhaps are deliberating about how to get a better grasp on them. Thus, well-defined proce-

---

[12] We are of course capable of regarding a single deliberation as arriving at a general result that covers a whole class of actions. There is no reason to suppose that, on Aristotle's theory, every action has to be immediately preceded in time by an actual process of deliberation, if it is to be regarded as resulting from a deliberation.

dures (reading and writing, for a literate adult), familiar cases (a doctor diagnosing ordinary strep throat), and uncomplicated matters (an accountant filling out the short-form tax return) are not matters of deliberation. Rather, as Aristotle observes, we can intelligibly be said to deliberate only about: "things that hold typically" (if they held always, there would be nothing we could do about them, and if randomly, there would be nothing we could intelligibly suppose about them); "things in which it is unclear how they will turn out" (since then there is something we need to figure out for ourselves); and "things that lack well-defined parameters" (since then we cannot simply apply some previously settled procedure) (1112b8–10).[13]

Recall that Aristotle is interested in how reason manifests itself as a cause in individual cases, not in the abstract. Aristotle thinks that deliberation is the principal manifestation of the practical effectiveness of intelligence. A child who employs an algorithm for long-division, although he is following a very clever set of rules, is making use of someone else's reasoning, from long ago, and thus is not actively exercising his *own* intelligence in practical matters (though we can congratulate him on mastering the method); yet if he has to work out (say) an apt outline for an essay about his summer vacation, then his own practical intelligence is indeed brought into play. We see his own intelligence at work in the essay but not in long-division, once that has been mastered. Aristotle adds,

And we deliberate not about goals but about things that contribute to goals – since a physician does not deliberate about whether he will heal; or an orator whether he will persuade; or a politician whether he will work for civil order; or any other expert as regards his end – but rather, taking the goal as given, they investigate how and through what things it will come to be. (1112b11–16)

This remark requires some care in interpreting. Aristotle is certainly not claiming, in the spirit of David Hume, that reason is purely "instrumental," and that we therefore can never evaluate goals on reasonable grounds: recall that, for Aristotle, a goal is simply a good, and the entire *Ethics* is a project of reasoning about the relative worth

---

[13] We may need to deliberate about *which* settled procedure to apply, but the application of that procedure is not itself an instance of deliberation.

of goods (not to mention that, by this point of his treatise, he has given several clear examples of such reasoning).

Rather, this remark should be understood as implicitly involving what logicians call "reduplication." Reduplication is where we make it clear that we want to speak about something precisely with respect to that attribute by which we pick it out. Typically we express a reduplication with the term "*qua*" or "as": "a physician *qua* physician," "a physician as physician." The phrase, "a physician *qua* physician" indicates a physician precisely in that respect in which she has the attribute of being a physician. A sentence which has such a phrase as the subject expression is therefore true only if what it claims is true of physicians and furthermore is true of them precisely because they are physicians. Thus, for instance, "A physician *qua* physician is a healer" is true, but "A physician *qua* physician is a respected member of the community" is false, even if, in fact, all physicians are respected members of their communities – because it is not being a physician itself which makes them so.

The claim that "A physician *qua* physician does not deliberate about whether he is to heal" is therefore the claim that, insofar as someone is a physician, she does not thus deliberate – that, if she were to deliberate about that, to that extent she would not be acting as a physician. This is easy to see: someone acts *qua* physician if she makes use of medical training in acting, but nothing about someone's medical training makes her better prepared to decide whether someone should be treated or not. Anyone who was engaged in that kind of inquiry would not be making use of *medical* expertise. Suppose a military doctor in the field establishes a triage and makes judgments, based on his medical training, about which wounds are either too dire, or too minor, to be given treatment: he would be acting *qua* physician in assessing the injury, but acting in some other capacity (say, under military guidelines) in utilizing those assessments in a triage.

But why does Aristotle make this claim about deliberation and goals? His point needs to be understood in relation to themes in *Republic*, book 1 about the nature of a skill or craft (*technē*), as well as in relation to the ideas Aristotle had put forward earlier in *Ethics* 1.1. Generally goals, and practices for attaining those goals, come in pairs: we seek goals through acquiring definite skills directed at those ends.

Our practical deliberations therefore typically take the form not of our throwing everything up for calculation, but rather of our inquiring whether, given that some goal is taken for granted, we should adopt some other goal which contributes to that. If we take seriously the analogy between skills and virtues, what Aristotle is maintaining is that goals of virtuous action are correlated with virtues directed at achieving them. Thus, the deliberation of a virtuous person simply takes this goal for granted; it does not expose that goal to deliberation as well. Just as, *qua* physician, a person does not deliberate about whether he is to heal, so, *qua* courageous, a person does not deliberate about whether he should be doing what is admirable in battle: he simply takes that for granted. In important respects, then, to be virtuous requires that we *not* expose some matters to deliberation.

Aristotle likens deliberation to the process of finding the correct construction for a geometrical figure. By this he seems to mean that:

1. Deliberation proceeds backwards, from goal to task at hand, constructing a series of intermediate goals.
2. When there are multiple paths to any intermediate goal, deliberation requires that we locate the best path, where what counts as best can vary.
3. We may come to recognize that paths cannot be completed, especially the path which leads from where we are now to the first intermediate goal, in which case we need to construct (one might say) a plan which gets us to a place where we can implement the plan.

All of these remarks are familiar enough to anyone who has ever tried to devise a flow chart or develop an action plan.

Yet, as was said, we might wonder whether this description of practical reasoning, admirable though it may be in capturing administrative rationality, has a good application to moral reasoning. Does not moral reasoning seem to be distinctive in relying on such devices as universalization ("what if everyone did that?"); taking an impartial viewpoint; acting fairly and without groundless discrimination; and so on? Aristotle might well respond that *that* sort of reasoning represents only one species of moral rationality, the sort displayed by a legislator setting down fair laws for political society: it has more to do with justice than with the other moral virtues. (We shall look at

Aristotle's account of justice in detail in chapter 6 below.) The reasoning of someone who is aiming to be courageous or generous has different characteristics, and at this point in his treatise he wants merely to give a very general characterization of deliberation, which could apply to all the virtues of character.[14] And any lingering impression that Aristotle's account covers only administrative rationality may perhaps be removed by pointing out that a "path" to a goal need not be an instrumental means or even something prior in time to the goal. Rather, any case in which one could claim that "in doing X he achieved Y" would be a case in which a path was taken to a goal; for instance, "In falling on the grenade, the soldier acted heroically" – but his falling on the grenade is not an *instrumental* means of heroic action.

The final definition is cryptic: "Since that which is brought about by *prohairesis* are those things, up to us, which are the objects of deliberated conation, *prohairesis* itself would be conation, having a deliberative character, of things that are up to us, since it is by making a judgment based on our deliberation that we have conation that is controlled by that deliberation" (1113a9–12). ("Conation" is a technical term in English, sometimes used in psychology, which corresponds well enough to Aristotle's own coined term, *orexis*, which means generally some striving for some aim.) The passage is obscure, but Aristotle's basic point seems to be that we are so constituted that we impose reasonability on our actions precisely through deliberation. If a character-related virtue is, as I have said, a kind of responsiveness of the non-rational part of the soul, or openness to persuasion, then deliberation can be understood as the way it becomes so persuaded.

---

[14] But consider this passage from General Patton's famous speech to soldiers of the Normandy invasion army. He regards courage apparently as involving the universalization, "what if everyone did that?," but then he immediately likens the appropriate course of action to playing one's part and contributing to the whole effort: "All of the real heroes are not storybook combat fighters, either. Every single man in this Army plays a vital role. Don't ever let up. Don't ever think that your job is unimportant. Every man has a job to do and he must do it. Every man is a vital link in the great chain. What if every truck driver suddenly decided that he didn't like the whine of those shells overhead, turned yellow, and jumped headlong into a ditch? The cowardly bastard could say, 'Hell, they won't miss me, just one man in thousands.' But, what if every man thought that way? Where in the hell would we be now? What would our country, our loved ones, our homes, even the world, be like? No, Goddamnit, Americans don't think like that. Every man does his job. Every man serves the whole." (See Charles M. Province, "The Famous Patton Speech," at http://www.pattonhq.com/speech.html.)

WISH

Aristotle's discussion of wish (*boulēsis*) in 3.4 is brief and aims to make a single point only, rather than give a general theory.

A common but apparently incorrect view should be put aside at the start. Sometimes it is supposed that Aristotle takes wish to have a single object, namely the ultimate good (happiness). All of us, then, wish for only one thing, and we are doing so constantly: we wish for happiness. On this view, 3.4 is concerned with the difficulty of whether every human being has the same ultimate goal.

But this interpretation seems mistaken. (i) Aristotle evidently thinks of wish as the same sort of thing as *prohairesis* and deliberation, but, as we have seen, these are general capacities which are exercised in the achievement of particular actions, so wish would presumably be that sort of thing as well. Moreover, (ii) the doctrine that "we do not deliberate about goals" implies that each person, at any time, would have various goals for which he would "wish," corresponding to the various roles he occupied: for instance, a physician who was also a loyal citizen of Athens would take for granted and therefore wish both the end of healing and the end of observing Athenian law. Furthermore, (iii) as we saw from Aristotle's discussion of mixed actions, Aristotle thinks of an agent as typically pursuing a variety of goals, in a rank-ordering, each wished for. Again, (iv) Aristotle's comparison of wish to a sense faculty also confirms this view. He says that wish is like a sense, which naturally yields correct perceptions and intuitive judgments, but which can give misleading reports if it is no longer in good natural condition. Yet just as we can sense different objects of sense, and take them into account, all at once, so on this picture we can "sense" a variety of goods and take them into account all at once.

It is precisely this comparison of the faculty of wishing with a sense organ that is the chief idea of the chapter. So let us look at this point more carefully. Aristotle begins his discussion of wish with a dilemma. (a) Suppose we say that wish is a power which takes as its object things that are really good. If so: if we wish for something, then *ipso facto* it is good. But then when someone wishes for something which is in fact bad, that thing would be both bad and good, a contradiction. So then, (b) suppose we say that wish is a power which takes as its object things that merely seem to be good. If so, then wish will never fail to attain its object (since we shall always be wishing for what seems good to us), but then we can never make a mistake in wishing, and it would make no sense to claim that what someone has wished for is actually good.

The dilemma is similar to: when we see that an object has a color, do we see the color that the object *actually* has, or do we see only the color that the object *appears* to have? If the former, then, an object might have two different colors at the same time: as when we have an after-image and see the wall which is white as also colored, or when the same wall looks white to one person but yellow to someone with jaundice. If the latter, then any claim that an object actually has a particular color would make no sense – colors exist just in our perceiving of them.

Aristotle's way out is to propose that there is a natural harmony between our faculty of wish and objects of wish, not unlike the natural harmony he thinks holds between our sense organs and objects of those senses. The eyes, Aristotle thinks, are naturally constituted to report the colors that things actually have, when these are viewed under the natural conditions for the operation of that organ: a healthy eye therefore reports the actual colors of a thing, whereas the reports of a diseased eye are untrustworthy. Similarly, the faculty of wishing is naturally constituted to wish for ends that are in fact good: when it develops well and correctly, what it wishes for is reliably counted as good; but when it has deviated from its natural condition, its reports are unreliable and reflect rather the subjective condition of the person whose wish it is.

Call a view of this sort, which regards our faculties as directed naturally at corresponding objects, a Teleological-Faculty view.[15] This view is of great importance for the entire *Ethics* and is the reason for Aristotle's frequent assertion that a good person serves as a kind of measure or standard in ethical matters (cf. 1166a12–14 and 1176a17–18). That a good person is such a standard would imply, among other things, firstly that we are justified in relying on the insight of a recognizably virtuous person in a difficult matter where we cannot ourselves discern the correct course; and secondly that

---

[15] On this, see the helpful discussion in Price (1989), 129–30.

there is some point in trying to imagine how an ideally virtuous person would perceive things and react, and then deciding a difficult matter from this viewpoint.

Aristotle remarks that "each condition has its own attractive (*kala*) and pleasant (*hēdea*) objects" (1113a31). This hearkens back to his doctrine about habituation and training, that each subjective condition implies a liking for those things to which it is accustomed. But when he adds that "the good person is set apart from others to the greatest extent by seeing what is truly so in each case" (a31–32), he is invoking the Teleological-Faculty view and suggesting that the phenomena of wishing for the good should be understood according to a focal or central-case analysis: the various bad conditions of wishing should be interpreted as various ways of falling away from the naturally good condition.

Aristotle then adds: "in most cases the illusory perception seems to have originated from pleasure, which, although it is not good, appears to be good, and so people seek after pleasant things as good, and they avoid painful things as bad" (1113a33–35). This too seems to hearken back to his doctrine of habituation and training. Suppose someone becomes accustomed to doing something that in fact is not good; because he has become accustomed to this, however, he *likes* acting in that way; he therefore will tend to regard the pleasure he gets from acting in that way (that is, pleasure in the broad sense – "satisfaction" or "contentment") as simply *constituting* what is good about that course of action.

DOES A PERSON ACQUIRE GOOD OR BAD CHARACTER "OF HIS OWN ACCORD"?

Consider two men who commit homicide. One kills a man he catches committing adultery with his wife: unexpectedly discovering them, he grabs a gun in a fit of passion, shoots the man, and immediately afterward cries out in agony over his action, "What have I done?" Another man, when he inadvertently discovers that his wife is having an affair, plots over a long period of time to have his wife killed: he hires an assassin, devises a ruse to lure his wife to a lonely spot, where the assassin kills her brutally, and afterward he helps the assassin destroy the body and hide the evidence. All the while he shows absolutely no remorse. Everyone would take the second crime to be worse than the first and deserving of greater punishment. But why? Both were homicides.

One might wish to explain the difference in terms of features of the action itself – how the latter was more "intrinsically bad," perhaps. Aristotle's view, rather, is that we should trace the two actions to the two sorts of character that produced them: the second man's action is indicative of a much worse character than that of the first, which is why he deserves a greater punishment. The very point of law is to produce good character in those governed by the law; hence, the law punishes more severely actions which spring from a worse character.

Yet one might wonder whether this way of proceeding would make sense if we were not responsible for our characters. Aristotle's view is that it would not: if we do not acquire our character "of our own accord," then the moral censure and punishment directed at an action cannot reasonably vary depending upon the character which produced that action. So in 3.5, as a kind of follow-up to his entire discussion of the relationship of action to character, Aristotle defends the claim that a person does acquire the character that he has of his own accord.[16]

The argument of the chapter is complex, but we can distinguish four basic stages: the fundamental argument (1113b3–21); a confirming argument (1113b21–1114a13); a diagnosis of why people are attracted to the false view (1114a13–31); and an afterthought (1114a31–b25).

Aristotle's fundamental argument is placed at the very beginning of the chapter and may be represented as follows:

1. Any action involving wish, deliberation, and choice is up to us.
2. Virtuous actions are like that.
3. Thus, virtuous actions are up to us.[17]

---

[16] Aristotle is not concerned in this chapter with the problem that we call "freedom of the will." This problem arises only once it begins to seem that some general, deterministic account of the world is true, e.g. causal determinism, divine predestination, or even the theory that Aristotle considers in *De Interpretatione*, ch. 9, that if the Law of Excluded Middle is true, then all future events must already be fixed and unchangeable. But no such deterministic theory is at issue here; and surely Aristotle would regard a metaphysical discussion of freewill as foreign to his present, practical inquiry, just as are other metaphysical questions.

[17] In 3.5 Aristotle makes liberal use of the idiom, "up to us," which we should understand in terms of his notion of an action being taken of the agent's own accord: an action is up to the agent just in case the performing of it was of his own accord; and, if he had not done it, his not doing so would also have been of his own accord.

4. But if virtuous actions are up to us, so is being virtuous.
5. Thus, being virtuous (that is, having a virtue) is up to us.
6. But there is parity between virtue and vice.
7. Thus, being vicious is up to us.
8. Thus, what character we have is up to us.

Here is the text in which steps 1–5 are presented: "Since the goal is something we wish for, and what contributes to the goal is something we deliberate about, then any action that involves these things would be performed by choice and be of the agent's own accord. But the actions through which any virtue is actualized involve these things. Thus, virtue as well is up to us" (1113b3–14).

The crucial step is clearly 4, and Aristotle gives no explicit justification for it. Perhaps the following is his thought. Recall that a virtue is a "state" or *hexis*, and, as we saw, one meaning of the word *hexis* is that it is a kind of potential or power, which finds its full existence in an actualization. So one might therefore wonder how it is that the *virtue*, a potential to action, could not be up to us, if the actualization of that potential were entirely up to us. The virtue, one might say, hardly has more reality than its series of actualizations. How, then, could *every single actualization* of a virtue be up to us, but not our having the virtue? Or perhaps Aristotle's view is the simple thought that the virtue-like actions by which we acquire a virtue have to be carried out of our own accord if they are to contribute to our acquiring that character, and then that same mark would have to carry over to the character as well. (But admittedly it is unsatisfactory that he fails to provide explicit support for the step in the argument that most needs it.)

Yet if the virtue is up to us – the argument now continues – then vice is as well, because, for every action the carrying out of which would be virtuous, we could just as well have omitted it, and for every action the omission of which is virtuous, we could just as well have carried it out. Here is the relevant text for steps 6–8:

But vice is similarly up to us. Here's the reason. In cases in which it's up to us to carry out an action, it's also up to us to refrain from carrying it out; and in cases in which saying "no" is up to us, saying "yes" is also up to us. It follows that:

[i] if carrying out an action, supposing it's admirable for us to carry it out, is up to us, then also refraining from that action will be up to us, given that it's shameful to refrain from carrying it out; moreover,

[ii] if refraining from carrying out an action, supposing it's admirable to refrain from carrying it out, is up to us, then also carrying out the action will be up to us, given that it's shameful to do it.

Thus, if carrying out admirable actions is up to us, then carrying out shameful actions is also up to us, and similarly also not carrying them out. But this was just what being a good or a bad person consisted in. The upshot is that whether we are good or bad is up to us. (1113b6–14)

This settles the matter for Aristotle. The only alternative to accepting the conclusion, he thinks, is "to call into question everything we've just now been maintaining and deny that human beings are the origin of their actions and beget them much as their children" (1113b17–19). We either affirm that we are responsible for our character, or we make nonsense of human action and indeed all of ethics.

Next comes what I have called the "confirming argument," which may be sketched as follows:

1. It is a presupposition of punishment that what gets punished is up to the agent.
2. But people in authority punish *character traits* as well as actions.
3. Thus people in authority presuppose that character traits are up to us.
4. Hence, character traits are up to us.

The inference from 3–4 reflects well Aristotle's philosophical attitude: he thinks it absurd that what is generally accepted in so indispensable an institution as legal authority could be in fact groundless. Recall that he thinks human beings by nature live in political society and that therefore political authority is an essential and naturally arising element of distinctively human life. But such a natural arrangement could not depend upon some systematic error.

As for 2, as we have seen, Aristotle regards it as a general truth about punishment: the sound assignment of punishment (as the example about the two sorts of murder showed) requires that we make a judgment about the relationship between a deplorable action and an agent's character in performing an action. But to clinch the case for 2 he puts forward what he surely regards as a very clear example in which a condition itself is punished, namely, culpable ignorance. Those who do something wrong because they are culpably ignorant – for instance, people who commit a crime when inebriated (drunk drivers who strike pedestrians), or who have avoided learning the relevant law (tax evaders) – are typically given an extra punishment. Aristotle thinks we should interpret this as: they get one penalty for the wrongdoing and another penalty for placing or keeping themselves in ignorance. They get this additional punishment because we recognize, rightly, that it was up to them not to be ignorant. In the same way, Aristotle suggests, if we punish people in other cases for their character, it is because we recognize that these conditions are similarly culpable.

It will not work to excuse someone for placing himself in a bad condition by blaming that on another antecedent bad condition, because this leads to an unsustainable regress. Suppose we say: "It wasn't his fault that he didn't know the relevant law, because he's just the sort of person who doesn't take sufficient care about such things" (cf. 1114a3–4). In saying this, we are excusing his bad condition of *ignorance of the law*, by blaming that on an antecedent bad condition, *carelessness in learning about the law*. But then what of *that* bad condition? We might perhaps excuse *that* by shifting blame to some more fundamental carelessness, say, "general carelessness." ("He was careless about the law, because he was never the sort of person to care about anything.") But eventually that sort of maneuver becomes incredible. Eventually what we have to say is that he was careless about acquiring bad traits of character at all. But, Aristotle says, it is not possible that anyone of sound mind could fail to recognize that his actions influence his character, and fail to consent to that influence in carrying out actions of a certain sort: "not to *know* that we acquire a condition from carrying out corresponding actions would be the height of obtuseness; and it makes no sense to say that someone, in acting unjustly, doesn't *wish* to be an unjust person, or in acting self-indulgently, doesn't *wish* to be a self-indulgent person" (1114a9–12).

After presenting these arguments, Aristotle gives his diagnosis of why we are tempted to think that traits of character are not up to us. We do so because we apply to traits of character a criterion that is appropriate only for actions. As regards actions, it is true that:

If an agent's doing X is up to him, then while he is doing X it is up to him to stop doing X.

But as regards traits of character and bad conditions generally, it is not true that:

If an agent's having condition Y is up to him, then so long as he has Y it is up to him to stop having Y.

The reason is that a condition is up to us if its *acquisition* is, that is, if each of the various steps by which we acquire that condition is up to us. But a condition once acquired is not revocable at will, and so it may no longer be up to us to rid ourselves of a bad condition. It is just like: once we ruin our health by a series of unwise decisions, we can no longer by a single decision regain our health. In short, the view that we are not responsible for our character depends for its force upon a confusion between actions and conditions. We wrongly suppose that, because we are "bound" by a condition once we have it, we were bound to acquire it.

The chapter concludes with what I have labeled an "Afterthought," aimed apparently at refuting the suggestion that we have no real control over what we do, and of what sort of character we acquire, on the grounds that all of us simply pursue things in accordance with how the end appears to us, and we have no control over that (1114a31–b25). Presumably Aristotle examines this suggestion carefully because it relies on premises similar to views that he himself endorses. Recall that in 3.4 Aristotle had maintained that "each state of character has its own things that are admirable and pleasant." So perhaps what seems admirable and pleasant to a person actually settles what his character is?

Aristotle in effect replies as follows.[18] It is true that there is a correlation between someone's character and what appears good to him, but correlation is not yet causation. In fact, there are two possibilities: either (i) a person's character (whether he has virtues or vices) causes how "the end appears to him"; or (ii) how "the end appears to him" causes a person to have virtues or vices.

If (ii) is untenable, then we should accept (i). So Aristotle turns to the investigation of (ii). Suppose, he says, that we have no control over how the end appears to us, and that, once the end is fixed, then

[18] The passage is one of the most obscure in the *Ethics*. The interpretation given here traces one possible interpretive path through it.

what actions we should choose, in order to attain this end, are also fixed. (Aristotle now changes the tone of his language, writing in an exaggerated manner that is designed to draw his interlocutors in.) If so, then "someone is 'well born' if he is naturally good in this way. The greatest and finest good – which cannot be acquired or learned from anyone else, but by nature is such as to be that way – is what he will have. Indeed, to be so well and finely gifted by birth, would be to have the perfect and genuine form of natural endowment" (1114b6–12).

So then, will such a person be admirably virtuous and deserving of our respect and praise? One might think so, but if his virtue followed directly from his natural endowment, in fact he would not deserve admiration and praise. The point is that we simply cannot sustain belief in (ii): the moment we assume it, we are inclined to praise and admire people who would not be deserving of praise and admiration at all if (ii) were true. Thus we should accept (i) after all.[19]

In the end, Aristotle's point is that virtue and vice must together be up to us, or not so, and we cannot succeed in making ourselves believe that virtue is not up to us.

FURTHER READING

Kenny (1979, ch. 3) gives a reliable overview and assessment of 3.1–5; Broadie (1991, ch. 3) is characteristically subtle and perceptive. Meyer (1993) is distinctive in taking Aristotle to be proposing a "theory of moral responsibility."

For particular discussions, one might begin with Austin (1970) on responsibility, a piece of ordinary language philosophy which aims to carry out more thoroughly what Aristotle began, although Austin does not (as I have argued that Aristotle does) examine excuses in order to arrive at some positive conception of human agency.

---

[19] Aristotle additionally points out that there is another possibility that has been overlooked, namely, that although the end is fixed, there is nonetheless considerable leeway in how we attain the end, and the difference between good and bad character depends on what path a person takes to that end. But clearly he is not interested in arguing here for some definite picture of how we become responsible for our character; he simply wants to defeat the contrary view that we are not.

Hursthouse (1984) gives a subtle and insightful reading of 3.1 in the manner of an Anscombe or Wittgenstein.

A pair of articles that are usefully read together, on the question of whether Aristotle is concerned with what we call "freewill" are Hardie (1968) and Huby (1967), and Sorabji's (1980) book-length discussion is valuable throughout.

CHAPTER 5

Some particular character-related virtues (Nicomachean Ethics 3.6–4.9)

Aristotle begins examining particular character-related virtues in 3.6. He looks first at courage, then self-mastery (or "moderation"), then generosity and magnificence, magnanimity and an unnamed virtue dealing with honor, before examining various minor social virtues. He reserves special treatment for the virtue of justice, which he considers a character-related virtue as well, but which he thinks is set apart in interesting ways from the others. I shall follow his practice and consider his treatment of justice separately, in the next chapter.

Let us review the argument once again. The reason why Aristotle wishes to examine the virtues, paying special attention to the sorts of actions a virtuous person does, is that he thinks that the ultimate goal of human life is some kind of action or activity that we can accomplish only through our having virtue. As was said, this goal should be understood as taking the form of an activity, repeated at intervals, which would rightly serve to organize and direct everything else that we do. But *which* activity of that sort should serve as our ultimate goal? It is that activity, Aristotle has argued, which satisfies the criteria of Ultimacy, Self-Sufficiency, and (perhaps) greatest Preferability. But we cannot determine which activity satisfies those criteria until we become clearer about the activities that are indeed distinctive of the various virtues. So this now is Aristotle's task, which he carries out in 3.6–6.13. He considers first character-related virtues, and then thinking-related virtues (in book 6).

Aristotle's discussion of the particular character-related virtues, like the rest of the *Ethics*, needs to be seen against the background of Plato. It was the tendency of Plato's thought to hold that any apparently *particular* virtue, if it were to be entirely adequate and wholly good, had to be understood so expansively that it effectively became identified with the *whole* of virtue. Thus, in the *Protagoras*, Plato argues that courage must involve an ability to discern and weigh correctly present versus future pleasures and pains, and that the general application of this ability, outside the particular circumstances of courageous action, would simply be virtue in general (see for instance *Protagoras* 359a–360e). Again, by the end of the *Charmides*, a dialogue in which a definition of self-mastery (or "moderation") is sought, Socrates has his interlocutor agreeing that real self-mastery would involve a completely general ability to discern the extent and limits of any expertise, including that very expertise itself (see *Charmides* 171d–172c). Such a skill appears to be so comprehensive, that anyone who possessed it would hardly need anything more in order to be entirely good.

Plato's view that any apparently particular virtue, if it is to be wholly good, must somehow be equivalent to the whole of virtue is sometimes referred to as the thesis of "the Unity of Virtue." Aristotle's tendency, in contrast, is to restrict and localize the virtues, or, at least, the various character-related virtues. Consonant with the notion of an *analysis* of virtue, which was examined at the beginning of chapter 2 above, Aristotle views a character-related virtue as some rather restricted goodness in functioning, which, however, contributes in some way to the good functioning of the whole person. Courage, he thinks, has a specific function: it enables us to act well on the battlefield. Self-mastery too is limited in its purpose: it enables us to act well in dealing with our basically animal desires for food, comfort, and sex. Generosity helps us to deal well with money, as it enters into our day-to-day association with others. Magnanimity enables us to deal well with significant honors. Each virtue has a rather restricted "domain," as I called it, because each deals with some restricted good that human beings characteristically or inevitably seek in daily life.

But this is not to say that Aristotle lacks resources for regarding the particular character-related virtues as having a general aspect as well. Courage, for instance, has a role when we are not on the field of battle: with courage, we can deal well with dangers generally. Other particular virtues similarly have extended or analogous functions, outside their principal domain of action. Aristotle, however, making use of his "central-case" method of analysis, will hold that the various extended phenomena have to be understood precisely in relation to the central case – that if we fail to discover the central case, then we shall fail to make sense of the whole range of phenomena of the virtue. (Indeed, Aristotle might claim that this points the way out of the difficulties Socrates discovered in trying to formulate "strict definitions," as I called them, of the various virtues. One will not find some attribute that all actions ascribable to a certain virtue, and only those actions, have in common. But such actions will have in common that they are the effect of precisely that power or "state" that the virtue is; and we clarify the nature of a particular "state" by looking at its principal and extreme actualization.)

The other main resource Aristotle has, for regarding particular character-related virtues as involving virtue more generally, is his notion of practical wisdom (*phronēsis*) – shrewdness and intelligence as regards the ordering of one's own actions. This virtue, he thinks, must be in place, if any particular virtue is to work as it should, since practical wisdom serves to harmonize and direct all of the particular virtues. The fact that practical wisdom plays such a role, Aristotle considers, is what is true about the thesis of the Unity of Virtue. He argues for this in 6.12–13 (which I shall consider in chapter 7 below).

THE ROLE OF THE *KALON* IN CHARACTER-RELATED VIRTUE

In considering what Aristotle has to say about character-related virtue, we should start by looking briefly at his doctrine that such virtues aim at what is noble, admirable, and pleasing to consider in action. He refers to this aspect of action as what is *kalon* in an action. It is evidently of the highest importance for Aristotle that character-related virtue aims at this, yet, unfortunately, what this means is somewhat obscure, and Aristotle says little about the matter directly.

Kalon (pronounced kal-ON) means, literally, "beautiful." It indicates something pleasing to contemplate, admirable, wonderful, and even glorious. The term is typically rendered "noble" but sometimes also "fine" or "admirable." ("Admirable" gets at the feature indirectly, through the response that such an action ought to evoke in someone perceiving it: admiration.) Something *kalon* is attractive; we are drawn to it; we want somehow to possess it. The opposite is an action's being *aischron* (ice-SCRON) – "ugly," "disgraceful," "shameful." Something *aischron* is, correspondingly, "offensive," "disgusting," and "repulsive."

Aristotle's use of these terms seems largely derived from Plato, who relies on the notions of *kalon* (and *aischron*) in four important contexts. The first is in Socrates' refutation of Polus in the *Gorgias*, where Socrates gets Polus to admit that whether an action is admirable (*kalon*) or disgraceful (*aischron*) is a distinct ground for evaluating an action, besides whether it is pleasant and painful, and that considerations of *kalon* and *aischron* have priority. To commit an injustice is worse than to suffer it, Polus ends up admitting, since the latter is merely painful, but the former is disgraceful (*Gorgias* 474c–475c). Aristotle follows Plato in this and similarly holds that an action's being *kalon* is a distinct ground for evaluating it, which has priority over whether it is pleasant or materially advantageous.

The second context occurs later in the same dialogue, where Callicles enters the argument and challenges Socrates' refutation of Polus, claiming that Polus had exposed himself to being refuted only because he had mistakenly agreed that unjust actions were in reality or "by nature" *aischron* (483a). Callicles insists, rather, that unjust actions are *aischron* only because of human conventions, not in reality; in reality, unjust actions are *kalon* if carried out by a person with sufficient strength and capacity (483b–d). Socrates' answer involves arguing that there is a real basis for our judgments that certain actions are *kalon* or *aischron*, depending upon whether or not they fit into a kind of mathematical harmony, which, he claims, human and divine actions should observe: "Partnership and friendship," Socrates says, "orderliness, self-control, and justice, hold together heaven and earth, and gods and men, and that is why they call this universe a world-order or *kosmos*" (508a). Aristotle similarly holds that an action is *kalon* not by convention merely but also depending upon whether it displays the right sort of order, and manifests an appropriate principle. He sometimes expresses this by saying or suggesting that an action is *kalon* insofar as it is fitting (*prepon*), or somehow deserved (*axion*), or appropriately due (*deon*) to a thing. Perhaps the clearest case of this would be a just action, which, Aristotle thinks, displays an appropriate equality.

The third context is from the *Symposium*, where the character Diotima argues that the most fundamental motive of all living things is a striving to reproduce, which she construes as a desire to "make something" (*poiēsis*) and, in particular, to make a copy or extension of oneself or one's own kind, which is an imitation of immortality. She claims that this yearning is stimulated or precipitated by our being attracted to beauty (*kalon*), and our desiring to possess beauty:

Pregnancy, reproduction – this is an immortal thing for a mortal animal to do, and it cannot occur in anything that is out of harmony, but ugliness is out of harmony with all that is godly. Beauty (*kalon*), however, is in harmony with the divine ... That is why, whenever pregnant animals or persons draw near to beauty, they become gentle and joyfully disposed to give birth and reproduce ... (206d)

Note that the desire for possessing beauty does not present itself to us as a desire to reproduce: the reason that we desire beauty, Plato thinks, is not the reason we would at first give for our attraction. And Diotima's reference to animals is important too, because it reveals that, as Plato sees it, non-rational beings can be attracted to beauty: this motive is in fact shared by all living things.

Aristotle, it seems, similarly brings in the notion of *kalon*, precisely to indicate some attraction that we have to virtuous actions, which is not attributable in the first instance to "the part of the soul that has reason." Recall that the character-related virtues, as Aristotle thinks of them, all involve how "the part of the soul that does not have reason but which listens and responds to reason" becomes suitably responsive to rational indications in action, in different domains of life. This part of the soul, then, needs something to respond to, some basis for being drawn to an action that is related to reason, but which does not involve its rehearsing or judging reasons. He is supposing that the *kalon* is a more satisfactory basis of attraction for this part of the soul, and thus, throughout 3.5–4.9, he describes character-related virtues as aiming at the *kalon*, and not at the "rational" or the "reasonable." And yet, in referring to a virtuous action as *kalon*, Aristotle also means to suggest that such an action carries with it a rational justification, which could in principle be discovered and made explicit.

The fourth context is a passage in the *Alcibiades*.[1] At one significant point in the dialogue, Alcibiades claims that courage is something bad, because sometimes it leads to the person who has it being killed

---

[1] The *Alcibiades* (or "First Alcibiades") is regarded by some scholars as not written by Plato, but the view that we are concerned with here, which that dialogue expresses particularly well, is common enough elsewhere in Plato.

in battle. As against that claim, Socrates gives the following argument: courage leads people to rescue their friends and relatives in battle; but to act in that way is admirable (*kalon*); and insofar as something is *kalon*, it is among the greatest of goods; but by acting admirably we obtain what is admirable, and thus the greatest of goods; and to get the greatest of goods is to do well in life; thus, courage *qua* courage is good and helps us do well in life (115c–116c). The passage is a kind of Function Argument in miniature, carried out with respect to one virtue only, courage. But what is important about it for present purposes is that Socrates supposes, and Alcibiades grants, that the greatest goods are ones that we come to possess and claim as our own, not through receiving, but rather through acting. This idea was already implicit in Plato's claim in the *Symposium*, that the most fundamental yearning of living things was for some kind of *making* – reproduction, in fact. Aristotle similarly holds that what is *kalon* in action can be possessed, and that we come to possess it by deliberately carrying out a *kalon* action, intending it as *kalon*.

Thus there is in Plato already an implicit theory of the *kalon* in action, which Aristotle takes over for his purposes, and which we may summarize as follows.

1. That an action is *kalon* is a distinct ground for our favoring that action (it is something good about that action); and this ground is reasonably to be preferred over other grounds, such as an action's pleasantness or material advantageousness.
2. Actions are *kalon* or *aischron*, and this depends on whether or not the action in some way fits into or conforms to an appropriate order.
3. That an action is *kalon* makes it attractive, potentially even to non-rational powers or agents, and yet that it is so attractive can in principle be given a rational account.
4. An action's being *kalon* is a good that we come to possess, and can claim as our own, simply by deliberately carrying out an action of that sort.

That the elements of this theory are already in Plato may go some way toward explaining why Aristotle does not discuss the notion of the *kalon* directly.

We have seen earlier (pp. 122, 128) that Aristotle takes a virtue of character to involve (i) a sensitivity to a good in some domain; and (ii) a certain ranking of that good over other sorts of goods. For instance, if a man is to be courageous, he needs to regard heroic action as something valuable or worthwhile, and he needs further-more to prefer heroic action over other goods that he might gain for himself in battle, such as his safety or life. We can understand this now as a claim about the *kalon*: a virtue of character requires that we recognize some sorts of actions as *kalon*, and that we show a pre-ference for the good that we obtain from performing that sort of action, over other goods available to us (such as pleasure or material advantage) in some domain.

It is useful to have a synoptic view of the various passages in which Aristotle mentions the role of sensitivity to the *kalon* in virtuous action:

(Courage) Someone who is courageous holds his ground, and performs actions characteristic of courage, for the sake of the *kalon*. (1115b23–24, cf. 1116a11–12)

(Self-mastery) That's why it's a necessary requirement that, in a man with self-mastery, the part of the soul that has desires should be in harmony with his reason, since the *kalon* is the target at which both of these aim. (1119b15–16)

(Generosity) All actions in accordance with virtue are *kalon* and for the sake of the *kalon*, and therefore a generous person will confer gifts for the sake of the *kalon* and in the right way. (1120a23–26)

(Magnificence) Someone who has the virtue of magnificence will make these sorts of expenditures for the sake of the *kalon* – this is common to all the virtues. (1122b6–7)

(Amiability) The fellow with this virtue will associate with others as is appropriate, using the *kalon* as his reference point. (1126b28–29)

(Truthfulness) Falsehood is in itself bad and to be avoided, but truth is in itself *kalon* and deserving of praise. (1127a28–30)[2]

---

[2] See also, for magnanimity, 1125b10–11; for wittiness, 1128a6–7, 19. Aristotle presumably takes it as obvious that the quasi-mathematical equality sought in just exchanges (see next chapter) is *kalon* and attractive, but he does not say this explicitly.

Similarly, here are various passages in which Aristotle mentions or suggests that a preference for the *kalon* is implicit in virtuous actions:

(Courage) A courageous man prefers the *kalon* that is attained in battle to [remaining alive and the greatest goods]. (1117b14)[3]

(Self-Mastery) Someone like that [sc. a self-indulgent person] cares for such pleasures more than they are worth. But a person with self-mastery is not like that; rather, he cares for them just in the way that sound reason indicates. (1119a18–20)

(Generosity) A person who confers gifts to those to whom it's not appropriate to do so, or not for the sake of the *kalon* but for some other reason, is not generous . . . nor is someone who confers gifts, but is distressed at doing so, since he would prefer money to *kalon* actions, and that's not the way of a generous person. (1120a27–31)[4]

(Magnificence) He's more concerned with figuring out how he might spend money in the most appealing [*kalon*] and most fitting [*prepon*] way, rather than how much he's spending or how he might minimize his expenditures. (1122b8–10)

(Amiability) [An amiable person, in his conversations with others] will aim to promote what benefits them, rather than aiming at not being unpleasant, or at being always agreeable. (1126b29–30)[5]

(Wittiness) [Buffoons] aim at getting a laugh rather than at propriety in speech and at not offending anyone else who looks on. (1128a6–7)

It should be noted, however, that in the *Ethics* Aristotle relies only informally and generally on this notion of preferring the *kalon* in action to anything else. He does not, for instance, try to explain this principle with sufficient definiteness that we might use it to resolve problem cases (he perhaps regards that as impossible), and he works out no particular examples. Yet he does begin to develop something of a theory of rational preference in his logical writings, in *Topics*, book 3.

---

[3] Compare the ranking displayed by "citizen soldiers": "To such men, death and avoiding disgrace are preferable to keeping safe in that way" (1116b19–20).

[4] See also: "[A liberal person is] not the sort of person to care for money for itself but rather for the sake of giving it away" (1120b16–17).

[5] And see the lines immediately before these, quoted above, where Aristotle says that such a person will "take the *kalon* as his reference point."

COURAGE

As mentioned, the first virtue of character that Aristotle examines is courage. He does not say explicitly why he examines it first, but there are various good reasons why he would do so: (i) On Plato's theory of human psychology, developed in *Republic,* books 2–4, there are two non-rational parts of the human soul, spiritedness or vigor (*thumos*) and felt desire (*epithumia*), and two corresponding virtues, courage and self-mastery. Aristotle remarks at the beginning of 3.10, "After courage let us discuss self-mastery, since these are regarded as the virtues of the non-rational parts of the soul" (1117b23–24), which apparently indicates that he examines these virtues first in deference to Plato. (ii) Courage was the chief virtue promoted among the Spartans, and Sparta was regarded by Aristotle as well as Plato as being distinctive, among city-states, for actually giving careful attention to the promotion of virtue among its citizens (see 10.9.1180a24–26). By dealing with courage first, then, Aristotle emphasizes his view that virtues have a social role and are meant to be sought in common and promoted by sensible legislation. (iii) Moreover, courageous action and cowardliness are *evident,* and typically the inference from an action to the agent's purpose in these cases is reliable and quite direct. Both the hero and the coward stand out fairly markedly on the battlefield; indeed, a battle is a kind of test of courage. Courage therefore displays well the connections among wish, deliberation, and action that Aristotle had discussed in 3.1–5.[6] In contrast, there are few clear tests of other virtues. It would be difficult, for instance, to draw inferences about an agent's generosity from some particular use of money by him. (iv) Again, courage is the virtue which probably best conforms to Aristotle's general account of character-related virtue in 2.1. The process by which someone may be given "training" to act courageously is obvious and familiar: in a military training camp officers require recruits, probably against their wishes, to do the sorts of things that courageous persons would do easily in various circumstances. As recruits advance in the program, what they are required to do more closely approximates action under "battle

---

[6] There are relatively few cases of only "apparent" courage, which Aristotle takes pains to identify and distinguish in 3.8. We should imagine, I think, that Aristotle regards "apparent" displays of other virtues as too numerous and varied to tabulate.

conditions." The desired result of such training is that a recruit have a settled disposition to carry out actions that fall between extremes (not charging recklessly and not running away), and that he have a character or outlook that falls between extremes (not tending to panic but also not being too relaxed). All of this tends to confirm Aristotle's general observations about character-related virtue.[7]

Aristotle begins his discussion of courage by defining the virtue narrowly: courage involves doing what is intermediate in circumstances in which death is near at hand in battle, and when dying would be *kalon* (here especially the term means "glorious" or "heroic").

As a preliminary, take note that courage for Aristotle is not a matter of *not feeling fear* but rather of feeling the right amount of fear and of doing what one should, given that one feels appropriate fear. Presumably, the right amount (and we can speak of a "right amount," Aristotle thinks, only when someone has to face fearful things that match our human scale, not such things as earthquakes and tidal waves, which we cannot be expected to deal with in a controlled way) is just enough fear to motivate vigorous and aggressive action, but not too much to hinder rational control of that action. For example, you are fearful enough to "fight for your life," with skilled swordplay, but you are not so fearful that you panic and "forget" the skills you were trained in, or make foolish mistakes because you "overreact." Aristotle considers, moreover, that feelings of boldness as well as fear are relevant to courageous action. Courageous action typically involves our *approaching* a danger, warily. We have "fight or flight" impulses, but to fight means actively to engage and "take on" the danger, and nature has given us emotions to assist in this. These "feelings of confidence" must be strong enough to stimulate a prompt action, but not so strong as to inspire

---

[7] As mentioned above (see chapter 1, note 15), Aristotle regards males as the best examples of human nature and male virtue, therefore, as the best example of virtue. Courage in Greek is *andreia*, literally "manliness." The word itself might therefore be taken to suggest – it surely had this connotation for many of Aristotle's contemporaries – that courage is the distinctive virtue of males and therefore the best virtue of the best sort of human being. So a first task of Aristotle (one sees this also in Plato's *Laws*) is to dethrone courage from this position of prominence. Aristotle's account aims to do so by putting courage in its proper place as important, but ancillary.

headlong, ill-considered rushes at the enemy with a view to "getting it over with" because you "can't take it any longer."

Aristotle's definition might strike us as unreasonably narrow. It seems to overlook or rule out the myriad expressions of courage which are shown in ordinary life, or in circumstances less extreme than battle: for instance, a homeowner needs to investigate a strange noise at night, to confirm that it is not a burglar; or someone needs to dispatch a wasp that has entered the room. Neither situation approaches hand-to-hand combat in war. Moreover, one might wonder how someone might expect that courage should be generally acquired, if its manifestation were so narrow. If, as Aristotle claims, the very sorts of actions with which we acquire a virtue are those by which it is manifested, and courage is shown only in battle-type circumstances, then presumably those sorts of circumstances are the only ones in which it can be acquired. Thus, no one who had not served in the armed forces could be accounted courageous. Even worse: no one could acquire courage *before* fighting in battle.

But these difficulties can be largely addressed, it seems, by placing suitable emphasis on Aristotle's notion of virtue as involving an intermediate that is *relative to us*. That qualification is naturally taken to imply a dynamic and flexible standard of correct action. It is dynamic when we are considering someone still acquiring a virtue, as an analogy from athletic training illustrates. Suppose someone – call him "Vance" – wants to become a skilled cyclist. Suppose also that he counts the Tour de France as representing the very pinnacle of cycling skill. Clearly it would not be advisable, or practicable, when Vance has just taken up cycling, for him to attempt to ride a race like the Tour de France – that would be far too much for him. Nor would it be sensible for him to attempt simply half of the race (the inter-mediate amount *as judged by the thing itself*). Rather, he should take racing in the Tour de France as his ideal; fix some time at which he would like to achieve it ("I'd like to qualify for the Tour de France three years from now"); and then plan a training regimen which, if followed successfully, might reasonably be expected to take him from where he was now, to achieving his goal in the set time. Count that regimen (which undoubtedly would need regular adjustments) as marking "the intermediate amount relative to him." At each point along the way he could over-train out of impatience or excessive eagerness, or he might under-train out of discouragement, despondency, or laziness. Yet what the regimen required would, of course, be changing dynamically over time, since the better Vance became at cycling, the more the regimen would demand of him.

Similarly, we should understand the notion of an "intermediate amount relative to us" as implying in typical cases a kind of path leading from someone's present position to an ideal goal. Such a path could not be traced unless some ideal were first set down, and the role of Aristotle's apparently narrow definition of courage would be to set down such an ideal. When Aristotle claims, then, that courage is a state that finds the intermediate mark between two extremes in heroic, mortal situations in battle, he is not attempting to give a formula which is satisfied by all and only courageous actions so much as delineating the extreme or maximal instance of the trait, which is what anyone who was striving to attain the virtue would aim at. This goal then becomes that with respect to which anything is properly judged courageous or not: roughly, when someone is aiming to acquire the virtue, his action counts as courageous if it is the sort of thing that he would do in those circumstances, if he were on a path taking him to the ideal of courage. Thus, whenever someone does something in circumstances where fear and boldness come into play, he is potentially performing a courageous sort of action: it is so, if it is the sort of action that would be taken by him if he were on the path to displaying courage in the ideal sense.[8]

Yet we might still wonder why Aristotle settles upon "heroic action in mortal danger on the field of combat" as the ideal goal for that virtue. Is it not arbitrary to take that as a goal that pertains to every human being? Why should not courage be defined relative to something more common, or which is a part of ordinary life? Aristotle does not explicitly address this point, but two answers would be available to him, one internal to our practices of aiming to be courageous, and the other external.

The internal answer concerns our practices of praising and blaming, and the manner in which we speak. As a matter of fact, we liken

---

[8] And for someone who has reached maturity and would be expected to have acquired the virtue already: then whether his action was courageous or not would depend, rather, upon whether it was the sort of action that someone with courage would do in those circumstances.

other sorts of courageous behavior to the case of heroic action in battle, but we do not do the converse, and this suggests that the latter is central and primary. Consider, for instance, a cancer patient who has to undergo a painful course of chemotherapy: let us say that he is half-way through a course of treatment which requires that he take an unpleasant drug once a week for six weeks. It would be natural to exhort him, "Be brave. There are only three more doses to go – just three more battles. You've come out the victor every time before. You'll beat this enemy." But suppose now that a general wants to exhort his troops. They have captured three key positions and need to capture only three more in order to finish the war. It would be absurd for him to say, "Soldiers, be brave. There are only three more battles to go – just three more 'doses' of chemotherapy, as it were. Be like those patients who stand firm in the hospital. You'll prevail over this 'illness'." That the one series of metaphors makes sense and the other does not indicates that we take heroism in battle to be the more fundamental thing.

But an "external" account could be proffered as well, with regard to the fact that (for Aristotle) human beings are intended by nature to live in city-states, and yet not all of us can live in the same city-state. A city-state may be understood as a society which aims to make the ordinary life of its citizens as free as possible from danger. Typically cities are not founded in locations which are threatened by danger,[9] and one of the first purposes of government is to remove dangerous risks from civic life: gaping holes in the road are repaired; wild beasts on the loose are captured; and so on. Life in a city-state is structured and designed in such a way that threats to life and limb are removed.

However, a city-state, Aristotle thinks, is naturally meant to be relatively small, only a couple of hundred thousand or so, so that its citizens can associate as familiars (*Politics* 1326b8–26). Thus it is inevitable that the bulk of human kind will live in city-states other than one's own. Any other city-state besides one's own, however, is potentially a competitor and aggressor. Thus the only danger that, in the typical course of things, is not in principle controllable by civic government, will be attacks from other city-states.

---

[9] It is considered something that needs special explanation when they are; for instance, "Why in the world would they have built this city on a major fault line for earthquakes?"

Given this context, we can give an interpretation of the priority that action in battle enjoys in our notion of courage. We observe that we are provided by nature with feelings of fear and confidence to deal with danger. We can infer that we are so provided in order to deal especially with the sort of danger in particular that remains as a threat to someone living as a citizen, namely the danger that comes from the attack of those outside one's own city-state. Thus the relevant virtue, which enables us to carry out this work well, will be that trait which enables us to act correctly in defending against such attacks – which is courage.

If this is a correct reconstruction of the purpose of courage, then this reconstruction provides the "order" in which an act of courage fits. And this would explain why, for Aristotle, courage seems to be principally manifested in actions which are *kalon*, because they are appropriately described as actions by which someone "gives" or "gives up" his life (cf. 9.8.1169a19–20). Recall that Socrates in the *Alcibiades* praises courage precisely as a trait which leads people to rescue their friends and relatives; consider also that courage in battle usually takes the form of fighting *for* one's comrades. But in cases of danger besides battle, either this notion does not apply, or it applies less well. Suppose, for instance, that a mountain climber dies while attempting a very dangerous ascent along a previously unconquered ridge of a mountain: there was something admirable and noble about his efforts; yet it makes little sense to say that "in dying he gave up his life for ___" (although people might try later to console themselves for his death with language like that: "he gave himself up for mountain-eering"). Again, the cancer patient who faces chemotherapy heroi-cally is not, for all that, in any obvious sense "giving up his life" for others in doing so.

According to Aristotle, as we saw above, the fact that a courageous action is *kalon* has to be the reason why one chooses to perform it. Suppose, then, we take heroic risk of one's life for one's friends and city-state to be what is *kalon* about a courageous action. Yet one might wonder what precisely the motive is supposed to be. Let us take a concrete case to fix ideas. A commander sends some men on a dangerous combat mission to destroy a bridge. The bridge is a vitally important military objective, but it is heavily guarded, so it is quite unlikely that it could be destroyed without substantial loss of life.

Now how should we describe the aim of a courageous soldier on such a mission? Is it (i) to destroy the bridge; (ii) simply to execute his commander's orders (which might involve at some point giving up on destroying the bridge and heading back); (iii) to *risk* his life to do either of the preceding; or (iv) to distinguish himself in heroism by *giving up* his life, if necessary, to achieve these things?[10]

The difficulty is not unimportant, because Aristotle thinks that the aim for which a courageous act is properly done sets it apart from other, spurious forms of courage. Aristotle distinguishes five spurious forms in 3.8: (1) civic courage; (2) experience in battle (or being "battle-hardened," as we would say); (3) pugnacity; (4) sanguinity; and (5) simple ignorance. Each of these conditions leads in some circumstances to actions that are characteristic of courage. But no one in any of these conditions acts from the motives that are distinctive of courage; and this deficiency will typically become apparent over time. Thus, most obviously, a soldier who is merely ignorant of the dangers of a situation will move boldly forward, as if he had courage. (How many of the men who charged boldly out of the landing vehicles at Normandy would not have been able to do so if they had vividly realized then what they were later to encounter?) A sanguine soldier, in desperation rather than from realism, tries to see everything optimistically; but when such an attitude is no longer tenable, even for him, he panics and flees. The civic-minded soldier is perhaps the closest to a truly courageous person. Since he recognizes what actions are regarded as courageous, and he tries to carry them out – not for the reason that they are courageous, and *kalon*, but for the reason that he will be treated with contempt by his peers if he does otherwise – his actions will resemble those of a courageous person almost exactly.

---

[10] We should perhaps use actual evidence about courage to decide such questions. For instance, General Patton's famous speech to soldiers newly arrived at the Normandy front cites three aims of courageous action: "Men, this stuff that some sources sling around about America wanting out of this war, not wanting to fight, is a crock of bulls–t. Americans love to fight, traditionally. All real Americans love the sting and clash of battle. You are here today for three reasons. First, because you are here to defend your homes and your loved ones. Second, you are here for your own self-respect, because you would not want to be anywhere else. Third, you are here because you are real men and all real men like to fight. When you, here, everyone of you, were kids, you all admired the champion marble player, the fastest runner, the toughest boxer, the big league ball players, and the All-American football players. Americans love a winner. Americans will not tolerate a loser. Americans despise cowards. Americans play to win all of the time."

The one case in which they might come apart would be when he is entirely confident that no one will find out how he behaves.

Aristotle concludes his discussion of courage with remarks about the pleasures of courage, which respond to an implied difficulty. In 2.3, as we saw, Aristotle claims that our likes and dislikes are indications of whether we have acquired a virtue or not: someone has a virtue if he enjoys performing the sorts of actions that are characteristic of that virtue. But it seems ridiculous to say that courageous actions are enjoyable, especially as regards the central case of courage – heroic action in battle – because a battle is a scene of death, mayhem, destruction, and much suffering. Who could enjoy that?[11] To reply to the difficulty, Aristotle concedes that courage always brings some pain with it, since fearful things are painful, and courage primarily involves standing firm when confronted by fearful things. But insofar as someone does what is courageous in spite of the pain, he achieves his goal, and this is something he likes and enjoys. That he enjoys his action in this respect can be missed precisely because of the pain that surrounds it. The passage, not unlike Socrates' point about courage in the *Alcibiades*, shows that Aristotle is committed to a theory of action that enables him to distinguish the kind of action that the agent *performs* from what *happens to him* in performing an action of that kind.

SELF-MASTERY

As I have said, Aristotle turns from courage to discussing self-mastery, remarking, "After courage let us discuss self-mastery, since these are regarded as the virtues of the non-rational parts of the soul" (1117b23–24). The remark seems to be in deference to Plato, but the fact that Aristotle so defers seems to indicate that he recognizes some truth in Plato's account of the human soul. Aristotle apparently picks out felt desire (*epithumia*) and spiritedness or vigor (*thumos*, involving both feelings of fear and feelings of boldness) as especially important motives pertaining to the non-rational part of the soul, and he thinks that these motives in particular have virtues correlated with them in some distinctive way.

[11] Notwithstanding Patton's "All real Americans love the sting and clash of battle."

He gives no explicit reason for his view, but two reasons suggest themselves naturally. First, some non-rational motives seem so persistent and strong, and their objects so definite, that we might seem to need habits of deliberation and willing that in some direct sense inform and constrain these motives. Felt desire, and feelings of fear and boldness, seem to be like that. In contrast, other non-rational motives are relatively transient, less persistent and forceful, more fluid in their objects, and capable of reinforcing and complementing one another in various ways: as regards all of these, it makes better sense to regard the relevant virtues as simply governing types of *action* – say, how we use money, or the way in which we strive for honor and distinction.

Second, it is a mark of both fear and the desire for sense pleasure that these impulses, if not controlled, unsettle someone's reason; but apparently not quite the same thing can be said of any other motive. Courage and self-mastery would deserve a special title as "virtues of the non-rational part," then, in the sense that they keep certain non-rational motives from entirely *subverting* reason (see 3.12.1119b7–18 and 6.5.1140b12).

"Self-mastery" renders the Greek word *sōphrosunē*. Although *sōphrosunē*, along with courage, justice, and prudence, is classically regarded as one of the four "cardinal virtues" – called such because classically regarded as those virtues on which all others hinged ("cardinal" is from *cardo*, Latin for "hinge") – there remains no good word in English for this trait, as classically understood.[12] *Sōphrosunē* connotes sobriety and chasteness; a certain humility; a tranquility, ease and serenity that comes of self-possession. Consider the way we describe the transition that someone undergoes, as he recovers from a fit of drunkenness: we say that such a person has "sobered up," "come to his senses," "become himself once again," "realizes what he is about," or is "once more of sound mind." The term *sōphrosunē* similarly suggests a certain clarity and self-possession in reason, which a person maintains even while enjoying the satisfaction of bodily appetites. "Moderation" is inadequate as a translation, because *sōphrosunē* can take the form, for instance, of hearty and

---

[12] Plato frequently lists these four virtues together and gives them special importance, although the term "cardinal virtue" seems to have originated with St. Ambrose of Milan (AD 340–397).

vigorous revelry amidst friends at a celebration – not immoderate behavior, to be sure, but also not the sort of thing we would naturally describe as "moderate." Likewise an extremely passionate but chaste lover could display *sōphrosunē*. Moreover, "moderation" misses the suggestions of self-reflection that the Greek term carries with it (which is why in Plato's dialogue, *Charmides*, the interlocutors so naturally take the virtue to be some kind of self-knowledge).

The term is sometimes rendered "temperance" or "self-control." But "temperance" is no longer an ordinary English word, and if it suggests anything definite, it means the resolve of not drinking alcohol. "Self-control" is misleading, because the term wrongly suggests a division in the agent: he wants something, but he controls himself and abstains from it. But, on Aristotle's view, *sōphrosunē*, although it can be displayed in this way, is most characteristically shown in someone who is entirely at ease in not taking or even wanting to enjoy some pleasure that it would be unreasonable for him to enjoy. For Aristotle it is a mark of the corresponding *vice* to be distressed at not enjoying illicit pleasure when one abstains from it, whereas the activity of *sōphrosunē* has no pains associated with it (1117b26–27). "Self-mastery" perhaps avoids these problems, since it can be taken to suggest someone who is completely at ease in what he does.

The Greek word for the principal corresponding vice, *akolasia*, is also difficult to translate. The word means, literally, "the condition of being undisciplined"; in effect, being spoiled. The usual translation is "self-indulgent", which, once again and unfortunately, carries with it the suggestions of a division in the agent, with part of him being indulged, and another part of him doing the indulging. But although the condition, as Aristotle sees it, typically arises by our doing actions that are "self indulgent" in this sense, once the condition has formed, however, there is no longer any part of the agent which does anything like indulging. Someone with *akolasia* is generally oblivious as to the immeasured character of his wants. As an instance of the phenomenon noted by Aristotle in 2.8, he will conflate the true intermediate condition with the extreme that is opposite to himself: he takes his own actions to be acceptable and regards a person with self-mastery as someone who fails to enjoy pleasure as he should (cf. 3.12.1119a33–b7). However, despite these shortcomings, I shall use the term "self-indulgent" for lack of a better alternative.

As he did with courage, Aristotle examines self-mastery by getting clearer about its scope and central case. It is concerned with pleasures, but not all of them. To establish that there are some sorts of pleasure that are irrelevant to the virtue, Aristotle can rely on his Greek readers' sense of the proper usage of the terms *sōphrosunē* and *akolasia*. We have no such guide and need to think instead, for instance, of those circumstances in which it would make sense to say such things as "He's really lost his head over that," "That pleasure has made him quite insensible," "There's really nothing that can explain what he's doing except the pleasure," or "That shows a wanton desire for pleasure, nothing more." It is clear that there are some pleasures for which it would be ridiculous to claim any such thing. One would not say, for instance, of someone who carried on with an interesting conversation much too long and missed an appointment as a result, that "He showed a wanton desire for the pleasure of that discussion" or "The pleasure of it befuddled him."

Aristotle makes a crucial distinction between "pleasures distinctive of the soul" (or "psychical pleasures") and "pleasures distinctive of the body" ("somatic pleasures").[13] The former, he says, involve our undergoing some change in the mind, not in the body (1117b30). He perhaps takes the distinction to have been introduced already implicitly, by his treatment of the pleasure of courage: whatever pleasure someone feels when acting courageously, as he is being hacked down by an enemy's sword, seems not to be a distinctively bodily pleasure. But Aristotle seems uninterested in explaining the distinction and mentions pleasures distinctive of the soul simply to put them aside: self-mastery and self-indulgence clearly have something to do with pleasure that we take in the functioning and operation of the body.

But they do not deal with all bodily functions and operations, nor with some of them in every respect. Again, relying on a Greek speaker's sense of what it would be appropriate to say, Aristotle notes that, even though there is excess, deficiency, and an appropriate, intermediate way of pursuing the pleasures that come from

---

[13] This distinction perhaps corresponds to the two treatments of pleasure that are found later in the *Ethics*, the former class being the primary concern in the book 10 discussion, and the latter in the book 7 discussion. But see chapter 10 below.

looking at works of art, or listening to music, we do not use the term "self-mastery" to pick out the intermediate enjoyment in these cases. (One might, rather, say such things as, "Art (or music) plays an important role in his life," and describe the extreme as a "fanaticism" or "obsession," and the deficiency as "being uncultured" or "lacking good taste.")

In fact, Aristotle claims, when one attends carefully to the usage of the words, one sees that the point of "*sōphrosunē*" and "*akolasia*" is to pick out a virtue and a vice that deal specifically with bodily pleasures of the sort that we share with animals. Animals do not find any pleasure in the formal aspects of sights, sounds, and scents: Pavlov's dogs might have been conditioned to salivate upon hearing not a bell but rather the opening bars of Beethoven's Fifth, but they would not, for all that, have been taught to enjoy classical music. The only senses they find pleasure in are touch and taste, but not formal aspects of taste, or *flavors* (leftover gourmet cooking goes unappreciated by your pet), and not formal aspects of touch, such as *textures* or *patterns* (Fido will never care enough about raised dots to be trained to recognize Braille). In short, Aristotle thinks, "self-mastery" deals with pleasures of the sort we might refer to as "brutish" or "animal-istic" when they are sought apart from any concern about appropri-ateness or rightness. For pleasures of this sort, there is nothing *kalon* about *what* one is taking pleasure in. These pleasures are principally feelings of comfort and satisfaction involving the sense of touch, and especially those involving consumption and the sex organs.

Yet to say that self-mastery deals with pleasures of consumption and sex still does not quite get it right. Distinguish, Aristotle says, "common" from "private" appetites. A common appetite is shared among all human beings: for instance, it is common to all of us to require three meals a day or the equivalent. Eating about three meals a day suffices to bring about a satisfaction of the appetite for food for nearly everyone.[14] So it is not correct to say, simply, that people are self-indulgent by going to excess as regards the pleasures that come *from consuming food.* Rather, one should say that self-mastery is

---

[14] Certainly, Aristotle concedes, there are a few people who seem to care simply about having an excessively large *bulk* of food, but this is unusual and does not get at the distinctive character of self-indulgence.

concerned with how we handle our "private" appetites, some preference or fancy which a particular person has and pursues: for
instance, someone especially likes chocolate, and thus too large a
proportion of his daily consumption of food comes to consist of
chocolate – and perhaps, *then*, as a consequence he takes in *too much*
food.[15] As regards these pleasures that come from private appetites,
Aristotle says, "most people go astray, and in many different ways"
(1118b22), and then he gives the usual list of particulars: they "like
things they should not, or they like them more than most people do,
or they like them not in the way that they should."

In fact, a self-indulgent person will tend to go astray in all of these
dimensions. The reason, Aristotle thinks, is that pleasure in eating
should be sought as a kind of side-effect of doing what is healthful
and sensible. Someone with the virtue of self-mastery, when he is
eating, aims to do "what contributes to health, or to good condition,"
and he seeks only the pleasures that are side-effects of these things,
and pleasures that come from activities that are not incompatible
with health or good condition, subject to the provision that these
things are not themselves hateful (1118b25), or beyond his means, or
contrary to what is *kalon* (1119a18). In doing so, he is only acting
sensibly (as "sound reason," *orthos logos*, indicates) (1119a20). A self-
indulgent person, in contrast, seeks the pleasure of these bodily
functions directly, not as a side-effect subject to the above-mentioned
constraints; consequently, he prefers it to the goods that come from
those constraints. Since he prefers the pleasure available in bodily
functions over attaining the *kalon* (or avoiding the *aischron*) in such
things, he easily goes to excess in each of the various particulars
involving pleasures of food and sex. This also explains why a self-
indulgent person is distressed when he is required to observe those
constraints, or it is otherwise impossible to obtain that sort of
pleasure (1119a1–5). In contrast, as I said, a person with self-mastery,
because he is not aiming at the pleasure directly, feels no such distress
when he abstains: there is nothing he wants that he fails to gain, when

---

[15] It is because self-indulgence arises as regards private appetites that the opposite vice, of
pursuing such things deficiently, is extremely rare. All that is required, for self-indulgence to
be a possibility, is that a person like some things especially more than others, since he can
then go astray by assigning a disproportionate place to these. But "even the animals make
discriminations in their food, liking some things but disliking others," 1119a7–10.

he acts as good sense indicates. "A person with self-mastery is characterized by *not* being upset by the absence of pleasure, or when he needs to refrain from pleasure" (1118b32–33).

Near the close of his discussion of self-mastery, Aristotle draws an astute comparison between that virtue and courage, which sheds some light on his subtle notion of acting "of one's own accord," which, as we saw, is introduced in 3.1. Suppose Curt is a coward, and Sal is self-indulgent. Aristotle claims, in effect, that (i) "Curt has made himself a coward of his own accord" is less appropriate than "Sal has become self-indulgent of his own accord," and also that (ii) "Curt dislikes the fact that he is a coward" is likely to be less appropriate than "Sal dislikes the fact that he is self-indulgent." Aristotle takes these truths to confirm both his view that conditions of character arise from corresponding acts, and his construal of what it is to act "of one's own accord". (i) holds because actions that produce the condition of cowardice are less the sort of thing that someone does "of one's own accord" than actions that produce the condition of self-indulgence. It is less easy to blame someone for not having acquired the virtue of courage, since opportunities for practicing it are less common; moreover, everyone wants to avoid the pain that is involved, and extreme danger tends to produce extreme distress, which is actually debilitating. But the opposite is true of self-mastery: ordinary life contains many circumstances in which to acquire it; and there is no debilitating distress involved in any of its characteristic activities. Yet, on the other hand, a coward is more likely to be complacent about his bad condition, because it is not something painful to him (and, insofar as he is a coward, he aims precisely to avoid suffering), but a self-indulgent person, in contrast, finds his own condition unpleasant: "no one wants (*epithumei*) to be self-indulgent" (1119a33).

GENEROSITY

Courage and self-mastery, as we have seen, involve persistent, natural motives, which are roughly concerned with goods involving the welfare of the body: protection from harm and maintenance of life. It makes sense that Aristotle would turn next to virtues that are concerned with property and its use, another fundamental constant of human existence. Aristotle in fact recognizes three virtues of character involving how we use our property (defined as "everything the worth of which can be measured by money," 1119b26–27): justice, generosity, and magnificence. Justice deals with property as it enters into definite exchanges and, as I said, is discussed in a separate treatise (book 5). Justice deals with the use of one's property, but it is not limited to this, because some just acts involve, rather, decisions about how the property of others is to be distributed or taken away. Magnificence (sometimes called "munificence") involves large-scale expenditures of a certain sort. Generosity ("liberality," "open-handedness") is the standard or typical virtue governing the use of possessions. Aristotle seems to regard it as the virtue by which someone expresses his view as to the point or purpose of having possessions at all.

Regarding this last virtue, once again, there are difficulties in translation. The relevant Greek term is *eleutheriotēs*, which means literally "being in a free condition," that is, in the condition characteristic of a free citizen, as opposed to a slave. This contrast is the clue to Aristotle's governing insight. *Eleutheriotēs* is the virtue by which someone is not, as we would say, "bound" or "tied down" by concerns about his possessions; it is meant to be a posture by which someone "rises above" his possessions, and, with a certain lack of concern, puts them to good use, in order to achieve admirable goals. It protects a person from being "driven" by his possessions or beholden to them. *Eleutheriotēs* keeps useful goods in place as subordinate to things that are *kalon*. To translate this as "generosity" is not entirely apt, because "generosity" carries the suggestion, perhaps, of "giving more than what would be expected," which is not essential to the virtue; "open-handedness," on the other hand, suggests indiscriminate giving; and although "liberality" gets at the correct fundamental notion, it is now an old-fashioned word. So "generosity" seems the least objectionable choice.[16]

Aristotle takes generosity to be concerned both with how we use possessions (both by spending and by giving them away), and with

---

[16] Of course, these and other issues in translation, persistent as they are, eventually raise the question: why exactly do we lack straightforward analogues to so many important Aristotelian ethical terms?

how we obtain them – appropriately enough, because a person can be "in servitude" or "overly dependent" with respect to the inflow as well as the outflow of wealth. Such a person spends or gives for the sake of those he should, as he should, when he should, and so on; and he acquires wealth only from the right sources, to the proper extent, at the appropriate time, and so on. The vice of excess is "wastefulness" ("profligacy," "prodigality"); the vice of deficiency is "avaricious-ness." There are many species of the latter, and Aristotle goes into much detail: the miser, the skinflint, the niggardly person, and so on (1121b17–1122a13). We can imagine these vices as manifested both in characteristic actions (skulking away from the group when it comes time to pay the bar tab; impulse buying) and typical outlooks or "frames of mind" (constant worry about your portfolio value; being cheerful only when you are considering buying something).

Although generosity is concerned with the use of money generally, and thus with both inflow and outflow, Aristotle is at pains to establish that "conferring one's money on the right persons is more characteristic of a generous person than receiving it from the right sources or not taking it from inappropriate sources" (1120a9–11). In fact he gives seven arguments for this claim (1120a8–23). It is instructive to take note of these:

1. Generosity is related to the use of money, but how we *receive* or *take in* money involves rather its possession and conservation than its use.

2. It is more characteristic of virtue generally for you to *do* something well, than to have something *done to you* well, but spending and giving are more like doing, whereas receiving and taking in are more like having something done to you (cf. 9.7.1168a19–20).

3. Actions that attain the *kalon* are, in general, more characteristic of virtue than those that merely avoid something *aischron*; but spending and giving correctly are a matter of achieving something *kalon*, whereas receiving money correctly is largely a matter of avoiding things that are *aischron*.

4. We may take people's tendency to allot praise or show gratitude as a good mark of virtue, but no one pays much attention to a person who refuses to acquire money in shady ways, whereas everyone praises and thanks a person who gives and spends his money well.

5. It is more difficult to part with something that has belonged to you than not to acquire something that has so far not belonged to you; thus, it is more difficult to spend and give money correctly than to acquire it correctly; yet it is distinctive of a virtue to accomplish what is difficult.

6. In fact, if we look at how "generous" is used as a term of praise, people get praised for being "generous" on account of how they spend and give money, whereas someone who refuses money from a bad source is praised for being "just," if anything, and no one is praised at all for taking in money only from appropriate sources.

7. We characteristically show love in response to perceived virtue, and we think that nearly the most loveable of all virtuous traits is generosity, but by this we mean, more precisely, the good way in which someone gives and spends money, not the way he acquires his money; that which we love most, then, is more characteristic of the virtue (cf. 9.7.1168a20–21).

It is useful to look at this repertoire of arguments for two reasons. First, the arguments are an excellent example of how Aristotle is examining the various virtues always *for a purpose.* There is a dialectic implicit in his examination of generosity and of the other virtues, consonant with the goal of the *Ethics.* Aristotle's general procedure is to isolate the features of a particular virtue that make it valuable, and then to look for that single virtue which most exemplifies these features. For instance, if generosity consists more in giving, which is active, and less in receiving, which is passive, and if it is especially valuable precisely insofar as it involves giving, then is there a virtue which in some analogous way is the most "active" and least "passive"?[17]

Secondly, the passage gives a valuable glimpse into the *nature* of moral reasoning, as Aristotle conceives it. He clearly regards moral reasoning as essentially diverse. Such reasoning is not a matter of applying a uniform calculus, and, rather than appealing to some single rule, it makes use of a variety of principles, including:

---

[17] In fact, the general argument of the *Ethics* seems to be that the activity of the virtue of philosophical wisdom contains in the fullest degree what makes other types of virtuous actions valuable.

 (i) Analogues in ethics of general principles from physics and metaphysics: for instance, that the utilization (*chrēsis*) of money must consist more in a doing (*poiein*) than in a being done (*paschein*). This is an analogue in ethics of the metaphysical truth that, in an activity, the passion is derivative upon the action (cf. *Euthyphro* 10a–c).

 (ii) Principles involving the general notion of a virtue: for instance, that since there are many ways in which something can go astray, the way which counts as "good" is in a sense unique, and thus difficult to attain (cf. 2.6.1106b9–12).

(iii) Principles involving human moral psychology, broadly construed: for instance, that we tend to love what we regard as good, and thus that we can use a reaction like that, properly interpreted, as a kind of measure of the virtue manifested in an action (cf. *Rhetoric* 2.4).[18]

Aristotle's treatment of generosity is throughout filled with keen insight into human character. He tells us, for instance, that it is not easy for a truly generous person to be wealthy, since he is so keen on conferring gifts upon others (1120b14–17); or that we can judge whether we in fact have the virtue, by our reactions of satisfaction or distress, since if we are distressed when we spend or give our money, it shows that, to that extent, we prefer our money to the *kalon* we could acquire through spending (1120a29–31); or that, of the two corresponding vices, wastefulness is easier to cure than avariciousness, since it tends to be self-correcting (1121a20–25). Once again, Aristotle would take the practical implications of his theory to be a partial confirmation of its truth.

MAGNIFICENCE AND MAGNANIMITY

There are two virtues that Aristotle sets apart for separate treatment because, he tells us, they involve great matters. "Magnificence"

---

[18] None of Aristotle's arguments 1–7 would naturally occur to us today. Hence part of the task of understanding Aristotelian ethical theory, for us, must be to recognize and recover a familiarity with such principles, and to acquire an intuitive ease in employing them, so that we become practiced in similarly accounting for our moral experience. To understand Aristotle's approach to ethics, it is not sufficient merely to articulate his doctrines, since generally the content of a doctrine is inseparable from its manner of justification.

(or "munificence," *megaloprepeia*, literally "tastefulness on a grand scale") is related to the use of money, as is generosity, but to expenditures solely, and only those that are "great." "Magnanimity" ("highmindedness" or "great-heartedness," *megalopsucheia*, literally "greatness of soul") is related to our attitude toward great honors. (In 4.4 Aristotle recognizes an unnamed virtue as concerned with ordinary honors, analogous to generosity in the realm of money, but I shall not discuss it here. We may think of it as "reasonable ambition.")

It is sometimes held that Aristotle thinks that these are aristocratic virtues, which can be possessed only by very wealthy or especially privileged persons; and it is thought that, besides perhaps being repugnant in itself, his view poses a problem for the thesis of the Unity of Virtue – since clearly we can imagine someone who had only average wealth and status, and who had all of the rest of the virtues, but who lacked these virtues involving greatness. But this seems not to be Aristotle's view, because he will argue later, in book 10, that happiness and the practice of virtue do not require large amounts of wealth or great influence:

> Just because it's not possible to be happy without external goods, one should not think that, for someone to be happy, he will need many things, and great things (*megalōn*). Neither the requisite self-sufficiency nor the required action consists in some kind of extreme: it's possible well enough to carry out *kalon* actions without ruling over land and sea. In fact, a person is quite capable of acting in a way that displays virtue with modest resources. That's easy enough to see: compare private individuals to people in power, and the former seem not to do fewer exemplary actions, but rather more of them. (1179a1–8; cf. a12–13)

As we shall see later (in chapter 11 below), this claim is one of his chief conclusions of the treatise. The passage would be bizarre if Aristotle actually held that some virtues did require great wealth and power.

Moreover, nowhere in his treatment of magnanimity does he claim that extreme wealth is necessary for it: he says, somewhat ambiguously, that goods of fortune can "make a separate contribution to magnanimity" (1124a21); and generally his view seems to be that wealthy people, and those who enjoy status and rank, tend *mistakenly* to think themselves great, and worthy of especial honor, on account of such things, with the result that they become puffed up and insolent (a26–30). In reality, he warns, only goodness of character deserves honor (a25, cf. 1123b19–20).

As for magnificence, Aristotle's view is not that a person needs to be rich to have it, but only that he cannot be poor, since then the disparity between the expenditure he attempts, and his means, would mar that very attempt (1122b26). In fact, Aristotle says, magnificence is displayed in such things as throwing a sumptuous wedding banquet, or setting up a household (1123a6–9) – expenditures that are within the reach of persons of average wealth – or even picking out an especially precious toy as a gift to a child (a14–16). Admittedly, for Aristotle the central case of magnificence is observed in grand expenditures to benefit the public or in service to the state, as carried out by people of vast resources and independent means. But we might similarly say that the best examples of philanthropy today are donations from the wealthy to opera houses or universities – without thereby denying that nearly everyone can practice philanthropy in some form or another.

Aristotle closes his discussion of magnanimity by giving what is sometimes called his "portrait" of a magnanimous man, 1124b7–1125a16. This "portrait" has come in for some serious criticism: a description of "a prig with the conceit and bad manners of a prig," as an Oxford don is alleged to have said.[19] But all or most of the apparent offensiveness of the portrait vanishes when we read it as accomplishing what Aristotle intends to show by it. Aristotle claims that magnanimity works so as to increase and refine the operation of the other virtues (1124a1–2). But how precisely does it do so? As Aristotle explains, someone who has magnanimity regards himself as worthy of honor, on account of his virtue. But this implies that he have a measured attitude toward external goods generally: he will not be especially concerned about honor as bestowed by competent judges on good grounds; he will not care at all about honors not linked to virtue (that is, most honors that are given out in society); dishonor will not affect him; and all other external goods, which he judges less valuable than honor, will likewise have little claim on him (1124a4–20).[20] At the same time,

---

[19] Hardie (1980), 119.
[20] He has an attitude of "contempt," Aristotle maintains – not for persons, but rather for those goods which, if he were attached to them, would hinder him from acting rightly.

precisely because such a person continues to aspire to true greatness, as he conceives it, he has an additional motive for performing *kalon* actions, namely, that they are exemplary. As a consequence, with respect to each of the virtues, a magnanimous person is both less attached to the goods that are given up through the practice of that virtue, and more greatly concerned to act in an exemplary way as regards that virtue.

Aristotle's famous "portrait" is meant to show this in detail. It runs through the various virtues and argues, in each case, that someone with the virtue of magnanimity will, for that reason, display that virtue to a greater degree and with greater refinement. Thus, for instance, a magnanimous person shows especial refinement in generosity, because he is quick to benefit others, without drawing attention to himself (b9–15). His sense of justice is magnified because he does not put himself forward for awards and distinctions (b23–24). Again, he easily forms friendships precisely because he does not care excessively about being loved, and he has traits that make him a good friend, such as a propensity to avoid gossip and slander (1125a1–8).

Courage deals with actions to protect life; self-mastery with actions to sustain it; generosity and magnificence deal with possessions; magnanimity with honor. Family and friends, or our life among them, constitute yet another external good of sorts, for Aristotle, and there are virtues too which govern this good: wittiness, amiability, and truthfulness. There are a few other incidental traits that Aristotle recognizes, which bring Aristotle's discussion of particular character-related virtues to a close – except for justice, which deals not with our own orientation to goods, but with those goods as they enter into our dealings with other persons, regarded as equals. To Aristotle's treatment of this virtue in book 5 we next turn.

FURTHER READING

The papers of Young (1977, 1988, 1994) on various particular virtues are recommended. Pears (1980) on courage raises some important difficulties. Magnanimity and whether it poses a problem for the Unity of Virtues in Aristotle may be examined via Irwin (1988b),

Gardiner (2001) and Pakaluk (2002). Curzer (1991a) gives an effective response to critics of Aristotle's treatment of magnanimity; see also Pakaluk (2004). The *locus classicus* for discussion of the virtues is, of course, Thomas Aquinas (1947), *Summa Theologiae*, II–IIae, qq. 47–170.

CHAPTER 6

Justice as a character-related virtue (Nicomachean Ethics, *book 5*)

THE PLATONIC CONTEXT

Aristotle's discussion of *justice*, which he regards as one among other character-related virtues, is quite different from a treatment of justice which one might find in John Stuart Mill or John Rawls. Aristotle devotes much labor, for instance, to defining justice as a "particular" rather than a "general" virtue. In order to appreciate why, we need (once again) to understand the Platonic context in which he is evidently writing.

Aristotle begins book 5 by remarking,

We observe, then, that everyone intends, in referring to "justice," to mean that condition of character which makes someone the sort of person who does just actions, and responds justly, and who likes to see justice done. In the same way, by "injustice" they mean that which makes someone the sort of person who acts unjustly and likes to see injustice done. Very well, then, for a start, let us adopt these as schematic definitions. (1129a6–11)

By the end of chapter 5 he has filled in those schemata, and he gives the following as his finished definitions:

Justice is that with respect to which a just person is said to be the sort of person who, of his own choice, does what is just, and who distributes goods, both to himself in his dealings with others, and to others in their relations to one another, not in such a way that he gets more of what is desirable, and his neighbor gets less (and contrariwise for harmful things), but rather in such a way that he gets an equal amount (that is, a proportionately equal amount), and, likewise, when he distributes goods to others, and he's not himself involved, he does so in such a way that the others each get an equal amount (again, a proportionately equal amount). And injustice is the opposite of this. (1134a1–7)

This filled in and relatively complex definition has five components. Justice is: (1) a distinct state of character; (2) involving deliberate purpose or choice; (3) dealing with distributable goods; (4) concerned with two sorts of distribution; (5) which distributions, when just, are marked by equality. We want to understand these five components, and why Aristotle regards them as important.

Once again, we need to begin with some remarks on language. The English word "justice" can mean: (i) a just state of affairs, that is, an arrangement or situation which is just ("let justice be done"; "with liberty and justice for all"); (ii) the intention with which an action is performed ("justice was served"); or (iii) the state of character, or virtue, which leads someone to aim at just states of affairs from a just intention ("The magistrate displayed exemplary justice – that is, he showed he was a just person – when he refused the bribe"). In Greek, there are separate words for each of these:

- *to dikaion* (pronounced *toh DICK-eye-on*): a just state of affairs
- *to dikein* (*toh dick-CANE*): acting justly, with a just intention
- *hē dikaiosunē* (*hay dick-eye-oh-SOON-ay*): the virtue of justice

Usually it is possible to mark these distinctions in English by suitable circumlocutions; or the context makes clear precisely which sense of "justice" is intended. So, for instance, Aristotle's elaborate definition of "justice" given above is clearly intended to be a definition of that state of character. But note that it defines the state of character by reference to equality as a mark of a just state of affairs, and also by reference to the correct intention of an agent in carrying out a just action. One might therefore say, somewhat perversely, that Aristotle's definition boils down to: "Justice is seeking justice with justice."

Aristotle begins to construct his definition by taking pains to clarify yet another ambiguity. We can get a sense of his concern if we consider that there are some terms of praise in English which, it seems, can be used generally, to praise any kind of good conduct, but which it seems can also be used especially to identify certain restricted types of good conduct. Consider, for instance, the term "proper." Any good action may be said to be proper, and someone who performs any sort of good action may be said to have acted properly: "It was proper for the soldier not to run away at that point" (courage);

"It would not be proper to claim honors beyond those you in fact deserve" (magnanimity); and so on. But the term has a special use when applied to financial transactions: "That was an improper distribution of funds," "The investment banker acted improperly (even: 'with impropriety') in not disclosing the conflict of interest." In the same way, the English word "just," used as a term of praise, can mean either "all round virtuous" or something like "honest in handling money."[1] So, then, if we wish to say that justice is yet another character-related virtue, do we wish to say that it is a state of character which helps one to be virtuous all round? Or do we wish to claim that it has a restricted field of operation, in the same way that self-mastery, according to Aristotle, deals only with pleasures of taste and touch?

The issue was murkier for Aristotle and his contemporaries than for us, because of Plato's important work on the subject. Aristotle thinks that Plato's work contains serious, yet subtle confusions; hence he painstakingly tries to clear these up. And it is because we do not approach the subject from within the same context that these efforts may seem to us belabored and in some respects unnecessary.

Call the character-related virtue which involves virtuous action all round "general justice"; call the character-related virtue which aims at a restricted type of good action "particular justice." In both the *Meno* and *Protagoras* Plato exploits what Aristotle would consider a confusion between general and particular justice, to advance his philosophical goals. In the *Meno* Socrates insists that before one attempts to determine whether or not virtue can be taught, one should try to define "virtue," on the grounds that only after we know what virtue *is*, can we determine whether it is the sort of thing that *can be taught*. So Meno proposes a definition of virtue: virtue, he says, should be defined as "the ability to rule" (73d). But Socrates quickly points out, and Meno agrees, that this definition fails to distinguish good behavior (ruling well) from bad. Hence Meno revises his definition and says that virtue is, rather, "the ability to rule *justly*." Socrates next asks Meno to name the various virtues, and Meno gives a list including self-mastery, philosophical wisdom, magnificence, and justice; at this point Socrates, naturally

---

[1] The former sense is rare nowadays although it is not uncommon in religious contexts: "Joseph was a just man" does not mean that Joseph's scales and balances were true, but rather that his conduct was generally upright.

enough, complains that Meno has defined virtue in terms of itself. He has taken one sort of virtue, justice, and defined all of virtue in terms of it, much the same as if someone were to define shape as "roundness" (74b). The refutation brings to an end Meno's attempts to define "virtue" and leads the way for Socrates to claim, later in the dialogue, that virtue is some sort of knowledge. But Aristotle would resist this conclusion and the way that the dialogue gets there: he would maintain that Meno's definition was basically sound, and that it could have escaped refutation if Meno had only distinguished between general justice and particular justice. Virtue in general (general justice) has justice (particular justice) as one of its parts.

In the *Protagoras*, the character Protagoras adopts a view of virtue not unlike Aristotle's: human virtue is a single thing which, however, has parts, in much the same way that a face is a single thing but has a mouth, nose, eyes, and ears as parts (329e). Each part of the whole of virtue, Protagoras insists (again, like Aristotle), is distinct from other parts and from the whole, because it has its own power and function (330a). But then Socrates, arguing against this, observes that some words indicating a particular virtue, such as "just," are such that they can be predicated of other types of virtuous action: we can say of any act of piety that it is *just* (331a), and in the same way also wisdom is just, and temperance is just, and so on. But, in contrast, we would not wish to predicate a term which we apply to one part of the face to some other part of the face: we do not say such things as "The eye is ear-like" or "The nose is mouth-like." But, Socrates argues, if this is so, then the different virtues are not related to one another as parts to a whole (331b). Socrates goes on to suggest, rather, that all of the putatively separate virtues are different aspects of one and the same thing. But here again Aristotle would want to resist both the conclusion and the argument leading to it. Aristotle would say that Protagoras could have avoided being refuted if he had made a distinction between "just" used in a general sense and "just" used in a particular sense. The latter alone indicates a particular virtue, and "just" when used in that special sense *cannot* be applied meaningfully to other virtues, whereas "just" used in a general sense *can* be so applied.[2]

---

[2] As we shall see, according to Aristotle, the reason why "just" can thus be used generally, is that it picks out a good action in a certain respect – insofar as it involves the agent's relation to a distinct other – and an action of *any* virtue can be regarded and referred to under this description.

But in book 5 Aristotle seems to be reacting above all to Plato's great dialogue on justice, the *Republic*, which traditionally carried with it the subtitle *Peri dikaiosunēs*, "On the Virtue of Justice." A brief word about this dialogue is therefore in order.

The *Republic* aims to show that the virtue of justice is inherently desirable, and it argues for this by developing an elaborate analogy between an ideal political society and the human soul. An ideal political society, Plato maintains, would contain a ruling class (the Guardians), a military class (the Auxiliaries), and a working class, which correspond to what (as we have seen) Plato regarded as the three parts of the human soul: reason (*logos*), spiritedness or vigor (*thumos*), and felt desire (*epithumia*). He thinks that by observing what makes such an ideal political society good, we will be able to see clearly what it is that makes a good human soul good. And if we can see *why* it is that something that makes the ideal political society good would be inherently desirable, then we can see *why* it is that the corresponding thing that makes a human soul good would be inherently desirable.

In the main part of his argument, which constitutes books 2–4 of the *Republic*, Plato assumes the doctrine of the four cardinal virtues and identifies the virtue of justice by a process of elimination. In the ideal political society, he argues, the ruling class arranges things well: this is the analogue of the virtue of *wisdom*, the good condition of the rational part of the soul. Similarly, the military class supports the decisions of the ruling class and fights off threats from without: this is the analogue of the virtue of *courage*, the good condition of the spirited part of the soul. Again, the working class labors at its business assiduously and does not claim anything beyond this: and that is the analogue of the virtue of *self-mastery*, the good condition of the appetitive part of the soul.

But what then of justice? There are four cardinal virtues, but only three naturally distinguished classes in an ideal political society (or so Plato thinks), and only three parts of the soul. Justice, he claims, involves the *arrangement* of the parts one to another, which explains why the virtue is so hard to discern and to recognize as valuable. That every part of society carry out its proper function, and that the lower parts obey the commands of the ruling class, Plato argues, simply *is* justice in the ideal political society; thus, similarly, that the parts of the soul keep their place and remain properly submissive to reason *is* the virtue of justice in an individual. Plato concludes his argument by pointing out that for the soul to exist is simply for it to have this order; hence the virtue of justice is desirable for the reason that one's own existence is – and clearly existence is inherently desirable, if anything is (443c–444e).[3]

This is a powerful and attractive argument. Nonetheless, one can see how, from Aristotle's point of view, the *Republic* might seem to involve a systematic confusion between justice as a particular virtue and justice as somehow encapsulating the entirety of virtue. Plato begins the dialogue, in book 1, by having his characters discuss what it means to be just in the modest and restricted domain of using money appropriately (331c–336d). However, as the dialogue proceeds, justice becomes something much grander: justice is now the correct ordering of the entire soul, implying all the virtues. Furthermore, the dialogue begins with the question of why a person should be just, in the sense of not seeking more than one's fair share in one's dealings *with others*, but it ends by giving an account of justice, which applies simply to a person *in relation to himself*, quite apart from his dealings with others. As a result of the analogy between political society and the individual, justice becomes a virtue that governs the relationship of a whole to its parts, or of parts of a thing to one another, whereas initially it seemed to be a virtue that governed the relation between distinct and independent individuals.

MARKING OUT JUSTICE AS A PARTICULAR VIRTUE OF CHARACTER

This is the context in which Aristotle wants to discuss what he thinks is a particular trait of character, on a par with all the various other virtues of character, which may appropriately be called "justice." His first step, then (in 5.1), is to mark out some other, broad sense of the term "justice," roughly corresponding to Plato's understanding of the virtue, and to explain that he is *not* going to be discussing that. To do this, he sets down three principles:

---

[3] And similarly someone who aims to become unjust therefore aims to subvert himself.

1. A state or condition of a thing (*hexis*), unlike a branch of knowledge, or a technical capacity, is typically productive of only one among opposites. For instance (to use modern examples): physics reaches conclusions about positive as well as negative electric charges; a civil engineer is the best person to hire both for building skyscrapers and for demolishing them. But the condition of health, of itself, is productive simply of health, not illness. Health leads to healthy signs, appearances, and actions. "We say that someone walks in a healthy way," Aristotle remarks, "when he walks in the way in which a healthy person walks" (1129a16–17), that is, the phrase "walks in a healthy way" would have no definite sense if health could lead to either of two opposite results.

2. Thus, we can identify a condition of a thing either by referring to the characteristic results of that condition (since these will be consistent), or by drawing a contrast with the opposite condition (since the effects of a condition will be consistently set apart from those of its opposite), if that is better known (1129a18).

3. Moreover, in cases where there are two or more distinct conditions, ambiguously designated by a single word, there will be the same number of distinct conditions opposed to these (perhaps, however, designated ambiguously by a single word indicating an opposite) (1129a23–25).

These principles would hold true of any of the virtues of character, but Aristotle articulates these principles now, especially in connection with justice, because they are useful given some peculiar features of justice.[4] As will be discussed below, Aristotle thinks that, unlike other virtues of character, justice has to be defined solely with regard to its characteristic effects, and in contrast to the characteristic effects of injustice. But this implies that we have to get at the trait or state (*hexis*) simply through its characteristic effects.

Principle 3 corresponds to a technique that Aristotle describes in his *Topics* for detecting ambiguity (106a9–621). Sometimes, he says, when it is difficult to recognize an ambiguity in a word, it is easy to spot the ambiguity that affects the corresponding opposites. For

---

[4] His argument at this point seems a self-conscious adaptation of an argument that Plato had employed to a nearly opposite effect, at *Protagoras* 332a–333a, as Aristotle aims to display in 5.1 how that sort of argument is *correctly* carried out.

instance, it might seem at first that "clear" means the same thing when applied to an *argument* and to a *pane of glass*. But the opposite of a clear pane of glass is a *dirty* pane, whereas the opposite of a clear argument is not a dirty argument but a *confused* one. The distinction between *dirty* and *confused* is much easier to see than that between "clear" in its two uses.

Similarly, Aristotle thinks, a difference in sense is difficult to discern for the word "just" but easy for "unjust." We call someone "unjust" either because he is, as we might say, "unprincipled" or "takes himself to be above the law" or "is always making an exception for himself" (the Greek is *paranomos*); or because he is a greedy person (*pleonektēs*), who is always trying to get something for nothing (*anisos*). Since variation in sense as regards a condition will be matched by a similar variation of sense in its opposite (principle 3 above), we can be confident, then, that there are two corresponding types of justice. If it holds true, furthermore, that the characteristic results of opposite conditions will be opposite (principle 2), then one sort of justice involves being principled and lawful, and the other form of justice involves not being greedy and not trying to get something for nothing: in short, observing a kind of equality in one's dealings with others. Finally, if the characteristic results of a condition allow us to infer the presence of that condition (principle 1), then the first form of justice can be provisionally defined as that state of a character by which someone acts in a principled and lawful way, and the other form of justice can be provisionally defined as that state of character by which someone brings about equality in his dealings with others.

The first sort of justice, Aristotle says, is not really a single state of character, but rather all of the virtues, as being put to use in a certain way. That explains why he is not, after all, particularly interested in this sense of "justice"; it is a spurious virtue, he thinks, and not one of the virtues of character. Justice in this broad sense is, as he puts it, "complete or mature virtue as exercised toward others" (*teleia aretē pros heteron*). By "others" Aristotle does not mean "other persons generally," but rather those who are at first strangers, that is, persons other than those whom you know from private life. (It would be absurd to regard any of the moral virtues, as Aristotle has character-ized them – except perhaps self-mastery – as having any existence apart from their being exercised for the good of other persons.) That is why Aristotle cites Bias in support, "Acquired authority reveals the man" (1130a1–2): that is, when someone takes on responsibilities outside the household, then it becomes clear, from whether he acts justly (in the broad sense) or not, whether he had the virtues *before* he took on that responsibility.[5] These reflections make it clearer, too, why Aristotle did not regard justice in this broad sense as a distinct virtue: no one acquires a virtue simply by expanding the scope of operation of his virtues, any more than, say, a concert pianist acquires any new skill in performance when finally playing in a major concert hall.

That we apply the name justice to "complete virtue as shown toward strangers" explains, Aristotle thinks, the extravagant things said about justice, which would be unaccountable if the term "justice" were applied only to one among various virtues of character. People say that justice is "the best of all the virtues," and "the high point" or "extreme" of virtue (1129b30) – yes, because virtue is most attractive and best when put to broad use. People also say, cynically, that justice amounts to "doing what is good for someone else" (1130a3); but they say that, Aristotle explains, because they are thinking of virtue only in its public employment (in private life it is at least as obvious, Aristotle would hold, that a person's virtue works out for his *own* benefit).

Yet one might wonder why people refer to "complete virtue shown toward strangers" as *justice*: why do they transfer the name of *that* particular virtue to the complete virtue in this way? Why do they not, for instance, use "generosity" in two senses, broad and narrow? Why do they not refer to the public employment of virtue as, say, "courage" or "magnificence"? The reason, Aristotle holds, is that the particular virtue of justice, alone among the virtues of character, contains as part of its definition that it is exercised "toward others" (that is, again, toward persons not of one's own household[6]). It is not possible to effect the kind of equality at which this particular virtue

---

[5] This notion of the exercise of virtue "toward others" requires exactly the same notion of "distinct others" as is involved in what Aristotle calls "political justice," – about which more below.

[6] Or, toward members of one's household, but not insofar as they are treated as such.

aims, Aristotle believes, except among those who are related to each other initially as strangers. Because of this shared element in common, he thinks, the name of the one is transferred to the other. As regards the other virtues of character, however, nothing prevents them from being exercised even toward family and friends; hence it would be incongruous to pick one of those virtues to signify our acting virtuously toward those other than family and friends. "It is clear that there is a particular sort of injustice, different from that which involves going against virtue in its entirety. It has the same name, because its definition, in its genus, is the same, since both are exercised in relation to others (*pros heteron*)" (1130a32–b1).

We should consider briefly Aristotle's three additional arguments, found at the beginning of 5.2, that "justice" signifies a distinct and particular virtue of character. Aristotle's strategy, in each case, is to argue that there is a distinct and particular vice of injustice, which he takes to imply that there is a corresponding virtue. Two of the arguments exploit the fact that the distinctive motive of particular injustice is *pleonexia*. This means, literally, "grasping for more." It is not unfairly thought of as "greed" or "covetousness." But, as mentioned above, we can get a good idea of what Aristotle means by it if we understand it as the attitude of someone who wants, or expects, or thinks he is entitled, to get something for nothing in his dealings with others.

The first argument (1130a16–24) is this. There are various sorts of wrongdoing people can do: throwing down one's weapons in battle and running away; saying something nasty to another; not giving financial help to a friend in need. Each sort can be referred to broadly as "doing an injustice" (and, indeed, each sort of wrongdoing involves inflicting harm on others). Yet, over and above this, we ascribe more particular explanations to these actions: "He was acting *from fear* when he ran away"; "He's a *difficult* person, and that's why he said that nasty thing"; "It's not surprising he left you in the lurch, since he's so *tight-fisted* with his money." Now each sort of ascription serves to identify a particular vice, which corresponds to a particular virtue of character. (And each of these vices is clearly distinct from the broad sense in which something is "unjust.") Yet among our repertoire of such ascriptions, there are also phrases such as "He did that because he's a *cheat*," or "That's just like him, always *trying to get something for nothing.*" And we find that: (i) only this sort of explanation makes sense for some sorts of action ("The reason he only gave you change for a ten, not a twenty, is that he's *tightfisted*" is inappropriate in *that* sort of case); and (ii) this sort of explanation makes no sense for the sorts of wrongdoing appropriately handled by the other ascriptions ("He threw down his weapons and ran because he's a cheat" makes little sense). Aristotle thinks that the best explanation of these facts about how we account for wrongdoing is that there is a distinct vice, which involves being a cheat, and a distinct virtue, which involves not being a cheat – or being "just."

The second argument (1130a24–28) is that two resembling actions, both "unjust" in the broad sense, may differ as to whether they are "unjust" in the narrow sense. Sleeping with your neighbor's wife is "unjust" in the broad sense of harming the man to whom (we presume) the woman covenanted exclusive fidelity. Yet we can imagine two scenarios. In the first, someone is desperate for money, and, conveniently, the wife of his very wealthy neighbor just happens to be obsessed with him; he therefore pretends to be in love with her, and, when she sends expensive gifts his way, he sells them for cash, which he immediately puts into an investment account. In the second, a man has lots of money, and his neighbor's wife is poor; but, scandalously, he leaves his lavish home and prestigious job to move in with her in a disreputable neighborhood, living in poverty. Suppose now that both relationships come to an end. Both women could claim to have been in some sense *deceived*, but the former could in a special sense claim also to have been *defrauded*: "That guy was little more than a petty thief."

The third argument (1130a28–32) again begins with the observation that there are different sorts of wrongdoing, call them "categories of injustice." Now for each category we operate with an expectation that a particular vice will typically be the cause of it: call this the "default explanation." The default explanation of adultery (Aristotle thinks) is self-indulgence: hence we might say, "The usual reason for this sort of injustice is self-indulgence." The default explanation of running away in battle is cowardice: hence, "The usual reason for deserting one's post in battle is cowardice." But another category of injustice involves wrongdoing for the sake of making an unfair gain. But what is the default explanation in this case? Aristotle says that we take injustice to be the typical cause: hence we should say, "The usual reason for this sort of injustice is injustice." But then (in this case only) we would be giving a tautologous, and therefore empty, explanation, that is, unless "injustice" takes a different sense in its second occurrence in the explanation. Thus there must be some *particular* virtue of justice and a corresponding form of injustice.

THREE FORMS OF THE VIRTUE OF JUSTICE

Once he has established in 5.1–2, as he thinks, that there is a distinct and particular virtue of justice (which I shall, from this point on, refer to simply as "justice"), Aristotle tries to define it more carefully. The vice associated with it (only one vice? – more about this later), involves "grasping for more" and "getting something for nothing" rather than aiming at equality. It is concerned with making an unfair gain. But a gain in what sorts of things? Here Aristotle might have carried on his discussion as he did with self-mastery, pointing out that we do not call someone "grasping" if he aims always to get the greater share of, say, the *kalon* in his action, and so on. But instead Aristotle cuts to the chase and says that justice involves "goods – not every sort of good, but those that constitute good or bad fortune" (1129b4–6). Later he is a bit more precise: it involves "honor, money, and security – it's not clear that we have a single name that covers all of these – even pleasure, that is, the pleasure people get from prospering" (1130b2–4). He sometimes calls these goods "divisible goods" (1130b32), "unqualified goods" (1129b5), or "unqualified goods which are shared" (1137b26).

Although Aristotle, as we have seen, takes *pleonexia* to be a distinctive mark of the unjust person, the account he prefers is that such a person aims at distributions of goods that are unequal (1129a33, b10; 1131a10). Hence Aristotle's fundamental description of an unjust person is that he is an "unequal" man. We might more naturally say that he is "unfair" or "doesn't deal fairly" with others. But this core ascription of inequality is important, because it is the basis for Aristotle's differentiation of three forms of justice.

Aristotle reasons: justice involves (as we have seen) divisible goods; and justice clearly involves *persons*; and, furthermore, it produces *equality* – a relation which fundamentally requires a distinction of two. Thus, justice must essentially involve the bringing about of an arrangement of four terms: two packages of divisible goods, assigned to two persons, which might be represented pictorially as follows (where "A" and "B" stand for persons, and "x" and "y" stand for packages of divisible goods):

Aristotle was clearly pleased with this conclusion and regarded it as of the first importance, which explains his belabored geometrical pictures of just arrangements. We might in contrast be tempted to dismiss it as trivial. Yet we can begin to grasp its significance if we ask: *where* is equality, so essential for justice, to be found in the above picture? Presumably the picture represents a just state of affairs; yet justice is an equality; and an equality holds between two terms. So we need to place an equality sign somewhere in the diagram. But if we place it between the x and the y, we get the wrong result: as Aristotle points out, justice does not consist in giving equal portions to everyone, because people will rightly be indignant, not only if equals get unequal shares, but also if unequals get equal shares. And if we place the equality sign between the A and the B, then the distributed goods become irrelevant: A and B were *already* equal, in some sense, *before* the distribution. Hence, Aristotle points out, the equality sign should actually be placed, not between things, but between the *relations*, or the proportions, of x in relation to A, and y in relation to B. (Thus, as Aristotle says, justice involves achieving "proportionate equality," that is to say, an equality of proportions.) And the equality which is justice is therefore irreducibly a four-term relation, in which each term plays its role in constituting the arrangement as just.

The significance of this account becomes especially clear in Aristotle's discussion of reciprocity in 5.5. In the immediately preceding chapters, Aristotle sets out his view that justice consists essentially in equality. In chapter 5 he takes on a challenge to his view: the competing view that justice consists, rather, in "repayment" or "reciprocity." There seems to be some merit in this view, which brings in the notion of retaliation – the *lex talionis* of "an eye for an eye" – and common notions and proverbs (such as, as we would say, "what goes around, comes around").

In reply, Aristotle first observes that repayment simply does not work in some cases: in Greek law generally, if a citizen were to strike a member of the government, justice would require that he be punished by something more severe than being hit in the same way in return; and if a member of government were to strike a citizen, he would be punished with something other than being struck. (Even our law recognizes this kind of disparity: a private citizen who assaults a government official is open to greater punishment than if he assaults merely another citizen.[7]) That the punishment is different if the "proportion" between agent and patient is evidently different suggests that some underlying notion of proportion is present even in cases in which the punishment would be the same.

But then Aristotle gives an elaborate argument at 1132b33–1133b28 – too complicated to follow in its details here – that even in those instances in which we rely upon some notion of reciprocity (and Aristotle acknowledges that reciprocity is crucial for human association), we are depending upon more fundamental, proportionate equality. Reciprocity works especially in contractual, business relationships: for instance, a shoemaker trades a certain number of shoes to a carpenter, in exchange for the carpentry work involved in enlarging his shoe shop. The exchange is amicable only if the shoemaker believes that he has received goods of equal worth in return. But, Aristotle observes, that sort of arrangement requires that, beforehand (or *ex ante*, as economists say), shoes be regarded as *commensurable* with buildings: say, a building

---

[7] For instance, the United States Code, title 18, section 111, chapter 7, contains the following provision:

(a) In General. – Whoever –

  (1) forcibly assaults, resists, opposes, impedes, intimidates, or interferes with any person designated in section 1114 of this title while engaged in or on account of the performance of official duties; or

  (2) forcibly assaults or intimidates any person who formerly served as a person designated in section 1114 on account of the performance of official duties during such person's term of service, shall, where the acts in violation of this section constitute only simple assault, be fined under this title or imprisoned not more than one year, or both, and in all other cases, be fined under this title or imprisoned not more than three years, or both.

is regarded as worth roughly two pair of shoes per square foot. Moreover, for the exchange to be regarded by both as fair and just afterwards (or *ex post*), then both the shoemaker and the carpenter have to agree that the worth of the shoes exchanged was *equal* to that of the carpentry work performed.

It is first of all an important discovery on Aristotle's part that such an arrangement admits of being evaluated from two viewpoints, *ex ante* and *ex post*, which must be considered separately. But his account has two other important implications. First, because the relevant equality is that of the proportions involved, reciprocity involves crucially a kind of "meeting of minds," where each party to the exchange appreciates the interests of the other, and understands that the exchange appears equal to the other: both carpenter and shoemaker have to come to see the worth of the carpentry work, *in the eyes of the shoemaker*, as equal to the worth of the shoes, *in the eyes of the carpenter*. Second, for this to happen with reliability in particular cases, no particular case is isolable. It is expedient for both shoemaker and carpenter, or for any other persons involved in a similar exchange, to regard their products as commensurable in a similar way with *every* good and service available on the market. That is to say, any single commercial exchange, correctly understood, implies the possibility of a *market*. (Aristotle astutely remarks that money was invented for precisely this purpose, of generalizing exchanges. He even describes money as constituting an "intermediary" for market transactions: "it becomes in a certain manner an intermediary, since it measures everything," 1133a20.)

In short, the fundamental economic notions of a *market*, which allows all goods to be commensurated through *pricing*, and provides a measure of their worth, and of a *market equilibrium*, whereby the worth of those goods is settled, each with respect to the others – and then too the possibility of a mathematical treatment of these relationships – all of this comes directly out of Aristotle's apparently trivial notion of "proportionate equality."

Aristotle thinks that there are three ways of producing an equality of divisible goods, and thus three forms of the virtue of justice.[8] The

---

[8] It is not entirely clear why these are to be regarded as three forms of a single virtue, rather than three related but distinct virtues.

first ("distributive") is for someone to distribute to individuals goods that are taken from a common stock: for instance, a general awards the medal of honor to a handful of soldiers who distinguish themselves in battle; or a professor awards grades to students. The second ("commutative") is for persons freely to exchange goods, in the manner described above. The third ("corrective") is for a judge to correct for an inequality that is created through an act of injustice, by taking goods away from the offender and restoring goods to the victim, or by simply punishing the offender.

Although Aristotle argues at some length that the third sort of equality is distinctive in being "arithmetic," because the correction takes place simply by making it so that the offender gained nothing from his offense (and note, by the way, that Aristotle, following Athenian practice, tends to look at an injury as only a "civil" offense, comparable to our notion of "tort"), this case too should presumably be seen as indirectly involving proportionate equality as well (cf. 1134a5–6). The reason is that it is a presumption of corrective justice that the distribution of goods prior to the offense is fair and therefore equal, but the standard implicit in this presumption is that of proportionate equality. (If B took ten dollars from A, but separately from this A crashes his car into B's car, creating damages worth thousands, we would not think that everything had been settled if we simply required B to return the ten dollars.)

THE DOCTRINE OF THE MEAN AS IT APPLIES TO JUSTICE

At the very start of his treatment of justice, Aristotle signals that, as he sees it, this virtue involves an intermediate in a different way from the other virtues of character: "We need to examine the virtue of justice and the vice of injustice, especially what sorts of actions they extend to, and what sort of intermediate condition the virtue of justice is, and of which things a just state of affairs (*to dikaion*) is an intermediate mark" (1129a3–5). But how exactly is it different?

Aristotle's first observation on the matter is unhelpful. He uses language similar to 2.6 and makes it seem as though the virtue hits the intermediate mark in this case in just the same way as in others:

In every sort of action it's possible to do more or less, and it's possible as well to do what is equal. So then, if something is unjust because it's unequal, it will be just because it's equal (which is exactly what everyone believes, though without going through this argument). And since what is equal is intermediate, the just thing to do would be a kind of intermediate mark. (1131a11–15)

At first glance, Aristotle's idea seems to be: any intermediate at all which is aimed at implies a kind of equality, since to hit the intermediate is to achieve something equal to it, and to go beyond it or to fall short is to achieve something "unequal" as regards that intermediate mark. Thus, to hit the bull's-eye of a target is like achieving an equality: the arrow falls at a height exactly *equal* to the height of the bull's-eye, and it diverges neither to the right nor to the left, hitting the target at a width exactly *equal* to that of the bull's-eye. And Aristotle apparently wants to argue from this that since any intermediate mark is a kind of equality, then any equality is a kind of intermediate; so justice, which involves equality, must involve something intermediate, and therefore conform to the Doctrine of the Mean. But the point, although true enough, seems trivial and uninformative. How precisely does an equality-that-is-intermediate differ from an intermediate-that-is-equal?

Aristotle moves on from this very general remark to argue for two differences between justice and the other virtues of character. The first (it seems) is that the intermediate mark and the extremes involved in justice are defined solely in terms of the distributions which justice is supposed to bring about, not in terms of any emotions, motivations, or impulses of the agent: "The virtue of justice is an intermediate condition, not in the same way as the other virtues of character, but simply because it is *of an intermediate*" (1133b32–33). Aristotle's point seems to be that the *virtue*, the trait of character itself, is something intermediate in an entirely derivative way: its being so is completely dependent on the fact that what it *aims at* is intermediate. In contrast, in the case of other virtues, Aristotle wanted to maintain that the actual state of a person with the virtue was somehow intermediate between the states of persons having the opposite vices. With courage, for instance, as we saw, the *action* which is right – neither charging precipitously against orders nor abandoning one's post – is roughly correlated with the agent's having emotions that do not themselves "fly to extremes" and so are not amenable to rational control. That the agent's emotions do not fly to extremes of fear or confidence, so that what the agent does is controllable by reason, is part of what Aristotle means in saying that the *virtue* of courage is itself something intermediate.

In various key texts Aristotle describes the virtues of character as concerning both actions and emotions (2.6.1106b16–17; 2.8. 1108b18–19; 2.9.1109a23; 3.1.1109b30; cf. 2.7.1108a30–31). His view seems to be that the virtues differ as regards the degree to which they deal with emotions: some virtues, such as being even-tempered (cf. 4.5), modulate emotional responses only; others, such as courage and self-mastery, modulate emotions with a view to correct action. But justice, Aristotle apparently thinks, modulates only actions and the equal arrangements they produce, and emotions not at all.[9]

The second difference, Aristotle thinks, is that there is only one vice corresponding to the virtue of justice, not two, as in the case of other virtues of character. Aristotle remarks that "injustice pertains to the extremes" (1134a1), yet as regards justice there are two extremes: having more than one should, and having less, which Aristotle appropriately describes as "acting unjustly, and being unjustly trea-ted" (1133b31). So whether there are two *vices* of injustice, depends upon whether there is a bad condition by which someone consis-tently treats himself unjustly, as well as a condition in which someone consistently acts unjustly. But this Aristotle denies, because, he claims, it simply is not possible for anyone willingly to treat himself unjustly. The reason in brief is that someone who deliberately wishes to have less of a good than he knows he can claim is simply giving that portion freely away, as a gift. Thus, any action which looks like it might be an instance of someone's "doing an injustice to himself" would be properly described as his making a gift to another. And, if so, then we should evaluate it according to the standards of friendship rather than justice, as follows: was this a close enough friend for a gift of that sort? Should he rather have given that gift to this other person, for whom it would be more appropriate? Has his having given that

---

[9] This is not to say that someone might not try to control his emotions as a *condition* of acting justly: "I'd better calm down, because, if I don't, there is no hope I'll see what is fair in this situation." But calmness might similarly be a condition of action for other virtues, without its being what those virtues "deal with" or have as their distinctive object.

gift made him unable to be of service to close friends who need his assistance now? And so on.[10] These two points are of course related, because the *virtue* cannot be intermediate, if there is only one vice to which it can be contrasted.

Aristotle devotes 5.9, then, to arguing that it is not possible willingly to be treated unjustly, and 5.11 to arguing for the related claim, that it is not possible to treat oneself unjustly, precisely to explain why there is only one vice associated with justice and thus why justice is an understandable exception to his Doctrine of the Mean. Many of his arguments in these chapters are exceedingly clever. Consider, for instance, the arguments at 1138a18–28, that a person cannot do an injustice against himself by assigning himself less of his fair share: (i) Suppose he did treat himself unjustly in this way. Then he would be allotting less to himself than is his due. But he would do so by holding something back from himself, which he ought to have. Yet in that case, since he is the one who is holding it back, he would have it after all! Again, (ii) anyone who receives compensatory repayment for some harm that he has done is treated justly in the end. Suppose, then, that someone harms himself: such a person admittedly commits an offense, but also he receives simultaneously a punishment exactly equal to the offense. Thus he treats himself justly after all! Again, (iii) every injustice, as we saw, can be assigned to some category of injustice. But it never makes sense to attribute to any such category an action that a person takes with respect to himself and his own belongings. For instance, "committing adultery with his own wife"; "stealing his own property"; and "home invasion, of his own dwelling" are all ridiculous descriptions. What they intend to pick out would have to be described differently, for instance, "not committing adultery after all, but attempting to do so," say, because it was his wife in disguise who met him at the rendezvous point, as, for example, in the folk song "Lamorna."[11]

---

[10] See chapter 9 below, for Aristotle's views on friendship.

[11] Admittedly, someone who accepts or brings upon himself some sort of disadvantage as a result of (say) his timidity or laziness, or some other such inhibition, can be said to be "Doing himself an injustice." But then this should be understood as: he acted without reason in such

EQUITY

Given that the upshot of chapters 5.9 and 5.11 is that no one commits an injustice if he deliberately takes less for himself than he may rightly claim as his due, we can appreciate why Aristotle wedges between these chapters his examination of "equity," because equity often takes precisely the form of taking less than one rightly could take.

Equity is a correction of the law in particulars, undertaken with a view to the purpose of a law, or the intention of the lawgiver. A stock example, which illustrates the notion well, is that of a prince of a walled city which is under attack, who sets down the law that the city gate is never to be open between dusk and dawn. In fact, one day the militia of the town, with the prince at its head, forays out to engage the enemy; but, after a long battle, in which the prince is killed, it retreats back to the city after dusk, with the enemy in hot pursuit. You are the gatekeeper, and the law instructs you to keep the gate closed. Do you follow the law, letting your city's troops get trapped and slaughtered, or do you break the law and open the gate? And if you do break the law, are you being unjust in doing so?

Aristotle claims that such difficulties will inevitably arise as regards any law. The reason, he thinks, is that law consists of instructions with a view to the attainment of some end; but no set of instructions will ever be suitable for all contingencies; and, in any case, law must be relatively simple, so that it can be easily and generally grasped and put into practice. Hence it is the very nature of law that it must be *intelligently* followed, through grasping its purpose, and then departing from the strict letter of the law, when that would defeat its purpose as regards unforeseen contingencies.[12] In our stock example, the gatekeeper can reason that to let the city's army be slaughtered (which would inevitably lead to the fall of the city to the enemy)

---

a way that others rewarded him with less than he might easily have merited. (I owe this clarification to Maximilian Pakaluk.) We would not use the phrase "injustice" except as having in mind how others deservedly treat him, or would treat him.

[12] Equity involves the interpretation of the law as regards contingencies that were not foreseen. It does not allow private citizens to go against the letter of the law in circumstances that were clearly foreseen. For instance, it is not an exercise of equity for a motorist to drive through a red light when clearly no other vehicles are in the area of an intersection – since legislators could easily foresee that this would happen and allowed no exceptions to this. Similarly, it is not an exercise in equity for a motorist to turn right after stopping at a stop light, where the law has left this to the driver's judgment.

would defeat the purpose of the prince's command. If you will: the gatekeeper can imagine what the prince would have included in the law when it was framed, if the contingency confronted by the gate-keeper were presented to the prince at that time.

Aristotle's discussion of equity is extremely brief and merely opens up the subject. A fuller treatment would need to consider such things as: can the letter of the law be neglected only when not doing so "defeats the purpose" of the law, or, more broadly, in cases in which neglecting the letter would (apparently) be an improvement on the law? Under what conditions is a private citizen, on his own authority, justified in neglecting the letter of the law (included in this is the area that we call "the necessity defense" in law)? How can we reliably determine the purpose of the law, or the intention of the lawgiver? Is civil disobedience an example of equity? If so, how do we distinguish such cases from lawlessness?

We tend to regard equity as a matter of legal claim or process: so, for instance, "Courts of Equity" have arisen in English common law to provide a remedy for cases in which the strict observance of the law would yield an intolerable injustice. But Aristotle regards it as a trait of character, which is the form that the virtue of justice takes when practiced with suitable refinement, describing it as the trait of "deli-berately aiming at and achieving in practice what is equitable" (1137b35–1138a1). He says very little about this trait, perhaps because he sees it as closely connected with friendship (see 8.1.1155a28, an apparent reference back to equity), and therefore as an area of joint actualization, of both the virtue of justice and those traits of character involved in friendship.

Perhaps the most striking manifestation of this trait, as I said (and to which Aristotle gives attention at the end of 5.10), is how equity leads someone to claim less for himself than the strict letter of the law would allow – which amounts to making a gift to the other. For instance, although you were first in line at the grocery store, with your basketful of groceries, you allow the man who only wants to buy a gallon of milk to step ahead of you in line. You are not required to do so, in fact the relevant rule permits you to go first and forbids the man from cutting ahead of you, but you let him go ahead because you have a sense of what the rule is meant to accomplish (viz. the efficient payment for groceries). Again, someone makes a voluntary contribution to her town when, on account of a tax loophole, her large income is not taxed at all; and so on. Actions like that clearly require some general intention to foster the good of others through law and therefore they constitute, as Aristotle thinks, a kind of "civic friendliness."

Everything that Aristotle says about the incapacity of law to take into account all contingencies of action will hold similarly of contracts. (In fact, it holds for ethical reasoning generally. As we saw, one of the things Aristotle means when he says that generalizations in ethics typically hold "for the most part" is that they are subject to the same infirmities as any code of law.) Contracts are essentially open-ended and incomplete.[13] But this implies that an important expression of the virtue of equity will be precisely to recognize when a contract departs from what is reasonably fair, to one's own advantage, and in such cases to consent willingly to revise it; and also to be friendly and flexible in dealing with partners to a contract, showing a willingness to change the letter of a contract to cover unforeseeable contingencies which lead to unfairness. Since friendship relies to a large extent on implicit contractual arrangements, equity will turn out to be important for the practice of friendship.

POLITICAL AND NATURAL JUSTICE

This consideration of Aristotle's view of the virtue of justice may be completed by looking briefly at two dimensions of justice, which are important for his treatment: political versus metaphorical justice; and natural versus conventional justice.

The first distinction is familiar, since it concerns the requirement, which we have looked at already, that justice cover the actions of a person *pros heteron*. I glossed this as "towards those who are initially strangers," but this was not entirely accurate. It is true that, according to Aristotle, members of a person's own household, and his friends, are not "others" in the strict sense. But neither does this concept of "other" apply (say) to the entirety of the human race beyond one's household. Rather, and more precisely, it extends to those persons, not members of one's own household, who are *in the*

---

[13] See Hart (1995).

same political society.[14] This is an extremely important point. For Aristotle, political society makes possible a distinctive manner of association, not found elsewhere, which he describes as an association of persons who are *free and equal* (1134a27), who are *under law* (a30), and who *share* (or "take turns") *in ruling and being ruled* (b15). Two persons who are in a political association are, as such, related to each other in such a way that the actions of each toward the other are *pros heteron*. We might say that, according to Aristotle, the distinctness of persons is revealed best in political society, and in political society most of all we take this distinctness into account in our dealings with others. In families people do not deal with one another as distinct; outside political society, they do not deal with one another in any consistent way at all.

Aristotle says that political justice is justice "without qualification," and by this he means that justice in the improper and broad sense (what "general justice" takes as its aim) as well as the equality aimed at by the particular character-related virtue are centrally exemplified in the relations of members of political society to one another, precisely as members of political society. To say this is to deny that a person's relationships with members of his family, or with his friends, is an example of justice in the strict sense. Rather, these relationships display a qualified form of justice; and, in the case of the relationship between a person and those others who (Aristotle thinks) are akin to parts of him (we would say: "These people *belong* to him"), to say that justice exists is to use a metaphor, just as to speak of giving something to oneself is a metaphor. From this, of course, comes Aristotle's criticism of Plato, with which I began this chapter. The argument of the *Republic* involves a grand confusion: it begins, properly, by considering justice as involving the relationships among distinct others in an ideal political society, but it ends by claiming that justice as a virtue of the soul involves a supposedly similar relationship of the parts of the soul to one another. But justice cannot possibly be shown in a person's relationship to himself.

The distinction between natural (or "primary") and conventional (or "legal") justice is of course required by the notion of equity: the conventional is what exists by agreement or decision, and to act

[14] We should add the proviso: "or who in effect are in the same society," to cover resident aliens, ambassadors, visitors on friendly terms, and even members of other societies insofar as they are bound by a common law, say, through treaties.

equitably precisely means dismissing what has been agreed upon or decided, in favor of judgments about justice that concern the reality that presents itself to the agent. Equity also requires recognizing some constraints, principles, or orderings as in some sense "just" prior to the law, and as what the law aims to bring about. (As Aristotle remarks: "Primary justice is something distinct from legal justice," 1136b34.)[15] Already a distinction between conventional justice and legality, and something prior to that, had been drawn by Socrates. When in the *Apology* Socrates explains that he did not follow the command of the Thirty Tyrants to arrest and bring before them an innocent man, because their command was not *just* (32a–33b), he must be appealing to something other than positive law, because the command would have been legal by the conventions that established that government. Hence Aristotle would have regarded his discussion of natural justice, too, not as an innovation, but as another notion he was simply appropriating from Socrates and Plato.

Aristotle does not say much about natural justice. He is much clearer in his rejection of the opposing position of conventionalism, and in his grounds for rejecting it, than he is in his assertions about natural justice – perhaps because, in the end, he has little patience with conventionalism, and regards it as obviously wrong. Our own affirmations of natural justice take the form of declarations of natural rights or natural laws. But Aristotle seems to have had no notion of a "right" as an attribute possessed by an individual.[16] (He of course recognizes that there are things that it would be "right" and "not right" to do to others, even prior to law. But this is expressed in the Greek by a verb, *dei*, "ought," not a substantive, a "right," which is meant to indicate an enduring basis for claims located in a person.) And, although in the *Rhetoric* he acknowledges "unwritten laws" (1.3), which apparently would express requirements of natural justice, in the *Ethics* he says nothing about this, and instead likens natural justice to what we should call a "propensity," which can be resisted by

---

[15] This is clear from the character of what is called "the necessity defense": the mountaineer who breaks into someone else's ski chalet and uses the supplies there in order to survive an unexpected storm is judging (correctly) that a purpose of the law is to preserve and protect life, so that any law that hindered this would be, to that extent, "unjust." This kind of consideration would have been implicit, too, in Aristotle's understanding of "mixed" actions in 3.1.
[16] Yet see Miller (1995), who argues otherwise.

some of the people all of the time, perhaps, or all of the people some of the time, but not by all of the people all of the time. A good example of natural justice in this sense would be, for instance, the principle that a person should himself own what he produces through his own labor – "the *right* to private property," as we should call it. There are some small communes that have disregarded this principle for relatively long periods of time; and there have been large societies, too, which, very briefly and with little success, have attempted to disregard it; but by and large we do well and flourish by acknowledging it. We devise and develop legal conventions which constitute property law, then, precisely to give concrete expression to this principle of "natural justice"; and likewise in other cases.

FURTHER READING

A provocative critique which considers how precisely justice involves emotion or non-rational motivation is Williams (1980), to which O'Connor (1988) aims to respond.

Meikle (1995) is a thorough study of Aristotle's contribution to the beginnings of economics. Judson (1997) is invaluable on the fairness and equality of exchanges. For whether Aristotle accepts some notion of natural law or natural rights, see Miller (1995). For the long tradition on "natural law" which regards itself as developing remarks in Aristotle, the *locus classicus* is again Aquinas (1947), I–IIae, q. 94. But the general spirit of Aristotle's remarks is perhaps best developed in the work of the Scottish moralists, especially Reid (1969).

CHAPTER 7

Thinking-related virtue
(Nicomachean Ethics, *book 6*)

Let us recapitulate Aristotle's argument once more. He is looking to identify the ultimate goal of human life, which he conceives of as some activity, regularly repeated, which appropriately serves to organize everything else that we do, and which has the marks of Ultimacy, Self-Sufficiency, and Preferability. He argued in the Function Argument of book 1 that activity like that will be something that only a good human being can do, that is, it is activity that can be accomplished only by someone who has the "virtue" of a human being. Thus he turned in book 2 to an examination of human virtue.

But human virtue turns out to be complex; it admits of analysis; it has various "parts." One such "part," related to character, makes someone good at following or carrying out what he reasonably thinks he should do. It does this, Aristotle claimed, in two ways: by maintaining a person's motives in a condition of responsiveness falling between irrational and excessive extremes, and by assisting a person in crafting his action with refinement, so that it is appropriate as regards all of the various dimensions of an action.[1] All stable conditions by which we become like this are particular character-related virtues, and Aristotle regards these as including courage, self-mastery, generosity, particular justice, and a handful of other good traits.

But just as a human being can be good at *following* or *carrying out* what he reasonably thinks he should do, so he can be good at *thinking* — thinking about how he should *act*, but also thinking about how to

---

[1] Recall Aristotle's remark when he introduces the Doctrine of the Mean: a virtue both "puts a thing in a good condition" and "makes its characteristic work come out well" (2.6.1106a16–17). He thinks that a character-related virtue is itself intermediate and assists in actions that are intermediate.

make something, or simply thinking about subjects such as geometry, which often have no evident application as regards action or production. Aristotle had claimed at the beginning of book 2 that to be good in these various ways is a distinct part of human virtue. He called this "thinking-related" virtue and claimed that it is acquired through instruction and learning rather than through some process of training and practice. In book 6 of the *Ethics* he turns his attention to virtue of that sort. He identifies five such virtues, argues that they are really distinct from one another, and, in a preliminary way, argues that some of these virtues are subordinated to others.

The five thinking-related virtues Aristotle distinguishes are:

1. craftsmanship (*technē*);
2. knowledge (*epistemē*);
3. administrative ability (*phronēsis*);
4. sound intuition (*nous*); and
5. wisdom or "profound understanding" (*sophia*).

He apparently holds that these are subordinated one to another as follows. Craftsmanship is subordinated to administrative ability, on the grounds that the latter deals with *acting* well, and the former with *making things* well, and generally we make things as instruments of action: doing is prior to making. But administrative ability is subordinated to knowledge on the grounds that the former aims to *bring about* something, relative to our interests and needs, but the latter need not aim for any result beyond itself, and it can be concerned with matters that are not relative to or restricted to our interests. Yet knowledge is subordinated to wisdom, on the grounds that, in aiming to know anything at all, we thereby aim above all to know the most basic causes and reasons of things, and this is what wisdom is directed at.

Thus already in book 6 we find an implicit argument for the view that wisdom, a profound understanding of things (*sophia*), is the best and most fundamental human virtue. And thus, it is implied, the activity that human beings can engage in through having this virtue – the activity of actually thinking about, dwelling upon, and reflecting upon those matters of which we have a profound understanding – is the best activity available to us.

This argument is, however, implicit in book 6 and carried out only indirectly, through what on the surface seems to be a mere project of classification. Aristotle's chief aim, in the first instance, is simply to classify: how many thinking-related virtues are there? What are they? How are they distinct from one another? What good traits should be counted as ancillary and not really as thinking-related virtues in their own right? He seems to think that the primacy of wisdom, among the thinking-related virtues, becomes evident once we develop a satisfactory classification.

His concern with classification must be understood, once more, as directed against Plato and in a Platonic context. As we have already seen, Plato describes virtue variously as *knowledge, craftsmanship, administrative ability*, and *wisdom*, as though these were interchangeable. Plato regards virtue as knowledge in recognition of the security, stability, and protection from error that virtue affords. Someone who has a virtue, he thinks, is thereby simply kept from going astray, just as a person with mathematical knowledge, to that extent, will not make mistakes in mathematical reasoning. So on these grounds virtue would be a kind of knowledge. Yet for Plato virtue also seems to be a master craft, a "craft of crafts," which provides criteria for our pursuit of those goods that we procure through crafts subordinate to it. (We saw how Aristotle in book 1 is himself attracted to this idea.) Yet virtue is also fundamentally the "good condition of the soul"; and the function (*ergon*) or task of the soul, Plato thinks, is to take command and put things in order; thus a *virtue* of the soul would enable us to do these things *well*, and virtue consequently must be some kind of administrative ability. Finally, according to Plato, if virtue is to be well-grounded, it must be based not on superficialities, but rather on an assured grasp of the most fundamental realities; but these are the Forms, and to achieve a grasp of the Forms seems to be a kind of wisdom.

There are not a few passages in Plato where he slides easily from one to another of these various ways of characterizing virtue. But then which of these things is virtue? Or is virtue all of these put together? As is typical, Aristotle wants to "save the appearances" by making distinctions. He distinguishes five thinking-related virtues, each having its own task, and he argues, in effect, that Plato was treating these distinct virtues as if they were all the same. Yet once these various virtues are distinguished, Aristotle thinks, then we can see that they have a certain order and priority.

This basically is what he aims to do in book 6, which has the following structure:

1. Introduction
   (chapter 1) "Sound reason" and its target
   (chapter 2) Some preliminary distinctions

2. The five thinking-related virtues
   (chapter 3) Knowledge (*epistēmē*)
   (chapter 4) Craftsmanship (*technē*)
   (chapter 5) Administrative ability (*phronēsis*)
   (chapter 6) Insight (*nous*)
   (chapter 7) Wisdom (*sophia*)

3. Some ancillary virtues
   (chapter 8) Varieties of administrative ability
   (chapter 9) Being good at thinking things through (*euboulia*)
   (chapter 10) Perceptiveness (*sunēsis*)
   (chapter 11) Sympathetic understanding (*gnōmē*)

4. The subordination of administrative ability to wisdom
   (chapter 12) The value of wisdom
   (chapter 13) The value of administrative ability

"SOUND REASON" AND ITS TARGET

In the opening lines of book 6 Aristotle makes a complaint and suggests a remedy. But what is the complaint, and what sort of remedy does he envisage? Here is the relevant passage:

[I] Since we said earlier that it's necessary to select the intermediate – neither the excess nor the deficiency – yet the intermediate is "as sound reason says," let's draw a distinction as regards this.

[II] The reason for doing so is that, as regards each of the previously mentioned sorts of actions (as in other matters), there's a particular *target* at which someone looks when he has the relevant principle in hand, tightening up or relaxing accordingly; also, there's a particular *standard* for intermediate conditions (those, that is, which we say are between excess and deficiency, on the grounds that they correspond to sound reason).

[III] Yet to speak in this way, although true, is not yet clear. Why? Because in other disciplines which involve things for which there is expertise, it's just as much true to say this: "it's necessary to strive and to relax neither more nor less, but rather to do intermediate things and as sound reason says." But if anyone were given this alone, he would know nothing beyond that – as, for instance, the sorts of things one should apply to the body, supposing someone were to say, "The sorts of things that *medical skill* recommends, and in the way that someone having that skill recommends."

[IV] That is why, as regards conditions of the soul also, it's necessary not only that we say this, correctly so, but also that we demarcate what "sound reason" is, and what its standard is.

A common view of this admittedly difficult passage – call it the "Standard View" – is that Aristotle is raising a difficulty about the Doctrine of the Mean, involving what I earlier called the "Problem of Guidance" (see p. 15 above). All of us desire concrete advice about how to act. Which actions should we carry out? Which should we avoid? Are there any actions that are in every case wrong? So far the only rule to which Aristotle has apparently appealed, in his account of the particular character-related virtues, is the Doctrine of the Mean. However, to say that "virtuous actions are intermediate actions" is obviously not yet to give any precise advice. Moreover, Aristotle in his earlier discussions was careful to say that what counts as intermediate ultimately gets determined by "sound reason." But then to say that "virtuous actions are intermediate, in the way that sound reason indicates" seems simply to put off the problem, since what is it, precisely, that sound reason typically "indicates"?

According to the Standard View, then, Aristotle is recognizing at the opening of book 6 that, in order to get real guidance, we apparently need more specific rules of conduct, or at least some concrete examples of sound reasoning. Aristotle proposes his comparison with medicine along these lines: the comparison is meant to suggest that a treatise on ethics should include specific prescriptions about how to act virtuously, just as a medical textbook has specific prescriptions about how to preserve and restore health.

But if this is Aristotle's complaint, what is the remedy that he provides? In fact, Aristotle in book 6 never gives any specific rules of conduct or specific examples of virtuous action. He never answers the problem which, according to the Standard View, he raises at the beginning of book 6, and which presumably motivates the inquiry of that book. And thus on the Standard View we are left with a gap between what Aristotle aims to do, and what he actually accomplishes. As one advocate of the Standard View puts it:

Book VI . . . seems to get off to a false start. In the first section of the first chapter, Aristotle clearly states that he is about to examine the nature of the principles of right reason that determine the mean between excess and deficiency. The remainder of the chapter, however, ignores this section . . . Nowhere does Aristotle tackle the problem set out in the first section of Chapter 1 . . . [2]

Indeed, on the Standard View the gap between what Aristotle says he is going to do in book 6, and what he actually does, is so great that some proponents of that view have even suggested that the opening of book 6 was not written by Aristotle, that it "should be regarded as probably either a false start by Aristotle or an unfortunate editorial insertion."[3]

However, an interpretation of a text that implies a large and inexplicable gap between what the author proposes to carry out, and what he actually attempts, should be avoided if possible. It would be better to close the gap, by changing how we understand the opening of book 6, so that what it says comes into alignment with what Aristotle actually does in the chapter.

And this seems the correct course to take. It seems incorrect, first of all, to understand Aristotle to be raising at this point the Problem of Guidance. In his discussions of particular virtues in books 3–5, Aristotle showed no signs of regarding virtuous action as, in general, especially obscure or hard to discern. (Certainly what is problematic on the battlefield is not *figuring out* what counts as courageous. And we all do a good job, for the most part, of figuring out what counts as equal and fair in our dealings with others – the virtue of justice.) Aristotle furthermore gives fairly clear sketches of what it is to be generous or courageous, or to show self-mastery. Moreover, even if these sketches were especially deficient or incomplete, and Aristotle thought so, it would be strange for Aristotle to be at this point demanding *additional* rules or principles as a remedy, since he has

---

[2] See Urmson (1988), 79.
[3] Urmson (1988), p. 79. That it is neither of these things, however, is indicated by the parallel passage in *Eudemian Ethics* 1249a21–b23.

emphasized up to this point that rules are open-ended. The way in which maxims must be left unspecified, because they require sensitivity to particular circumstances, is not something that could be remedied by giving *further* rules and prescriptions. But presumably it is precisely through this sensitivity to particular circumstances that "sound reason" makes its most important contribution to virtuous action.[4]

Again, we should expect that Aristotle would intend to deal with "sound reason" (which he ends up identifying with administrative virtue, *phronēsis*) in book 6 in the way that he deals with the other thinking-related virtues that he identifies. But, for the other virtues, Aristotle's interest lies in *defining* them, not giving their *content.* For instance, he says that craftsmanship (*technē*) is a thinking-related virtue, and he defines it, but he gives no handbook of any craft. One will not find in the *Ethics*, say, any direction about how to build a house. Again, knowledge is a thinking-related virtue, but Aristotle gives no axioms or deductions in any branch of knowledge. Indeed, to provide the *content* of any thinking-related virtue would simply be to give a *display* of that virtue, to expound that field of inquiry, and Aristotle might in any case maintain he was *already* doing that as regards administrative virtue, at the appropriate level of generality, precisely in writing the *Ethics*![5]

It seems better, then, to reject the Standard View and to understand Aristotle instead to be raising a much more restricted difficulty at the beginning of 6.1, which he does after all succeed in answering.

Aristotle begins in (I) by insisting that a distinction of some sort needs to be drawn. But with regard to what should a distinction be drawn? It seems that Aristotle is insisting that a distinction needs to be drawn as regards the notion of "sound reason." The reason is this. Earlier in the *Ethics* Aristotle had spoken as though just *two* things were relevant in character-related virtue: the virtue itself, which aims

---

[4] We might indeed complain that Aristotle does not say much about why some sorts of actions, such as adultery, theft, and murder, are to be regarded as "extremes" and explained as wrong because in some way belonging to an "extreme." Yet, in defense, his project in the *Ethics* is not explaining what it is to be bad, but rather to be good – and certainly he is not aiming to explain to a bad person why his badness is bad.

[5] At this point recall 1.2.1094b11, where Aristotle says that his very inquiry is an instance of the art of governance or "political skill" (*politikē technē*), which is indeed one manifestation of "sound reason" (6.8.1141b23).

at and falls within an intermediate area between extremes, and "sound reason," which adjusts and refines what counts as intermediate. But what he apparently now wishes to emphasize is that some *third* thing must be taken into account as well, which in (II) he calls the "target" (*skopos*) or "standard" (*horos*), to which sound reason refers when making appropriate adjustments. Sound practical reason is *for* something; it aims to *bring about* something. We administer, govern, command, rule, or give orders for a purpose. Thus, there must be some goal or target at which sound reason aims and which provides the rationale for its commands.

This qualification makes sense, because it often happens that what we regard as appropriate in an action depends upon the "context" of that action, which in turn is affected by some kind of long-range goal or purpose; for instance: you are at a friend's house for dinner, and usually you would have two or so glasses of wine with dinner, but a good friend of yours has just died in a car accident, and consistent with your sorrow, you decline to drink. Certainly having two drinks, you think, would display a kind of frivolity or thoughtlessness inappropriate to the circumstances. Or a friend asks to borrow some money, and ordinarily you would lend it without hesitation; but you and your spouse have been making many sacrifices to save for a down payment on a house, and, given those circumstances, you judge, appropriately enough, that this time your friend will have to look for help elsewhere. So our goal or purpose affects what we count as going too far or falling short in particular actions, and a special goal can lead us to make corresponding adjustments.

Suppose, then, that we make this further distinction and say that in matters of conduct and appropriate emotional response three things are necessary: (i) to do what is intermediate, (ii) by making the adjustments that sound reason indicates, (iii) which sound reason arrives at with a view to some target or standard. Yet, as Aristotle next points out in (III), to say this is to give a schema that holds of *any* domain of action in which there is some sort of expertise. In all such domains, it will be true that one needs to use sound reason – let us call it "good sense" – with a view to some ideal, when applying or interpreting relevant maxims. To advance beyond this truism, Aristotle then says in (IV), one needs to identify the specific *sort* of "good sense" that enters into play in some domain and also to indicate the relevant "target." This, then, becomes Aristotle's task: to identify the specific sort of "good sense" that is relevant for ethical deliberation and action, and to say what this should appropriately take as its target.

But once we construe Aristotle's purposes in this way, we see that this is exactly what he carries out in book 6. He devotes the bulk of the book to identifying the exact sort of "good sense" that is needed for character-related virtues, and then he devotes chapters 12–13 to explaining what sound reason takes as its "target." Good sense in these matters, he maintains, is appropriately called *phronēsis* ("administrative ability," "practical wisdom," "intelligence and foresight in action," cf. 6.12.1144b27–28), and it may be defined as that virtue which deals with what is good and bad generally for human beings (1140b5–7). Its target, Aristotle argues, is speculative or contemplative activity of the sort that we engage in when we exercise the virtue of wisdom. In just the same way that medicine makes the relevant adjustments in the balanced conditions of the body with a view to its target of health, *phronēsis* makes adjustments in emotions and conduct with a view to promoting the activity of *sophia* (cf. 1144a3–5; 1145a6–9). *Phronēsis* is for the sake of *sophia*.

Thus there is no mismatch between the problem Aristotle sets himself in 6.1 and what he subsequently argues for. He says that he needs to define what counts as "sound reason" in ethics and identify its target, and this is exactly what he does.[6]

A word should be said about points of translation. "Sound reason" renders the Greek, *orthos logos*, literally "correct reason" or "right reason." Sometimes the phrase is taken to refer to a sort of maxim or prescription: "the correct rule" or "the right principle." But it is better to take the phrase to refer principally to a power or faculty (just as, as we have seen, *logos* on its own typically indicates a power or faculty).[7] This is clear, first of all, from Aristotle's plain words. He says in 2.2, "Later we will discuss sound reason – what it is, and how it is related to the other virtues" (1103b32–34), implying that *orthos logos* is one of

---

[6] Yet we might wonder why Aristotle's project is an interesting one. Is it not relatively trivial simply to say what sort of thing sound practical reason is? Would it not be more interesting, rather, to give us some of its *results*? I consider these questions below.

[7] In fact, Aristotle sometimes refers to *orthos logos* as simply *logos* (see. 1114b29, 1115b12).

the virtues; and he says explicitly in book 6 that *orthos logos* simply is the virtue of *phronēsis* (1144b28). Moreover, he treats as equivalent the expressions "as sound reason indicates" and "as a person with *phronēsis* indicates" (cf. 1107a1); and he regularly speaks of *orthos logos* as something that commands (1114b30) and speaks (1138b20) – and it would be absurd to take a maxim or prescription to do these things, or to think that a *maxim* had the job of adjusting and refining other maxims to suit particular circumstances.

Phronēsis has a meaning which is contested and unsettled in Greek. As we saw, Aristotle's main goal in book 6 is to mark this good trait clearly off from related traits. It has been variously translated into English as "practical wisdom," "wisdom," and "intelligence." Perhaps "sagacity" would be the best English equivalent, if that word were not old-fashioned. For our purposes, we can think of *phronēsis* as "administrative virtue," on the grounds that, as Aristotle understands it, the point of this virtue is to bring into existence important goods in an orderly and efficient way, and in a way that does full justice to all of them, and this is what we think of as distinctive of good administration. The one drawback of this rendering is that we hardly think of a person's intelligent ordering of *his own* affairs as an instance of good *administration*, yet *phronēsis* in Greek applies just as much to that as to the intelligent ordering of a household or city-state. But the phrase will work well enough if we keep this caveat in mind.

Aristotle's point in 6.1 about the need for an appropriate target for character-related virtue – which, as we have seen, he thinks is speculative or contemplative activity – should be seen in the historical context of the *relatively recent discovery of science, pure mathematics, and philosophy* in the ancient world. Here is how Aristotle viewed the matter. From time immemorial, human beings had been engaged in difficult labor simply to procure the necessities of life. Century after century, people farmed the land, raised animals, and engaged in rudimentary commerce to continue staying alive and raise a succeeding generation. But what was all of this effort *for*? What was the *point* of it all? Note that our wanting to raise that question at all seems to indicate that the point could *not* be the courageousness, generosity, justice, and other virtuous activity that people could display in carrying out these activities. If character-related virtues supplied the point of life, then that would be evident on the face of it. But in fact it is natural to think of our effort and work as directed at some *other* point, which lies outside it.

This question of the point of human effort was answered, for Aristotle, with the discovery – very recently for him, a century or so prior to his life – of the possibility of pure mathematics, natural science, and philosophy. Before this discovery, it simply was not suspected that there was a substantive, non-practical use of reason – that human beings could investigate and discover truths that were, or that seemed to be, necessary, enduring, and universal. Prior to this discovery, it would have seemed reasonable for a young person with prospects for a successful life to devote himself exclusively to, say, military ventures or political advancement. After this discovery, Aristotle considers, we have considerably less reason to engage in anything else. To Aristotle it would seem vitally compelling that a young person should minimize the time spent on other things, in order to maximize time spent in speculative and contemplative thought. This new target implied a new standard for excess and deficiency in other activities. What previously would have been, for instance, a reasonable dedication to military or political activities, could now look excessive and inappropriate.[8]

THE CHARACTERISTIC WORK OF PRACTICAL REASON

What are the virtues, then, of the thinking part of the soul? In particular, how do we identify "sound reason" or "good sense" in ethics – that good trait that is brought to bear when people perform actions in accordance with the various character-related virtues?

A virtue is a trait which places a thing in good condition and makes it so that it does its characteristic work well. Thus Aristotle first tries to identify the characteristic work of the thinking part of the soul. In 6.2 he maintains that its work is to attain truth, which he expresses in two different ways. Sometimes he uses the verb "to see,

---

[8] Aristotle's attitude toward the discovery of a realm of pure inquiry is well displayed in his *Protrepticus*, which, as I said, is an extended exhortation directed at young persons to leave ordinary life, with its routines and necessities, and to devote themselves to a life of intellectual inquiry.

to contemplate, to view" (*theōrein*) and describes the characteristic work of this part of the soul as a kind of intellectual perception:

When things that can be otherwise fall outside our viewing of them (*theōrein*), they can exist or not without our noticing it. (1139b21–22)

Every sort of craftsmanship deals with bringing something into existence, devising and seeing (*theōrein*) how something that can be otherwise might either exist or not. (1140a10–13)

We think that Pericles and men like that have administrative ability, because they are able to see (*theōrein*) what things are good for them and what things are good for human beings generally. (1140b8–10)

Each group says that to see (*theōrein*) correctly what things are good for any of its members is to have *phronēsis*. (1140b25–26)

None of the things that lead to someone's being happy is something that wisdom looks at (*theōrein*). (1143a19)

At other times, he regards the thinking part of the soul as something that is actualized through particular acts of assertion or denial; he therefore describes its characteristic work as making true assertions and denials: "Let us set it down that those things by which the soul attains truth by assertion or denial are five in number. These are *craftsmanship, knowledge, administrative ability, wisdom*, and *intuition*. (We do not include *supposition* or *opinion*, since these can be drawn into falsehood.)" (1139b14–18).

The characteristic work of the thinking part of the soul, then, is to "see" or to assert the truth. To carry out this work *well* is to have a thinking-related virtue. As the last quotation indicates, Aristotle adopts a rather high standard for what it is to do this well: a thinking-related virtue is a state of the soul which is such that, when that virtue is operative, we never arrive at anything except the truth. A thinking-related virtue, as such, never leads us astray into error.

In this regard, we should look more carefully at Aristotle's view that "supposition" or "opinion" are not thinking-related virtues. Suppose Smith asserts some statement, P. What is it that makes P an opinion or supposition of Smith, as opposed to an expression of (say) his knowledge? Aristotle is presupposing that we cannot answer this question by looking at P alone and its content, but rather at the state which is operative when Smith asserts P. When that state is such that its being operative implies that what Smith says is true, then that state is an intellectual virtue. For instance, suppose Smith asserts P, and, in asserting this, Smith is in the state of *knowing* that P. It follows from this that P is true (since, if we indeed know something, then it necessarily is true). Because in this case the truth of P follows from Smith's condition in asserting it, the condition of *knowledge* is a thinking-related virtue. In contrast, suppose Smith asserts P, and, in asserting this, Smith is in the state of *opining* that P. It does not follow from this that P is true. Because it does not thus follow, opining is not a *virtue*.

A thinking-related virtue, then, is a condition such that the assertions in which it finds expression are reliably true. As I said, Aristotle picks out five such conditions, and he refers to them as those conditions "by which we attain the truth and never are drawn into falsehood, as regards matters that cannot be otherwise, or as regards also matters that admit of being otherwise" (1141a3–5).

Once we appreciate the high standard that Aristotle sets for a trait to count as a thinking-related virtue, we can understand better his distinction between two parts of the rational soul. His argument is the following:

1. Things that exist can be divided into (a) those the basic causes of which cannot be otherwise and (b) those that can be otherwise.
2. This difference is a difference in kind.
3. To grasp something involves resemblance and kinship between that which does the grasping and that which is grasped.
4. Since there are two kinds of things that exist, there are two kinds of resemblance and kinship to them.
5. The characteristic work of the thinking part of the soul is to grasp what exists.
6. Thus, it does so by the two kinds of kinship.
7. But it can have these two kinds of kinship only if it has two parts which differ in kind.
8. Thus, the thinking part of the soul itself has two parts – the knowledge-attaining part (*epistēmikon*) by which it grasps things the basic causes of which cannot be otherwise, and the reckoning part (*logistikon*), by which it grasps things that can be otherwise.

We might wonder why Point 3 should imply a distinction *in kind* within the soul, or a distinction into *only two* parts: the image in a mirror resembles that which is in the world, but there are not as a consequence different "parts" of the image, corresponding to kinds of things in the world; and horses differ in kind from dogs, but we do not wish to say that there is one part of the soul by which we know horses and another by which we know dogs. Yet Aristotle's conception of a thinking-related virtue explains why he adopts the view that he does. We have a thinking-related virtue, he says, when there is a reliable connection between our being in some condition and our seeing or asserting some class of truths. But how could this standard be met when we are dealing with changeable things? As Aristotle himself says, "When things that can be otherwise fall outside our viewing of them (*theōrein*), they can exist or not without our noticing it" (1139b21–22). How could there be a reliable connection, then, between our asserting something when in a certain condition as regards changeable things, and its being so? Aristotle's answer is to appeal to two sorts of kinship between the rational soul and the world. As regards things that cannot be otherwise, the soul cognizes and reliably attains truth by *the soul's becoming like them*; but as regards things that can be otherwise, the soul cognizes and reliably attains truth by making it so that *they become like the soul*. Take truth to be a correspondence between what the soul says and how the world is: one sort of truth results from the soul's coming into correspondence with the world; another kind of truth results from the world's coming into correspondence with the soul. These are plausibly two sorts of function or "characteristic work." Thus they would involve different virtues. Thus, on Aristotle's view there are two ways of grasping truth; two parts of the soul to do the grasping (theoretical and practical reason); and two principal virtues of the thinking part of the soul, which make it do so reliably:

The very same sort of thing that, in reasoning, is assertion and denial, in conation is pursuit and avoidance. As a result, since a character-related virtue is a state involving choice, but choice is deliberative conation, then, because of these things, the reasoning must be true and the conation correct, if the choice is to be good, and the very same things that reason says must be pursued by conation. So then, this is reasoning and truth in the realm of action. (1139a21–27)

Theoretical reason attains the truth simply through assertion and denial: if the world is as it says, then what it says is true. Practical reason attains the truth through making what it regards as good actually come to exist. If a soldier, for instance, thinks that "It would be noble and admirable for me to storm that outpost and secure the countryside," but then he runs away in fear, he has not so far attained practical truth, as Aristotle understands it, even though he had asserted correctly what ought to be done. Again, if, under the same circumstances, he is impelled by a sheer rush of fury to storm the fort, all the while thinking to himself (incorrectly) that it would have been better had he done something safe instead, then, once again, he has so far not attained truth through his practical reason. Practical reason is meant to be operative in the world and to change it reasonably; thus it functions poorly when either it fails to do so, or when it does so, but without consistency of thought and impulse.[9] "That is why choice is either *conative intelligence* or *ratiocinative conation*, and that is the sort of origin of change that a human being is" (1139b4–5).

Aristotle's notion of truthfulness of practical reason, although it may seem unusual at first, is not in fact very different from many of our own ways of thinking and speaking. If someone says that he thinks something is good, but does nothing to promote it when he has a chance, we suspect that he does not really mean what he says – that what he says is not *true*.[10] Or, if someone consistently pursues something, but always when asked takes pains to deny that he thinks it good, we take him to be hypocritical and *untruthful*.

So the characteristic work of the rational part of the soul is to attain the truth, and practical reason does this by regarding something as "to be pursued," and then pursuing it, consistently so. Merely to judge that something is to be pursued is not yet to attain truth in practice; rather, the thing actually has to be successfully achieved. Aristotle's picture is that we attain truth by a kind of grasping (*gnōsis*, 1139a11) or contact

---

[9] Hence Aristotle denies that someone can have *phronēsis* but show weakness of will: "The same person cannot at the same time have *phronēsis* and have weakness of will . . . a person has *phronēsis* not by having knowledge alone, but also by being the sort of person who acts accordingly. But someone who shows weakness of will is not the sort of person to act accordingly" (7.10.1152a6–9).

[10] What he says is not true, not because what he says is about himself and what he strives for ("This is good" said by Smith is not *about* Smith or Smith's desires) but because it is true only if it is consistent with what he strives for.

with it, and if we merely *think* that something is to be sought, we do not yet grasp it, since *that* does not yet exist.

I have said that practical reason "successfully pursues" or "promotes" what it takes to be good, but *how* does it do so? In an important passage at the end of 6.2 Aristotle argues that, although practical reason, so understood, can do so in either of two ways – either through action or by making – it does so primarily through action: "Choice is the originating cause of *action*... Practical reasoning (*dianoia praktikē*) is also the originating cause of technological or productive reasoning, since anyone who makes something, makes it for the sake of something. Moreover, nothing that is made is without qualification a goal: rather, it is made *for some purpose* and *for someone*. But things that we *do* are without qualification goals: good action is itself a goal" (1139a36–b4). So the characteristic work of practical reason is to attain practical truth primarily through our actions; and the virtue of this part of the soul would be a condition which makes it so that we do so reliably.

THE DEMARCATION OF "SOUND REASON"

As we saw, near the end of 6.1 Aristotle says that his task is to mark out clearly what "sound reason" (or "good sense") is in ethics and what its target is (1138b33–34). After describing in 6.2 the characteristic work of the thinking part of the soul, he carries out these two tasks.

As I said, he marks out "sound reason" by offering definitions for each of the five contenders for thinking-related virtue, and arguing that these are all distinct from one another. He is especially concerned to argue (in 6.7) that administrative ability (*phronēsis*) is something different from wisdom (*sophia*). In the course of his discussion he gives the following definitions:

- Knowledge (*epistēmē*): a state of the thinking part of the soul that makes one actively and reliably disposed to attain truth through devising demonstrative proofs (1139b31–32).
- Craftsmanship (*technē*): a state of the thinking part of the soul that makes one actively and reliably disposed to produce goods of a certain sort precisely through true reasoning (1140a9–10).

- Administrative ability (*phronēsis*): a state of the thinking part of the soul which makes someone actively and reliably disposed to attain truth in action as regards things ultimately good and bad for human beings, precisely through reasoning (1140b5–6).
- Sound intuition (*nous*): an active disposition reliably to grasp the first principles of some branch of knowledge (1140b33–35).
- Wisdom (*sophia*): insight and knowledge as regards those sorts of things that are best by nature (1141a19–20, b3).

Aristotle sets apart knowledge and wisdom, on the one hand, from craftsmanship and administrative ability, on the other, for the reason that the first two deal with "matters the basic principles of which cannot be otherwise," whereas the latter two deal with changeable things. Sound intuition, he claims, is simply a part of the virtue of knowledge. Of virtues that reliably reach truth in changeable matters, administrative ability is set apart from craftsmanship in its various forms, as I said, on the grounds that *doing* is distinct from *making*. Thus we see that in 6.3–7 Aristotle appeals to the various dimensions that he had just used to describe the characteristic work of the rational part of the soul (unchangeable vs. changeable things; making vs. doing) in order to demarcate the various intellectual virtues.

These chapters of the *Ethics* can appear prosaic and obvious to us. Yet ironically they have that appearance because of their great success as a piece of philosophical writing. The distinctions that Aristotle insists upon have since become so much a part of our intellectual culture that we accept them as obvious. Yet, as I mentioned earlier, these distinctions would not have seemed obvious to Aristotle's contemporaries, and especially not to those influenced by Plato.

Aristotle's identification of practical reason as a distinct sort of reasoning should be contrasted with attempts to conflate distinctively ethical reasoning with either demonstrative or technological reasoning. One might argue that modern accounts of ethical reasoning presuppose one or the other of these identifications. Indeed, it is commonly supposed today that there is something suspicious or defective about commonsense ethical reasoning – that ethics is not yet on solid ground; that it has not found a scientific basis; and that ethical reasoning will not *become* set on solid ground, until we come to see how reasoning in ethics is similar to that of a deductive system or a branch of technology. The two chief approaches to ethical reasoning today are "deontology" and "consequentialism": but deontological systems typically present ethical reasoning as a deductive system; and consequentialism is evidently modeled on technological science. Aristotle's demarcation of a distinct virtue of *phronēsis* is effectively the claim that neither of these alternatives could quite be correct.

We might wonder why Aristotle sets apart "sound intuition" (*nous*), the ability to see the truth of first principles in various disciplines, as a distinct intellectual virtue. Why should the ability to grasp first principles be a separate virtue, but not deductive skill – the ability to see whether inferences are valid? Is it not arbitrary to take one aspect only of knowledge and elevate it to a distinct virtue? Moreover, is there not something rather *straightforward* about grasping first principles? One reads the axioms of geometry in Euclid, and then one has grasped them: first principles are "self evident." It seems pointless to posit a separate intellectual virtue for *that*.

But presumably Aristotle is thinking of "sound intuition" as an active ability; it is the ability not simply to understand first principles when one is taught them, but also to *discover* or *formulate* them – if not for the first time, then at least "for oneself," as when one really begins to *see* that some principle is true and pervasively operative in a domain. Presumably, too, someone with "sound intuition" profits well from experience: he "learns the lesson" of something he experiences; he "draws a truth out of it." Moreover, recall Aristotle's remarks in book 1, that we should follow Plato in wondering whether we are reasoning to first principles, or away from first principles (1095a33–34), and that there are various ways in which we grasp first principles, by induction, perception, habituation, and other means (1098b3–5). Presumably part of what makes "sound intuition" a virtue is that it involves the ability to recognize when it is appropriate to invoke first principles, and also to recognize which approach, in a particular discipline, is appropriate for arriving at first principles.[11]

---

[11] It is not unreasonable, moreover, to hold that the same skill which enables us to see a universal truth in a particular instance also enables us to recognize particular instances of a universal truth. Thus *nous*, as Aristotle remarks, would be relevant as well for judgments

In his demarcation of *phronēsis* from other thinking-related virtues, Aristotle devotes the most effort to arguing that it is distinct
from wisdom (*sophia*). This is understandable, since he regards these
as the two chief thinking-related virtues. But wisdom is simply a kind
of knowledge, so a word should be said about how it occupies a
special position.

The term "knowledge," on Aristotle's view, indicates a *class* of
thinking-related virtues, not a single virtue, since, corresponding to
each branch of knowledge, there will be a distinctive ability to
produce demonstrative proofs, and a person might be proficient in
one such branch, without having mastery in the others. But, despite
this, Aristotle thinks that the various branches of knowledge are
hierarchically arranged, with some subjects being more fundamental,
because they are more explanatory than others. For Aristotle, the
most fundamental branch of knowledge, and what is therefore at the
top of the hierarchy of sciences, is "metaphysics," which studies, he
says, "being *qua* being," that is, existing things at the highest order of
generality. And within metaphysics itself there is also a hierarchy: the
most fundamental part of metaphysics is theology, the study of divine
beings, and especially the completely and essentially actualized being,
living a life of complete happiness, which is the First Cause or "Prime
Mover."[12] Thus, although for Aristotle there are a multiplicity of
sciences, and different branches of knowledge, there is a single sort of
knowledge which encompasses and unifies all the others. Thus, as he
sees it, there would correspondingly be a chief virtue of the part of the
soul that grasps unchanging things, a single virtue which, as it were,
encompasses and contains all the other virtues that are kinds of
knowledge. This is wisdom, as Aristotle understands it.

One of Aristotle's chief arguments that *sophia* and *phronēsis* are
distinct is that the former is the same sort of state wherever it is found –
in gods as well as human beings – but the latter is relative to the species
of thing in which it is found. For a member of a species to have *phronēsis*

---

pertaining to particular actions: "*nous* and not reasoning deals with both primary definitions
and ultimate particulars" (1142a36–b1). To posit a rule as covering instances might seem to be
the same skill as correctly interpreting particulars as falling under a rule.

[12] See *Metaphysics*, book 12 for Aristotle's theology.

(and here the rendering "sagacity" works best) is for it to pursue effectively and in an ordered way what is ultimately and basically in its own self interest, and this will vary across species.[13] A human being might know what is best (say) for a species of fish in general, and we might even make particular determinations about what course of action would most benefit some particular fish, but our doing so would not be the same as our exercising fish-promoting *phronēsis*; this, rather, would require a dedication above all to the most basic goods of that fish. (A human caretaker of fish is not devoted to the good of the fish above all; he is not, as it were, a *slave* to the fish.) *Phronēsis* therefore attains *qualified* truth in practical reasoning, truth which is relative to a species; but wisdom, in contrast, attains *truth* (full stop). And thus wisdom is preferable to administrative ability, in the way that an unqualified good is preferable to a qualified good of the same sort: "It would be strange for someone to suppose that political art or administrative ability was the very best state, unless he was supposing that a human being was the best good in the whole universe" (1141a20–22).

After demarcating *phronēsis* from other thinking-related virtues, in chapters 8–11 Aristotle says something directly about *phronēsis*, by giving a classification of it and then discussing incidental traits which resemble *phronēsis*, and which presumably are employed by someone who has *phronēsis*, but which nevertheless are slightly different. We can outline these chapters as follows:

6.6 Classification of forms and manifestations of *phronēsis*
6.7 Good at thinking things through (*euboulia*)
6.8 Perceptiveness (*sunesis*)
6.9 Sympathetic understanding (*gnōmē*)

In 6.8 he gives two classifications of administrative ability, which apparently are interlocking, and when put together look something like the following diagram (p. 226). But I shall not here discuss these chapters, which present no special difficulties.

---

[13] When Aristotle admits freely that the various species of non-rational animals each have their own sort of "sagacity," he must have in mind their instinctual behavior: 1141a25–26.

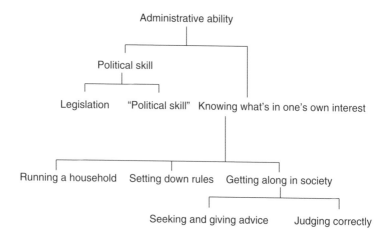

THE "TARGET" TO WHICH "SOUND REASON" LOOKS

Aristotle concludes book 6 by carrying out his second task, which, as we saw, was to identify the "target" to which *phronēsis* refers as it adjusts and refines actions done in accordance with virtue. I should perhaps say something more about this role of adjusting and refining. It seems possible to distinguish various ways in which *phronēsis* does this, all of them somehow involving ordering.

We are not here concerned with actions of the sort that, Aristotle claims, are never to be done in any circumstances, such as murder, theft, and adultery. As we have seen, Aristotle thinks that such actions already have built into their specification that they involve irrational extremes (perhaps if only the sort of extreme that marks any injustice), so that they could *never* be done correctly. It makes no sense to give the recommendation, "Murder someone only in the way that sound reason bids," which suggests that there is a sensible way of murdering someone. Aristotle is concerned, rather, with the broad field of actions that are not ruled out *tout court* and principles that might be taken to direct or guide actions like that. Such principles hold "for the most part" and therefore admit of being suspended or overruled (e.g. "repay friends before strangers"; "give freely to relatives in need"); or they can be formulated only in outline and therefore need to be interpreted given the circumstances (e.g. "don't talk about yourself in conversation"; "avoid offensive humor"); or they are dependent upon some condition, which might not be appropriately satisfied (e.g. "when it is necessary to fight, act courageously"). *Phronēsis* would presumably adjust and refine the operation of the character-related virtues in all of these ways.

Aristotle conceives of *phronēsis*, insofar as it takes on this role, as like medical skill in relation to the body. The principles that govern the body in its functioning – principles of balancing and exchange – are not "rules" that the body follows consciously, but rather regularities of action.[14] When these regularities need redirection or adjustment, and only then, medicine intervenes with its deliberate skill. Similarly, a character-related virtue is a "state" which involves the habituation of non-rational elements; consequently, the principles that it follows are regularities of feeling and response: we are *disposed* (say) to repay friends before strangers; that is a person's *instinct* or *gut feeling*; he *feels right about* taking care of things in that way. No doubt there are maxims implicit in these habitual regularities of action (such as the very maxim cited above, "Repay friends before strangers"), but for all that a virtuous disposition is not simply a maxim.

But precisely because a virtuous disposition is a habit of a non-rational element in us, it needs direction and guidance. Yes, to be sure, typically we ought to repay friends before strangers, and we would not do so effectively and consistently unless that was what, in usual circumstances, "felt right" to us. But in some cases to follow this principle would lead us astray, and in such cases our habitual tendency needs to be checked or suspended, for instance, when the stranger to whom we owe money is in much greater need than our friend. In such cases it becomes necessary for *phronēsis* to intervene rather directly, and, Aristotle wishes to insist, it could not do so unless it had in view some sort of target, which yields an appropriate ordering or "prioritizing" of principles of action.

That the operation of the character-related virtues needs to be regulated is especially clear if one considers that the virtues of character are operative, as we saw, only *given* that we are *already engaged* in some sort of activity;[15] therefore, it cannot be their task to say whether or not we should engage in that activity. We show justice on the supposition that we are exchanging

---

[14] Although note that for Aristotle these regularities will be underwritten by structures and systems: something works in a balanced way because its parts and actions display balance.

[15] Recall Aristotle's important principle that it is by the same sorts of actions that people become virtuous or vicious, that it is therefore *how* we do them that counts for character.

or distributing divisible goods; therefore, justice does not decide whether
and to what extent we should engage in business or assume public
responsibilities. We show courage when at war; therefore, courage itself
does not decide whether we should or should not engage in war. We
apparently need a virtue distinct from the virtues of character, then, which
says in effect up to what point we should engage in those activities in
which those virtues are displayed. This presumably is the role of *phronēsis*.
It initiates or curtails those activities with a view to some order, and this
order is formulated with respect to some standard or target.

In 6.12–13 Aristotle reveals his hand and briefly states what he takes
this standard to be, although his more extended discussion and explanation will be found later, in book 10. He reveals his view in the course of
responding to a puzzle: if wisdom (*sophia*) is the best virtue a person can
have, how can it be that administrative ability (*phronēsis*), as it seems,
plays the role of directing and governing all human affairs? "It would
seem strange," Aristotle observes, "if, although administrative ability is
worse than wisdom, it nonetheless has more authority" (1143b33–34).

Aristotle's reply is that administrative ability has authority over wisdom, only in the way that medical skill "has authority" over health.
Medical skill "has authority" over health in the sense that it aims at health
and orders everything else in its domain so as to promote health;
likewise, administrative ability aims at wisdom and orders everything
else so as to promote the acquisition and actualization of wisdom:
"Administrative ability does not employ wisdom as an instrument;
rather, it looks to how wisdom might come into existence. It gives orders
then, *for the sake of* that; it does not give orders *to* that" (1145a7–9). The
Eudemian Ethics, as we saw, is even more explicit on this point:

Since a physician makes use of a definite standard, to which he looks and
judges that the body is healthy or not . . . so also a good person makes use of
a definite standard as regards his actions and choices . . . [W]hatever choice
or possession of things that are good by nature (goods of the body, money,
friends, or any other good) best results in the contemplation of God, this is
best – and that is the best standard. But whatever, through deficiency or
excess, hinders our service to and contemplation of God – this is bad. Our
soul is that way (and this is the best standard of the soul), when we perceive
the non-rational part of the soul, as such, as little as possible. (1249a21–b23)

Yet if we think that this view firmly tips Aristotle toward Selection
in finding the ultimate goal, matters are not so clear elsewhere in

6.12–13, where Aristotle argues that a person needs all of the virtues of character if administrative ability is to succeed in directing his actions toward the appropriate target. Aristotle begins those chapters by raising difficulties about the value of administrative ability and wisdom: wisdom deals with metaphysics and theology, not with human happiness, so what use does it have? It seems to be worthless. As for administrative ability, it is of no use to people who already have good character, any more than medical skill is useful to the healthy persons; yet if someone were not yet good, but wanted to become good, then he himself would no more need to acquire administrative ability than he would need to go to medical school in order to get cured. To become healthy, it is enough to follow the advice of someone else who has medical skill; similarly, to become good, it is enough to follow the advice of someone else who has *phronēsis*.

Aristotle's response to these difficulties has three parts.

1. First he denies the premise on which the difficulties are based. The difficulties presuppose that something should be sought and acquired only if it produces something good. But Aristotle maintains it might be the case that something should be sought, simply because *it* is good. In fact, a trait is good, if it puts that which has it in a good condition, and wisdom and administrative ability are themselves good for this reason at least: "We should say that these two virtues are required just on their own, because, at very least, they are virtues, each of a distinct part, even if neither produces anything else" (1144a1–3).

2. But, in any case, Aristotle wishes to insist, each virtue *does* produce something. Here he recalls the familiar maxim from 2.6 that a virtue of a thing "places it in a good condition and makes it so that it carries out its characteristic work well." Wisdom and *phronēsis* both make it so that a human being carries out his characteristic work well and achieves happiness. Wisdom produces happiness, not as something distinct from it, in the way that medical skill produces health, but in the way that health produces health (1144a3–5): it is constitutive of happiness.

As for *phronēsis*, Aristotle claims, it makes a person such that wisdom can play this role, in two ways: first, by presupposing the goal that is inherent in character-related virtue; and, secondly, by supplying whatever is relevant to attaining that goal. Character-related virtue, Aristotle remarks, has the task of "making the target correct" (1144a8), and administrative ability then brings about "those things that promote this" (a9): "[Character-related] virtue makes a person's choices correct, but that which is suitably done for the sake of this is not the work of [character-related] virtue but of some distinct power" (1144a20–22).

This is cryptic and puzzling. Apparently Aristotle wishes to maintain that the various character-related virtues – courage, generosity, magnanimity, justice, and so on – all point someone in the right direction, in the sense that they dispose him to seek happiness in the right way, and that *phronēsis*, through its work of governing and ordering one's affairs appropriately, helps one to achieve that goal.

What is especially puzzling about this is that Aristotle has maintained that wisdom is the goal to which *phronēsis* refers, yet he has so far not said anything about how the character-related virtues dispose someone to regard wisdom, or its actualization, as one's final goal. But how would courage keep someone on the course toward wisdom? How would generosity do this? What is the relationship between justice and wisdom? Is Aristotle's view the strong claim that philosophical contemplation is somehow aimed at implicitly by anyone who acts virtuously? Recall that Aristotle maintains that character-related virtues aim at the *kalon*, at what is admirable and noble in action, a kind of moral beauty. Does he think that we possess this moral beauty only through some activity that is similar to contemplation? On this view, to seek the *kalon* in action, above everything else, would be thereby to be committed, implicitly, to the preferability of contemplation above everything else as the goal for one's life. This is a tantalizing suggestion, but Aristotle says nothing about it. Or is Aristotle's view the more modest claim that character-related virtues dispose someone to achieve the right "target" only in the sense that they do not allow the target to become wrong. Arguably, someone who acts unjustly or out of cowardice, to that extent definitely does *not* take his ultimate goal to consist in philosophical contemplation, but rather in something like material prosperity or bodily safety. Aristotle even claims in 6.5 that self-mastery (*sōphrosunē*) has received its name from administrative

ability (*phronēsis*), because the former saves or preserves administrative ability (*sōzousan tēn phronēsin*):

Pleasure and pain destroy and corrupt not every grasp that we have on
things – for instance, that a triangle contains or does not contain two right
angles – but the grasp that we have on matters involving action. The first
principle of action is that for the sake of which actions are to be carried out;
but when someone is corrupted by pleasure or pain, immediately the first
principle fails to show itself, nor is it clear that one ought to choose and do
everything for the sake of that and on account of that. Bad character is after
all corruptive of the first principle. (1140b11–20)

3. Aristotle concludes his consideration of the difficulties by a
discussion of the way in which administrative ability adjusts and
refines the operation of the character-related virtues. In explaining
this point at some length (1144a22–1145a11), Aristotle maintains that
administrative ability and the character-related virtues are mutually
dependent. Administrative ability cannot exist without the character-
related virtues, because these supply the correct target, and *phronēsis*
cannot exist if it has the wrong target: when effective deliberative
reasoning is directed at a false good, it can be no more than shrewdness or cleverness.[16] But the habits and dispositions that constitute
character-related virtues similarly cannot exist without administrative ability, since (as we have seen) these would lead to incorrect and
harmful action if they were not adjusted and guided by administrative ability – this would be as if someone had only "natural virtues,"
inborn tendencies to act generously, magnanimously, and so on,
without these ever being refined or corrected.

Aristotle uses this remark about the mutual dependence of *phronēsis* and the virtues of character to give his solution to the question of
the unity of virtues, which he poses in this way: is it the case that
someone cannot have one virtue without having all the virtues? As we
have seen, Socrates and Plato had maintained that the virtues were
thus united, because they took all of the virtues to be facets or aspects
of a single sort of knowledge. On the view that Aristotle has
defended, in contrast, it would appear that the virtues need not
occur together: if virtues are simply good habits, which are actualized

---

[16] As we saw, *phronēsis* is a virtue of practical reasoning, which has both a reasoning and a
desiderative component; therefore, both must be good for the virtue to exist.

relative to distinct domains, then there would seem to be no reason why someone might not display justice when engaging in business, but lack (say) generosity when associating with friends. Aristotle's solution is that the virtues as occurring naturally are not united – a person could have inborn impulses and a temperament that would yield much the same actions as a virtue – but considered strictly, as tendencies to action that are appropriately shaped and refined, they are united. A person cannot have even a single virtue of character, in the strict sense, if its operation is not adjusted and governed by administrative ability, yet no one can have administrative virtue, if he lacks the correct first principles, and these are supplied and preserved by the virtues of character. Thus to have a single virtue of character implies having all of the virtues.

This solution is clever and appealing, but at the same time it is perplexing, since it relies on the claim, which Aristotle does not fully or clearly explain, that administrative ability has its first principles supplied for it by the various virtues of character.

FURTHER READING

Broadie (1991), chapter 4 is a good general guide to book 6. Anscombe (1965) gives a provocative account of distinctively practical reasoning and truth attained in action. See also Wiggins (1980).

There has been something of a revival of interest in "intellectual virtue": see Zagzebski (1996) for a recent theory meant to be Aristotelian in spirit. For two very different and recent attempts to account for practical reasoning as non-instrumental, see Hampton (1998) and Richardson (1994).

CHAPTER 8

Akrasia, *or failure of self-control* (Nicomachean Ethics *7.1–10*)

By the end of book 6 Aristotle has completed his examination of the virtues, both the virtues of the non-rational part of the soul that is responsive to reason (books 3–6) and those of the rational part of the soul (book 6). One would think that, at this point, he would be in a position to bring his investigation in the *Ethics* to an end. He had said (in book 1) that the ultimate goal of human life is some activity, or activities, of the sort that we can carry out through having the virtues. With a view to determining this, he identified and described the various virtues. Should he not now simply make a decision on this matter? Yet he does not attempt to do so until book 10, chapter 6.

For the moment, Aristotle puts on hold his search for happiness, in order to discuss three topics which he regards as closely related: pleasure, friendship, and *akrasia*. He discusses pleasure (7.11–14; 10.1–5), because he wishes to argue that happiness is the most pleasant as well as the best good. Friendship (books 8 and 9) is important, because relationships involving friendship are the ordinary context in which good persons exercise their virtue; moreover, since human beings are social animals, human happiness will be essentially social and therefore something that must be shared among friends, if possessed at all. But *akrasia*, the subject of 7.1–10, requires discussion, as will become clear, largely as a kind of follow-up to his account of the virtues.

But first we should say what *akrasia* is. This is not a straightforward task, and indeed Aristotle's discussion is largely aimed at becoming clear about how to characterize and classify *akrasia*. The term in Greek means literally "not in command" and is variously rendered in English as "lack of control," "weakness," "moral weakness," "weakness of will," or even (as in older translations) "incontinence." The opposite of *akrasia* is *enkrateia*, which means literally "being in command" and is rendered as "self-control," "strength of character," "moral strength," "strength of will," or (again archaically) "continence." The Greek terms were contested in Aristotle's day, and today the English analogues are similarly contested. What counts as "lack of self-control"? What happens when someone loses self-control?

It should be noted that, although commentators frequently speak of *akrasia*, or "lack of self-control," as a particular psychological process or event, Aristotle is apparently even more interested in *akrasia* and *enkrateia* as persistent states of the soul, just as vice and virtue are persistent states. Admittedly, someone with *akrasia* acts in characteristic ways, but the condition is distinct from that sort of action, and the term applies principally to the condition. That there should be such enduring conditions is implied by Aristotle's theory of the virtues. Recall that, for Aristotle, when someone has a virtue of character, his non-rational impulses are harmonized with what the rational part of the soul requires. A virtuous person has no desire to do things that are wrong or bad, Aristotle holds, and this is why such a person is pleased by doing what is right, but would be distressed to do something wrong. Yet we may easily imagine someone who was very much like a virtuous person in what he *thinks* he should do, but who had persistent *desires* to do things that he thinks he should not do. Someone who had such desires but typically did not control them, and was prone to act on them, would have *akrasia*; someone who had such desires, but who typically could control them, not acting on them, would have *enkrateia*.

We can capture this in the following chart, where a check indicates that a person having the condition is as he should be in the relevant respect.

	Virtue (*aretē*)	Self-control (*enkrateia*)	Lack of self-control (*akrasia*)	Vice (*kakia*)
What he thinks he should do	√	√	√	X
What he has impulses to do	√	X	X	X
What he in fact does	√	√	X	X

As persistent states of character, then, *akrasia* and *enkrateia* fall between virtue and vice. This explains why Aristotle would want to examine these conditions at length. *Virtue* and *vice* are, so to speak, ideal conditions, of which there will be few pure instances; one would expect that most people fall somewhere between the one and the other. *Akrasia* would presumably be the category into which the largest portion of human action and character must be sorted. Whether Aristotle's entire framework of ethics is a satisfactory way of understanding the strengths and foibles of actual human beings will, to a large extent, hinge on the plausibility of his account of *akrasia* and *enkrateia*.

That these conditions fall in between virtue and vice puzzles Aristotle (see 1145b1–2; 1154b33–34) and probably explains the elaborate method that Aristotle adopts for his discussion. This is described in a famous methodological passage, already noted, at the beginning of book 7:

> We should discuss lack of self-control and effeminacy (or softness), as well as self-control and toughness, since none of these conditions should be regarded as involving quite the same condition as virtue or as vice, or as a different kind of thing. As in other cases, what we should do is set down how things appears to people (the *phainomena*), then, after going through all the difficulties (*aporiai*), to vindicate – that's the best case – all of the reliable opinions (*endoxa*) about the subject, but, failing that, we should vindicate the bulk of them, or those that are most authoritative. The reason is that, if the difficulties are dissolved and the reliable opinions are preserved, then our view will be sufficiently established. (1145b2–7)

The discussion of 7.2–10 follows this plan exactly. Aristotle first sets down at 1145b8–20 "what seems to be the case" (*ta phainomena*), that is, what seems to be true to people and finds expression in what they say. He presents in fact fourteen distinct opinions about self-control and lack of self-control.[1] Next he formulates five difficulties about

---

[1] It is useful to distinguish and number the *phainomena*. Aristotle groups some of these views in pairs; we may follow this arrangement and number them as follows:

Φ1.
  (a) Self-control and toughness are good.
  (b) Lack of self-control and softness are bad.

Φ2.
  (a) To have self-control is to abide by your reasoning.
  (b) To lack self-control is to abandon your reasoning.

akrasia.[2] And then the subsequent discussion is devoted to resolving these in such a way as to clarify what is true in the various *phainomena.*

Often, in the above methodological passage, interpreters take the phrase "as in the other cases" in an unrestricted sense as meaning "as in any philosophical investigation whatsoever." On this interpretation, Aristotle is describing in that passage a universal 'dialectical method' which is to be employed generally in philosophy: he is maintaining that the method recommended here, which he employs in book 7, is the sole method to be used in philosophy. Yet such an interpretation is hardly plausible and furthermore unnecessary. It is hardly plausible because (as scholars have often pointed out) Aristotle rarely uses this method even elsewhere in the *Ethics,* and he does so only infrequently in other works.[3] It would be odd for him to claim that this is the only method to follow always in philosophy, when he hardly uses it himself. Moreover, Aristotle is remarkably flexible and

Φ3.

    (a) To lack self-control is to do what you think is bad, because of emotion.

    (b) To have self-control is not to follow desires that you regard as bad, because of reason.

Φ4. Anyone who has the virtue of self-mastery also has both self-control and toughness.

Φ5.

    (a) Anyone with self-control and toughness has the virtue of self-mastery.

    (b) It is not the case that anyone with self-control and toughness has the virtue of self-mastery.

Φ6.

    (a) Self-indulgent persons are just those who lack self-control.

    (b) Self-indulgent persons and those who lack self-control are different.

Φ7.

    (a) Someone who has practical wisdom might lack self-control.

    (b) No one with practical wisdom can lack self-control.

Φ8. There is such a thing as lack of self-control with regard to keeping one's temper, seeking honor, and seeking profit.

---

[2] Difficulty 1 is given at 1145b21–1146a9; Difficulty 2 at 1146a9–16; Difficulty 3 at 1146a16–31; Difficulty 4 at 1146a31–b2; and Difficulty 5 at 1146b2–5.

[3] Bostock concludes a thorough review of Aristotle's method in the *Ethics* by saying that "despite the fact that he advocates it as the right method to pursue on all issues, he does not in fact rely upon it in any other major discussion [sc. besides 7.1–10]," p. 234.

inventive in his philosophical investigations, and it would therefore seem strange, and in need of further argument, for him to claim that his various kinds of investigation are at bottom instances of the single form of investigation that he describes here.

But furthermore it is not necessary to take the passage in this implausibly expansive and unrestricted sense, since it may easily be understood in a narrow sense, as bearing principally upon the task at hand.[4] As we have seen, as Aristotle views it, *akrasia* and *enkrateia* are not quite the same as either virtue or vice, nor yet are they entirely different. One might therefore wonder: how should we deal with kinds of things that, curiously, fall in this way *in between* other kinds? In cases like that, in fact, people will sometimes treat the intermediate kind as though it were the same sort of thing as the other identifiable kinds, but sometimes also people will distinguish it from them. That people deal with the intermediate form in this way will inevitably lead to apparent contradictions and "difficulties." How, then, should we best handle this lack of clarity and decisiveness in ordinary ways of speaking?

Let us say that one kind of thing is *analogous* to others if it does not fall under a common genus with the others (that is, it is not one among several species of the same genus as the others) and yet it is not so distinct as to count as unrelated. The methodological passage can be understood as describing the best way to proceed when we wish to describe and classify a kind of thing that is thus analogous to other identifiable kinds: the first thing to do is to get clear about the contradictory things that are said about it; next, one should find a precise description of the analogous kind which is under investigation; and, if this description is correctly framed, it will consequently reveal the extent to which what people say about it is true. The correct account therefore "leaves standing" those apparently conflicting views, and that it does so is the best proof of its correctness. Since *akrasia* and *enkrateia* are analogous kinds, in this sense, Aristotle deals with them in this way.

That this narrow reading of the methodological passage is correct is supported by the fact that the handful of passages in the *Ethics*

---

[4] That is, we understand the phrase "as in the other cases" in a restricted sense to mean "as in the other cases *like this one*."

where Aristotle uses something like the method described are those in which he deals similarly with the classification of things that differ in kind but nonetheless are analogously related: his discussions, namely, of pleasure (7.11–14), friendship (8.1–4), and of self-love (9.8).[5]

HOW THE PROBLEM OF *AKRASIA* APPEARED TO ARISTOTLE

Let us say that there is an instance of *akrasia* when:

(i) a person grasps correctly what he should do (or: his reason says that he should act in some way), but
(ii) he does something else, and
(iii) it is appropriate to say that he does this other thing *because of* some impulse or emotion.

Aristotle's first concern in book 7 is: how is *akrasia* in this sense possible?[6]

In saying that Aristotle's first concern is with how *akrasia* is possible, I do not mean to suggest that Aristotle seriously entertained the suggestion that, perhaps, *akrasia* either did not occur or was impossible. In fact, Aristotle thinks that it is obvious that *akrasia* occurs: we observe instances of it all the time, and therefore it certainly exists and is possible. His very division of the soul in 1.13 into rational and non-rational parts was based upon remarks about *akrasia*. One might therefore say that his entire theory of virtue and vice presupposes the possibility of *akrasia*. Yet, although he never doubts its existence, Aristotle thinks there are serious difficulties in the notion of *akrasia* and that therefore some subtlety is needed in accounting for it correctly.

We may begin to get a sense of Aristotle's concerns by considering first the view he ascribes to Socrates:

It would be astonishing if, when knowledge is around (so Socrates used to think) some other thing took control and dragged it about, as though it were a slave. Socrates for his part fought indiscriminately against that notion,

---

[5] Aristotle's remark at 9.8.1168b12–13 seems to recapitulate the method: "Presumably, then, as regards these sorts of claims, one needs to draw a distinction and determine to what extent and in what way each claim so distinguished is true."

[6] From this point on for convenience I shall use *akrasia* to mean the condition or the corresponding act indifferently; in what sense it is meant will be clear from the context.

through maintaining that *akrasia* does not exist. Why? Because no one acts against what he takes to be best; rather, it's because of ignorance [that a person fails to do what is best].(1145b23–27)

That is to say, Socrates was so much concerned with protecting the truth of the idea that "knowledge cannot be overpowered" that he adopted the much stronger position, that we never act against what we *in any way* take or recognize to be what we should do. Aristotle regards this stronger view as clearly false. He thinks that there is something right about Socrates' concern, yet he disagrees with the way Socrates frames the problem and with Socrates' solution.

Aristotle rejects the way Socrates frames the problem, because for Aristotle the difficulty is not whether *knowledge* might be overpowered, but (roughly) whether human *reason* might be overpowered by an emotion.[7] That is, Aristotle takes *akrasia* to raise difficulties more broadly about the nature of human irrationality. Aristotle's view is apparently that the power or faculty of reason cannot be overpowered by emotion. Yet of course Aristotle does not wish to deny that *akrasia* exists, and that a natural way of describing *akrasia* is just to say that someone is "overcome" by his impulses and emotions; in fact, Aristotle speaks in this way himself (e.g. 1149b3). On the other hand, it would be problematic also to say that reason is not *overpowered* by emotion, but rather *gives way* or *concedes ground* to it – since how could it do so, unless it somehow consented to or affirmed what the emotion was aiming at? But in that case it would be difficult to see how an *akratic* person would be different from a vicious person, who *deliberately* aims to satisfy his desire to do bad things.

Thus, the problem of *akrasia*, for Aristotle, is to describe a condition in which someone acts irrationally, and does what an emotion provokes rather than what his reason indicates, but where the emotion does not "overpower" his reason, nor does his reason accede to

---

[7] That this is Aristotle's concern is shown by how he handles the view that it is *true belief* rather than *knowledge* which is at stake in an instance of *akrasia* (see 1146b24–31; cf. 1145b35–1146a4). To make this change, he claims, does not remove the difficulty. Suppose someone believes, but with strong conviction, that he should not do something, yet he does it anyway. That would apparently still be an instance of his reason being overpowered by an emotion. In fact Aristotle freely interchanges talk of belief (*doxa*) and of knowledge (*epistēmē*) in his discussion of Socrates' view, as if the distinction were unimportant for his purposes. And he commonly discusses the problem of *akrasia* with respect to the role that reason (*logos*) plays in it, e.g. 1145b10–14.

the emotion. As Aristotle puts it: "There is a kind of person who tends to depart from sound reason and who is such that, although his emotion so controls him that he acts against what sound reason says, nonetheless the emotion does not so control him that he comes to accept that he should pursue such pleasures without restraint" (1151a20–24).

Aristotle does not explicitly state his reasons for agreeing with Socrates' basic intuition and holding that the human power of reason cannot be overpowered by an emotion.[8] Yet we may speculate as to his grounds. In the *Ethics* he generally holds that reason is divine in character (see for example 1177a15–16, b30–34); if so, then it would be absurd for something not divine to prove more powerful, for if the non-divine could overpower the divine within human nature, then it could do so elsewhere as well.[9] Furthermore, Aristotle takes reason to be naturally authoritative in a human being (cf. 1102b32), yet one might hold that nothing could have a natural authority, unless that authority were operative *always* (otherwise, the authority would be in some way *acquired*); but that authority would be empty, if it did not carry with it the possibility of control. Again, Aristotle thinks that it is *possible* that we be virtuous (cf. 3.5) and that, in some sense, it is the intention of nature that human beings be virtuous; but virtue, he thinks, implies the uniform governance of actions and emotions by reason; yet if emotions could overpower reason in *some* cases, then in principle they could do so in *any* case – and thus virtue would be either impossible or, at least, unstable (cf. 1100b15–16). And his view is probably based as well on more metaphysical considerations: if reason is not a material faculty (as Aristotle apparently argues in *De anima* 3.4–5), then it would seem that if it had control over something material at all, it would have it without restriction, since what could serve to limit it in *some* cases only? Its operation certainly could not be checked as if it were in conflict with some other material power. Or, again, it seems to be even a conceptual truth that someone we count as a rational being has control over his own activities:

[8] In fact, he does not in book 7 even explicitly affirm this view; rather, he takes this for granted, as becomes clear in the course of his discussion.
[9] Some line of thought like this, too, seems to underlie the famous Final Argument of Plato's *Phaedo*: if a single life could be overpowered by death, then all living things, even the gods, would be threatened (see *Phaedo* 106d).

"someone is said 'to have control' (*enkratēs*) or 'to lack control' (*akratēs*)," Aristotle remarks, "depending upon whether his mind is in control or not, on the presumption that this is what each person is" (1168b34–35) – and so one might simply regard it as an absurdity that *something else* other than that person be in control of *himself,* as if he could be that person, without the possibility of self-control.

The problem of *akrasia* for Aristotle, then, is as follows: reason has control over the emotions; something that has control can come to lack it only if either something else takes away its control (it is "overpowered") or it relinquishes control; but an emotion cannot take control away from reason; nor could reason relinquish control to an emotion, except by acceding to what the emotion aims at, in which case there would no longer be any important distinction between *akrasia* and *vice.* (*Akrasia* on this last suggestion would simply be another form of vice, one that makes more of a fuss, or puts on a better show, before it goes ahead anyway with the bad action.) This is the context of Aristotle's discussion in 7.3 of Socrates' view, and it explains why Aristotle insists that "the fundamental basis of the investigation" (1146b14) is being clear about the distinction between *akrasia* and the vice of self-indulgence: "a self-indulgent person is deliberately (*prohairoumenos*) led about [by his desires], accepting that 'I should always pursue the pleasure that's before me'; an akratic person in contrast does not accept this, yet he pursues it anyway" (b23–24).

ARISTOTLE'S REPLY TO SOCRATES: INITIAL DISTINCTIONS

We should begin with an observation about Aristotle's language in his response to Socrates, which potentially can cause confusion. In his discussion Aristotle uses the terms "knowledge" and "ignorance," and he even says that what is at issue is whether, when *akrasia* occurs, the agent *knows* that he should not do what he is doing and, if he does, how it is that he knows this (1146b9). Yet in saying this Aristotle is using "knowledge" (and the opposite term, "ignorance") in an informal sense, as he often does elsewhere in the *Ethics* (e.g. 1094a26, 28; 1105a31), to mean simply some kind of "grasp" or understanding of something. He is not using this term in the technical sense which he had just defined in 6.3 – that an agent knows something just in case he has an active capacity to devise proofs as regards necessary and unchanging subject matter (1139b31–32).[10] The reason why he uses this language is in part a point of *charity* in argument: that one should not use a mere difference in terminology to gain an upper hand in a philosophical debate. But, more deeply, Aristotle's own concern, to explain how reason cannot be overpowered by an emotion, is a concern about reason *insofar as it is successful.* He is not interested in deliberative reasoning, which might be at a loss as to what to affirm or seek (1112b18–25), or calculative reasoning, which can make mere mistakes in calculating (1111a33–b3). He is interested, rather, in reason insofar as it *sees* something and is prepared to stand by it, and the term "knowledge" suggests this well enough.

Aristotle's procedure is first to point out exactly what would be involved for knowledge in this informal sense to be "present" or operative, because clearly there would be no question of knowledge being overpowered by emotion, if it were not even, so to speak, in the field. To this end, he makes three distinctions:

1. Knowledge as a possession versus knowledge that is "activated" or put to use (1146b31–35); for example, you understand that adultery is wrong, but (almost certainly) you were not actually thinking it was wrong five seconds before reading this sentence.[11]

2. Knowledge of a universal truth versus knowledge of particulars (1146b35–1147a10); for example, you understand that adultery is wrong, but you do not know that the other person is married (or: you do know it, but the other person is wearing a disguise, so your knowledge is not operative as regards this person before you, cf. 1147a7).

3. Knowledge when sober versus knowledge when affected with a "mind altering" bodily condition (1147a10–24); for example, you understand that you should not commit adultery with this married person, but, when you have had several drinks, there is a sense

---

[10] Hence, as was noted, he is happy even to call this grasp a "belief" (1147a25, b3), even though belief implies a lack of knowledge.

[11] An example such as adultery is helpful as providing a clear case of someone's going wrong (by Aristotle's lights). Philosophers will often use as an example of *akrasia*, say, eating a piece of cake when one is on a diet. But, from Aristotle's point of view, one could not in advance rule out in such an example that it might be best after all to eat the cake.

in which you do *not* understand this, even though you might even say that it is wrong if someone were to ask you.

Each distinction supplies a sense of "knowledge" in which it evidently is possible for someone to have knowledge, but for his knowledge not to be in some worrisome way "overpowered," since it is not even in play. Each distinction, then, can serve as the basis for a reply to Socrates. Thus, after presenting the first distinction only, Aristotle declares, alluding to Socrates' original objection, "This is what seems astonishing – for someone not to do what he's *actually thinking* he should do – but it's not astonishing if he's not actually thinking about it" (1146b35), as if this point alone resolves Socrates' problem. Again, as he introduces the second distinction, Aristotle notes that "nothing hinders" someone from acting contrary to his "knowledge" – if by that one means merely his knowledge *of universal truths*, when he lacks knowledge of particulars (1147a1–2) – because actions have to do with particulars, and thus, if someone's knowledge extended only to universals, it would not, so far, even have a chance of being "overpowered" by some emotion that was influencing action. The third distinction similarly clearly gives a sense in which we might "know" something, yet in which that knowledge would not be operative as regards action: we are not, after all, in the slightest bit tempted to say that knowledge (or reason) is overpowered whenever someone gets drunk.

But Aristotle takes the third distinction to be the most relevant, and he goes on to develop it in more detail. Referring to people who "have but do not have" their usual understanding of what they should do, because of some change in their body, Aristotle claims: "Clearly we should say that akratic persons are in a condition similar to these" (1147a17–18). Yet why does he claim that only this third distinction is the one that is relevant, when the first two distinctions, as we have seen, also supply a response to Socrates?

The reason, it seems, is that Aristotle accepts the common view (indeed, it is one of the *phainomena*) that *akrasia* is to be attributed to an impulse or emotion:[12] it is *because of* an emotion that the akratic person does what he previously thought he should not do

---

[12] A *pathos*, literally an "induced change" or "affect" undergone by the agent.

(1145b12–13). Thus, from the start, Aristotle has insisted that, however *akrasia* is explained, one needs to take account of the *change* that the agent undergoes, in relation to the impulse or emotion that he feels. For instance, when Aristotle initially states Socrates' view, that *akrasia* does not exist, and then points out that this view "is at odds with evident reality" (1145b28), Aristotle goes on to note that "We need to investigate the emotion (*pathos*) involved, if *akrasia* is a result of ignorance. What is the usual process (*tropos*) by which the ignorance arises? –since it's clear that, until the very point when the emotion takes hold, the person who lapses into *akrasia* thinks he should not act as he does" (1145b28–31). That is to say, the emotion is the more fundamental explanation of *akrasia* than (as on Socrates' view) the ignorance, because the emotion apparently causes the ignorance. Yet, of the three distinctions that Aristotle proposes, it is only the third distinction that seems related to any such change.

To say, as Aristotle in effect does as regards the first two distinctions, that nothing hinders a person from doing what he "knows" is wrong, in either of these two senses – that there's no impossibility in that – is so far simply to show that Socrates' denial of *akrasia* was groundless. But that was evident already. What one wants is a positive account, which appeals to relevant principles and causes, but subject to two constraints, which are familiar to us already. One needs to give a positive account of *akrasia* according to which it is clear, firstly, that knowledge (or reason) is not overpowered by emotion, and, secondly, that someone who lapses into *akrasia* differs from a self-indulgent person insofar as he never affirms an incorrect principle of action. Although Socrates' view has been rebutted – which was hardly necessary anyway – Aristotle's own difficulty remains: how can reason fail to be in control over someone's bad behavior if it neither is overpowered nor accedes to the bad behavior? This is why Aristotle at 1147a24–b17 goes on to give a fuller account of *akrasia*, which he characterizes now as appealing "even more to the relevant principles of change" (1147a24, cf. 1167b29, 1170a13).[13]

---

[13] It seems plausible that *eti kai . . . phusikōs* at 1147a24 constitutes a single linguistic unit and has the sense given in the translation here, not unlike *phusikōteron*, as at 1167b29, 1170a13. (The resulting *asyndeton* is consistent with the sentence's marking a fresh line of thought.)

ARISTOTLE'S POSITIVE ACCOUNT OF AKRASIA

It seems that Aristotle's account of *akrasia* at 1147a24–b17 should be understood dynamically: he is interested in the process (*tropos*) by which someone lapses into *akrasia* (*akrateuesthai*, 1147b1). A particular episode of *akrasia* is something that arises (*ginetai*, 1145b29); it involves timing (*hama*, 1147a31); it has elements that take a progressive course (*agei, kinein*, 1147a34–35). An episode of *akrasia* eventually dissipates (*luetai*, 1147b6). How exactly it dissipates requires a physiological explanation (1147b6–9). In its onset, course, and alleviation it is comparable to an illness (1150b29–36). A person can be more or less disposed to develop *akrasia*, depending upon his underlying bodily temperament and humors (1152a27–33, cf. 1154b11–15). So, then, Aristotle's positive account of *akrasia* should be understood as giving a sketch of a typical process.

His account has three parts: (i) some preliminary observations, which provide criteria for a satisfactory account of *akrasia* (1147a25–31); (ii) the account itself (1147a31–35); and (iii) five observations deriving from the account (1147a35–b17).

(i) The preliminary observations are as follows:

(a) One kind of belief is general; another kind is about particulars. As regards particulars, it is sense perception which is directly decisive.

(b) Whenever a single belief is made from these, it is necessary that the soul immediately thereafter assert the conclusion, and, in matters involving action, that it act immediately. For instance, supposing "All that is sweet is to be tasted, and this (particular thing) is sweet," then it is necessary (assuming he is able to act and is not hindered) that he simultaneously also do this (1147a25–31).

One way to understand this is the following. Regard a 'general belief' as one that we would be disposed to assent to at various times and in various places; regard a 'belief about particulars' as one that we would be disposed to assent to only at a particular time or place, or in the presence of a particular person or thing. Since any action is something particular, it needs to be cued to particulars. But this requires beliefs about particulars; and beliefs about particulars will depend upon what I perceive with my senses. For instance, I may have the general belief that, in order to hear the daily news, I should turn on the radio at 1pm; moreover, I may have various general beliefs about how to turn on the radio, and how the radio works. But I will not actually turn on the radio, until I believe that *it is now 1 pm*.[14] Moreover, I believe that it is now 1 pm, because of something I presently perceive with my senses – I actually *see* the town clock reading 1 o'clock.

Particular beliefs are "directly decisive" for action, because whether or not we act on a general belief will depend upon particular beliefs. Hence, we can sometimes rule out that someone has a general belief, given the particular belief that he has, or that he has a particular belief, if we know that he has a general belief of a certain sort yet does not act correspondingly. For instance, consider Aristotle's own example: if someone does not taste the sweet thing before him, but (we know) he believes that "All that is sweet is to be tasted," then he must lack the particular belief that *this thing before him is a sweet thing*; moreover, if he does have that particular belief, yet fails to taste the sweet thing before him, then we can conclude that he must not have the general belief that *all that is sweet is to be tasted*. In a person who is able to act and is not hindered, his failure to act implies a lack of either the general or the particular belief.[15]

But this has immediate implications for *akrasia*, as follows. In *akrasia*, someone has a lapse in which he changes from acting well to acting badly. That is to say, any case of *akrasia* involves someone who, beforehand, is perfectly able to act and is not hindered, and is

[14] The example is from Mellor (2001, 312): "Now suppose more specifically that I want to hear the one o'clock news, so I push the switch at one o'clock. Why did I do that at one o'clock and not some minutes or hours earlier or later? Well, obviously, because I wanted to hear the one o'clock news. But that on its own is not enough, even given that I know that pushing the switch turns the radio on. I could have been wanting to hear the one o'clock news for hours, and I could have mastered the radio years ago. Something more than these two steady states of desire and belief is needed actually to propel my finger to the switch at a specific time. Obviously, what I also need to believe is that it is now one o'clock. Until I acquire that present-tense belief, I shall do nothing, however much I want to hear the news and however strong my tenseless belief in the efficacy of the switch."

[15] Once more, Mellor: "If a man wants above all else to do something at a particular time, knows how to do it, and is able to do it, it makes no sense to suppose he believes that time to be present but still does nothing because he is too feckless to act on his belief. If in those circumstances he does not act on that present-state belief, he does not have it" (313).

fully aware of everything relevant yet does not do some wrong thing, but then, a little while later, he does do it. That he at first does *not* do it, implies that he does *not* have the general belief that he *should* do it. Presumably also (Aristotle assumes this) he has the general belief that he should *not* do it. But that he later *does* do it, implies that he then lacks the particular belief that would be decisive for his not doing it. The very lack of consistency in an akratic person's action – his hesitation and delay, no matter which path he takes – shows that he lacks both a general belief of an incorrect sort and (at a later time) the right sort of particular belief.

(ii) This then leads Aristotle to posit at 1147a31–35 the following schema:

Therefore, whenever:

[a] a general belief is present in [the soul] hindering something from being tasted,

[b] and also another, that "All that is sweet is pleasant, and this particular thing is sweet," and

[c] this is activated, and

[d] as it happens, sense desire is present in [the soul],

then, although the one belief issues the command, "Get away from this," sense desire nonetheless exerts its pull, since each part of the soul is capable of initiating movement.

Note that the passage at no point mentions an akratic person's *action*, his doing something that he thinks he should not. Rather, as the final sentence of the passage indicates, Aristotle is here aiming to give an account simply of the *conflict* such a person experiences: it is not, so far, an account of how that conflict gets resolved. The passage might therefore serve just as well as a description of the condition of an enkratic person, prior to his doing the right thing. Moreover, as was said, Aristotle's schema is meant to describe something that is dynamic. When Aristotle says, for instance, that sense desire "exerts its pull," surely we should think that it does so progressively, say, by first causing someone to rehearse even the line of thought, "All that is sweet is pleasant, and this particular thing is sweet," which leads to the conclusion that "This is pleasant," and which in turn increases sense desire for the thing. That is, the schema to this extent identifies a positive-feedback loop.

Understood in this way, Aristotle's schema serves in effect as a "model," which tells us whether or not someone is likely to be akratic, depending upon how we alter the elements of the model. Let us consider a particular case, to fix ideas. Suppose a man needs to lose weight and judges therefore that he should not eat between meals, as has been his usual practice. He therefore forms the general belief, "Nothing is to be tasted between meals." For this general belief to be effective, he has to believe additionally various particular beliefs, each time the possibility of eating something arises: "It is *now* between meals," " *This* is not to be tasted," and so on.[16] Suppose one day he is working from his home, and that therefore at various times he goes into the kitchen, when he takes a break or fixes coffee. Each time he does so, he notices food in the kitchen, and he must believe, at that time and with respect to that particular food, such things as that it is *now* between meals and that *this* particular food is not to be tasted. Perhaps, to help himself believe this, he thinks about how many calories the food has (and thus he thinks about how *this* food *now* has lots of calories), or he uses his imagination and tries to picture that if he ate the food, it would be transformed into fat and deposited directly onto his waistline. Nevertheless, he becomes increasingly hungry as the morning wears on. By the end of the morning, in fact, because of this hunger, when he enters the kitchen and sees the food, he begins to dwell upon it: "This food is tasty. Tasty things are pleasant to eat. It would be very pleasant to eat this food." As he thinks about the food in that way, he stimulates his hunger. He therefore becomes even more disposed to dwell on how pleasant it would be to eat it. Perhaps by this point he finds himself even walking over to a cabinet, mindlessly taking out a box of snacks (as he is half thinking about a problem from his work), and fingering the box – before he comes to his senses, repeats his resolution to himself, puts the box away, and leaves the room.

Aristotle's schema describes a conflict such as this. Now, will this person eat a snack before lunchtime or not? The schema obviously does not lead to such a prediction. However, it does identify which factors tell for or against each side of the conflict, and thus which

---

[16] Note that therefore it will be more difficult to follow a prohibition rather than an admonition: the prohibition must *repeatedly* be made effective.

variations would make it more or less likely that the man eats the food. For instance, the man is less likely to eat it: to the extent that he has strengthened his resolve by deliberating in advance; to the extent that he can avoid seeing or smelling food (or puts himself in a position where he cannot see or smell it); to the extent that he can manage or dampen his hunger (say, by drinking water to fill his stomach); to the extent that his imagination is less susceptible to the influence of his appetites. On the other hand, he is more likely to give in, insofar as his situation is altered in any of the opposite ways.

(iii) After giving his schema, Aristotle comments upon it:

[1] It follows that a person lapses into *akrasia* through the power of reason, somehow, and of belief. But the belief is not contrary of itself to sound reason, but only incidentally so, since it's the agent's sense desire that is contrary to sound reason, not his belief.
[2] It follows also, for this very reason, that wild animals are not akratic, because they have no grasp of anything general but have only representations and memories of particulars.
[3] As to how his lack of knowledge dissipates, and an akratic person becomes once again someone with knowledge – this gets the same explanation as does a drunk or sleeping person's [return to knowledge], and it's not something special for this sort of change. We need to turn to natural scientists for the explanation.
[4] The last premise is a belief about an object of sense perception and is decisive for action. Since that is so, either he does not grasp that premise, once he begins to undergo the change, or he grasps it in such a way that, as we said, he does not grasp it – but he *says* it in the way that someone who has had too much wine recites verses of Empedocles.
[5] Moreover, because the last term is not general and doesn't look like the sort of thing one has knowledge about, as a general term does, one gets something like the result that Socrates was looking for. The change takes place, not where what is thought to be knowledge in the strict sense is present (and that sort of knowledge is not "dragged about" because of an emotion), but rather where "sense knowledge" is present. (1147a35–b19)

In these comments, Aristotle is chiefly concerned with showing that his schema describes *akrasia* in a way that resolves the difficulty he was concerned about, namely that, in *akrasia*, reason is neither overpowered nor accedes to any bad principle.

In *akrasia* reason is not overpowered, because, rather, reason actually plays a role in the onset of *akrasia* (observation 1). On Aristotle's view, reason is no more overpowered in *akrasia* than when someone has too much to drink (although admittedly each subsequent drink makes him less unable to discern the effects of his drinking), or when a fatigued person falls asleep, and therefore stops reasoning, after he sits down on a comfortable chair. Yet note that Aristotle does not wish to say that the akratic person *deliberately* makes it so that his desire becomes effective. *Akrasia* is not like deliberately "getting drunk" or deliberately "making oneself" fall asleep. But if so, then the thoughts of an akratic person would be only *incidentally* contrary to the correct principle. On Aristotle's view, in *akrasia* we dwell on the pleasantness of something, and find ourselves thereby becoming increasingly affected by this, so that we are led with increasing desire actually to take pleasure in it, but all the while we are not deliberately *dwelling on its pleasantness in order to stir up an irresistible desire*. It is because of this point that *akrasia* occupies the puzzling position of being between virtue and vice.[17]

Aristotle takes reason's role in stirring up desire to be essential to *akrasia* (observation 2). One might say: if the desire were stirred up only through memories and mental imagery (and assuming this happened through no fault of the agent), then we would regard *akrasia* as a condition that deserved forbearance and understanding, rather than censure and blame – as with someone, for instance, who cannot but act on angry feelings which arise automatically, given certain stimuli, as a result of bad experiences in childhood.[18]

Yet, although reason plays an essential role in the onset of *akrasia*, once someone is beset by *akrasia*, his reason can do nothing to dissipate it; rather, the condition has to be dissipated through ordinary physiological processes (observation 3). However, that we cannot, by a deliberate act, free ourselves from an akratic episode, does not imply that we are not responsible for it, any more than that our inability to change our character immediately, by a single act, implies that we are

[17] Note that there is no reason why someone might not eventually change and want to make himself subject to overpowering desires. Then presumably he would have developed a vice: cf. 1154b15.

[18] "*Akrasia* is censured not as a defect simply, but also as a kind of badness, either as badness in a person without qualification, or as badness as regards some aspect of him" (1148a2–4).

not responsible for our character: an episode of *akrasia* is like the stone that, once released, cannot be recalled at will (cf. 1114a13–21).

As we have seen, it must be the case that someone who is being led by desire to enjoy a pleasure he thinks he should not enjoy *must* no longer be holding together the line of reasoning which forbids him from enjoying it. But it is not the correct *general* belief that he has abandoned: he held to it before the akratic episode; he holds to it afterward; and in the interim he does not undergo an intellectual conversion or corruption. Thus, during the akratic episode, some particular belief must be in some way lacking, of the sort which would have made his general belief effective. Note that Aristotle is not much concerned with describing the exact *manner* in which this particular belief is no longer available. It might simply be unavailable as a result of an ordinary instance of avoidance; for instance, the man in our example simply avoids looking at that part of the snack box which lists the calories and fat content of the snack, because this will make him think he should not eat it. Or, perhaps, the particular belief is unavailable because by some condition induced by the desire which is at work, he becomes so "absorbed" with the possibility of eating the snack that he ceases (this sort of thing happens) to have any effective sense that eating it would *count* as eating between meals. But after he has eaten half the box he 'comes to his senses' and wonders why he did that.

In any case, the preceding remark is enough to protect the claim that Socrates was concerned about, namely that nothing properly called "knowledge" can be dragged about by non-rational forces (observation 5). What can get dragged about are our particular beliefs. But, as we have seen, these spring fairly directly from perception, and they involve imagination and memory related to perception. It is hardly surprising that, as someone's sense desire for the pleasant thing increases, this has a direct effect on the direction and nature of his sense perception: he begins to look intently at and attend to what continues to inflame that desire, and his mental imagery and memories are stimulated correspondingly.

CENTRAL AND METAPHORICAL SENSES OF *AKRASIA*

As I said above, Aristotle's project in book 7 is in some sense principally one of classification. He regards *akrasia* as in some

curious way intermediate between virtue and vice, and he wishes to
give a description of *akrasia* which captures this. Yet because, as
Aristotle recognizes, the term "*akrasia*" is a disputed and controversial term, his theory of it at the same time gives his judgment as to
how that term is properly to be employed.

In fact, Aristotle holds a narrow and strict view about the proper
application of the term. '*Akrasia*' applies properly, he thinks, only to
lapses from correct conduct that are induced by the operation of
strong sense desire for the pleasures that come from taste and touch,
but primarily those of touch. He no doubt regards loss of self-control
involving sexual desire as the paradigmatic case of *akrasia*, and his
simplified examples involving sweet foods are perhaps intended as a
refined and indirect way of representing that sort of thing. That he
thinks of *akrasia* in this way explains why he can so naturally liken it
to episodes of mania or drunkenness, since sexual desire can have
similar manifestations.

All other applications of the term, he says, are metaphorical: "It is
clear, then, that *akrasia* and *enkrateia* involve only those things that
self-indulgence and self-mastery deal with, and that *akrasia* as regards
anything else constitutes a distinct form of *akrasia* – the term being
used in a metaphorical sense and not straightforwardly" (1149a21–24).
We correctly apply the term by extension to other conditions,
Aristotle says, only insofar as the emotion or desire (or, perhaps:
"induced change") is similar (1148b6–7).

Yet the emotion or desire involved in other conditions can hardly
be similar, because sense desire for the pleasures of touch is the only
human motive, Aristotle thinks, that we directly share with non-
rational animals. That was his argument, we should recall, in 3.10:
"Self-mastery and self-indulgence deal with the same sorts of pleasures in which all of the other animals share also" (1118a23–25). Even
hot-headed anger is set apart from sensual desire in this way, as
Aristotle takes pains to argue, and thus *akrasia* is only metaphorically
applied even to cases in which we lose control because of anger. The
reason is that anger takes as its object something that appears good
only as thought about in a certain way. You overcharge me for some
work, for instance, and I "boil over" when our conversation about it
turns into a shouting match, saying all kinds of nasty things I later
regret having said. In my anger I desire to attack you verbally in this

way only so long as I keep thinking of you as "unjust cheat." But in an episode of *akrasia* in the strict sense, the object of attraction is attractive because of features we need merely sense, not think about. Thinking about the food *stimulates* the senses and the imagination, but our continuing to do so is not necessary for the food to continue to have appeal:

His reason or imagination clearly represents the outrage or slight, and, as though rehearsing an argument – that this sort of thing is cause for attack – he immediately is in turmoil. But sense desire, in contrast, if reason or sense perception so much as indicates that "this is pleasant," presses on toward gratification. It follows that hot temper cooperates with reason, in a way, but sense desire does not. [*Akrasia* in the strict sense] is therefore more shameful, since in an episode of anger-*akrasia* a fellow is overcome by reason, in a way, but [in an episode of *akrasia*] he is overcome by sense desire, not by reason. (1149a32–b3)

Someone who suffers anger-*akrasia* correctly reasons that the fellow who committed an injustice deserves punishment; and he is right, too, to be indignant when he realizes this. He makes a kind of implicit mistake, however, if he attacks the other, as if he is the one who should rightly administer the punishment. His mistake is located in the usurpation, not the indignation: "Hot temper seems to listen in some way to reason, but to mistake what it says, like excitable servants who go off before hearing everything that one says and who later get your instructions wrong" (1149a25–28).

Naturally enough, any sort of departure from correct conduct on account of some emotion even less similar to sensual desire is called "*akrasia*" in an even more remote and metaphorical sense. Aristotle mentions a variety of such forms of *akrasia*: *akrasia* as regards gain, honor, money, or even as regards one's family members. We need not think that he has in mind a single emotion or desire that is operative in each case. He does say, however, that in these cases the emotion or desire that explains the lapse is not in itself bad, because it does not have for its object something that is in itself bad;[19] thus the emotion becomes bad only incidentally, when context or comparison would imply that acting on that emotion would be inappropriate – for

---

[19] It is clear that in making this distinction Aristotle is relying on points from his account of virtues of character.

instance, a father who, because of strong affection for his son (some-thing in itself good) cannot restrain himself from remonstrating with him not to join the army when his country has unjustly come under attack. This expression of his affection (Aristotle at least would think) is inappropriate.

This reflection should make it clear that, as Aristotle sees it, in the central case of *akrasia*, sensual desire is for a pleasure that would be (as we would say) morally wrong to enjoy. A good paradigm of *akrasia* involves, say, the pleasure of committing adultery rather than eating a chocolate eclair when on a diet, since wanting to taste a chocolate eclair is not something in itself bad. One might say that Aristotle takes the paradigmatic case of weakness of will to be *moral* weakness.

J. L. Austin famously objected against Aristotle's account that giving in to temptation need not imply lack of rational control:

I am very partial to ice cream, and a bombe is served divided into segments corresponding one to one with the persons at High Table: I am tempted to help myself to two segments and do so, thus succumbing to temptation and even conceivably (but why necessarily?) going against my principles. But do I lose control of myself? Do I raven, do I snatch the morsels from the dish and wolf them down, impervious to the consternation of my colleagues? Not a bit of it. We often succumb to temptation with calm and even with finesse.[20]

Other commentators have objected that Aristotle's theory is unrea-listic, because weakness of will need not involve any lack of clarity about the badness of what one is doing. The following passage from Bostock states the objection with force:

Suppose that I have a strong liking for cream, and someone offers me a chocolate eclair. Suppose also that I do stop to think, and what I think is: "I should not eat what is bad for me; cream is bad for me; eclairs contain cream; this is an eclair; so I should not eat it." In this way I complete a piece of deliberation. But suppose further, as we all know is entirely possible, that I nevertheless take the eclair and eat it. Then on Aristotle's account this must be because my desire for cream blots out some part of this deliberation ... But, as we all know, this is wholly unrealistic, for even as I bite into the eclair I may well be thinking to myself, "I should not be doing

[20] Austin (1970), 198 n. 1.

this." And there is no reason at all to say that I fail to understand these words that I think to myself; I do know perfectly well that I should not be doing what I am doing.[21]

But Aristotle would seem to have a handy response to objections like this. He can say, simply, that Austin's and Bostock's examples are remote from the central case of *akrasia*, whereas his own account is meant to describe the central case; it would hardly be surprising, then, if his account seems not to apply. If no emotion or impulse is, *to any degree*, leading us to act as we would not otherwise wish (as Austin is effectively suggesting, as regards his example), or if there is no limitation or alteration *at all*, as regards our sense perception or imagination (as in Bostock's example), then – on Aristotle's lights – the phenomenon is something other than *akrasia*, and it can be no objection to Aristotle's theory that it does not describe it.

Yet if Austin's and Bostock's examples are not cases of Aristotelian *akrasia*, what are they? Can we account for them nonetheless from within Aristotle's framework? It is not so clear, first of all, that these examples succeed in describing determinate cases. One can imagine a variety of reasons, motives, and thought processes that might be consistent with either example. As regards any particular interpretation, even we might wish to contest whether it should be counted as a genuine case of weakness of will – rather than, say, mere inconsistency, befuddlement, self-deception, rationalization, or peevishness. But within an Aristotelian framework, there would seem to be two ways to account for behavior which looks like *akrasia* but is not, namely vice and inappropriate self-love. To take two portions of the bombe at High Table, depending upon how one interprets the example, might conceivably be an instance of some vice: injustice, small-mindedness, failure of affability, or lack of good sense. Or again, it might be an expression of inappropriate self-love, which Aristotle discusses in 9.4, and which can look very much like weakness of will: for instance, someone takes the double portion simply because he lacks a stable conception of himself and his true good, and therefore he follows no consistent principle in such things.

[21] Bostock (2000), 133.

Yet this response on Aristotle's part then opens his theory to another objection. By restricting so narrowly the proper application of the term *"akrasia,"* has Aristotle made his job too easy? Does he give us an interesting and subtle account, only by ignoring most of the phenomena he needs to explain? Has he perhaps made it look as though he has explained human irrationality, only because he never defends the comprehensiveness of his theory? It seemed at the start that Aristotle needed to discuss *akrasia* in order to account for that broad area of human action which falls between virtue and vice; and yet if *akrasia* is such a restricted phenomenon, as Aristotle maintains, one might wonder whether that intermediate area, including most of the phenomena of irrationality, still remains unaccounted for.

FURTHER READING

The above "dynamic" interpretation of *akrasia* differs from usual accounts, which typically take Aristotle to be concerned with the "practical syllogism" (a pattern of reasoning supposed to govern inferences ending in action). See Bostock (2000), chapter 6, for an overview.

For the "practical syllogism," see Cooper (1975), chapter 1. Kenny (1966) maintains that there is only one practical syllogism at work in *akrasia.* That there are two competing syllogisms in play is the more usual view, but commentators differ as to whether the syllogism leading to correct action is rendered ineffective because correct perception is hindered (see, for instance, Robinson [1969]); because the relevant premises are never in fact put together (Charles, 1984, chs. 3–4); or because the agent fails in some way to make proper use of what he knows (Broadie, 1991, ch. 5).

Davidson (1969) is important for reviving the problem of *akrasia* as a puzzle about rationality in contemporary philosophy.

CHAPTER 9

Friendship
(Nicomachean Ethics, *books 8 and 9*)

FRIENDSHIP-FRIENDLY PHILOSOPHY

One of the merits of Aristotle's approach to ethics is that it aims to be practical and, therefore, faithful to how human beings actually are. This surely helps to explain why Aristotle devotes one-fifth of his treatise to a topic that is usually neglected altogether by contemporary moral theory – friendship. We do not often find ourselves having to make a snap decision about how to steer a runaway trolley car. It rarely happens in daily life that we are engaged in delicate surgery and must face the question of whether to carve up a patient for his separate organs, for distribution to other patients who just happen to be prepped for the operating room and waiting to receive them. But friendships and "personal relationships" constitute the very fabric of daily life. If our living well does not depend on the relationships we form with others, and how we typically treat those close to us, then it is difficult to see on what it could depend. And surely Aristotle is correct in holding that any ideal of *human* happiness must include within it enduring and satisfying friendships: if someone were offered every good thing – wealth, good health, pleasures, and endless life – on the condition that he would be alone, he would not accept the offer (1169b17–18).

However, what makes Aristotle not simply an astute and relevant moralist but also a great philosopher is *how* he deals with ordinary subjects such as friendship. Aristotle's chief philosophical strength is to see what is profound in what is very ordinary, in such a way as to conserve rather than destroy ordinary reality, and yet he does so not in an entirely "conservative" way. Consider an example from a different area of philosophy. After Aristotle in the *Physics* has given

258 ARISTOTLE'S NICOMACHEAN ETHICS

us his philosophical account of *change*,[1] and we come to appreciate its significance, we are not tempted to say – as after studying some other philosophers – that change does not exist; or that change is "nothing but" some other thing; or that what we took to be some real feature of change is to be located, instead, within our own minds. Rather, Aristotle's discussion affirms a commonsense understanding of change, while aiming to lead us to see in a new way what we had taken change to be; although undoubtedly our seeing it in this new light will require that we also refine what we had previously thought, and reject various confusions which had affected us. Yet, this new understanding that we achieve is not something static or closed, and therefore objectionably conservative, because, as Aristotle would have it, once we acquire that sort of understanding of change, we become disposed to think about, and in fact are prepared to think better about, matters that (Aristotle thinks) are beyond the realm of change, but to which the fact of change inevitably points. To be led on in this way is to pursue the discipline that Aristotle calls "metaphysics," literally "those matters that are to be investigated after investigating physics."

Aristotle's discussion of friendship has a similar character, since it deals with an ordinary reality in a profound way, conserving that ordinary reality, yet not conservatively so. Aristotle's account of friendship spans books 8 and 9 of the *Ethics*. The first and largest portion of this, 8.1–12, is concerned mainly with issues of definition and classification. As we have already seen, for Aristotle, matters of classification very often cloak a substantial philosophical point. Similarly here: there are many sorts of relationships that people call "friendship," and it is philosophically important, Aristotle thinks, to place these in order, by selecting one form of friendship that qualifies as "friendship" in the proper and strict sense. Once this central form has been correctly identified and described, Aristotle thinks, then we can make sense of the other forms and phenomena of friendship, in relation to this central case. In Aristotle's view, the central case of friendship is a relationship of reciprocal affection between two equal and similar adults, who have affection for each other because each

---

[1] He defines change as "the actualization of something in potentiality, in the respect in which it is in potentiality."

recognizes and enjoys the virtues of the other. All other sorts of relationships are secondary and derivative, such as friendships among unequals, or between people who lack the virtues, or relationships based on mere expedience. (Even affection within the family, for Aristotle, is a secondary case of *friendship*, although perhaps not of *love*.)

To identify the central case is to identify what needs to be looked at to draw general conclusions about the nature of friendship. Thus, after he puts the phenomena of ordinary reality in place, by putting them in relation to the central case (and after discussing some difficulties involving reciprocation in friendship, in 8.13–9.3), Aristotle attempts to give an account of the nature of friendship in 9.4–8; this is undoubtedly one of the more fascinating sections of the *Ethics*. It is here that Aristotle develops his remarkable idea that a friend is an "other self," because a good person, he claims, is related to his friend as he is to himself. This notion of "other self," for Aristotle, constitutes the fundamental ideal of friendship: insofar as someone counts as a friend, in any way or in any respect, he plays the role of an "other self." Moreover, there is a kind of intention or aim within any friendship for this ideal to be as fully realized as possible, given the nature and constraints of that particular sort of friendship.

This notion of a friend as an "other self" leads Aristotle to examine self-love. If friends love their friends in the way that they love themselves, and if they should do so, and friendship is something good, then it would apparently follow that self-love is something good as well. This implication seems to be at odds with the common idea that self-love is bad because it involves selfishness, and therefore in 9.8 Aristotle gives an extended argument that there is a good sort of self-love as well as a bad. In fact it is unavoidable, Aristotle thinks, not simply that a good person love himself, but also that he love himself more than he loves anyone else.

Yet Aristotle's discussion of friendship does not end with these reflections on ordinary phenomena of friendship. As I said, there is a direction or motion to Aristotle's discussion, which aims to recast how we think of ordinary realities.

Consider, for instance, Aristotle's view of reciprocity in friendship. Our initial view of the matter is likely to be something like this: reciprocity among friends takes its highest form as some sort of *exchange of action* – the friends take turns in doing good for each other. If A and B are friends, they need to reciprocate care and affection for each other; and this reciprocal care, we think, is best found in reciprocal service: A does a favor for B, and, at a later time, B in exchange responds with a similar favor for A. "You scratch my back, and I'll scratch yours." But Aristotle regards this sort of reciprocity as defective; it does not quite capture or express, he thinks, the ideal of reciprocity. To appreciate his reasons, we should consider: *why*, after all, do friends practice reciprocity in the first place? *Why* does the one friend aim to match or correspond to the actions of the other? The reason, Aristotle maintains, is that they wish to be "other selves" in relation to each other. To be an "other self" implies equality and some sort of sharing. However, an act of service or giving implies, rather, an *inequality:* the person who does the service is, to that extent, a superior, and the one who receives it is, so far, an inferior. Moreover, a reciprocal exchange that is extended in time involves no real sharing: the friends are not truly acting *together*, if they are simply taking turns.

Considerations such as these lead Aristotle to conclude that the best expression of friendship – that in which friends most of all stand as "other selves," each to the other – is not, as perhaps it first seemed, when the friends are busily engaged in "doing good" for each other, but rather when they are simply "spending time" with each other and "living life together" (*suzēn*), as Aristotle puts it. In the most elaborate argument of the entire *Ethics*, in 9.9, Aristotle argues that to "spend time" with a friend amounts to a kind of mutual sharing in perception and thought. Friendship, he thinks, finds its greatest fulfillment when friends are thinking about the same truths, and each recognizes that the other thinks the same as he, and each recognizes that each recognizes this. The reason, Aristotle claims, is that human perception and thinking is inherently reflexive: to think is always also to perceive that one thinks. Only in "spending time" with a friend do we enter into a relationship with another person that closely resembles this relationship that, at the same time, one has to oneself.

Because the highest expression of friendship is simply "spending time" or "sharing in thinking" with one's friend, and, as Aristotle argues, friendship is necessary for happiness, some striking results follow, for instance: since "spending time" with others requires leisure, happiness is especially connected to leisure; and since the best activity of friends is a sharing in thinking, then some kind of thinking is the best thing that friends can share. These results in turn support the conclusion that the ultimate goal of human life must be some kind of thinking that we engage in when we have leisure, which is exactly Aristotle's conclusion in book 10.

So once again we see that Aristotle is conservative, but not conservatively so. For Aristotle, a careful consideration of ordinary phenomena of friendship leads to rather unordinary results about the ultimate goal of human life. If we reflect carefully on the ordinary reality of friendship, he thinks, and appreciate its central manifestation and basic nature, we arrive at a transformed and even radical view of the purpose of human society and human life.

From this brief overview we can see, then, that the books on friendship have the following basic structure:

8.1.1	Introduction
8.2–12	Definition and classification of friendship
8.13–9.3	Reciprocity within friendships
9.4–8	The nature and causes of friendship
9.9–12	Friendship and happiness

GOODWILL, LOVE, AND FRIENDSHIP

Aristotle distinguishes goodwill (*eunoia*); love (*philēsis, philein*); and friendship (*philia*). So let us become clear about these first.

He uses the term "goodwill" in two senses. Most commonly he uses it in a fairly wide sense, but in some important contexts he uses it in a different and narrow sense, and it is good to be clear about the difference between these. Goodwill in the wide sense is a kind of positive or promoting attitude shown toward a person. As we have seen, Aristotle thinks that goodness is objective: each kind of thing actually has a characteristic work or function; something becomes *good* in fact if it has those attributes that enable it to carry out that characteristic work well; and it is *good for* a kind of thing that it be good and carry out its function well. Anything else which tended to promote its goodness would furthermore be "good for" that thing, in the extended sense of *contributing* to its good. We are capable, then, of recognizing the characteristic work of things and therefore recognizing what makes something good and what is good for a thing.

But suppose we go beyond simply recognizing that something is good and, moreover, take it as a goal for ourselves, in the minimal sense at least in which we take as a goal what we express sincerely in (what grammarians call) the optative mood as a wish: "That it might happen that ..." or "Oh that ... would occur." This would be to wish that it be so. Goodwill in the wide sense is a kind of wish: it is simply to recognize that something is good for some person and to wish that it be so. Clearly, that sort of goodwill is wide-ranging and implies no commitment or cost (1167a10; compare the expression, "Have a nice day!"). We show goodwill in that sense, as Aristotle remarks, for athletes who are complete strangers to us, when we cheer them on in contests, or even for fictional characters represented on the stage, when we want things to go well for them in the story.

Goodwill in this wide sense is superficial and transient (1166b35). Yet, for all that, Aristotle holds that we cannot have goodwill for non-persons. He does not explicitly state his reason for thinking this, but presumably his view is that wishing good for someone involves some kind of minimal identification with another, taking his good to be the same as one's own: "To wish wine well would be fairly ridiculous. If anything like that takes place, it's rather that a man wishes that it be preserved, so that he can have it" (1155b29–31).

Goodwill in the wide sense, then, extends to persons we hardly know, to persons in other places and times, and even to fictional characters. In contrast, *love* has a relatively narrow ambit and extends only to what is somehow consistent with our interests and aims: "Each person seems to love," Aristotle says, "a good that is related to him" (1155b23–24). Aristotle follows Greek usage and applies the term "love" to things and animals as well as to persons. (He does not observe a distinction between "loving" and "liking.") On this usage a person might love honor, money, or glory, as well as his dog, his parents, and his best friend. Yet, although we do love inanimate things and non-rational animals, Aristotle seems to hold that any love that we have for such things presupposes love for a person, whose welfare might genuinely be regarded as a goal or "end" of the love that we have (*telos*). In the most typical case, a person's love for an inanimate thing will presuppose love for himself: for Smith to love money, is for Smith to love himself – what he wants is that *he* have the money. (But clearly in the same way we could love money for someone else.) Unlike goodwill, love implies some kind of commitment and cost, although perhaps of a very limited sort. This commitment, Aristotle thinks, is marked by an engagement of our affections and an active disposition to *do something* to promote the good of the person or thing that we love (1166b32–33).

As for *friendship*, Aristotle seems to think of it in the first instance as a certain kind of affection that one person can have for another – what we might call "friendliness" or "affability" (cf. 1105b22, 1108a28). But there are two distinctive notes of this sort of affection, Aristotle thinks: first, it wants or expects reciprocation (*antiphilēsis, antiprohairesis*); second, it aims at and seeks the good of the other person "for his sake" (*autou heneka*). Aristotle sometimes calls this second note "goodwill" as well – this would be "goodwill" in the narrow sense, previously mentioned. "Goodwill" in this restricted sense refers to the special character of that affection which is distinctive of friendship.

Recognizing that the ideal of loving another "for his own sake" is rich and in need of further explanation, Aristotle works with a variety of expressions to capture its significance. He describes it also as love for another "on account of him" (*di' auton*). This phrase is concerned with what properly *explains* or *accounts for* the love that someone has. It is to attribute an explanation: when A loves B *on account of* B, then B rather than something else provides the explanation for A's love for him. Another expression that Aristotle uses is love for another "in his own right" (*kath' hauton*). This phrase is concerned with whether something just on its own is the object of the love. It is a remark about what the love responds to and aims to promote: when A loves B *in his own right*, then in particular A loves something about B that is independent of B's relationship to A.

Because the affection of friendliness expects reciprocation, it is typically found in reciprocal relationships, and therefore the word "friendship" is applied to such relationships as well: *friendship* (in this sense) is a relationship in which persons display friendship (in the other sense) to each other.[2] Note that, in referring to relationships as "friendships," Aristotle is much more generous in his use of that term

---

[2] That friendship admits of these two senses explains the passage in Plato's *Lysis* (211d–213d) in which Socrates ties Menexenus in knots over puzzles about reciprocation of friendly affection.

than are we. We tend to reserve "friendship" for intimate relationships between two persons. But since Aristotle uses the term for any affection that expects reciprocation, or that expects and finds reciprocation, no matter how extended or attenuated that affection, he applies it very widely: to families, clubs, clans, and even to reciprocal affections of loyalty and patriotism among citizens. These sorts of relationships – "associations" and "partnerships" of various sorts – do not rely so much on some direct acquaintance of one person with another but are mediated, rather, by structures of governance. The individual members of an association reciprocate affection and concern for each other primarily through the rules and structures of that association. Aristotle gives particular attention to this sort of affection as it is found among citizens and is typical of political association, mediated by the form of government of one's city-state; he calls this "civic friendship," and he regards this sort of affection as crucial to the unity and good functioning of political society.

These notions of goodwill, love, and friendship, then, are the basic notions of Aristotle's account of friendship.

THE THREE LOVES

Aristotle's argument about the central case of friendship (8.2–4) consists of certain preliminaries, which then lead up to the argument itself. We can refer to these preliminaries as Aristotle's account of: (i) the *standard* of friendship; (ii) the *schema* of friendship; and (iii) the possible *content* of a friendship. Aristotle's strategy is to argue that the only relationship that satisfies the standard of friendship is one in which the schema of friendship is given a certain content.

The standard of friendship. As we have seen, Aristotle thinks that the distinctive marks of friendliness are reciprocity and a love for the other "for his own sake." The latter is love that we have for another *because* of him; love for him as he is *in his own right*. Only a relationship which meets this standard, Aristotle thinks, can be regarded as friendship in the proper sense of the term. If a relationship looks like a friendship but fails to meet this standard, it can be called "friendship" only in some loose or extended sense.

The schema of friendship. A friendship is, at very least, reciprocated love. But, as Aristotle points out, the reciprocation of love has to be *recognized* by each person if they are properly to be accounted friends (1155b31–34): if A is a secret admirer of B and sends anonymous gifts to B, and B just happens to be a secret admirer of A who also sends anonymous gifts to A, there would be reciprocation of affection between A and B, but no friendship. For a friendship to exist, each has to recognize the love that the other has, and each has to regard his own love as in some way answering to the love of the other. Moreover, each of the friends must also recognize that the other recognizes his own affection. Thus the structure of a friendship is reciprocated love that is reflectively recognized as reciprocated.

The content of friendship. There are various sorts of love, Aristotle maintains, and thus various ways in which the schema of a friendship can be filled out. If we distinguish these sorts of love, Aristotle thinks, and then consider what sort of friendship would result if the schema of friendship were filled out by love of each sort, then we can determine which, if any such friendship, meets the standard of friendship. Aristotle's view is that there are three sorts of love, and only one of these, when it is reciprocated and mutually recognized, results in a friendship which meets the standard of friendship.

His argument that there are three sorts of love is as follows. Love is goal-directed, Aristotle thinks: love, as mentioned, engages the affections and aims to promote something. Therefore, love has as its object something that has the nature of a goal. But there are only two sorts of things that someone might intelligibly seek as a goal: goods and pleasures. Thus Aristotle proposes a preliminary classification of sorts of love into two: love for something as good; love for something as pleasant.

But love always implies some kind of relationship between the agent and the object of love, as we have seen: unlike goodwill (in the wide sense), love is not wide-ranging but pertains only to things that are somehow consistent with the interests and goals of the agent who has the love. Let us say that an object of love must therefore be something that "contributes to" the agent's goals, whether this be the agent's good or the agent's pleasure. That someone in this way does contribute to an agent's good or contribute to an agent's pleasure, Aristotle thinks, can itself conceivably become the reason why we love someone. That very relation that someone has to us can come to serve as a basis for love. And thus there are, Aristotle thinks, four distinguishable types of love that a person, A, may have for another, B:

(i) A loves B because A takes B to be good.
(ii) A loves B because A takes B to be pleasant.
(iii) A loves B because A takes B to contribute (in some way) to A's good.
(iv) A loves B because A takes B to contribute (in some way) to A's pleasure.

Let us consider these more carefully. What it is for someone to be *good* is clear enough: someone is good if he has those traits that enable him to do his characteristic work well; thus, for A to love B because A takes B to be good is for A to love B because B has the virtues. But what is it for someone to be *pleasant* (full stop) and loved for that reason? To explain this, we must appeal to doctrines about pleasure that Aristotle had introduced in his book 7 discussion of pleasure (and which I shall examine more carefully in the next chapter). Aristotle evidently relies on these doctrines in his discussion of friendship. In book 7 he adopts the view that, roughly, pleasures simply are good activities, insofar as these activities are "unimpeded": living beings are themselves simply pleasant, insofar as they are carrying out activities of their natural and good condition and without obstruction. One can get a sense of what Aristotle means by this, if we think, say, of a vigorous colt prancing about a field on a fine spring morning, or the look of delight on a child's face as he rides on a swing. We can easily enough come to regard these activities, and others like them, as *themselves* pleasant. It is true that we too can take delight in them – we can *share in* the pleasure of the colt or the child, and we might love to work with horses or spend time with children for this reason – but that there is a pleasure that we delight in or share in (one might think) depends upon the activity's already being pleasant. For A to love B because he takes B to be pleasant, then, is for A to regard B's activity as itself pleasant, in this way.

Aristotle's most important claim about these four types of affection is that love of type (iii), he thinks, can occur apart from love of type (i) (and therefore *a fortiori* apart from love of type [ii] or [iv]); and that love of type (iv) can occur apart from love of type (ii) (and therefore *a fortiori* apart from love of type [i] or [iii]); and yet love of type (i) and of type (ii) inevitably occur together. Thus these four types of affection reduce effectively to three.

To see that love of type (iii) can occur apart from love of type (i), consider a case where B contributes to A's good – that is, B is *useful* to A – and yet B is not good and is not regarded by A as such: for instance, A is a writer who needs to have her works edited; B is a good editor; but B is not a particularly good person. In this case, A maintains a relationship with B, then, because of B's usefulness. To see that love of type (iv) can occur apart from love of type (ii), consider a case where B contributes to A's pleasure – that is, B *amuses* A – and yet B's activity is not inherently pleasant: for instance, A needs to be consoled for some disappointment or loss; B is grumpy and irritable (and not *himself* pleasant); but B has a particularly mordant sense of humor which amuses A. In this case, A maintains a relationship with B, because B is amusing, not because B is pleasant.

In contrast, it is not possible to devise cases in which (i) and (ii) come apart. The reason, Aristotle thinks, is that any good person will be engaged in activities which are themselves pleasant. This follows trivially (as we shall see) from Aristotle's book 7 doctrine of pleasure: he claims there that something is in itself a pleasure, if it is the unimpeded activity of a living thing in good condition; therefore, virtuous activities which are unimpeded (and typically they will be so) are pleasures; and thus a good person's activities would be pleasures. The same result follows also from Aristotle's book 2 doctrine of virtue: a virtuous person wants to perform virtuous actions for their own sake and therefore is pleased simply in performing them: anyone who did not find them so, would not be virtuous.

Thus, (i) and (ii) will go together. But Aristotle also argues that (i) will typically imply (iii): suppose A loves B, and B is virtuous; but then because B is virtuous, B will prove of benefit to A; and then this benefit naturally becomes another reason for A to love B. The principal reason that B in this case will prove of benefit to A is that esteem for a virtuous person, and an admiration for what he does, implies a resolve, on the part of the person who has this love, to act similarly in a virtuous way (cf. 1172a10–14). The lover's very admiration implies a benefit to him, an improvement in his soul. And if A goes so far to befriend B, when B is virtuous and A loves B because of that, then of course A will become the frequent object of B's virtuous actions, benefiting from his generosity, affability, and so on, and it would prove impossible for A not to esteem B for this as well. Thus (i) typically carries along with it (iii).

Moreover, (ii) will typically imply (iv), according to Aristotle. Suppose A loves B because of the inherent pleasantness of B's activity: then A is inevitably himself pleased by B; and then that he is thus pleased by B naturally becomes another reason for A to love B. Suppose that A loves B because B's activity is inherently pleasant. But then it would be practically impossible for A not to sympathize with B and consequently to be pleased as B is pleased (compare: it is hardly possible to spend time with a cheerful child, and to admire the child's cheerfulness, without oneself becoming cheered up). But, beyond this, A could not join in B's pleasure without somehow sharing in B's intention, which implies A's taking a similar pleasure in B's action: for instance, a friend tells you with excitement her plan to hold a surprise party for her parents' anniversary, and you find it nearly as pleasant to hear of the planning and execution of the event, as if it were your idea and you were carrying it out. Thus (ii) typically carries along with it (iv).

Thus love of type (i) carries every other type of love along with it, because love of type (i) is inseparable from (ii), and (i) implies (iii) as well, and (ii) implies (iv). Yet love of type (iii) can occur on its own and does not bring (i) along with it; and love of type (iv) can occur on its own and does not bring (ii) along with it. Aristotle therefore claims that any relationship based on love of type (i) is "complete," because it contains every sort of motive and love that can be found between two persons, moreover it is "prior," because it implies every sort of love, whereas some sorts of love do not imply it. Thus, Aristotle thinks, a friendship consisting of reciprocated love of type (i) is the only complete relationship, and it is a relationship that is prior to all others. Clearly, it would be the central case of friendship.

As I said, because (i) and (ii) always coincide, Aristotle reduces the four sorts of love to three, and he assigns them commonsense names. The three basic forms of love, according to Aristotle, are:

- "Love because of usefulness": love of sort (iii) standing on its own.
- "Love because of pleasure": love of sort (iv) standing on its own.
- "Love because of goodness": love of sort (i) along with (ii).

The next step in Aristotle's argument, as I said, is to consider what sort of relationship results, when each of these three sorts of love is inserted into the schema for friendship.[3] Aristotle does so with especial attention to the principle that, as he puts it, "people who love each other wish good things to each other in that respect in which they love" (1156a9–10). That is to say, that particular feature about the object of love which serves as the reason for a person's love serves also as a kind of constraint or limit on what he does by way of promoting the object of his love. For instance, if what Smith likes about Jones is that Jones is an excellent musician, then Smith acts to promote the interests of Jones in the respect in which this advances Jones's musicianship or musical career, but not at all when his promotion of Jones's interests would be irrelevant to Jones's musicianship and career.

Using this principle, Aristotle argues that a friendship consisting of love based on usefulness, and a friendship consisting of love based on pleasure, do not satisfy the standard of friendship. We shall consider his argument as regards usefulness; the other is similar. Suppose A loves B because of usefulness. Then the "respect in which" A loves B is B's contributing to A's good. (This simply makes explicit what "love because of usefulness" amounts to.) But then this has several implications for the way in which A treats B. Aristotle presents these in an extremely compressed passage. We do well to tease them out:

1. A does not love B in his own right (*kath' hauton*). Why? Because it is not something about B on his own that A loves, but rather B's being in a certain relation to A. B's remaining in that relation, then, is a condition of A's love, and A will not promote B's good in a manner inconsistent with this (1156a10–12).
2. A in fact loves B because of A himself, not because of B (not *di' auton*). Why? Because the reason that A esteems B's being in a certain relation to him, is that this promotes his own good. His promotion of B's good is therefore fully accounted for as, simply, love for himself (1156a15).

---

[3] Aristotle examines first, and primarily, relationships in which each friend has toward the other the same sort of love, "friendships which are uniform" (1156b33–35, cf. 1163b32–33), because these are closer to the ideal of reciprocation in friendship.

3. A does not love B, except incidentally (*kata sumbebēkos*). That is, his wishing of goods to B misses the mark, since this serves to advance an incidental feature of B rather than B's good.
4. And if B himself is not the target of A's well-wishing, then A does not in fact wish goods to B *for the sake of* B (*autou heneka*) (cf. 1156a15–19).

So this sort of friendship does not satisfy the standard of friendship as regards the mark of wishing goods to the other for his own sake. But neither does it satisfy the requirement of reciprocity, Aristotle argues, because such friends rarely reciprocate in similar ways (1157a2–4); people can engage in this sort of friendship and not even want to spend time with each other (1156a28–29); and their exchanges typically falter on misunderstandings or lead to quarrels (1162b16–25).

In contrast, friendship that consists of reciprocated love based on the goodness of the other does satisfy the standard of friendship, or so Aristotle wishes to maintain. His argument is as follows. Suppose A loves B because B is a good human being, and indeed B is good. That B is good remains so, independent of any relation that B has to A, that is, A loves B in his own right (*kath' hauton*, 1156b9). Thus, A's promotion of B's good is not constrained by any relationship B has to A and, in particular, A might promote B's good even if this were inconsistent with A's interests. Furthermore, B's goodness explains A's love: A's love is *because of* B (1156b10). Again, B is in fact good, and B's goodness is what A loves, therefore B's goodness is the target of A's love: thus A loves B *for the sake of* B (1156b10).

Moreover, the reciprocation displayed by such a friendship involves similarity and unity. Each friend finds good, useful, and pleasant in the other basically the same sort of thing that his friend admires in himself. Furthermore, since love for someone because of his virtue is "complete" and implies all three other reasons for loving someone, then the relationship has "exactly what one looks for in a friendship" (1156b35); nothing from outside the relationship need attract them, and the relationship consequently has great stability (which is reinforced, too, by the inherent stability of good traits of character, 1156b12).

Aristotle's conclusion is that only friendship that involves reciprocated love based on the virtues of another is a friendship in the proper sense of the term. He is half-tempted to say that no other relationship should even be called friendship, but, as a concession to ordinary usage, and by way of uncovering what is right about that usage, he concedes that any other relation may be counted as a friendship, to a greater or lesser degree, to the extent that it resembles this ideal (1157a25–32; 1158b5–11).

Some commentators have objected that Aristotle's account of friendship sets an absurdly high standard for relationships, that, in fact, according to his account, hardly any human relationships would count as true friendships. Aristotle would presumably accept this conclusion: he thinks that true friendship is rare, much as virtue is rare. But recall that most of the *Ethics* is concerned with setting down ideals of action, and thus what is really at issue is whether Aristotle has sketched correctly the ideal of friendship. That such relationships are rare would not imply that they are not an ideal against which ordinary relationships should be measured.

FAMILY AND CITY

One of the more curious discussions in the books on friendship is Aristotle's rather extended comparison of the family with political society, at 8.9–12. It is apparently his treatise on civic friendship. Yet what is the point of the comparison? Aristotle maps forms of family association onto forms of political association, and vice versa, but to what end? He gives very few guidelines as to the nature and direction of his argument, yet the following seems a plausible reconstruction.

Chapters 8.9–12 present Aristotle's theory of friendship as existing in a *koinōnia*. *Koinōnia* means literally "a sharing," and the term may be variously translated as "association," "community," or "partnership." People form a *koinōnia* when they individually want or need something, and they cannot possibly, or cannot easily, procure it as individuals working independently, yet they can do so if they cooperate. The want or need which motivates their cooperation is the original good that motivates their associating; their achieving this through cooperation is their common good.

It is not each person's getting the original good which is the common good of the association, but rather each getting it according to the plan of their cooperation, since the common good implies a

kind of exchange, which transforms what each member of the association aims at. A simple example will make this point clear. Imagine
an agragrian society consisting of citizen farmers in a rural community. Each farmer wishes to defend his own farm against marauders;
this is a good for each of them. Each recognizes, too, that he cannot
achieve this good if he works solely on his own: an uncoordinated or
inconsistent defense will not be effective. So the farmers in the
community, or the bulk of them, band together (compelling
would-be freeloaders to go along) and form a militia. The militia
requires a plan of cooperation and some kind of government to
oversee and execute the plan. Under this plan, each farmer gives up
his own defense of his own plot of land, in exchange for protection by
the militia as a whole. It may turn out that, under the plan of
common defense, some particular farmer happens to be assigned to
guard his farm and only his farm, which is exactly what he would
have been doing anyway, had no militia been formed. Nonetheless,
his good (or goal) is now different, because now he aims to protect his
own farm *as part of a plan* that, if executed, protects everyone's farm
all at once. Since this new goal is shared by everyone else it is a
"common goal" or common good.

It is clear that a *koinōnia* of this sort, if it is to be fair, requires that
everyone be able to achieve that which was the reason for the formation of the *koinōnia* in the first place; otherwise a member of the
association, through being a member, would be forced to give something up without receiving anything in exchange. And since everyone
in the *koinōnia*, through wishing for the common good, wishes that
this be done for everyone else, and each recognizes that everyone else
so wishes it, there is an analogy between any *koinōnia* and the
structure of a friendship. Thus we may follow Aristotle and speak
of the friendship that is "constituted by" or "exists in" that *koinōnia*
(1159b27–30, cf. 1161a10–11). This friendship will depend, as was said,
on the fair construction and implementation of a plan for joint
action. Thus, as Aristotle remarks, the friendship of a *koinōnia*
depends upon the justice of the arrangement.

Although the friendship of a *koinōnia* requires that there be justice
in the plan of cooperation, does it follow that the *virtue* of justice is all
that will be needed, for people to associate well in a *koinōnia*?
Aristotle denies this. He believes that the virtue of justice will be

insufficient for guaranteeing satisfactory corporate action among persons:

> It seems that it's friendship that holds together a city-state, and that legislators are more concerned about friendship than about the virtue of justice ... Moreover, suppose people are friends: then they have no need of the virtue of justice. But suppose they are just: they still need friendship. Furthermore, those actions of ours that excel in point of justice seem similar to friendliness. (1155a22–28)

Why does Aristotle think that people need friendship if they have the virtue of justice? Justice presumably leads someone to watch out for his own interests and defend against injuries; it makes people prone to nurse resentments, seek revenge, or regard themselves as aggrieved. These resentments and grievances will only compound over time, if love and friendship do not in some way moderate them. And as Aristotle emphasized in his discussion of equity, every law and every principle of justice requires a sound interpretation given particular circumstances, with reference to the intention of the legislature, yet good sense and refinement in doing so require that we are able to see things from the point of view of our neighbor, and "walk in his shoes," very much as in a friendship.

For these and other reasons, human social life would not be practicable if people had the virtue of justice only and lacked friendliness toward one another. But Aristotle affirms the natural sociability of human beings: "human beings are by nature city-dwelling animals" (1097b11; 1169b18–19). And nature would not prompt to something for which it failed to supply the means. Thus, there must be some naturally supplied means by which human beings acquire those affections that equip them to show friendliness in the various associations in which they participate, including political society. And Aristotle seems to think that it is the family which naturally plays this role.

The family and political society occupy a special place and are set apart from every other *koinōnia* insofar as they are natural associations: "Human beings are by nature disposed to pair off in marriage (*sunduastikon*) even more than to form cities (*politikon*)" (1162a17–18). To say that these associations are by nature is to say such things as that we are prompted to form them by motives that are enduring and practically unavoidable in human life (romantic attraction for marriage; economic need for the city-state, cf. 1160a12); it is to say that these motives typically prompt, or appear to prompt, to something more immediate than the associations to which they lead, so that the associations look as though they have arisen indirectly and without deliberate aim (a man and a woman can fall in love and have intercourse without intending to found a family; various free farmers can trade in a market without intending to found a city); yet that we can, upon reflection, recognize these associations as good and endorse them for that reason (a couple might later come to regard their children as much the best reason why they fell in love; the city-state, as Aristotle remarks, arises out of need but continues in existence "for the sake of the *kalon*," *Politics* 1252b29-30; 1278b15-18; 1281a2; 1291a18). Furthermore, both family and city-state are comprehensive associations, insofar as they involve the sharing of all goods necessary for human life: the city-state, according to Aristotle, is simply the basic self-sufficient social unity, the smallest large-scale association which can provide from within its own resources all of the basic material goods required for living well; and the family is correspondingly the association in which all of these various goods are applied to daily life.

So political society and the family stand out and are set apart from other associations. Yet curiously there is a correspondence in the structures of these associations and, Aristotle suggests, it is implausible to hold that this correspondence is accidental (cf. 8.10–11). And thus Aristotle's argument proceeds on the supposition that there is a point to the correspondence. There are three basic sorts of political constitution, Aristotle thinks, depending upon whether a single person governs, or a few, or many: these are *kingship*, *aristocracy*, and *timocracy*, respectively. (We would want to call this last form "democracy," but Aristotle reserves that term for *corrupt* government by the many.[4]) Yet analogues of each of these forms of government

---

[4] His view is that good government differs from corrupt government, depending upon whether virtuous or non-virtuous people hold office. A "democracy," as he understands it, is government in which anyone whatsoever has a say in the government, regardless of whether he has virtue, and mere numbers win the day. But this would be corrupt. A "timocracy" in contrast is rule of the many in which a person has to satisfy a minimum property requirement in order to have a say in government; someone's having accrued and preserved a minimum of property is taken as a mark or sign of some minimum of virtue.

are found within the family (1160b22–23). Kingship is mirrored in the relationship between father and children; aristocracy is mirrored in the joint governance of the affairs of the household by husband and wife; and timocracy is mirrored in the self-governance of siblings in their own affairs. The correspondence, we are supposing, is not coincidental: therefore, what is its purpose? Aristotle suggests: in the family, we learn and acquire habitual affections that are appropriate for governments having the corresponding structure. These affections arise naturally and spontaneously in a healthy family, and they are transferred by analogy to the government of political society, and by this means to fellow citizens. The affections that animate citizens in a monarchy are simply those that they initially have cultivated toward their fathers within a family.[5] The affections that are proper to an aristocracy are those that are cultivated initially within a family for husband and wife as having distinct roles. And the affections that should animate citizens in a timocracy are like those originally developed toward brothers and sisters in a family.

Note that on Aristotle's conception it is not simply that political society relies upon the family, insofar as civic friendship depends upon familial affections in the way that I have sketched.[6] He thinks that family life, too, relies upon political society, insofar as the structures of governance in a family are clarified by their resemblance to political constitutions. For instance, a father in a family is guided in how he leads his family, by conceiving of himself as similar to a king, and then measuring his actions against how a good king acts: he regards himself as being an analogue of a king. Likewise husband and wife together regard themselves as having a quasi-aristocratic share of

[5] Aristotle could use "central-case" analysis to handle cases where a child is raised as an orphan or under a negligent or abusive father. It is possible to learn the requisite affections vicariously, but not if fathers throughout a society were not "for the most part" good fathers. Needless to say, he is supposing that there is one chief authority in a family, the father.

[6] Aristotle's critique of Plato's communism in *Politics* 2 should be read in connection with his discussion of civic friendship in the *Ethics*. Plato argued that the abolition of the family in his ideal Republic would lead to citizens' treating one another as if they were all members of the same family. In the *Politics* Aristotle maintains that someone can succeed in looking upon other citizens "as brothers" only if he has experience in dealing with *actual* brothers: we cannot but understand civic affections as analogues of familial affections.

authority over the household;[7] and brothers look upon their association as being akin to equal citizens in a timocracy. The chief point to
stress here is that for Aristotle a family does not exist in isolation; it is
meant to be part of political society, and it leads to political society;
and therefore the family can be properly understood only in its
natural relation to political society.

OTHER SELVES

After his discussion of friendship as it exists in a *koinōnia,* and
after his account of reciprocity and failure of reciprocity in friendships (8.13–9.3), Aristotle presents in 9.4–8 an extended discussion
of the relationship between self-love and friendship. These chapters in effect give Aristotle's view on the nature and origin of
friendship.[8]

The argument in 9.4 is that, for a good person, any friendship he
enters into is an extension of his self-love.[9] Let us sketch the argument, and then look at some difficulties concerning it.

The argument is deliberate and carefully constructed:

1. There are four "marks of friendship" (*philika*).
2. A good person exhibits these toward himself.
3. A bad person, to the degree that he is bad, exhibits the opposite of
these.
4. Thus, a good person is related to himself as he is to his friend.
5. Thus, a good person is related to his friend as he is related to
himself.
6. Thus, a friend is an "other self."
7. Thus, friendship is an extension of and derived from self-love.

---

[7] Clearly, Aristotle's understanding of the authority of husband and wife applies better to an
estate, or large household, in which each partner has authority over a separate domain, and
presumably also over servants and workers in that domain.

[8] Book 9, chapter 9 in some ways belongs to this section, yet it also serves as a bridge to the final
section in the books on friendship, on the relationship between friendship and the ultimate
goal of human life, and therefore also as a bridge to book 10, on happiness.

[9] That this is Aristotle's thesis is clear both from the opening of the chapter (1166a1–2) and
from his reference back to it at 9.8.1168b5–6.

The "characteristic marks of friendship" as distinguished by Aristotle are:

(a) *Assistance.* A friend wishes good things, and things that appear to be good, and does them, for his friend.
(b) *Joy.* A friend finds the mere existence and life of his friend something good.
(c) *Association.* Friends spend time with each other.
(d) *Sympathy.* A friend is pleased by his friend's pleasure and feels distress at his friend's distress.[10]

We need not quarrel about the list, which is plausible enough. The list in any case originates with things that Aristotle has already claimed about friendship. (a) was part of Aristotle's original definition of friendship; (b) looks a lot like the core intuition underlying "goodwill," of wishing someone good for his own sake; (c) looks related to the points Aristotle had made about friendship's close relationship to *koinōnia,* and Aristotle has been insisting all along that simply spending time with someone else is the most distinctive activity of friendship (cf. 1157b22–24); and (d) looks like a special case of (a).

As regards the argument, steps 5 and 6 look non-controversial. If there is a similarity of relations, of friend-to-friend and self-to-self, then 5 follows, and the phrase "other self" becomes simply a shorthand, albeit somewhat paradoxical way of expressing this similarity of relations.

The controversial steps of the argument are 2 (and 4, which depends on this), and step 7, the conclusion. The conclusion is controversial because, as the maxim goes, "correlation does not imply causation." If self-love and friendship are correlated, in the way that the argument claims, then there are at least three explanations for this: either friendship is caused by self-love; or self-love is caused by friendship; or self-love and friendship both have some distinct cause. That the first explanation is correct, as Aristotle holds, would apparently require further argument.

---

[10] The labels given here are not Aristotle's but rather represent how we might refer to these characteristics.

Step 2 (and therefore 4 as well) is controversial, because of the oddness of the claim that a person can have to himself a relation similar to that which he has to a friend. Can a person *give* something to himself, for instance (as Wittgenstein wondered)? But, if not, how can he *assist* himself? Aristotle is aware of the difficulty (1166a33–b2). But he suggests that we ought to be able to speak of friendliness toward oneself: after all, how could the extreme of friendship be *like* the relation that a person has to himself, if that relation were not itself *like* friendship? And it makes sense to posit something like friendliness toward oneself insofar as an individual can be regarded as *in some way* two, and indeed an individual can in various ways be regarded as two: the same individual at two different times is in some way two; and also two parts of an individual at a single time; and also a part of an individual in relation to the whole.

And this is the way that Aristotle argues that marks (a)–(d) are exhibited by a good person in relation to himself, looking at how a single individual may be regarded as in some way two. He does so, it seems, by presupposing the model of human virtue that, as we saw, was sketched and developed in book 6 (especially in 6.12), according to which there are three basic parts of a human soul: theoretical reason, practical reason, and the non-rational part that is potentially obedient to reason.[11] Corresponding to these are three basic virtues: philosophical wisdom, practical wisdom, and virtue of character. When each part has its appropriate virtue, then the soul works in the following way: practical reason gives orders to the non-rational part of the soul, which obediently carries them out, in the service of the activity of the theoretical part of the soul. Aristotle also presupposes that an individual human being appropriately identifies himself with his reasoning part generally, which, as Aristotle says, puzzlingly, each person is "most of all." Thus the way in which some other part of his soul or his entire soul treats his reasoning part, as Aristotle wishes to maintain, is an analogue of the way that one person treats another.

---

[11] It should be noted that scholars debate to what extent 9.4–8 presupposes or relies upon a distinction between theoretical and practical reason. The view adopted here is that Aristotle's acceptance of the distinction is apparent at various points, but that his argument hardly relies upon it.

Aristotle's argument that mark (a), *assistance*, is exhibited by a good person in relation to himself, when fully spelled out, is something like the following. A good person aims to act virtuously. But this is to do what is *kalon*. But the *kalon* is a good that is attained by and appreciated by his thinking part, and each person is correctly identified with his thinking part. Thus, a good person wishes good things to himself. Furthermore, he carries them out, because he has virtue of character, and consequently his non-rational part obediently carries out what his reason dictates.[12]

Likewise, a good person exhibits mark (b), *joy:* all of us inevitably wish for what we take to be good for ourselves; but a good person *is* good; thus his continued existence is good; thus, a good person wishes that he continue to exist. But he does so only on the condition that he act rationally. Why? If he were to act irrationally, he would be gratifying his irrational part and, to that extent, treating that part as though this were himself. Yet "no one chooses even to have everything on the condition that, to possess it, he become someone different from who he now is" (1166a20–21). Thus, he wishes himself existence only *as* rational. But since he is especially his reasoning part (Aristotle claims), his doing so is an analogue of someone's wishing mere existence to another.

Likewise, a good person exhibits mark (c), *association*. To associate or to spend time with another (as Aristotle will argue in 9.9) is simply to share in perception or thought. But a virtuous person, because of the consistency of his good action, can at any time in his life enter into and endorse his outlook and motives from any other time of his life. But this is simply for his thinking part at one time to share in the thoughts of his thinking part at some other time. Furthermore, his thoughts in the present moment are similarly ones that he wants to dwell upon. But this is simply for his thinking part to share in its own thought, because of the reflexivity of thought (discussed at greater length in 9.9). Again, because each person can be identified with his reason (as Aristotle asserts), these are analogues, in a single person, of association between two or more persons.

---

[12] Aristotle does not spell out this point by introducing his notion of the *kalon*, but his later discussion of self-love in 9.8 justifies this.

Finally, a good person exhibits mark (d), *sympathy*, because of the harmony of his non-rational soul with his rational soul. That is to say, his non-rational part responds with pleasure to the same things as his rational part is pleased with, and it is pained by the same things as his rational part is distressed by. Since (once again) each person is especially his reason, this is an analogue of a good person's sympathetically sharing in the delight and distress of another good person.

Aristotle's arguments gain in force and plausibility if we construe them in terms of the notion of "identifying with" someone. Aristotle does not use that idea explicitly, but it seems implicit in his notion of "other self." To take someone as an "other self" is to identify with that person. Aristotle's basic argument then becomes: to possess virtue requires that a person "identify himself" with his thinking part; and this identification then enables that person to identify, similarly, with the thinking part of another person. In contrast, insofar as a person "identifies himself" with his non-rational part, he is blocked from identifying with another, since the non-rational part of the soul simply lacks the capacity to identify with anything distinct from it.

When Aristotle's arguments are viewed in this way, is his conclusion justified, that friendship is an extension of self-love to others? Why does Aristotle claim that self-love is *prior* to love of others and friendship? Well, he may not mean that self-love is prior *in time*. He may intend his claim to be "ontological" merely: just as the category of substance is prior (in existence or reality) to that of relation, so a trait of a single substance is "ontologically" prior to any similar relation it has toward others. (For instance: two patches of yellow color are created simultaneously, and yet it is true of each that its being similar in color to itself is *ontologically prior* to its being similar in color to the other.) Or, Aristotle may have had in mind only the obvious and commonsense truth that we acquire our character while growing to adulthood, but we develop friendships in the strict sense, that is, those based on virtue, only once we have become adults. People can become friends because of virtue only if each has *already* acquired virtue, to which the other can be attracted (cf. 1166b25–29). This would imply nothing about the relation of self-love and love for another during the formation of virtue, say, for a young child within the family.

But whichever way self-love is prior to friendship, it still turns out on Aristotle's theory that self-love is something good. This, however, implies a difficulty, as I said, because self-love is widely deprecated as being something bad. So Aristotle needs to explain the appearances and vindicate self-love. This he does in 9.8, arguing that there are two sorts of self-love depending upon whether a person identifies himself with his thinking part or with his non-rational part and that the former is in fact admired and appreciated, whereas the second sort only comes under criticism.

We may understand Aristotle's view of the matter by considering an example of a just distribution of external goods (1168b15–28). Suppose someone takes less of some external good than he might help himself to, because he prefers that the distribution be equal, rather than that he get more of the relevant good. In preferring this, Aristotle thinks, he prefers and favors – thereby identifying himself with – the part of the soul for which the sheer equality is a good. This is to display love for that part of him which (Aristotle thinks) he principally is, and thus this is a good sort of self-love. In contrast, someone who preferred to have more of a material good, even when his having so required an unequal and therefore an unjust distribution, would be favoring his non-rational part, to that extent identifying himself with that, and displaying a censurable sort of self-love.

As Aristotle sees it, people get it wrong about self-sacrifice just as much as they do about self-love. If taking more of a material good instead of an equal amount counts as *not* loving oneself, then giving away a material good when appropriate, instead of holding onto it, counts *especially* as loving oneself. In fact, Aristotle argues, if we understand self-love correctly, we see that it is impossible to love another more than oneself. Someone might do so in either of two ways: either by conferring a material good upon another, or by sharing a rational good with him. If he confers a material good upon another, assuming that it is correct to do so (that is, that to do so would be an expression of either justice or well-ordered friendly affection), then to confer that good is *kalon*, and the person who does so obtains something *kalon*, whereas the person on whom it is conferred obtains only a material good. But a good that is *kalon* is a greater good than any material good; and any person to whom we distribute the greater good, when we have a choice, is the one we love more; thus, the giver, in conferring the gift, displays a greater love for himself than for another.

If, however, someone were to love another by *sharing* a good with him (say, sharing a good conversation, or sharing an insight into a mathematical theorem), then, as Aristotle had argued in 9.4, self-love serves as the very *standard* for that sort of thing, to which friendliness between two distinct persons could only approach as an ideal – which implies that a person shows that sort of love to himself above all.

This is effectively Aristotle's philosophical construal and defense of the idea that "it is more blessed to give than to receive." Aristotle's arguments rely crucially, as we have seen, on the claim that the *kalon* is a true good, which benefits and is appreciated by the rational part of the soul. As was said above in chapter 5, this doctrine is not explicitly explained or defended in the *Ethics*, but Aristotle relies upon it throughout.

FRIENDSHIP AND HUMAN HAPPINESS

So, as we have seen, according to Aristotle, persons can have a friendship in the proper sense of the term only if both have virtues: another person would not be loveable, and would not be particularly good at the reciprocation necessary for friendship, if he had vices. It follows that, if happiness is not possible without friendship, then happiness is not possible for anyone who lacks the virtues. This would remain true even if happiness did not itself *consist* in friendship or consist in the activity of any of the virtues.

Yet Aristotle apparently wants to argue in 9.9 for the stronger result that that activity in which happiness consists must have a social character. He gets at this result by three sets of arguments. We need not be much detained by the first set, which appeals to very general considerations as regards happiness:

- if a happy person lacks no important human goods, he cannot lack friends, which are regarded as "the greatest of external goods";
- happiness is a kind of prosperity, but we enjoy prosperity by doing good for others, and it would hardly be satisfying to be helping strangers instead of friends;

- human beings are naturally social, and it would be absurd to think someone could be happy who is deprived of a basic natural good (1169b8–22).

Aristotle is evidently not satisfied with these arguments, perhaps because they make no use of his definition of happiness, and they consider friends as if only instrumentally valuable for happiness. So he begins a second stage of argument (1169b28–13) by appealing to his book 1 definition of happiness as "activity of the soul in accordance with virtue." If friends help us to be *active* in virtue, then we need them for happiness. But it is obvious that they play this role: we can be more continuously active when we do things together with friends; our activity goes more easily; friends encourage and support us; their competition spurs us on to accomplish even more; and so on.

Furthermore, friends increase the *scope* of the virtuous activity that we can enjoy as and take to be our own, or so Aristotle seems to argue in a very difficult passage at 1169b30–1170a4. Aristotle had argued in 9.4 and 9.8 that the chief good that someone obtains through virtuous activity is the *kalon*. Therefore, if friends significantly increase our acquisition of the *kalon*, then they contribute to the goodness of a happy life and are to that extent "needed." But we acquire the *kalon* simply through our apprehension of a *kalon* action as something that is "our own." In the typical case, an action counts as "one's own" because it was in fact *done* by that person; but the identification of friend with friend (Aristotle supposes) is another way in which something can become "one's own": if someone successfully identifies with another, then the *kalon* actions of the latter can be regarded as "one's own" by the former. Thus, through friendship, the scope of *kalon* action that we can appropriate and enjoy is considerably expanded. And if anything is lost by the fact that we ourselves do not *perform* the virtuous actions of our friends, this is compensated for by the greater clarity of a friend's action, because (as Aristotle puts it) "we are better able to view our neighbors than ourselves, and their actions than our own" (1169b34).

Yet even this argument leaves Aristotle unsatisfied. Although this argument appeals to Aristotle's definition of happiness, it does not appeal to his definition of a friend as an "other self," except indirectly, when it supposed that a friend's actions counted as "one's own."

Furthermore, this sort of argument still counts friends as only extrinsically contributing to a happy person's happiness. Yet Aristotle wishes to argue, as he tells us, that "a friend is by the nature of the case desirable to a good person" (1170a14). To this end, he gives one of the most intricate arguments in the Aristotelian corpus, at 1170a13–b12.

We may understand that argument as involving three presuppositions. The first might be called a principle of "greater preferability":

Greater Preferability. If A and B are both desirable on condition C, but B contains C to a greater degree than does A, then B is more desirable than A.

The second might be called a principle of "amplification" for relations:

Amplification. When the same or a very similar relation exists between two things, and between one thing and itself, then the relation as between two things is an actualization of that relation.

The third is a principle of "relevance to happiness":

Relevance to Happiness. If A is necessary for someone's happiness, and B is more desirable to him than A, then B is necessary for his happiness.

Aristotle then argues in something like the following way:

1. Each person desires that he live.
2. But living is perceiving.
3. And perceiving is an inherently reflexive activity, that is, to perceive is to perceive that one perceives.
4. In fact, the reflexivity of living is a condition of its desirability.
5. Assume: the most distinctive activity of friendship is "living life together."
6. But to live life together is to share in perception.
7. When two friends share in perception, the relation between them is the same as or similar to that which each has to himself in reflexively perceiving; it is a kind of reflexivity shared between them.
8. Thus, the reflexivity as shared between friends is a fuller actualization of that relation than the reflexivity of an individual's perception alone. (Amplification)
9. However, both living on one's own and sharing in perception with one's friend are desirable on condition of reflexivity.

10. Thus, sharing in perception with one's friend is more desirable than living on one's own. (Greater Preferability)
11. But living on one's own is necessary for happiness.
12. Thus, sharing in perception with a friend is necessary for happiness. (Relevance to Happiness)

The core of the argument is that what friends aim at is simply spending time with their friend; but, when we analyze "spending time with someone" carefully, we see that it is a relationship in which each person takes on a role as regards the other, that each has in relation to himself, simply on account of the reflexivity of his own thought and perception; thus, this distinctive activity of friends is a fuller actualization of the life that each of them has individually, precisely in the respect in which their life was worth choosing for them in the first place. We therefore arrive at the result that it is, so to speak, inherent in the structure of human consciousness that we want to live our lives with others.

For Aristotle, it is ultimately because thinking is reflexive that human beings are social animals – a rather extraordinary result from an investigation into something that is very ordinary. And, as we saw, for Aristotle this result has important ramifications for civic friendship and for the role of theoretical investigation in a correctly governed city-state.

FURTHER READING

Book-length studies of Aristotle on friendship, which can be consulted for comments on particular passages, are Price (1989), Stern-Gillet (1995), Pakaluk (1998), and Pangle (2004). For the forms of friendship in particular, see Fortenbaugh (1975), Cooper (1977), and Walker (1979). For friendship and self-love, Annas (1977) was already mentioned, but see also Annas (1988, 1993) and Madigan (1985). For civic friendship, Cooper (1990) gives an interpretation of Aristotle, and Schwartzenbach (1996) looks at the matter within political philosophy. Aristotle's *De anima* 3.2 should be consulted in connection with *Ethics* 9.9 on the reflexivity of perception.

CHAPTER 10

Pleasure
(Nicomachean Ethics *7.11–14 and 10.1–5*)

UNPLEASANT DIFFICULTIES

What can be so common and so well known to us as pleasure? Do we not seek it throughout the day? Does it not frequently guide or even sway our actions? Many people apparently even live for pleasures of a certain sort.

And yet it seems almost impossible to say what pleasure is. Is it a sensation, like seeing a patch of blue sky? Or is it a feeling, like joy and delight? If it is feeling, can it be enduring, like a "mood," or is pleasure something passing, more like an emotion? But perhaps pleasure is not a "thing" that we are related to at all, but rather our *being related* to something in a certain way, so that to be pleased simply is to "take pleasure" in something that is not itself a pleasure. Yet is it not also pleasant to take pleasure in something? (How could it not be?) But then, if it is pleasant to be pleased, a pleasure *could* serve as an object of pleasure.

Moreover, what is the relationship between pleasure and attraction? Might we be *repelled* by a pleasure, *qua* pleasure, or is that suggestion nonsense? But if we are necessarily attracted to a pleasure, must we not in some sense inevitably take it to be good? It would be, if a good is a goal. Or at least this much seems true: the fact that something is pleasant seems to be some kind of *sign* that it is good. (We typically take it to be so – but why?) Yet then why do we not take *extreme* pleasure to be a sign that something is *extremely* good? In fact we are often suspicious of that sort of pleasure and think that it is probably bad. (Should we regard pleasure, then, as *prima facie* good or bad? When I said above that "many people apparently live for pleasures of a certain sort," it was natural to take such a life as

286

censurable. But perhaps we *should* live for pleasures – "good pleasures"?)

Again, if pleasure is ineffable and hard to grasp, what difference does it make whether we have it? Why should it be so important? When we think about it carefully, pleasure can seem a kind of nothing. And yet we could hardly live without this "nothing"; moreover, its opposite, pain, hardly strikes us as nothing.

This perplexity about pleasure goes fairly deep, as can be confirmed if we turn to any dictionary.[1] Even the best dictionaries give no coherent definition:

PLEASURE.

1. The state or feeling of being pleased or gratified.
2. A source of enjoyment or delight: *The graceful skaters were a pleasure to watch.*
3. Amusement, diversion, or worldly enjoyment: "*Pleasure . . . is a safer guide than either right or duty*" (Samuel Butler).
4. Sensual gratification or indulgence.
5. One's preference or wish: *What is your pleasure?*[2]

Pleasure is a state, or perhaps it is a feeling. Or it is neither of these, but rather the *source* of the "enjoyment" (that is, of the *pleasure*, so pleasure is the source of itself). Or pleasure is not a passive object of experience, or our experiencing something, so much as a guide to action, if not the aim. (But then is the pleasure of the action *distinct* from the action?) On the one hand, pleasure is associated with the senses ("sensual gratification"); on the other hand, it is so closely connected to the rational capacities of wish or choice that we can even say that one's reasonable preference simply is one's *pleasure.*

---

[1] Usually it is hazardous for students of philosophy to introduce a dictionary definition into a philosophical discussion, since a genuine philosophical problem will be deeply controversial, whereas to quote a dictionary is simply to appeal to an authority – the authority of a chance lexicographer. Yet, for all that, in an Aristotelian spirit, dictionaries can provide useful material for philosophy. They tell us at least how things seem to people (*phainomena*), and they convey "trustworthy opinions" (*endoxa*) inherent in language, especially for something so familiar as pleasure, as regards which everyone is something of an authority.

[2] *American Heritage Dictionary of the English Language*, 4th edn.

PLEASURE TWICE OVER

We need hardly be surprised, then, to find a discussion of pleasure in the *Ethics*. The subject is inherently interesting, yet also directly relevant to action. What is surprising, however, is to find *two* discussions of the subject. The first is at 7.11–14, after Aristotle's discussion of *akrasia* and immediately before his two books on friendship. For convenience I shall adopt the convention of scholars and call this the "A" discussion (or simply "A"). The second is at 10.1–5, after the books on friendship and just before Aristotle draws his final conclusions of the treatise. Let us similarly call this the "B" discussion (or simply "B").

The two passages lead to two difficulties, one "editorial" and the other "philosophical." The editorial difficulty is to explain why two distinct discussions of pleasure turn up in a work which, as we have seen, is otherwise exceedingly well-planned and coherent. The discussions are distinct not simply because they occur in different locations, but also in the strong sense that neither seems to show any awareness of the other. For instance, A seems never to flag a topic as something to be discussed later, and B seems never to say that it is relying upon, or summarizing, or clarifying certain things that were mentioned earlier. Yet in what they maintain and wish to refute, A and B sometimes overlap.

What is worse, each seems even to *exclude* the other, since each begins as if it is the sole discussion of pleasure in the neighborhood. We have seen how, when Aristotle begins a new subject in the *Ethics*, his usual practice is to justify his examination of that subject relative to the goals of the treatise as a whole – typically by referring to his definition of happiness, or virtue, or to the aims of a practitioner of "political skill" or "the art of governance," which is the discipline he thinks the *Ethics* exemplifies (recall 1.1.1094b11). But he seems to do this at the beginning of both A and B. Here is the opening of version A:

It's appropriate that a philosophical practitioner of the art of governance should examine pleasure and pain. The reasons are:

[1] Such a person is a master craftsman of our goal, and it's by attending to our goal that we call each thing, without qualification, either good or bad.
[2] It's moreover even necessary that he inquire into it, because character-related virtues and vices (as we claimed) deal with pains and pleasures.
[3] And happiness (most people say) involves pleasure. (1152b1–7)

This passage refers explicitly back to 2.3 and implicitly to 1.1 and 1.8. Thus it refers back to other material in the book, yet nowhere in A does one find a reference to anything in B. Compare with this the parallel passage at the start of B:

After these matters, it presumably follows that we discuss pleasure. Why?

[1] Because nothing seems to be so carefully adapted to the kind of thing that we are as pleasure. This is why people educate the young through steering them with pleasure and pain. And it seems a big help for acquiring character-related virtue, too, that a person like the things he should do and dislike the things he should not do.
[2] Pleasure and pain completely pervade life; they are crucially important and influential for virtue and a happy life, since people choose to do pleasant actions, and they avoid doing painful ones.
[3] And, besides, it would seem that a discussion of pleasure and pain should least of all be overlooked, especially as they involve many difficulties. (1172a19–28)

The B version as well justifies a discussion of pleasure by noting its connection with happiness and virtue, and, although B does not explicitly refer to identifiable, earlier passages in the *Ethics*, it does rely upon theses that Aristotle had defended earlier, such as the importance, for acquiring virtue, of doing actions typical of that virtue. So both A and B apparently refer to earlier material in the *Ethics*, but neither refers to the other.

The *philosophical* difficulty involves an apparent contradiction in the views adopted by A and B. Both passages, it seems, purport to define what pleasure is, and yet they apparently give incompatible definitions. Here are the definitions[3] which Aristotle seems to give:

A: Pleasure is the unimpeded activity of a living thing in its natural condition (1153a12–15).
B: Pleasure is an end which supervenes upon and completes an activity (1174b31–33).

These definitions need some explaining. By "in its natural condition" Aristotle means the way a thing is when it does not need to be

---

[3] There is some difficulty in understanding and even translating these definitions correctly; it is not even clear that Aristotle is intending to give proper definitions when he gives these characterizations. But here I give the standard view of the matter.

"restored." Aristotle regards the life of an animal as going through cycles of activity, on the one hand, and rest and replenishment, on the other. Rest and replenishment are defective conditions, and a living thing which is replenishing itself is not yet doing what it is supposed to do. It is only insofar as it is replenished and well rested that it is in condition to do its work or characteristic activity. If at that point it were to encounter hindrances or obstacles, it would experience pain; therefore, it is that activity as unhindered which is the pleasure – or so, roughly, seems to be Aristotle's view in A.

Thus, Aristotle in A seems to identify pleasure with certain sorts of activities. The pleasure of seeing a beautiful landscape, for instance, is just that activity of seeing; the pleasure of a vigorous walk on a fine spring day is just that activity of walking. But in B the activity and the pleasure are regarded as distinct. The seeing of a beautiful landscape is one thing; the pleasure of seeing it is another. The pleasure "follows upon" or is "yoked together with" the activity, Aristotle says (see, e.g., 1175a5, 19), yet no pleasure is identical with the activity of which it is a pleasure. True enough, the pleasure and the activity in which we take pleasure are so closely related that people sometimes think they amount to the same thing; but in fact such a view, Aristotle seems to say, is "absurd" (1175b34–35). Thus, B apparently not merely contradicts but also regards as absurd the view adopted by A.

The standard ways of answering these difficulties all seem unsatisfactory. A common response to the editorial difficulty is to hold that A is anomalous, because it did not originally belong to the *Nicomachean Ethics*. Recall that *Nicomachean Ethics* 5–7, the so-called "Common Books," coincides with *Eudemian Ethics* 4–6; and A falls within this material. If the Common Books belonged originally to the *Eudemian Ethics*, then A did as well. Thus one might hypothesize: the *Eudemian Ethics* was written first; the Common Books originally belonged there; the books peculiar to the *Nicomachean Ethics* had their own discussion of pleasure (version B); and when the Common Books were later incorporated into the *Nicomachean Ethics*, the duplicate discussion was retained.

But this is hardly an explanation. Who made the editorial decision to retain A, while recognizing that it duplicated but contradicted B? Was it Aristotle? But it is as inexplicable that Aristotle would make that sort of poor decision as an editor as that he would have done so as an author. Was it someone besides Aristotle, then? But presumably this editor also revised the rest of the Common Book material when incorporating it into the *Nicomachean Ethics*. Yet why should such an editor have adapted so well the material which does not overlap other material in the *Nicomachean Ethics*, while neglecting to harmonize precisely that text (version A) which, because it does duplicate and contradict something in the *Nicomachean Ethics* (version B), stands in greatest need of editing? To postulate an editor who fails to edit hardly explains anything.

As to the philosophical difficulty, there are two common responses, one minimizing the difference between A and B, the other emphasizing it. The minimizing view denies that there is a difficulty because, it holds, the A and B definitions are actually consistent. The two formulations, it is claimed, say the same thing in slightly different words. The A version defines pleasure as "unimpeded activity," that is, as activity *insofar as* it is unimpeded. The pleasure, then, is not to be identified with the activity, simply, but rather with the *unimpededness* of the activity. Pleasure is, so to speak, adverbial: to have a pleasure is to engage in an *activity in a certain way*. But the B version defines pleasure as something which "perfects" an activity. This at first looks different, but it should be considered that, for an activity to be done *perfectly* is just for it to be done without hindrance. That an activity be *perfect*, and that it be *unimpeded*, amount to the same thing. In both cases, the pleasure is the marginal difference between merely carrying out an activity (perhaps in a hindered or frustrated way) and carrying it out in an untrammeled way. Thus A and B say basically the same thing in slightly different ways.

But this response is not entirely satisfactory. In B Aristotle holds that a pleasure is distinct from the activity of which it is a pleasure: but the unimpededness of an activity is *not* distinct from it. Furthermore, in B Aristotle says that the pleasure of an activity constitutes a goal distinct from that of the activity. Yet it would seem strange to say that unimpededness is any kind of goal at all, or that, if it is, it presents a goal that is distinct from simply doing the activity.

The second response[4] is to admit that A and B give different definitions, but to insist that the definitions are not incompatible,

[4] Developed in a famous paper by Owen (1971/2).

because they aim to define different phenomena. On this view, which emphasizes the differences between the definitions in the hope of rendering them complementary, we first observe that the term "pleasure" is ambiguous and can mean either something objective – what sorts of activities or things give you pleasure – or something subjective – what it is for you to take pleasure in an activity or thing. (This ambiguity affects Greek as well as English.) Then one claims: Aristotle's project in A is to define pleasure in the objective sense; his aim in B is to define pleasure in the subjective sense. That is why in A he defines pleasure as a certain sort of activity, namely, those activities that, he thinks, we properly take pleasure in. Yet in B he defines pleasure as something distinct from the activity but perfecting it, because our taking pleasure in an activity is distinct from that activity, follows from it, and serves as an additional motive for engaging in it. In sum, being pleased is relational: it involves a person being pleased by something. Version A looks at one relatum of the relation; version B looks at the other, or perhaps at the relation itself.

But this reply, although appealing, also seems problematic. The reply maintains in effect that "pleasure" is used in two basic ways. But Aristotle typically is extraordinarily sensitive to the various meanings of terms, especially when this has philosophical importance. And, as we have seen in many instances, when he notices an important variation in the use of a term, he typically tries to determine what sense of the term is primary and central. If Aristotle indeed wrote both the A and the B accounts, and these accounts are different, it would have been strange for him not to notice the difference, and even stranger that he not argue that one sense of the term is more basic or more proper. Moreover, if one maintains that the A and B versions are not incompatible but rather complementary,[5] then the editorial difficulty becomes even more pressing. Why was their complementary character not noticed by whoever included both of them in the *Nicomachean Ethics*? A single line indicating the distinction between pleasure in the objective and pleasure in the subjective sense would presumably have been sufficient to harmonize the two accounts.

---

[5] Owen writes: "They are neither competing nor cooperating answers to one question, but answers to two quite different questions" (1971/2, 335) – yes, but *cooperating* answers to two questions.

FINDING PLEASURE SOMEWHERE ELSE

Perhaps we would find some help in these matters if we looked first at what Aristotle says about pleasure elsewhere in the *Ethics*, outside A and B. In fact he puts forward significant claims elsewhere, and presumably A and B should be understood in this context. We can distinguish six basic claims, which are closely interrelated.

1. *Pleasure necessarily involves appearance* – perhaps not the appearance of pleasure, but the appearance of something. Something can be good or useful without its appearing in any way to any living thing. If a tree in a forest is good, it need not appear to be good, or appear to be anything else, to any living being. But the tree could not be pleasant, without its appearing in some way to some living thing. Thus pleasure involves essentially some relation to a percipient or thinking being. Aristotle calls this the relation of "being pleased" and remarks that "To be pleased is something that pertains to the soul" (1.8.1099a8). On Aristotle's view, apparently, if no living thing existed, there would be no pleasure.[6]

It is natural to speak of something's appearing *as* something. In this sense an appearance has "content." Aristotle's view seems to be that when something appears to be good or useful to a living being, then it appears as pleasant: the content of that appearance is, or at least includes, pleasantness, or so he seems to say: "What is *kalon* and what is useful appear pleasant" (2.3.1105a1). Because this is so, we can take pleasantness as a sign of goodness. Yet when something is not in fact good, but appears to be, and therefore is pleasant, we can be led astray by the pleasure: "In many cases the cause of deception seems to be the pleasure, since it appears good, although it is not. People therefore choose what is pleasant as good, but they avoid pain as bad" (3.4.1113a33–35).

2. *The relationship of being pleased is teleological.* Each kind of thing is naturally meant[7] to be pleased with certain kinds of things; those are the things that are pleasant "by nature" to it. For instance,

---

[6] In the *Metaphysics* Aristotle clearly maintains that God's activity is extremely pleasant, and God is a mind; but Aristotle would not accept that God has a soul. That "pleasure pertains to the soul" is true of sublunary beings, at least.

[7] Aristotle uses the Greek term *bouletai*, "wishes," where we would more naturally say that something is "meant" to act or be in a certain way.

different species of animal have different habitats and foods which are pleasant to them. An apple is by nature pleasant to eat for a human being; garbage is not pleasant for us to eat (although it is for pigs). Similarly, the characteristic activity (*ergon*) of a kind of animal is by nature pleasant to it. These claims about what is pleasant by nature are meant to apply primarily to things that are in good condition. To say that an apple is by nature pleasant to eat for a human being is to say that an apple in good condition (a ripe, not bruised apple) is pleasant to eat for a human being in good condition (a healthy person with a good appetite). Again, to say that the characteristic activity of a kind of animal is by nature pleasant to it is to say that a good instance of that kind will find that activity pleasant.

We are therefore required to draw a distinction between "pleasant by nature" and "pleasant to this particular animal." What is pleasant by nature is what is meant to be pleasant to something of that kind. What is pleasant to that particular animal is what it in fact finds pleasant. For an animal in good condition, what it finds pleasant is what is pleasant by nature. But unhealthy animals, or animals given unusual training, may take pleasure in activities other than those which are pleasant by nature. "The pleasures of most people are in conflict with one another, because these are not the sorts of things that are pleasant by nature, but for those who want to perform noble and admirable actions, what is pleasant to them are things pleasant by nature" (1.8.1099a11–13). It is clear that Aristotle regards nature as a harmonious system, so that an animal that enjoys something pleasant by nature will not thereby be hindered from enjoying other things pleasant by nature.

Only in an animal in good condition is there an alignment between what it finds pleasant and what is pleasant by nature. It follows that if we know that an animal is in good condition, we can infer, from the fact that it finds something pleasant, that what it finds pleasant is pleasant by nature. This is one reason why Aristotle claims that a good person serves as a standard: "A good person discerns each class of thing correctly, and what seems to be so to him is what is true, as regards the various classes of things. The reason is that, corresponding to any condition are distinctive attractions and pleasures. And presumably a good person is most distinguished in seeing what is true for each class of thing – as though he were a standard or measure of them" (3.4.1113a30–33).

Note that the notion of things pleasant by nature requires that we draw a distinction between pleasure in the objective sense (what we take pleasure in) and pleasure in the subjective sense (our taking of pleasure in it). That something is pleasant by nature is a claim about its pleasantness in the objective sense: it is something that animals of a certain species naturally take pleasure in. That a good person serves as a standard is to say that what is pleasant for him in the subjective sense is a standard of what is pleasant in an objective sense.

3. *We may take pleasure either in an activity itself or in something incidental to it.* Aristotle takes this distinction to follow from his notion of activities that are pleasant by nature. A good human being takes pleasure in what is naturally pleasant. The characteristic actions of a thing as done by a good instance of that kind are naturally pleasant. For a human being, according to Aristotle, this is to act virtuously. But, as we have seen, to act virtuously is simply to do well in those sorts of actions that occupy the bulk of human life: work, business, administration, spending time with family and friends, seeking knowledge and culture. Thus, simply living life well is pleasant for a good person. At the end of the day, she will not find herself thinking that she had not lived pleasantly: "The way of life of good persons will not, then, stand in need of additional pleasure – as some kind of thing stuck onto it – but rather it contains pleasure in itself" (1.8.1099a15–16). Someone who is not good, in contrast, will not be able to take sustained pleasure from her ordinary activities. She is in a bad condition and takes pleasure, therefore, in doing bad things. But these "are in conflict with one another": she wants to shirk work, for instance, but she also wants money to spend. At the end of the day, she finds that she has not lived pleasantly and looks to add pleasure artificially to her life from amusements and diversions.

4. *The ultimate coincidence of goodness, attractiveness, and pleasant-ness.* From reflections of the sort that have just been considered, Aristotle thinks that it follows that happiness, the ultimate human goal, involves a harmony of goodness, attractiveness, and pleasant-ness. Aristotle is evidently pleased with this result and considers it an important consideration in favor of his view: "Then it's the best and most attractive and most pleasant thing – happiness is – and these things do not stand on their own . . . since all of these things belong

to the various activities of the best sort, and we say that happiness consists of these, or of the single best activity from among these" (1099a24–31). It is clear that Aristotle takes the unity of goodness and attractiveness to be straightforward and obvious. The more important result, and the one he argues for at length, is the unity of pleasantness with both of these: "If these things are so, then actions corresponding to virtue would be pleasant in their own right" (1099a21–22).

5. *Pleasure is invariably related to motivation.* Aristotle thinks that if we love or want something, we find it pleasant; and if we find something pleasant, we are drawn to it. Thus, we love or are attracted to something just in case we are pleased with it. Here are two passages where he maintains that loving something implies finding it pleasant:

When someone is said to be a "lover of such-and-such," then such-and-such is pleasant to him. For instance, horses are pleasant to lovers of horses; and visual spectacles are pleasant to lovers of such things. In the same way also, just actions are pleasant to lovers of justice, and, in general, the various actions corresponding to the virtues are pleasant to lovers of virtue. (1099a7–11)

Again,

Pleasures may be divided into those pertaining to the soul, and those pertaining to the body. Consider love of honor or love of acquiring knowledge. Each person takes pleasure in that which characteristically he loves, even if his body does not undergo any change but rather his thinking does. (3.9.1117b28–31)

Similarly it is a familiar theme in Aristotle, and an obvious truth, that taking pleasure in something makes someone want it or want to do it: pleasure provides a reason for choosing something, and its opposite, pain, is a cause for avoiding something (2.3.1104b30–33); and it is difficult to contend against pleasure (1105a8). Besides goodness, Aristotle says, pleasantness is the only reason that something can be loved as a goal (8.2.1155b21).[8]

6. *The doing of a pleasant action has an inherent complexity.* I said above that Aristotle is required to draw, indeed, must take for

[8] As was said, if one takes being good to be simply being a goal, then pleasantness *must* be something good.

granted, a distinction between pleasure in the objective sense and pleasure in the subjective sense. Pleasure is the taking of pleasure (subjective) in some activity, which is itself pleasant (objective) or not. But our being pleased by something is itself capable of becoming an object of attention and its own motivation. As we saw, according to Aristotle we tend to take our being pleased by something as a sign of its goodness. Someone can take this condition of being pleased as itself an object of striving, thus becoming a "lover of pleasure": "What is pleasant, too, is a good – for those who love pleasure," Aristotle remarks (8.4.1157a33). What happens in that case is that a person takes his own internal condition as a goal of his action, rather than traits and features in the persons or things he is dealing with, which contribute to their goodness. As Aristotle comments: assume that B is a witty person and entertaining in conversation; suppose that A loves B out of love for pleasure; then what A loves is not something about *B* – that B is a witty sort of person, which is something good about B – but rather something about *himself* – that he himself, A, is pleased by B's company (1156a12–14). To love something out of pleasure, then, is to take one's own subjective response of being pleased as the goal of one's action.

But Aristotle is drawn to acknowledge a yet further sort of complexity in the experience of pleasure, through his reflections on friendship. Recall that Aristotle holds that a friend is an "other self," a claim which, as we have seen (in 9.4), he wishes to understand as: it is possible to find analogues, in a good person's relation to himself, of the various friendly relationships that a good person has to his friend. One friendly relationship that a friend has to his friend is that a friend takes pleasure in the actions of his friend; for instance, when B performs a just action, A takes pleasure in B's performing that just action. But what is the nature of this taking pleasure? It seems to be something more than a "disinterested" pleasure, the sort of pleasure, say, that A might take in *any* just action. Rather, with friends there is something more, a kind of "sympathetic" pleasure. We want to say that A *shares in* the pleasure that B takes in his own action.

I said that B finds his own action pleasant, and that A, if he is a friend and therefore an "other self," adopts a relation toward that action, not unlike the relation that B has to it himself. What this requires, then, is that some relation that B has to himself be an analogue of the relation that A has toward him, precisely insofar as A shares in his pleasure, which implies that B's taking pleasure in his own action has an added level of complexity, or such apparently is one of the themes in the difficult passage of 9.9 (1170a13–b17).

Here is how we may understand it. Suppose that when B takes pleasure in his own action, there were only two elements: B's action, and B's taking pleasure in it. Then, for A to adopt toward that action the same relation that B has toward it, it would be enough for A to take a disinterested pleasure in it. However, as we saw, friends take pleasure in each other's actions in a fuller sense than that: A *shares in* B's pleasure. We can construe this as: A and B *together* take pleasure in B's action. But for that relationship to be analogous to the relationship that B has to himself, there must be a sense in which B and B "together" take pleasure in B's action. B has to *share in* his own pleasure. Aristotle maintains that this is what happens through the reflexivity of consciousness. When B performs a just action, B takes pleasure in that action. Yet, because of the inherent reflexivity of consciousness, whenever we do anything, we also perceive that we do it. Thus, when B performs a just action, B perceives that B has performed that just action. This perceiving is itself naturally pleasant and something B takes pleasure in ("the perceiving that one is living is to be counted among things that are pleasant in their own right," 1170b1). So when B performs a just action, B takes pleasure in that action, and takes pleasure in perceiving that action. In this way B, so to speak, shares in his own pleasure in acting justly. This seems to be the way in which, according to Aristotle, when A shares in the pleasure of B's action, he is occupying a role as regards that action analogous to B's posture toward himself: A takes pleasure in B's action through taking pleasure in B's taking pleasure in his action, and this is analogous to B's reflexively taking pleasure in B's taking pleasure in his action.

Admittedly, Aristotle's discussion in 9.9 is tangled and somewhat difficult to sort out as regards the exact details of reflexive perception. Is the reflexive perception of an inherently pleasant action simply to be identified with the agent's taking pleasure in that action, or is it something besides that? Is the reflexive perception merely objectively pleasant – something in which the agent *can* take pleasure – or does it also carry along with it its own subjective pleasure, distinct from the agent's taking pleasure in his action? But regardless of these details, it follows from this sort of analysis that there are at least three "pleasures" in an action whenever a good person takes pleasure in a naturally pleasant action: the objective pleasure of his action as something naturally pleasant; his subjective taking pleasure in the action; and his reflexive taking pleasure (in some way) in the action. Aristotle's discussion in 9.9 displays a considerable sophistication about the subjective experience of friendship, and it takes for granted, as I said, a distinction between pleasure in the objective and subjective senses.

THE "A" DISCUSSION OF PLEASURE IN BOOK 7

The context of Aristotle's separate discussions of pleasure, in books 7 and 10, is therefore this. Aristotle takes it as established that there is a coincidence between goodness and pleasure. This coincidence is to be expected given that nature is teleological. If the two did not coincide, then they might even typically diverge, and animals would therefore have pervasive motivation to do what was not good for them. The natural system which is an animal would be pulled in various and conflicting directions. Of course the chief good of a human being and pleasure would similarly also have to coincide. They coincide, Aristotle thinks, in the strong sense that the chief good is also the most pleasant thing. This explains why people think that a happy life involves pleasure (1.8.1098b25), and why people regard a happy person as "divinely blessed" (*makarios*). Moreover, as we have seen, Aristotle presumes and relies upon distinctions between natural and peculiar pleasure; between objective and subjective pleasure; and between inherent and adventitious pleasure. He acknowledges a complexity in our experience of pleasure.

If this is the general context of the book 7 discussion, it would seem incorrect to interpret it as an attempt to establish similar views, as though for the first time. It is not Aristotle's usual practice to call into question, as if doubtful, something that he has already taken as established. We might speculate, rather, that the point of book 7 is this: to show that nothing that had been said in the immediately preceding discussion of *akrasia* counts against Aristotle's views, already set out, that pleasure is good, and that the chief good is something pleasant by nature.

7.11–14 has a relatively simple structure. In 7.11 Aristotle presents a variety of arguments that pleasure is not good, and that the chief good cannot be a pleasure. In 7.12–13 he argues that these arguments do not show what they purport to show. And in 7.14 he explains why, if pleasure is in fact good, and the chief good is a pleasure, people have come to think that pleasure is bad. The discussion is therefore defensive and negative. It aims to show that Aristotle's views on pleasure are not affected by considerations that might seem plausible given his discussion of *akrasia*, and by its emphasis on pleasure as something that leads us astray in action.

That the discussion has this limited, defensive character is not at first clear, because it seems to begin with a general introduction, and then to raise what seem to be general concerns about the nature of pleasure and pain. Yet if we look at the introduction once more, this time with the context of the passage in mind, it seems not to be that sort of general introduction. "It's appropriate that a philosophical practitioner of the art of governance should examine pleasure and pain"; that is, it is not appropriate that this be decided by abstract metaphysical arguments (as Platonists and others have wished to do). "Such a person is a master craftsman of our goal, and it's by attending to our goal that we call each thing, without qualification, either good or bad"; that is, only in this sort of investigation do we have the orientation, and can we claim the expertise, to determine without being gainsaid whether a kind of thing, such as pleasure, is not in fact good. " . . . character-related virtue and vice (as we claimed) deal with pains and pleasures. Moreover, happiness (most people say) involves pleasure" – and surely this comment brings in earlier conclusions and is meant to establish a burden of proof: some powerful arguments would be needed, Aristotle intimates, to overturn what had already been arrived at.

So the introduction to the A discussion is not general at all. Rather, it leads up to this narrow question: is pleasure not in fact something good, as has been claimed?

Then three versions of the view that pleasure is not good are put forward:

1. Pleasure and goodness are distinct; hence pleasure is not-good; hence pleasure is not good (1152b8).

2. Most pleasures are bad, and so (it is suggested) that is the sort of thing that pleasure generally is (1152b10).[9]
3. The chief good cannot be a pleasure, but (it is suggested) only the chief good is *truly* good (cf. 1096b10–14); and thus (for all intents and purposes) one might say that pleasure is not good.

Aristotle then remarks, by way of summary, that the underlying reason why some philosophers take pleasure not to be good is the metaphysical view that a pleasure is a sort of *genesis* – a process by which something comes into existence (call this a "process" for short) – but no process can be good, because a process always has a terminus or goal, and (as has been set down) only that which has the nature of a goal can be good. The *goal* of the process is perhaps good, but not the *process* which leads to that goal (1152b12–15). Note that this argument is made especially relevant by the preceding discussion of *akrasia*, because the pleasures of eating and sexual gratification chiefly involved in *akrasia* seem to be connected with "processes" in this sense.

But then Aristotle brings in a variety of subsidiary arguments, most of which similarly take their start from his discussion of *akrasia*, for instance, that anyone who has the virtue of self-mastery apparently aims to *avoid* pleasures; but (the argument presupposes) a good person serves as a standard of the goodness and badness of things; and so his avoidance of pleasure shows that pleasures are bad. Again, anyone who wishes to show responsible leadership and governance (a *phronimos*) aims to live a calm life, detached from pleasures; and pleasures are an obstacle to thinking; but (the argument presupposes) some sort of thinking is the highest good; thus pleasure is incompatible with that (1152b15–18); and what is incompatible with the highest good is bad. (And if we furthermore consider that Aristotle had just been claiming that the desire for pleasure can induce a kind of *mania* that brings about a temporary state of *ignorance*, given which we become capable of doing the most shameful things, then these arguments will appear to have even greater force.)

After giving arguments like these, Aristotle announces what he wishes to show: "That it does not follow from these arguments that

[9] This view trades on Aristotle's own notion that in the *Ethics* generalities tend to be true for the most part: that pleasures are for the most part bad licenses the assertion that "pleasure is bad."

pleasure is not good, or that it is not the best good, is clear from the following considerations" (1152b25–26). He then devotes 7.12 to rebutting the various arguments that pleasure is not good, and 7.13 to rebutting the view that the chief good is not a pleasure.

His largest stretch of argument in 7.12 concerns the relationship between pleasures and processes (1152b2–1153a17). The passage is tangled and difficult, but its principal ideas seem to be the following:

1. Not everything is a process: there are states and activities as well as processes, and some activities are pleasures. The goal of an activity is not distinct from that activity, in the way that the goal of a process is distinct from the process, and, Aristotle suggests, a pleasure can be a goal of an activity.[10] Thus, even if no process is good, this would not imply that no pleasure is good.

2. But in fact some processes are good. A process should be regarded as good, if it leads to a good nature or condition (1152b27–29). Thus, if a process of this sort is a pleasure, then it is good.

3. But any process which looks like it is both bad and a pleasure is either good in some respect – the very respect in which it is pleasant – or not a pleasure. By something which "seems to be a pleasure but is not," Aristotle apparently means something which is not itself pleasant but which has something pleasant associated with it, so that we mistakenly attribute the pleasure to that to which it does not properly belong. An example of this would be the pleasure we get from eating when hungry. It is not "eating when hungry" which, properly speaking, is a pleasure, because this involves pain, and pleasure and pain are contradictories. Rather, what happens in this case is that the hunger is painful and our nature insofar as it is restored, and is operating as restored, is pleasant. Thus, it is something "underlying" the replenishment and associated with it that is the pleasure, not the process of replenishment itself. The replenishment is only incidentally pleasant, because it is accompanied by this pleasure (1152b33–1153a6).

Note that Aristotle keeps the distinction between objective and subjective pleasure firmly in view throughout the discussion. He is

---

[10] Note that this consideration implies *some kind* of distinction between the activity and the pleasure.

aware that it sounds strange to say that something that seems to be a pleasure is not. But, he says, "In the way that pleasant things are related to one another, so also are the pleasures derived from these" (1153a6–7). That is, we should make talk of subjective pleasure consistent with talk of objective pleasure.[11] People when sick take pleasure in acidic things. People when healthy take no pleasure in these. If we were to count the former as a pleasure, then it would turn out that the same sort of thing is both a pleasure and not a pleasure. It is better to say, then, that it is not a pleasure – except *to* a sick person.[12]

Aristotle's rebuttal of the view that pleasure is not good also removed the major argument for thinking that pleasure could not be the chief good – the view that all pleasures are processes. Thus he begins 7.13 with a summary restatement of his own view:

I. *Pleasure is some sort of good.* Pain is to be avoided and bad (as everyone agrees); pleasure is the opposite of pain; and the opposite of something bad is a good: "It is necessary, therefore, that pleasure be some sort of good" (1153b4).

II. *The chief good is a pleasure.* Pleasure is the unimpeded activity of something in good condition; actions in accordance with the virtues are activities of a human being in good condition; if these are unimpeded, they are pleasures; happiness is either all of these together or some one of these; thus, happiness is a particular pleasure (1153b9–14).

Argument (II) evidently restates material from 1.8, but with a twist, since it adds the idea that a necessary condition of an activity's being pleasant is that it be unimpeded.

Does book 7, then, define pleasure in the objective sense as "unimpeded activity of something in its natural condition"? Does it

---

[11] Aristotle's usual principle is that, when X is related to Y, then judgments about the nature of X are dependent upon judgments about the nature of Y. X's taking pleasure in Y, then, counts as a pleasure, depending upon whether Y counts as a pleasure ("by nature," "without qualification") or not.

[12] Other instances of his relying upon the distinction would be his talk of pleasures of things that are by nature pleasant (1154b16); his talk of people taking pleasure in pleasures (1153a2, 1154b3); his remark that God takes pleasure in a single pleasure (1154b26); and his mention of pleasures *of* contemplating (1153a1), that is, *derived from* contemplating (a22), whereas presumably contemplating is itself a pleasure (cf. 1153b10–12).

rule out that there is anything that counts as a pleasure, which is distinct from the activity that is pleasant?

It should be said, first, that it is not clear that Aristotle intends to propose a definition of pleasure at all. He takes over a formula from his philosophical opponents, "a pleasure is a perceptible process"; remarks that this is incorrect; mentions that it would be better to say "activity of a natural condition" rather than "process"; and adds, as if in an afterthought, that it would similarly be better to say "unimpeded" than "perceptible" (1153a12–15). It is not clear that the formula that results from such substitutions is what Aristotle would give if he were proposing his own definition from scratch. It is plausible, rather, that he regards the new formula as simply an improvement on the earlier one, serviceable enough for his present purposes, and he makes use of the revised formula in later arguments in a largely *ad hominem* manner; the revised formula represents what his *opponents* would be bound to recognize as a pleasure, once they had made certain minimal but necessary concessions.

Yet even if Aristotle would endorse the revised formula without hesitation, it is unclear what precisely it means. As we noted earlier: does the formula mean that a pleasure is just a pleasant activity, or that the pleasure of an activity is the unimpededness of the activity? Presumably it means the latter, for two reasons. First, when one and the same activity goes from being impeded to being unimpeded, it goes from being painful to being pleasant; thus the pleasure cannot be simply the activity. Secondly, presumably what Aristotle says about pain applies correspondingly to its opposite. Yet he says that "some pain is bad without qualification; other pain is bad only in the respect in which it serves as an impediment" (1153b2). It is not entirely clear what this means; presumably it means something like the following. A pain is bad "without qualification" when it is something bad that we also find painful, say, the distress that a just person would feel in acting unfairly toward another. (In that case the distress of performing the action corresponds in the right way to the badness of the action; it is the sort of action that a good person, who is the standard in such things, would find distressing.) A pain is bad "only insofar as it is an impediment," when someone is pained at something good, say, the distress that a bad person would feel in acting justly toward another. In the latter case, the proposed action is good; therefore it is by nature pleasant; and the pain is just the bad person's being impeded from doing it: his bad character and background, and his badly governed emotions, render him incapable of carrying out the action directly and effortlessly. But if this is the correct way of construing what Aristotle says about pain, then we must reason about pleasures correspondingly, and we should say that there are some actions that are pleasant "only insofar as they are unimpeded," say, the satisfaction that a bad person feels in doing something bad. But if this is correct, then it is clear that Aristotle regards an activity's being impeded or not as, so to speak, correlated with, or a cause of, our finding it painful or pleasant (pleasure in the subjective sense). But then the formula "unimpeded activity of a natural condition" should be interpreted as including *both* the subjective and objective elements of pleasure: "activity of a natural condition" is what it is for something to be pleasant by nature; "unimpeded" signals that, furthermore, the activity is pleasant to the agent.[13] This makes sense: the qualification "unimpeded" was Aristotle's replacement for "perceptible" in the original formula. Presumably, then, it plays the same role, as indicating our experience, or the appearance, of pleasure.[14]

Thus my conclusion about the A discussion of pleasure in book 7 is as follows. The A discussion is an *ad hoc* discussion of pleasure, and it regards itself as such: it is narrowly constructed to respond to objections to Aristotle's view of pleasure which seem to arise once we hold, as Aristotle does in his treatment of *akrasia*, that the desire for pleasure leads people to act wrongly. The A discussion does not overlook but rather presupposes the distinction between objective and subjective pleasure. The "definition" of pleasure it offers need not be understood as excluding the subjective element of pleasure, but perhaps should even be regarded as including it. In style and

[13] Note that in book 7 Aristotle thinks it is coherent to consider the activity of *eudaimonia* as *not* being pleasant (1154a1–5). Note too that MS Mb at this point has Aristotle saying, "unless the pleasure and the activity are good, a happy person will not be living pleasantly," as if the pleasure is a good that is distinct from the activity.

[14] In fact, Aristotle does not say why he regards "perceptible" as inadequate. For all we know, he objects to it on the narrow grounds that "perceptible" suggests that pleasure involves something like an internal sense perception, or that a pleasure (in the objective sense) must be bodily, or located somehow in the sense organs.

content A is therefore, for its part, entirely consistent with both the rest of the *Ethics* and the book 10 approach to pleasure.

We saw that in the A discussion Aristotle freely appealed to the distinction between pleasure in the objective sense and in the subjective sense. The same is true in B: (i) He distinguishes between the (activity of) being pleased and the pleasure itself (1173a17, 22), the former varying in degree, the latter being a mixture and having a formal structure, varying in its "purity." (The language he uses for the latter is similar to that he uses to describe objects of the senses as they exist in reality.) (ii) In connection with the theory that pleasure is the "replenishment of a natural need," he distinguishes between what the pleasure would be on that theory (a replenishment) and what the subject would be that would *take pleasure*. Aristotle argues that on the replenishment view the subject would be the body, absurdly so (1173b9–10). (iii) He draws a distinction between a pleasant thing, and the pleasure taken in it (1173b20–28). Aristotle speculates that perhaps we can explain away apparently bad pleasures by maintaining that, although the pleasures people take in such things are good, the pleasures from which they are derived are not. (iv) He maintains that *pleasant things* are those in which a good person takes *pleasure* (1175a18–19), clearly taking the distinction between objective and subjective pleasure for granted.

It should not be surprising that this distinction is taken for granted in B as well as A, since Aristotle holds in both discussions, as he does throughout the *Ethics*, that pleasure involves appearance – and there can be no appearance without the possibility of a distinction between objective and subjective.

If the difference between the A and B discussions, then, is not that A is concerned with pleasure in the objective sense, and B with pleasure in the subjective sense, what is the difference? At first glance we may say: A argues that pleasure is not bad; B argues that pleasure is a good which we should aim at directly and deliberately. Discussion A aims to clear pleasure of charges against it; discussion B aims, in a sense, to argue for hedonism (of a certain sort). B's view is that pleasure provides an additional and correct reason for performing a good action, and that pleasure is meant to play this role. The outlook of B is that nature has attached pleasures to good activities for a purpose – in order to stimulate and encourage those activities – and that we are right to pursue those pleasures along with the activities.

That this is B's purpose is clear from its introduction. B's opening remarks are about the natural teleology of pleasure: the pleasures we enjoy are closely matched to the kind of animal we are (1172a20); pleasures of the right sort stimulate us to act well, just as the right sort of distress helps us to avoid bad action (a21–23); pleasures, in fact, as they pervade human life, draw us on to happiness (a23–25). They do so by becoming a distinct object of pursuit: "people deliberately seek pleasures, and they are careful to avoid pain" (1172a25–26). These remarks are all naturalistic observations about the role that pleasure plays in our actions. It is pointless and harmful, Aristotle adds, to pretend otherwise – like those misguided philosophers who among themselves hold that pleasure is good, but outwardly maintain that it is bad, because they hope thereby to encourage ordinary people to become less attached to pleasure. Such philosophers will inevitably be caught seeking pleasure, to bad effect: "If someone who censures pleasure is even once seen to be seeking it, then – people think – he takes all pleasure to be like the pleasure he's abandoning his principles for" (1172b1–3). At that point, it will be useless for him to protest that only select pleasures are good, since "making distinctions is beyond the capacity of the great bulk of people" (1172b2). Thus, one really needs to teach explicitly that "pleasure is good." The only issue is how to cast this: how can we maintain that pleasure is good, and encourage others to seek pleasure deliberately, yet without leading them to seek the wrong sorts of pleasures? It is this task that the B account aims to carry out. The B discussion's principal claim in carrying out this task, occupying 10.4–5, is that pleasures differ in kind. If pleasures differ in kind, Aristotle considers, then it is possible to pursue some *kinds* of pleasures, without thereby becoming devoted to *pleasure*, generally. The claim that pleasures differ in kind is essential for establishing the ethically good sort of hedonism that Aristotle wishes to advocate.

Note that the difficulty about how to pursue pleasure selectively becomes more pressing once the subjective side of pleasure is given greater emphasis. So long as we think of pleasure as primarily that *in which* we take pleasure (in the manner of book 7), then it remains easy to think of pleasures as differing in kind, since things in which we take pleasure evidently differ in kind. But, as we saw, in his discussion of friendship, in order to highlight how an individual's relationship to his own pleasure, when he takes pleasure in something, is analogous to his friend's sympathetic appreciation of his pleasure, Aristotle was required to give particular attention to the experience of taking pleasure in something. The view then begins to threaten that the only thing that matters in pleasure is its subjective side: the taking of pleasure is itself good, and pleasure in the subjective sense is the same sort of thing, whatever the activity or object that occasions it. Perhaps then, too, a bad person experiences as much (or more) pleasure in this subjective sense as a good person.

The passage in which Aristotle explains why he wants to establish that pleasures differ in kind begins with standard book 7 doctrine:

In reply to those who bring forward pleasures that should be reproached [sc. as an objection to the view that pleasure is good], one might say that these things are not pleasures – their being pleasant for people who are in a bad condition should not make one think that they *are* pleasant, except *to these people* ... (1173b20–22)

But immediately Aristotle puts forward another possible reply, which looks plausible now that the subjective side of pleasure has been given more prominence in his discussions:

Or might one say this: that the *pleasures* are desirable, yet not *as derived from* these things – in the same way that acquiring wealth is desirable, but not in payment for a betrayal, or that being healthy is desirable, yet not regardless of what one has to eat? (b25–28)

But in fact Aristotle does not welcome this approach, the view that pleasure in the objective sense is merely the instrumental cause of undifferentiated pleasure in the subjective sense. Aristotle aims to reject it through emphasizing that pleasures differ in kind (b28). The view needs to be rejected, Aristotle insists, for ethical considerations:

- There needs to be a distinctive pleasure that is available only to those who have a virtue – which presumably can serve as a kind of reward and encouragement of virtue (b28–31).

- We need to be able to mark a distinction between the sort of pleasure a flatterer provides and that which a friend provides (a consideration clearly following from 8.2–4) (b31–1174a1).
- It cannot be the case that the pleasure we take in a bad action can ever be equal in worth to, or outweigh the worth of, the pleasure that we take in good actions, since then it would become correct to perform the bad action for the pleasure. That is, the pleasures of doing good must be better than and incommensurable with the pleasures of doing something bad (a1–4).

Aristotle's task, then, is to make out a difference in form among pleasures, sufficient to sustain these ethical considerations, while still preserving the point that the goodness of the activity is one thing and the goodness of the pleasure derived from it (*ap' autōn hēdonē*, 1174a8) is something else.

The way that Aristotle argues for this is to give, as it were, a *functional* definition of pleasure. He is not in the B discussion so much interested in what pleasure *is* – the putative "content" of pleasure, or its ontological standing – but rather with how pleasure *works*. He seems to presuppose that, because pleasure is a good, and any good has the nature of a goal, to inquire into what pleasure is, is properly an inquiry into how it functions as a goal. His basic argument is apparently the following:

1. The pleasure of an activity functions as a distinct goal, the attainment of which is correlated with the full execution of an activity.
2. But pleasure could not play this role, unless it were matched precisely to the activity to which it is thus correlated.
3. But pleasure could not be so matched, unless it varied in form with the activity.
4. Thus, the pleasure derived from an activity varies in form with the activity from which it is derived.

And if it thus varies in form, then the objectionable ethical consequences sketched above are blocked.

He prefaces his discussion with some preliminary arguments against views that would imply that pleasures do not vary in kind with the activities from which they are derived, especially the view that a pleasure is a kind of movement or process.[15] He begins by drawing an analogy between perception and pleasure: to take pleasure in something, like an act of seeing (*horasis*), is complete in form at any time; but a movement (*kinēsis*) – and the special case of generation (*genesis*) – is not something that is complete in form until it reaches its end, when strictly the movement no longer exists. For instance, the building of a house is incomplete in form throughtout the process of its construction; and when there is something formally complete, the house, the process is over. In contrast, seeing is something that has its form from the start and maintains it for the course of that activity.

Much has been written about this distinction and whether Aristotle properly states the criteria for making the distinction. It is not possible to examine this here, nor would it really be to the point. What is important for present purposes is what would be implied if pleasure were a "movement" or a "process." If a pleasure were that sort of thing, then the form of the pleasure, if it had a form, would not be concurrent with the form of the activity. In that case, the pleasure could not, in virtue of its having a certain sort of form, play the role that Aristotle wants it to play. If, for instance, the pleasure of thinking did not have a form that was appropriately matched to the activity of thinking, which existed just as long as the thinking did, then the pleasure of thinking, *as having that form*, could not play the role of stimulating us to think with greater clarity and intensity. This is why Aristotle wishes to maintain that pleasures are not movements or processes. Whether he is entirely successful in maintaining that is not quite relevant for understanding his intentions.

The crucial passage in which he makes an observation about the function of pleasure is 1174b14–23. First, he makes an observation about how the activity or "actualization" (the more technical metaphysical term is perhaps preferable here) varies in degree, and the conditions under which it reaches a maximum; then he notes that the pleasure of the activity is correlated with this; and from these he draws a conclusion about the function of the pleasure. The passage,

---

[15] There is some overlap between this material and the A account, but Aristotle's purpose in B is quite different.

for the sake of perspicacity, may be translated with numbering and indentation as follows:

[1] Every power of perception is actualized when directed at an object of that power.

[2] It is completely actualized, when it is in good condition and directed at the best thing within its scope.

(Why? Because this is the sort of thing that seems to be the complete actualization of that power, to the greatest degree. And it makes no difference whether we say that the *power* is actualized or *that in which* the power is located.)

[3] Hence, as regards each power of perception, its actualization is the best, when it is in the best condition and directed at the best thing within its scope.

But this would be the most complete and the most pleasant. Here is why:

[4] There is pleasure corresponding to the actualization of any power of perception.

(The same holds true of thinking and intellectual perception.)

[5] The most complete such actualization is the most pleasant.

But the most complete is that of a power in good condition directed at the best thing within its scope.

[6] Thus,[16] the pleasure brings the activity to completion.

The conclusion of this argument is often translated as "The pleasure completes the activity." But this is ambiguous: does it complete it as a formal constituent, or rather is its function to complete the activity? The former cannot be the case, because Aristotle has already argued that an activity is not incomplete in form at any time; therefore, the pleasure of the activity cannot complete it as a constituent. But an activity, as having the same form, can be more or less acute or intense – just as a thought can be more or less clear, even though it is one and the same thought (and therefore has one and the same "form"). The acuity of an activity is correlated with its degree of pleasure. But the pleasure is a distinct goal, which accompanies the activity (1174b33). Thus the

---

[16] Reading *dē* at 1174b23.

pleasure has a function such that, in seeking it, we engage in the activity with greater acuity. The pleasure functions as a distinct goal not unlike beauty in relation to bodily fitness: we typically reach the peak of fitness through aiming to reach the peak of beauty (b33).[17]

Pleasures could not be thus correlated with intensity of activity if they were not matched in form to the activity; otherwise, for all we knew, by aiming at the pleasure of doing geometry we might be stimulated (say) to play the flute better. "Things that differ in form, we consider, are brought to completion by things that themselves differ in form – that it works that way is evident from things in nature and from matters pertaining to technical skill" (1175a23–25). And Aristotle's discussion about the way in which the pleasure proper to an activity increases the intensity and accuracy of the activity, but alien pleasures work as impediments (1175a30–b24), is meant to confirm this point.

He brings the entire discussion to an end with two results relevant to ethics. First, if activities vary in form as good and bad, and the pleasures of activities vary in form with the activities, then pleasures as well vary in form as good and bad (1175b24–28).[18] Thus even though pleasures are "derived from" the activities of which they are pleasures, pleasures are not *qua* pleasures good. Thus the pleasures of bad actions cannot even be entered into a calculus of *goods*.[19] Secondly, just as there is a characteristic activity (*ergon*) for each sort of thing, so there is a characteristic pleasure for each sort of thing. Thus there are distinctive human pleasures. These pleasures are precisely the pleasures that accompany activities in accordance with virtue. We may, and we should, deliberately aim at such pleasures, since in doing so we are stimulated to act virtuously with even greater intensity and concentration. And, because pleasures differ in form, it will not follow that,

---

[17] Commentators puzzle over Aristotle's metaphor at b33, but the meaning seems plain once we interpret his remarks about pleasure functionally. What is important about "one's prime" (*akmaios*) and "bloom of youth" (*hōra*) is that these are both maxima, which are correlated.

[18] In confirmation: if the desire for a good thing is good, and the desire for a bad thing is bad, then, on the same principle, because a desire is matched to its object, but the pleasure of an activity is closer to it and therefore even more closely matched, the pleasure of a good activity would be a good pleasure, and the pleasure of a bad activity would be bad (1175b28–32), albeit good "to him." See the repetition of this idea at 1176a19–24.

[19] One might say: the function of a pleasure, fully specified, is to stimulate toward something good; a pleasure that stimulates toward something bad is good insofar as it still works to stimulate – it still functions as a goal – but it is bad because that to which it stimulates is bad.

because we pursue such pleasures, we will become at all disposed to value other kinds of pleasures.[20]

A PLEASANT ENDING

What, then, of the difficulties with which I began this chapter? I distinguished a philosophical and an editorial difficulty. The philosophical difficulty was largely dissolved by the consideration of the significance of the formula "unimpeded activity of a natural state" in the A discussion, since we saw that the A discussion acknowledges a subjective as well as an objective side of pleasure, and the term "unimpeded" seemed to have been included in the formula precisely to account for the subjective side.

Some commentators, as I said, have held that the B account at one point actually contradicts the A account. The relevant passage occurs at a point where Aristotle is arguing that the pleasure of an activity is closely matched in form to the activity of which it is a pleasure. That it is so closely matched, he says, explains why people may even think that the pleasure and the activity are the same thing:

The pleasures are very closely related to the activities; in fact, they are so hard to distinguish, that it's debated whether the activity is just the same thing as the pleasure. But pleasure surely doesn't look like thinking, at least, and it's not a perception (that's absurd), yet because it doesn't exist separately, it seems to some people to be the same. (1175b32–35)

Yet what Aristotle here regards as absurd is not the identification of the pleasure of an activity with the activity – that is a common and understandable mistake, he says – but rather the implication that, if these are identified, then pleasure is a perception. Aristotle's implicit argument seems to be as follows. The activity of living things consists of either sense perception or thinking; these are the only two alternatives (1170a17). Thus, if pleasure is an activity, it is either a kind of sense perception or a kind of thinking. It is evident on the face of it

---

[20] Aristotle clearly thinks that it adds to the attractiveness of the pleasure to say that it is a "distinctively human" pleasure, as opposed to one that any animal might share (1176a24–26). Recall his setting apart of the pleasures of taste and touch, the domain of self-mastery, as those pleasures enjoyed by any animal, which therefore seem slavish and bestial (3.10.1118a23–25).

that taking pleasure is not the same sort of thing as thinking. And the suggestion that taking pleasure is a kind of sense perception is absurd, because that would imply, since thinking involves pleasure, that there could be no thinking without sense perception.

Admittedly, we are still left wondering what exactly taking pleasure in something is, as a matter of ontology. What exactly is taking pleasure in something, if it is something that a living thing does, yet it is not an activity of thinking or sense perception, and it is not quite the pleasant activity, but rather a goal distinct from the activity? Aristotle might reply that he has told us already: it is the unimpededness of the activity. He seems content to leave it at that, because the B account is concerned with motivation and teleology, not metaphysics. His view is perhaps ultimately unclear, and he does not always speak in such a way as to put off possible confusions, but that is not a difficulty arising from his two different treatments of the matter, so much as a difficulty in the subject matter – and in the subjectivity of pleasure.

The editorial difficulty remains, but only in a considerably diminished form. What needs to be explained is not why Aristotle, or some editor, failed to notice an important change in the meaning of "pleasure" between the A and B accounts, but rather a slight inaptness in the way that the two discussions are introduced and the doctrine of pleasure-as-process is twice attacked. If we were to imagine appropriate headings supplied for the two discussions – "Why Pleasure Is Not Bad" (for A); "That Pleasure Is to Be Pursued by a Good Person" (for B) – even this difficulty would largely go away. Since there is some slight repetition in B of content from A, and no explicit references back and forth, it is perhaps best to conclude that, in an otherwise coherent treatise, we find here two originally independent treatments, which were not in the end thoroughly adapted to the whole in which they were placed. Nevertheless that placement itself, as we have seen, is expert and even required by the argument of the treatise.

FURTHER READING

The few writings especially to be recommended in connection with pleasure in Aristotle are relatively dense and repay careful study. Owen (1971/2) was mentioned above. It is easily the most subtle and sophisticated discussion around. Gosling and Taylor (1982), chapters 11–15, give historical context and thorough exegesis and offer some criticisms of Owen.

Ackrill (1965) and Heinaman (1995) should be consulted to consider more carefully the distinction between a process and an activity. Bostock (1988) puts forward the important claim that only thoughts and perceptions can be enjoyed, according to Aristotle.

CHAPTER 11

Happiness
(Nicomachean Ethics *10.6–9*)

ARRIVING AT THE END

Perhaps the most puzzling sentence in the entire *Ethics* is one that Aristotle apparently thinks should be perfectly clear. It occurs at the beginning of 10.7, where he begins to give his final views on the ultimate goal of human life, happiness (*eudaimonia*): "If happiness is activity in accordance with virtue, it is reasonable that it be activity in accordance with the best virtue" (1177a12–13). This is puzzling, because Aristotle, as we have seen, has throughout the *Ethics* been deliberately maintaining a kind of indecision as regards what we have called Selection and Collection. Happiness is activity in accordance with virtue – granted – but is it some single such activity (Selection) or all such activities (Collection)? As late as 10.5 he was apparently keeping the question open: "So whether there is one sort of activity or several which are characteristic of a complete and blessedly happy man, the pleasures that bring these activities to completion would in the strict sense be referred to as 'human pleasures'" (1176a26–28). If anything, that passage tips toward Collection, since it speaks of the *pleasures* that bring these *activities* to completion (in the plural). Yet in 10.7 the matter is suddenly settled. Moreover, it is settled without argument. Look at that puzzling sentence in context, and observe that it is not followed, as is typical in Aristotle, by any argument in justification:

If happiness is activity in accordance with virtue, it's reasonable that it be activity in accordance with the best virtue. This would be the virtue of the best part. Whether this part is the mind or some other thing which is regarded as by nature governing and leading and taking thought of admirable and god-like things, and whether it's also godlike itself or the most godlike thing in

316

us – the activity of this part as carried out through the virtue proper to it would be perfect happiness. That this activity has the character of viewing [sc. it is speculative, contemplative] has already been said. (1177a12–18)

It is true that Aristotle, as we may recall, had remarked at the beginning of his treatise, immediately after giving his definition of happiness, that "if there are several virtues," then happiness would be activity "as carried out by the best virtue, the virtue which most has the character of a goal" (1.7.1098a17–18). But if it were already settled then that happiness was the best activity (and why not, since happiness is the best good?), why should Aristotle have remained at all open throughout the *Ethics*, as he does, to the possibility that happiness consists of a plurality of activities?

Yet another puzzling aspect of the passage is its use, for the first time, of the phrase "ultimate happiness" (*teleia eudaimonia*; see also 1177b24). What precisely this could mean is unclear. We have seen, in book 1, that the word *telos* tends to mean "goal," and words derived from it typically mean "goal-like." But "goal-like happiness" hardly makes sense: how could happiness, the ultimate goal, not be goal-like? In fact Aristotle draws a contrast in book 10 between *teleia eudaimonia*, which he claims is good contemplative or activity, and *eudaimonia deuterōs*, or "happiness in a secondary sense" (1178a9), which he says is activity as carried out through practical wisdom (*phronēsis*) in conjunction with the other virtues. So would the latter sort of activity be a kind of happiness which is *not* goal-like? The suggestion is absurd: if it is not goal-like, it cannot be happiness. Thus *teleia eudaimonia* must have a different sense. Presumably it means either "complete," that is, not lacking anything that is due to it, or "perfect," that is, occurring in its fullest form. But how can anything be lacking as regards happiness, which Aristotle had argued is something "self-sufficient" (1097b14)? And Aristotle has said nothing which would lead us to think that there could be different degrees of happiness, so that it could have a fuller and less full form. We saw, in fact, in 1.7 that Aristotle was willing to speak of degrees of goodness only insofar as one could *rank* goods: if good X is for the sake of good Y, then Y is good "to a greater degree" than X. It seemed to be Aristotle's view that this was the only way to compare goods, or goals. But happiness is that for the sake of which we do whatever else that we do. It is never for the sake of anything else (1097a33–34), and it must lie at the end point of any structure of "for the sake of" relations (1094a18–22). But clearly in this sense there could not be any "degrees" of happiness.

Moreover, Aristotle's talk of "happiness in a secondary sense" looks like a fudge. He had been deliberately keeping open the issue of Selection versus Collection, it seems, and then he decides suddenly, and apparently without argument, in favor of Selection: happiness is activity in accordance with (simply) the virtue of philosophical wisdom. That is, happiness consists in the exercise of knowledge about theology and metaphysics – God and first principles – and perhaps also thinking about other things, through these. But then why not leave it at that? Why go on to say that anything *else* counts as happiness? If that sort of contemplative thinking is happiness, then nothing that is not like that would be happiness. (And Aristotle seems to agree: he seems to say that happiness extends only so far as activity does, 1178b28–29.) To say that other activities are "happiness in a secondary sense" looks as if we are bestowing upon them a merely honorific title. Indeed, the contest for being counted as happiness seems so important (cf. 1094a23) that coming in second should mean nothing. Determining what happiness is, Aristotle has declared in 10.7, is a matter of Selection: why then revert back to holding that in some sense (a "secondary" sense) happiness may also be a matter of Collection? This is to decide but not to decide what happiness is, leaving us with no clear guidance on the matter.

But there is another difficulty in "happiness in a secondary sense." We might think that Aristotle's view is that the Selection should be used to determine what happiness is in the full and "ultimate" sense, and that Collection should be used to determine what happiness is in a "secondary" sense. Yet in fact that is not his view, because the latter does not consist of activity in accordance with *all* of the virtues. That sort of happiness – Aristotle is explicit on the matter – does not include activity corresponding to philosophical wisdom. It is simply administrative virtue (*phronēsis*) working in conjunction with the various character-related virtues (1178a9–21). So *both* sorts of happiness are fragments, really: "ultimate" happiness is a fragment of virtuous activity, and happiness "in a secondary sense" is a complementary fragment. Neither of them is complete: so how can either constitute *happiness*?

THREE LIVES COMPARED?

Recall that in 1.5 Aristotle had said that we might judge what people
in fact take to be the highest good by looking at the sorts of lives that
they lead, and he distinguished three principal ways of life: a life
centered around pleasure; a life devoted to public service; and the
"theoretical" life. His book 10 discussion of happiness occupies three
chapters, which might seem to correspond to these three ways of life:

Chapter 10.6	pleasant amusements	the life of ease
Chapter 10.7	ultimate happiness: the activity of philosophical wisdom	the life of attaining insight (the theoretical life)
Chapter 10.8	happiness in a secondary sense: the activity of administrative and character-related virtue	the life of civic involvement

So a plausible suggestion is that we should understand book 10 to be
rendering a judgment about the relative worth of these various lives,
which were first introduced in book 1. In book 10, on this view,
Aristotle effectively establishes a ranking of these lives: the theoretical
is to be preferred to the life of civic involvement, which is to be
preferred to a life of ease. In book 10, then, Aristotle is not interested
simply in the *activities* which, he says, constitute complete or secondary happiness, so much as in "ways of life" that are centered
around these activities.

   This interpretation would seem to resolve some of the difficulties
I raised. Although the *activities* around which these lives are centered
may be "fragments" of virtuous activity, the *lives* themselves are not
fragments; rather, we can conceive of them as coherent wholes. And
the reason why secondary happiness, although it is inclusive in
character, does not involve contemplative activity, is presumably
that the way of life centered around that sort of happiness – a life
of public service – is the sort of life that should be pursued precisely
by someone who has little aptitude for metaphysics or theology. After
all, people have different aptitudes, and there is no reason why
someone who lacks talent in metaphysics or theology should be

barred from happiness altogether. There is a way of life open to him in which he can exercise various practical virtues and thereby still attain some sort of happiness, although admittedly not the best sort. This is "happiness in a secondary sense."

That this is the correct way of understanding Aristotle's argument in book 10 appears to be supported by his language. At 1177b26 he begins an extended argument, apparently for the view that a life centered on theoretical activity is better than a life centered on practical virtue, on the grounds that the former is godlike activity, whereas the latter is distinctively human, and gods are better than human beings:

> A way of life like that would be better than a life suited to a human being. Why? Because it's not insofar as someone is human that he will live like that, but rather insofar as there's something godlike within him. The extent of the difference between this godlike part and the composite which he is, is the extent of the difference between this activity [viz. of philosophical wisdom] and that of the other virtue [viz. of practical wisdom]. Hence, if the human mind is godlike, in comparison with a human being as a whole, so also is the way of life corresponding to that part godlike, in comparison with a merely human way of life. (1177b26–31)

However, there are various difficulties in this interpretation of book 10 as proposing a comparison of "lives." For instance, the pleasures of relaxation and amusement which Aristotle discusses in 10.6 seem not to be the same sorts of pleasures around which a life of pleasure is said to be centered in 1.5; there the pleasures envisaged are evidently those of food, drink, and sex but in 10.6 Aristotle seems to have in mind such things as games and joke-telling. The different arguments deployed by Aristotle in the different passages confirm this point. As we saw, he gives no *argument* in 1.5: he simply dismisses the pleasures under consideration as slavish and animalistic (1095b19–20). Note that these terms suggest that a person pursuing that sort of life will typically have the vice of self-indulgence and act accordingly. In contrast, the amusements mentioned in 10.6 seem harmless in themselves and consistent with virtue – Aristotle even recommends them, as ways of relaxing prior to work (1176b33) – and in 10.6 Aristotle does use fairly sophisticated arguments, in order to show that, against what might seem to be the case, such pleasures do not constitute happiness.

Again, he dismisses the life of public service in 1.5 as aiming at the relatively superficial goal of honor; of course subsequently in the *Ethics* he maintains that someone who seeks honor apart from its foundation in virtue risks either having the vice of self-aggrandizement or falling prey to *akrasia* as regards honor. But the way of life described in 10.8 is a life of virtuous activity which apparently does not take honor as its ultimate aim.

Indeed, one would have thought that, by the end of 1.5, Aristotle had regarded all ways of life except the theoretical life as being no longer of interest for his inquiry. His remark dismissing the money-making life, that "it's clear that riches are not the good we are seeking," seems of a piece with his dismissal of the life of public service. But then if the one is no longer a serious contender for a happy life in the *Ethics* after 1.5, neither is the other. We saw in fact that Aristotle was engaging in a kind of process of elimination in 1.4–1.5. At the start of 1.6 there are only two contenders left for the ultimate good: the Form of the Good, the chief good on the Platonic theory, which immediately gets eliminated, and "activity in accordance with virtue," Aristotle's own view, which is the only view holding the field at 1.7. The task of the *Ethics*, as Aristotle says, is to fill in the details of this view (1098a20ff.), not to argue for it all over again. And the book 1 discussion provides no reason for thinking that Aristotle's definition of happiness will give rise once again to a new plurality of "lives," which will need to be compared and adjudged at some later point.

There is a difficulty, too, in taking 10.8 to be marking out a "life of political involvement" which putatively involves administrative virtue and character-related virtues alone. Aristotle was clear in book 6 that administrative virtue requires some "target" (*skopos*) at which it aims, if it is to play its role of issuing commands to the non-rational part of the soul. Later in book 6 it appeared that this "target" was in fact the activity of wisdom: Aristotle's view seemed to be that the point of administrative virtue is to provide for wisdom and its activity. But if this is so, and if 10.8 were describing a way of life that lacked the activity of wisdom, then it would be describing a life in which administrative virtue lacked a "target" – a strange way of life, in which someone employed his reason well insofar as his intelligence were applied to action, but in which he lacked altogether the ability

to use his reason well when not applied to action. It would additionally seem odd, by Aristotle's lights, that someone might be accounted
a *good* person – presumably it would be necessary for him to be good
if he were to have any prospects of happiness – and yet have only one
of the two chief intellectual virtues.

One might reply, once again, that Aristotle has in mind different
sorts of lives, which would be suited to persons with different
aptitudes, and that he thinks that the good of the better sort of
person, involving philosophical contemplation, should provide the
"target" for the practical wisdom of the less gifted sort of person. The
two lives are meant to complement each other and be coordinated
within political society. But it would be odd, if this were his intention, that he never says anything like this explicitly. He does not talk
(as did Plato) about different classes of persons corresponding to the
different ways of life, or of how we might identify into which class a
person should be sorted; and he does not hint at any kind of political
arrangement involving the two sorts of lives. Moreover, apart from
these considerations, it is unclear why we should count as happy at all
someone who had no "aptitude" for the best human virtue and
activity: happiness in the Aristotelian scheme is meant to be an
ideal, not a catch-all for people with different sorts of deficiency.

Again, just as it is odd, on Aristotle's scheme, to think of administrative virtue as embedded in a way of life without its having any
"target," so it is odd to consider philosophical wisdom as pursued
within a way of life in separation from administrative virtue. And
thus it looks as though the "theoretical life," so construed, could be an
immoral life. If the theoretical life were simply a life of a full-tilt
pursuit of philosophical contemplation, it is difficult to see why (on a
familiar example) a fellow should not murder his wealthy aunt and
collect her inheritance, if he could get away with it, if this increased
his possibilities for philosophical reflection. Once we divide up the
virtues in this way across different "lives," the one sort of life seems to
lack a point and the other to lack any constraints.

A SKETCHY CONCLUSION?

Another approach to book 10 would be to take seriously Aristotle's
remark at the beginning of 10.6, where he introduces his topic:

Now that the various virtues and types of friendship and sorts of pleasure have been discussed, our remaining task is to discuss happiness in outline, since we are proposing it as the goal of human concerns. (1176a30–32)

The word "proposing" here translates a verb that may also mean "setting up" or "instituting." Aristotle seems to be saying that he intends to give a sketch of happiness (presumably relying on what he has so far said) that can serve as some kind of practical ideal of action. If he is proposing it as a goal, but fails to say enough for it to direct our "human concerns," then he has failed in his task. His saying furthermore that he intends to sketch happiness "in outline" suggests a delineation of parts or aspects of a single thing, rather than a classification of kinds. Note too that his language of discussing happiness "in outline" seems to correspond to his stated intention earlier in book 1 (1098a 20) and suggests that now he will be consolidating and assembling rather than introducing anything new.

Suppose then that he is not in fact intending to introduce anything new, that he is taking for granted and importing into book 10 his sketch of the interrelationship of the virtues that he had already given in 6.12. Recall that his view there is that philosophical wisdom, or rather its activity, provides the "target" at which administrative virtue aims and with respect to which administrative virtue issues commands that guide the virtues of character. One might also recall Aristotle's frequent insistence that happiness requires some kind of equipment for its exercise, some degree of wealth and authority, as well as that happiness is somehow related to good fortune – that a happy life cannot at least be marred by bad fortune and generally needs to be seen through to some desirable end.

Putting all of this together, we could say that a sketch of happiness, as Aristotle had considered it in the *Ethics*, would require mention of four elements:

(i)   the activity of philosophical wisdom as the "target" and most highly ranked among the constituents;
(ii) the working of administrative virtue, in conjunction with character-related virtue, in service of the activity of philosophical wisdom;
(iii) some appropriate sufficiency of material goods;
(iv) some appropriate good fortune, or at least immunity from disastrous bad fortune.

In describing these four elements in suitable relation to one another, it would seem, one would have provided a sketch of happiness.

Suppose next that, instead of dividing up the material of 10.6–9 corresponding to chapter divisions (which are probably not original with Aristotle, in any case), we were to divide up the text in a manner fairly coordinated with these four elements so distinguished (see table 11.1).

If this is the sort of sketch Aristotle aims to be giving, then in book 10, it appears, he in fact gives fairly definite direction about how a life is to be lived if it is to be happy. First, a person must choose the appropriate "target," which is that which he aims to maximize. Aristotle urges that we should aim to live a life which gives the greatest possible scope to the exercise of the virtue of philosophical wisdom. This would seem to be the import of his insisting that "We should not go along with those who advise that mere human beings should think about human things – that 'mortals should think mortal

Table 11.1

Text	Theme	Element in the sketch
10.7	The activity of philosophical wisdom, as pertaining to the chief and godlike element in a human being	(i) Activity constituting the "target"
1178a9–22	The activity of practical wisdom and the virtues of character, as pertaining to a human being as a composite of intelligence and animality	(ii) Activity providing for the activity of philosophical wisdom
1178a22–1179a22	What amount of material goods are needed if one aims at the activity of philosophical wisdom above all	(iii) Appropriate sufficiency of material goods
1179a22–32	How someone who aims above all at the activity of philosophical wisdom will be loved by the gods	(iv) Immunity from disastrous bad fortune

thoughts' – but to the greatest extent possible we ought to act as do the immortals, and we should do everything that we do with a view to living in the manner of the best element within us" (1177b31–34).

Of course, it is impossible to spend all of one's time in philosophical contemplation. We are not simply our minds: we are human beings who are composite creatures, and thus that side of our nature needs to be taken care of (1178b33–35). But it needs minimal care. That we take philosophical contemplation as our target in fact implies that we live a simpler and more austere life than if we (misguidedly) took the exercise of the character-related virtues as our highest good: philosophical contemplation "requires either minimal equipment or less than does character-related virtue" (1178a23–25). We need not worry that such austerity will handicap us in any respect as regards the virtues, because no virtuous activity requires any great degree of wealth or influence: "it's possible to do admirable actions without ruling over sea and land" (1179a4), Aristotle observes, and "Anaxagoras too seemed to suppose that a happy person was neither wealthy nor powerful, since he remarked that it shouldn't be surprising if a happy person looked strange to most people" (1179a13–15). Of course in these matters the austerity and simplicity of life of the sages testifies to this truth even better than what they say (1179a17–22).

The goal is therefore philosophical contemplation; the material means required are minimal. The virtue which sees to it that appropriate means are procured for the maximal pursuit of this goal is administrative virtue (*phronēsis*), which trains and harnesses the non-rational impulses of human nature to achieve this purpose, by inculcating the character-related virtues. The maximization of contemplative activity, Aristotle thinks, is therefore subject to the constraint that it can be maximized only through actions that are consistent with the various virtues. Aristotle refers to this constraint generally as our always acting in a "fitting" or "appropriate" way: "In our dealings with one another we carry out just actions, courageous actions, and actions of the other virtues – amidst our business deals, interests, actions of every sort, and our emotions – by taking care to safeguard what is fitting in each case" (1178a10–13).

But the gods are fond of anyone who strives in this way to maximize philosophical contemplation, subject to the appropriate constraints. Although Aristotle does not say so explicitly, it seems reasonable to infer that, in the following passage, he is maintaining that such a person, then, will be kept safe by the gods from extremes of bad fortune that could mar his happiness:

Someone who actively makes use of his mind, who takes care of his mind and sees that it is in the best possible condition, would seem to be the sort of person who is most loved by the gods. Here is why. Suppose that there is such a thing as special care for human beings by gods, as it seems that there is. Then it would make sense that the gods both take pleasure in what is best and most akin to them (which would be the human mind) and return the favor of those who esteem and honor this most of all – on the grounds that such people show a special care for what the gods themselves love, and also that such people act correctly and admirably. That all of these things are true of a man who has philosophical wisdom is not unclear. The upshot, then, is that he is the sort of person who is most loved by the gods. It is to be expected that anyone who is most loved by the gods will be the most happy. (In this way, too, one may reach the conclusion that anyone with philosophical wisdom is the most happy.) (1179a23–32)

Aristotle's remarks here may therefore be taken to answer the question he had raised in 1.9, about the role that the gods play in conferring happiness (1099b11–14). His considered view is apparently that happiness is conferred by the gods indirectly and in a relatively limited sense: they do not confer virtue, nor the requisite training in virtue, but they will actively favor someone who has acquired the virtues and is exercising them for the right end.

That Aristotle intends in 10.6–8 simply to be consolidating a view he has already marked out would explain why his remarks about philosophical wisdom seem abrupt and without any justification. He takes it as obvious that that is the best "activity in accordance with virtue" and in this sense happiness.

But of course there are other loose ends. Why does he maintain until that point, as we have seen, an apparent indecisiveness as to whether happiness is a single activity or several? As we saw above, he uses that sort of language as late as 10.5. As another example, recall also the similar language in 7.13: "Presumably it's even necessary, if there are unimpeded activities of any condition, whether the activity of all of these is happiness or the activity of some particular one of these, that if it's unimpeded, it would be that which is to be preferred over anything else. And this is a pleasure" (1153b9–12). There seem to be two ways of construing such passages, besides indicating indecisiveness. First, he may be using the "either...or" construction simply to indicate *independence* rather than tentativeness: the point that he wishes to emphasize is independent of whatever position one adopts on the other matter. If this is how it should be understood, then it would be better to translate as, "regardless of whether happiness consists of all of these activities or some particular such activity, the point still holds that..." (His concern to emphasize independence might therefore indicate a standing dispute in his school rather than any wavering on his part.) Secondly, it often happens that Aristotle uses "either...or" to mean in fact "both.... and" when the conjoined elements have an ordering and therefore one element has a certain priority. We saw this already in Aristotle's discussion of friendship and self-love: each person "either is or is especially his thinking part" (1169a2). One might paraphrase this assertion as: "Each person is either his thinking part, or he is his thinking part together with his non-thinking part," that is, he is both parts, but the thinking part has priority. Thus, if this is the sense of the disjunction, then "happiness is either a particular activity or various activities" has meant all along that "happiness is both sorts of activities, but in a certain ordering."

But then why does Aristotle speak in book 10 of "ultimate happiness"? What does this phrase mean, and how is he justified in speaking of *degrees* of happiness? Note that on the interpretation of 10.6–8 as giving an outline of happiness, we do not take the phrases "a life lived according to the mind (or philosophical wisdom)" (1177b30) or "a life lived according to the other virtues" (1178a21) to mean separate ways of life, or possible biographies, but rather ways of carrying on with life, which coexist in the life of one individual. Aristotle when lecturing in philosophy is living "life according to the mind," and when he is writing his will, and exercising administrative virtue and justice, he is living "life according to the other virtues." Those phrases should be taken to indicate types of activity. His argument in 10.7 is that the former sort of activity has all of the marks of happiness, which is why it is "ultimate" (it has any attribute that people wish to attribute to a blessedly happy person, 1177b23), and those marks of happiness which the latter sort of activity has, it has to a lesser degree.

For instance, according to Aristotle the activities of the virtues of character are not as end-like, because we do them only on condition that we need to procure some good, such as protection from enemies or wealth, which then is put to use to promote philosophical contemplation (1177b3). Again, these activities are less self-sufficient, he claims, because they rely more on material conditions (1178a24–34).

But then why count activity in accordance with character-related virtues as happiness at all? Why not say that only philosophical contemplation is happiness, especially given that Aristotle holds that happiness extends only so far as theoretical activity (1178b28)? What is the difference if one maintains that there is only one activity that is happiness, but that there are also other sorts of activities which, although not happiness, nonetheless are similar to happiness?

His reason, ultimately – a deep but only implicit theme of the *Ethics* – would appear to be that actions corresponding to the various character-related virtues are "reasonable"; because they are reasonable they are themselves "goals" of action (which for Aristotle implies that they can never be acted against); and that their being goals somehow involves our being able to reflect upon or *see* them with reasonable satisfaction; this is not philosophical contemplation strictly, but some kind of intellectual perception, presumably of the *kalon*, namely what is admirable and attractive in action. It must be Aristotle's view ultimately that to carry out a fitting action is somehow to *see* that it is fitting, and that our seeing that it is so is the best part of the action, and that there is no point to life beyond *seeing* in this way.

ALL'S WELL THAT ENDS WELL?

These reflections bring us to the difficulties which were raised in the very first chapter of this book, the global difficulties about the interpretation of the *Ethics*, which, we may sense, have not been entirely resolved, even given Aristotle's frequently subtle and intricate analyses. I shall review them only briefly, because a full consideration would take us beyond the scope of an introductory book such as this. And I must be largely limited to expressing judgments, rather than reviewing the grounds for those judgments.

The Problem of Selection versus Collection as regards *eudaimonia*. Which does Aristotle hold? Both, it seems, but in an order. And the result is disappointing: as we have seen, without further argument, the reasons why Aristotle enthusiastically places philosophical contemplation in first position do not carry over and explain, with complete persuasiveness, why the activities of other virtues are counted as happiness at all.

The Problem of Order. This does seem to be resolved, at least in the sense that Aristotle's notion of order is *intelligible*. That we should use X to pursue Y while respecting the nature of X (doing only what is "fitting" or "appropriate" given what X is) makes good enough sense. It is perhaps less clear why X's nature should in such cases prove an unconditional constraint on action; yet if one is willing to grant that X as well as Y is to be regarded as an "end" or "goal," perhaps the matter may rest there. A "goal" in that sense is what one may never reasonably act *against*, even if some goals are what one should consistently act *for*.

The Problem of Egoism versus Altruism. For Aristotle there is no issue of the "possibility of altruism" because he takes it for granted that the human mind has the capacity to discern what the nature of a thing is and, therefore, what is good for it; furthermore he thinks that, once it has discerned this, it is able to wish that it be so. The mind's being able to do these things is a general intellectual capacity, of a piece with our knowledge of nature, and in principle independent of our interests and emotions. Neither does he think that a human being originally has self-interested desires only, which must somehow spread out to others. Rather, he regards a human being as originally a private person, with loves and concerns that in the first instance develop within a family, in which the other members of the family are regarded as not entirely distinct from oneself. Admittedly, after one's character has matured it becomes a task to extend one's concern analogously to fellow citizens conceived as free and equal. But this is a practical not a philosophical problem, which, although it may be difficult to achieve, involves no great mysteries.

The Problem of Moral Objectivity. It is clear that Aristotle thinks we can formulate moral judgments that are true or false; also that these judgments are true or false depending upon objective characteristics of persons and their actions. But he says little about the grounds of such judgments or so-called "moral epistemology." This seems to be simply a shortcoming of the *Ethics*: the treatise needs to be supplemented by a more thorough account of the *kalon*.

The Problem of Guidance. It should by this point be clear that the *Ethics* contains not a paucity but rather a surfeit of guidance; the difficulty is, rather, that it is not entirely evident how to balance the advice that Aristotle gives, or whether these various sources of guidance might be simplified or reduced to some more common or basic principles. We should aim to simplify our lives, Aristotle tells us, in order to maximize contemplation, within the constraints of virtue; we should cultivate distinctively human pleasures; we should spend time with friends; we should be careful to form a small number of close friendships, but not too many; relationships with friends should appropriately involve reciprocation; different kinds of goods are to be rendered to different sorts of friends on different bases; we should avoid putting ourselves in a position in which the availability of pleasures of taste and touch so affects our body that we cannot control our actions reasonably; we should acquire knowledge, especially metaphysical and theological knowledge, and use our leisure to make good use of that knowledge; we should be trained in relevant skills; equality of various sorts, tempered by equity, should guide our transactions with others; we should avoid those extremes of emotion that imply all-or-nothing responses on our part; we should take care to carry out actions typical of the good traits we wish to acquire; we should discount the pleasure of an action in deciding whether to carry it out – and so on, and so on.

The question that this varied advice and direction raises is: what is the nature of moral reasoning, and the moral life – and what must moral education be like – if becoming a good human being is as nuanced and subtle a matter as Aristotle's treatise implies? This at least seems clear: that progress in understanding an Aristotelian approach to ethics will be a matter of living a life within a culture and tradition in which that approach is taken seriously. We might expect a deeper understanding of Aristotelian ethics to be located less in works of philosophy and more in works of literature and culture, and in actual human aspirations and achievements.

In giving us a sketch only of human happiness and the requirements of ethics, whatever his other purposes, Aristotle has surely also left us room actually to put them into practice for ourselves.

FURTHER READING

Of the many good discussions of the perplexing final chapters of the *Ethics*, to be recommended as raising nearly all the important points, and covering the main alternative positions, are Broadie (1991), chapter 7; Keyt (1978); Curzer (1991b); and see also, already mentioned, Cooper (1975), Lawrence (1993), Kraut (1989), and N. P. White (1988).

References

The footnotes at the end of chapters in Broadie (1991) may be used as a good, select bibliographical guide, as also, for earlier literature, the additional notes in Hardie (1980).

Ackrill, J. L. (1965) "Aristotle's Distinction between *energeia* and *kinesis*" in Bambrough, R., ed., *New Essays on Plato and Aristotle*. London: Routledge, 121–41.
  (1972) "Aristotle on 'Good' and the Categories" in Stern, S. M., Hourant, A., and Brown, V., eds., *Islamic Philosophy and the Classical Tradition*. Oxford: Oxford University Press, 17–25. Reprinted in Barnes et al. (1977), 17–24.
  (1974) "Aristotle on Eudaimonia." *Proceedings of the British Academy* 60, 3–23. Reprinted in Rorty (1980), 15–34.
Annas, J. (1977) "Plato and Aristotle on Friendship and Altruism." *Mind* 86, 532–54.
  (1988) "Self-Love in Aristotle." *Southern Journal of Philosophy* 27, 1–18.
  (1993) *The Morality of Happiness*. New York: Oxford University Press.
Anscombe, G. E. M. (1965) "Thought and Action in Aristotle" in Barnes et al. (1977), 61–71.
Aquinas, Thomas (1947) *Summa Theologiae (or Summa Theologica)*. New York: Benzinger Bros.
  (1993) *Commentary on Aristotle's* Nicomachean Ethics. Translated by C. I. Litzinger. Edited by R. M. McInerny. Beloit, WI: Dumb Ox Books.
Austin, J. L. (1970) "A Plea for Excuses" in *Philosophical Papers*. 2nd edn., Oxford: Oxford University Press, 175–205; first published as "A Plea for Excuses. The Presidential Address." *Proceedings of the Aristotelian Society* 57 (1956–7), 1–30.
Barnes, J. (1980) "Aristotle and the Method of Ethics." *Revue Internationale de Philosophie* 133/4, 490–511.
  ed. (1984) *The Complete Works of Aristotle*, the revised Oxford translation. 2 vols. Princeton: Princeton University Press.
Barnes, J., Schofield, M., and Sorabji, R. (1975) *Articles on Aristotle*, vol. 1: *Science*. London: Duckworth.

(1977) *Articles on Aristotle*, vol. II: *Ethics and Politics*. London: Duckworth.

(1979) *Articles on Aristotle*, vol. III: *Metaphysics*. London: Duckworth.

Bolton, R. (1991) "Aristotle on the Objectivity of Ethics" in Anton, J. P. and Preus, A., eds., *Essays in Ancient Greek Philosophy*, vol. IV: *Aristotle's Ethics*. Albany: State University of New York Press. 59–72.

Bostock, D. (1988) "Pleasure and Activity in Aristotle's Ethics." *Phronesis* 19, 251–72.

(2000) *Aristotle's Ethics*. Oxford: Oxford University Press.

Broadie, S. (1991) *Ethics with Aristotle*. Oxford: Oxford University Press.

Broadie, S. and Rowe, C. (2002) *Aristotle: Nicomachean Ethics*. Translation, Introduction, and Commentary. Oxford: Oxford University Press.

Burnyeat, M. (1980) "Aristotle on Learning to Be Good" in Rorty (1980), 69–92.

Charles, D. (1984) *Aristotle's Philosophy of Action*. London: Duckworth.

Chroust, A. H. (1973) *Aristotle: New Light on his Life and on Some of his Lost Works*. South Bend, IN: Notre Dame University Press.

Cooper, J. (1975) *Reason and Human Good in Aristotle*. Indianapolis, IN: Hackett.

(1977) "Aristotle on the Forms of Friendship." *Review of Metaphysics* 30, 619–48. A slightly shortened version is part of "Aristotle on Friendship" in Rorty (1980), 301–40.

(1985) "Aristotle on the Goods of Fortune." *Philosophical Review* 94, 173–96.

(1990) "Political Animals and Civic Friendship" in Patzig, G., ed., *Aristoteles: Politik*. Akten des XI Symposium Aristotelicum. Göttingen: Vandenhoeck and Ruprecht, 221–42.

Curzer, H. J. (1991a) "Aristotle's Much-Maligned *megalopsuchos*." *Australasian Journal of Philosophy* 69, 131–51.

(1991b) "The Supremely Happy Life in Aristotle's *Nicomachean Ethics*." *Apeiron* 24, 47–69.

(1996) "A Defense of Aristotle's Doctrine of the Mean." *Ancient Philosophy* 16, 129–39.

Davidson, D. (1969) "How Is Weakness of the Will Possible?" in Feinberg, J., ed., *Moral Concepts*. Oxford: Oxford University Press, 93–113; reprinted in Davidson, D., *Essays on Actions and Events*. Oxford: Oxford University Press (1980), 21–42.

Foot, P. (1978) *Virtues and Vices*. Berkeley, CA: University of California Press.

(2001) *Natural Goodness*. Oxford: Oxford University Press.

Fortenbaugh, W. W. (1975) "Aristotle's Analysis of Friendship: Function and Analogy, Resemblance, and Focal Meaning." *Phronesis* 20, 51–62.

Furley, David J. (1980) "Self-Movers" in Rorty (1980), 55–68.

Gardiner, S. (2001) "Aristotle's Basic and Non-Basic Virtues." *Oxford Studies in Ancient Philosophy* 20, Summer, 261–95.

Geach, P. (1977) *The Virtues*. Cambridge: Cambridge University Press.

Glassen, P. (1957) "A Fallacy in Aristotle's Argument about the Good." *Philosophical Quarterly* 7, 319–22.

Gomez-Lobo, A. (1991) "The Ergon Inference" in Anton, J. P. and Preus, A., eds., *Essays in Ancient Greek Philosophy*, vol. IV: *Aristotle's Ethics*. Albany: State University of New York Press, 43–57.

Gosling, J. C. B. and Taylor, C. C. W. (1982) *The Greeks on Pleasure*. Oxford: Oxford University Press.

Hampton, J. (1998) *The Authority of Reason*. Cambridge: Cambridge University Press.

Hardie, W. F. R. (1965) "The Final Good in Aristotle's Ethics." *Philosophy* 40, 277–95.

(1968) "Aristotle and the Freewill Problem." *Philosophy* 43, 274–78.

(1980) *Aristotle's Ethical Theory*. 2nd edn., Oxford: Clarendon Press.

Hart, O. (1995) *Firms, Contracts, and Financial Structure*. Oxford: Clarendon Press.

Heinaman, R. (1988) "*Eudaimonia* and Self-Sufficiency in the *Nicomachean Ethics*." *Phronesis* 33, 35–41.

(1995) "Activity and Change in Aristotle." *Oxford Studies in Ancient Philosophy* 13, 187–216.

Huby, P. M. (1967) "The First Discovery of the Free Will Problem." *Philosophy* 42, 353–62.

Hursthouse, R. (1980–1) "A False Doctrine of the Mean." *Proceedings of the Aristotelian Society* 81, 57–72.

(1984) "Acting and Feeling in Character: *Nicomachean Ethics* 3.i." *Phronesis* 29, 252–66.

Irwin, T. H. (1981) "Aristotle's Methods of Ethics" in O'Meara, D., ed., *Studies in Aristotle*. Washington: Catholic University of America Press, 193–224.

(1985) "Permanent Happiness: Aristotle and Solon." *Oxford Studies in Ancient Philosophy* 3, 89–124.

(1988a) *Aristotle's First Principles*. Oxford: Clarendon Press.

(1988b) "Disunity in the Aristotelian Virtues." *Oxford Studies in Ancient Philosophy*. Suppl. vol., 61–78.

Jaeger, W. (1948) *Aristotle: Fundamentals of the History of his Development*. Translated by R. Robinson. Oxford: Clarendon Press.

Judson, L. (1997) "Aristotle on Fair Exchange." *Oxford Studies in Ancient Philosophy* 13, 147–75.

Kaczor, C. (1997) "Exceptionless Norms in Aristotle: Thomas Aquinas and Twentieth Century Interpreters of the *Nicomachean Ethics*." *Thomist* 61, 33–62.

Kenny, A. (1966) "The Practical Syllogism and Incontinence." *Phronesis* 11, 163–84.

(1978) *The Aristotelian Ethics*. Oxford: Oxford University Press.

(1979) *Aristotle's Theory of the Will*. New Haven: Yale University Press.

Keyt, D. (1978) "Intellectualism in Aristotle." *Paideia* 7, 138–57.

Kosman, L. A. (1980) "Being Properly Affected: Virtues and Feelings in Aristotle's Ethics" in Rorty (1980), 103–19.

Kraut, R. (1979) "Two Conceptions of Happiness." *Philosophical Review* 88, 167–97.

(1989) *Aristotle on the Human Good*. Princeton: Princeton University Press.

Lawrence, G. (1993) "Aristotle and the Ideal Life." *Philosophical Review* 102, 1–34.

(1997) "Nonaggregatability, Inclusiveness, and the Theory of Focal Value: *NE* 1.7 1097b16–20." *Phronesis* 42, 32–76.

(2001) "The Function of the Function Argument." *Ancient Philosophy* 21, 445–75.

MacIntyre, A. (1994) *After Virtue*. 2nd edn., London: Duckworth.

Madigan, A. (1985) "*Eth. Nic.* 9.8: Beyond Egoism and Altruism?" *Modern Schoolman* 62, 1–20.

Meikle, S. (1995) *Aristotle's Economic Thought*. New York: Oxford University Press.

Mellor, D. H. (2001) "The Need for Tense" in Loux, M., ed., *Metaphysics: Contemporary Readings*. London: Routledge, 304–20.

Meyer, S. S. (1993) *Aristotle on Moral Responsibility*. Oxford: Blackwell Publishers.

Miller, F. D. (1995) *Nature, Justice and Rights in Aristotle's Politics*. Oxford: Oxford University Press.

Moravcsik, J. M. E., ed. (1967) *Aristotle: A Collection of Critical Essays*. Garden City: Anchor Books.

Nussbaum, M. C. (1982) "Saving Aristotle's Appearances" in Schofield and Nussbaum (1982), 267–93.

O'Connor, D. (1988) "Aristotelian Justice as a Personal Virtue." *Midwest Studies in Philosophy* 13, 417–27.

Owen, G. E. L. (1960) "Logic and Metaphysics in Some Earlier Works of Aristotle" in Düring, I. and Owen, G. E. L., eds., *Aristotle and Plato in the Mid-Fourth Century*, Papers of the Symposium Aristotelicum held at Oxford in August, 1957. Göteborg: Studia Graeca et Latina Gothoburgensia, II; reprinted in Barnes et al. (1979), 13–32; and in Owen (1986), 180–99.

(1961) "*Tithenai ta Phainomena*" in Mansion, S., ed., *Aristote et les problèmes de méthode*, Papers of the Second Symposium Aristotelicum, Louvain, Publications Universitaires de Louvain, 83–103; reprinted in Moravcsik (1967), 167–90; in Barnes et al. (1975), 113–26; and in Owen (1986), 239–51.

(1971/2) "Aristotelian Pleasures." *Proceedings of the Aristotelian Society* 72, 135–52. Reprinted in Owen (1986), 334–46.

(1986) *Logic, Science, and Dialectic*. Edited by M. Nussbaum. Ithaca, NY: Cornell University Press.

Pakaluk, M. (1998) *Aristotle*: Nicomachean Ethics *Books VIII and IX*. Translation with Commentary. Clarendon Aristotle Series. Oxford: Clarendon Press.

(2002) "On an Alleged Contradiction in Aristotle's *Nicomachean Ethics*." *Oxford Studies in Ancient Philosophy* 22, 201–19.

(2004) "The Meaning of Aristotelian Magnanimity." *Oxford Studies in Ancient Philosophy* 26, Summer, 241–75.

Pangle, L. S. (2004) *Aristotle and the Philosophy of Friendship*. Cambridge: Cambridge University Press.

Pears, D. (1980) "Courage as a Mean" in Rorty (1980), 171–88.

Price, A. W. (1980) "Aristotle's Ethical Holism." *Mind* 89, 338–52.

(1989) *Love and Friendship in Plato and Aristotle*. Oxford: Clarendon Press.

(1995) *Mental Conflict*. London: Routledge.

Reid, T. (1969) *Essays on the Active Powers of Man*. Edited by B. Brody. Cambridge, MA: MIT Press.

Richardson, H. S. (1994) *Practical Reasoning about Final Ends*. Cambridge: Cambridge University Press.

Robinson, R. (1969) "Aristotle on *Akrasia*" in *Essays in Greek Philosophy*, Oxford: Clarendon Press, 139–60; reprinted in Barnes et al. (1977), 79–91.

Rorty, A. O., ed. (1980) *Essays on Aristotle's Ethics*. Berkeley, CA: University of California Press.

Schofield, M. and Nussbaum, M. C. (1982) *Language and Logos: Studies in Ancient Greek Philosophy*. Cambridge: Cambridge University Press.

Schwartzenbach, S. (1996) "On Civic Friendship." *Ethics* 107, 97–128.

Sorabji, R. (1980) *Necessity, Cause, and Blame*. London: Duckworth.

Stern-Gillet, S. (1995) *Aristotle's Philosophy of Friendship*. Albany: State University of New York Press, 1995.

Urmson, J. O. (1973) "Aristotle's Doctrine of the Mean." *American Philosophical Quarterly* 10, 223–30; reprinted in Rorty (1980), 157–69.

(1988) *Aristotle's Ethics*. Oxford: Basil Blackwell.

Walker, A. D. M. (1979) "Aristotle's Account of Friendship in the *Nicomachean Ethics*." *Phronesis* 24, 180–96.

Wedin, M. (1981) "Aristotle on the Good for Man." *Mind* 90, 243–62.

White, N. P. (1988) "Good as Goal." *Southern Journal of Philosophy* 27, 169–93 (Spindel Conference Supplement).

White, S. M. (1992) *Sovereign Virtue: Aristotle on the Relationship Between Happiness and Prosperity*. Stanford, CA: Stanford University Press.

Whiting, J. (1988) "Aristotle's Function Argument: A Defence." *Ancient Philosophy* 8, 33–48.

Wiggins, D. (1980) "Deliberation and Practical Reason" in Rorty (1980), 221–40.

Williams, B. (1980) "Justice as a Virtue" in Rorty (1980), 189–200.

Young, C. (1977) "Aristotle on Courage" in Howe, Q., ed., *Humanitas: Essays in Honor of Ralph Ross*. Claremont: Scripps College Press, 194–203.

    (1988) "Aristotle on Temperance." *Philosophical Review* 97, 521–42.

    (1994) "Aristotle on Liberality." *Proceedings of the Boston Area Colloquium in Ancient Philosophy* 10, 313–34.

Zagzebski, L. (1996) *Virtues of the Mind*. Cambridge: Cambridge University Press.

Index

identifying with someone 280, 283
insight, *see* sound intuition
Interdefinability of Goodness, Function, and
    Virtue 6

justice, general virtue of 188–89
    complete virtue exercised towards others
        188–90
    marked by lawfulness 188
justice, particular virtue of (*dikaiosunē*)
    181–205
    among free and equal persons 202–203
    commutative 196
    concerns actions not emotions 198
    corrective 196
    distinct from general justice 190–92
    distributive 196
    equity as corrective of 200
    how the Doctrine of the Mean applies
        196–99
    insufficient for human social life 273
    involves equality 192–93
    and just states of affairs 182
    natural or "primary" 203–205
    opposed by greed 188, 190–91, 192
    Plato's view of 185
    political 202–203
    three forms of 192–96
    without qualification 203

knowledge (*epistēmē*) 207, 209
    defined 221
koinōnia, *see* association

love 261
    for another "on account of him" 263, 269,
        270
    for another "for his own sake" 263, 264, 270
    for another "in his own right" 263,
        269, 270
    three forms of 265–69
Lyceum 20–21

magnanimity 176–79
    domain of 152
magnificence 176–77
Mean, Doctrine of the 105, 108–13, 210
    as applied to justice 196–99
    relative to us 110, 112–13
Metaphysics of Aristotle
    on *aporia* and *lusis* 28–29
    on goodness 67

Mill, John Stuart 181
moderation, *see* self-mastery

Nicomachus
    father of Aristotle 17
    son of Aristotle 4, 20
nobility (*to kalon*) 153–58
    derived from Plato 154–56
    how we possess it 156, 281, 283
    motive for virtuous action 157–58
    and objectivity in ethics 14, 154
    preference for 158
    sensitivity to 157

objectivity in ethics 13–15, 329–30
    contrasted with conventionalism 13
    of *eudaimonia* 48
    fact/value gap 14
opinion (*doxa*) 130, 133–35

pain 102
phainomena 25–28, 41, 235–36, 243
phenomena, *see* phainomena
Physics of Aristotle 257
Plato 14, 16, 17, 17–19, 85, 183, 223
    Alcibiades 164, 166
    Charmides 152
    founder of the Academy 18–19, 20
    his Function Argument 77, 82, 156
    Gorgias 70–71, 154
    Meno 183
    One Over Many argument 59–60,
        62–65
    Philebus 73
    Protagoras 152, 183, 184, 185–86
    Republic 16, 68, 77, 138, 159, 203
    Symposium 154–55, 156
    theory of goodness 6, 58–67
    theory of justice 185–86, 203
    Third Man problem 64
    Unity of Virtue 151–52, 208, 231
Platonic context of the *Ethics* 100, 151, 154–56,
        159, 204, 208, 222
pleasure 286–314
    coinciding with goodness 267, 295
    commonly taken to be happiness 55
    completes activity 311–12
    defined as "unimpeded activity" 303–305,
        313
    equivalent to "satisfaction" 103
    functional definition of 309, 310–11
    a good 307

virtue (*aretē*) (cont.)
  thinking-related 92, 118, 151, 206–32,
    207, 218
  Unity of 152–53, 177, 231–32

wisdom, philosophical (*sophia*) 9, 207–208,
  209, 214, 321, 323
  defined 222

in Plato 185
wisdom, practical (*phronēsis*), *see*
  administrative ability
wish (*boulēsis*) 130, 132–33,
  141–43
Wittgenstein 27

Xenocrates 19